D1595974

Transcendentalism as a Social Movement, 1830–1850

Transcendentalism as a Social Movement, 1830–1850

ANNE C. ROSE

New Haven and London: YALE UNIVERSITY PRESS

For my mother

Published with assistance from the
Frederick Jackson Turner Award of the
Organization of American Historians.

Designed by James J. Johnson
and set in Sabon Roman type.
Printed in the United States of America by
Edwards Brothers, Inc., Ann Arbor, Michigan.

Library of Congress Cataloging in Publication Data

Rose, Anne C., 1950–
    Transcendentalism as a social movement, 1830–1850.

    Based on the author's thesis (Ph.D.)—Yale
University.
    Bibliography: p.
    Includes index.
    1. Transcendentalism (New England)   2. Social
movements—New England.   I. Title.
B905.R67   974'.03   81–3340
ISBN 0–300–02587–4   AACR2

10 9 8 7 6 5 4 3 2 1

Contents

Preface

As long ago as 1888, Henry James called for a social history of Transcendentalism. He had just read the *Memoir* of Emerson by James Elliot Cabot, and although "Mr. Cabot's penciled portrait is incontestable," James felt that there must have been more to Emerson's life than its "enviable quiet—a quiet in which we hear the jotting of the pencil in the notebook." Might not the biographer say something about Emerson's society?

> I mean a greater reference to the social conditions in which Emerson moved, the company he lived in, the moral air he breathed. . . . I may overestimate the latent treasures of the field, but it seems to me there was distinctly an opportunity—an opportunity to make up moreover for the white tint of Emerson's career considered simply by itself.[1]

Undoubtedly James would have admitted that besides supplying the background for a great man, the subject held an interest in its own. Nor did he overrate the "latent treasures of the field." For the Transcendentalists were hardly the retired, literary gentlemen their name implies. They had wives and children, sisters and cousins, friends and enemies, and some were not gentlemen at all but women. Together they ate sparingly, talked prodigiously, and acted passionately. They were determined social reformers who lived at the outset of the urban industrial revolution, without question the decisive moment of transition of modern times, and their aspirations speak eloquently of human resilience in the face of tremendous social and moral dislocation. Far more than James suspected, the Transcendentalists were fully part of the social life of antebellum America.

Yet our impression of the Transcendentalists is altogether contrary to the facts, since they are consistently pictured as superior, aloof, for better

1. "Emerson," from *Partial Portraits* (1888), in Brian M. Barbour, ed., *American Transcendentalism: An Anthology of Criticism* (Notre Dame, Ind.: University of Notre Dame Press, 1973), p. 258. Cabot's study is *A Memoir of Ralph Waldo Emerson*, 2 vols. (Boston: Houghton Mifflin, 1887).

or worse transcendent. To argue, as I do, that they engaged wholeheartedly in the reforms of their day makes this study frankly revisionist, and it
is well to identify the sources of the standard interpretation. Though
successive generations have rewritten Transcendentalism in light of their
own preoccupations, individualism is a common theme, though what
began as praise became, over time, a reason for blame. In the works of late
nineteenth-century writers, the Transcendentalists stand out as heroic
figures of uncompromising integrity and high ideals, traits especially
precious in an age troubled by social conflict and religious doubt. O. B.
Frothingham's *Transcendentalism in New England* (1876), the best work
of the period and still immensely valuable for its sensitivity to the Transcendentalists as people, explains the way Emerson, Bronson Alcott, Margaret Fuller, and others adapted the ideas of European transcendentalism
to their personal goals.[2] Academic interest in the first half of the twentieth
century focused on the Transcendentalists as intellectuals and particularly
as writers. Here the Transcendentalists helped demonstrate that America
had a native intellectual and literary tradition, and the documents Perry
Miller collected in *The Transcendentalists* (1950) are indeed convincing
proof of the force and originality of their thinking.[3] Miller's major work
on the religious roots of American intellectual history created a context,
moreover, for William Hutchison's *The Transcendentalist Ministers* in
1959.[4] But Hutchison significantly changed the terms of discussion when
he described the Transcendentalists as reformers of religious institutions
as well as ideas. His study helped counter the charge of a number of
historians, most notably Stanley Elkins, that the Transcendentalists were
irresponsible individualists whose disdain of established political channels led the American people to the violence of civil war to resolve
sectional differences.[5] In part, the institutional critique drew its force from
the strong case already made for the Transcendentalists as leading thinkers; but its heart and soul was the faith that the normal democratic process
could be trusted to yield social justice, a presumption which in the past
two decades we have come less and less to believe.

From Vietnam and the disaffection of the Left to the Reagan presi-
dency and the alienation of the Right, Americans have learned a lesson

2. *Transcendentalism in New England* (1876; reprint ed., New York: Harper and
Row, 1959).

3. *The Transcendentalists: An Anthology* (Cambridge, Mass.: Harvard University
Press, 1950).

4. *The Transcendentalist Ministers: Church Reform in the New England Renaissance*
(New Haven: Yale University Press, 1959).

5. Stanley Elkins, *Slavery: A Problem in American Institutional and Intellectual Life*,
2d ed. (Chicago: University of Chicago Press, 1968), pp. 140–93. Other historians who have
made the same argument are Arthur M. Schlesinger, Jr., *The Age of Jackson* (Boston: Little,
Brown, 1945), pp. 380–90, and George M. Fredrickson, *The Inner Civil War: Northern
Intellectuals and the Crisis of the Union* (New York: Harper and Row, 1965), pp. 7–22.

without which Transcendentalism as a social movement cannot be grasped: established institutions too often sanction inequality, legitimate aggression, and restrict our freedom, so that commitments to a better society must be voiced by alternative means. The moral optimism of the sixties, which produced a rich variety of communal experiments, alternative families, and spontaneous organizations to agitate for every progressive cause, is especially akin to Transcendentalism. But the historical parallel should not obscure the fact that voluntary associations were an even more important agency of social reform in the early nineteenth century. This was the age of revolution, a double revolution, democratic and industrial, according to E. J. Hobsbawm, and undeniably social and religious, too.[6] So often were old traditions broken and new conditions met by the concerted action of individuals, in evangelical crusades, workingmen's associations, antislavery conventions, and utopian communities that these associations, rather than the far less flexible mechanism of party politics, must be judged the type of reform organization most appropriate to this society. Recently Taylor Stoehr's sensitivity to the similarity of Transcendentalism to the modern counterculture made it possible for him to see that they had a social critique.[7] Yet his conclusion, that the Transcendentalists were engaged in a purely retrospective search for individual integrity, loses its force once we recognize that the same voluntary tactics they consistently used were revolutionizing the early nineteenth-century world, at home and abroad. One reason Stoehr mistakes the nature of antebellum culture is that he has not taken account of the new social history.

The discovery of the Transcendentalists as reformers owes as much to new historiographical trends as to our more general experience. Recent social history is based on the insight that much important living is done outside institutions, where interest, desire, custom, and ideology are what determine action. The contribution of social history has been as wide-ranging as tactically significant, as urban, women's, family, and minority history have all grown up under its rubric. Yet, like any field, it has its limitations. Too often the individual is lost in the aggregate, the extraordinary man or woman is sacrificed to the quantifiable common man, and a passion for technique follows close on the heels of subjects simply too mundane to sustain an intellectual's interest. The result is faceless history, where we know more about how the conclusions were reached than about how people actually lived. Writing the social history of intellectuals is a chance to restore some balance. The life of the mind is hardly inimical to social experience but rather introduces deliberation into common affairs,

6. E. J. Hobsbawm, *The Age of Revolution: Europe, 1789–1848* (New York: Praeger, 1962).

7. Taylor Stoehr, *Nay-Saying in Concord: Emerson, Alcott, and Thoreau* (Hamden, Conn.: Archon Books, 1979).

which resonate, in turn, in thought. More important, the issues that command a thinker's attention cannot help but cast light on the society in which he (or she) lives, just as a full exposition of his ideas requires an accurate understanding of the social context as an indispensable first step. I began this study with more conventional expectations than these. I suspected that the Transcendentalists were more concerned with social issues than is generally credited, and I planned to write on their social thought. But I found that the connections between antebellum society, the Transcendentalists' personalities, and their thinking were as fascinating as they were intricate. My claims for the profitable coordination of social and intellectual history will be demonstrated, if at all, by this book itself.

Exactly who the Transcendentalists were would seem to present no problem until one sees that every historian has compiled a different listing of leading members of the movement, an activity in which I now indulge by naming Orestes Brownson, George Ripley, Elizabeth Peabody, Margaret Fuller, Bronson Alcott, and Ralph Waldo Emerson. I will not argue that these were the only Transcendentalists, but I am convinced that they are the most important if we are to understand Transcendentalism as a matter of social consciousness and action. Reform was the lifeblood of Transcendentalism as a social movement. In the public sphere, its members judged such new conditions as competition, class division, and alienation against traditional Christian values of cooperation, harmony, and spiritual fulfillment. They established two communities, Alcott's anarchic Fruitlands and Ripley's Fourierist Brook Farm, in the expectation that these would be prototypes for yet another social revolution, this time of millennial significance. Privately, too, they experimented with their vocations, friendships, and family relations in order to find a way of life satisfying to both inclination and conscience, in a society far different from the preindustrial towns and cities in which they were born at the turn of the nineteenth century. These personal choices had a decisive influence on their reform ideas. For there are clear connections between Fuller's friendship with Emerson and her feminist principles, Alcott's child-rearing practices and his dream of society as one harmonious family, and Ripley's decision to leave the ministry and his advocacy of structural social reform. The six individuals on whom I concentrate participated equally in these private and public reforms. Henry Thoreau, another likely candidate, has been given less attention because he was interested in social reform only by way of personal example, while Theodore Parker, despite his radical theology and energetic support of numerous causes, led a quite conventional private life.

Dating the Transcendentalist movement raises equally pertinent issues. The two decades between 1830 and 1850 were not the only ones of the urban industrial revolution, but they were critical for New England

and especially Boston from a social and cultural point of view. Boston Unitarians, hitherto advocates of reasonable religion, became committed evangelicals in the 1830s to counter the self-seeking, intolerant, indeed unchristian, spirit of a city composed of increasingly differentiated and mutually hostile social classes. The Transcendentalists began as the philosophers of this Unitarian awakening, who argued that the Christianity of the Bible simply restated the intuitive truths of the heart. They intended to make religion personal, immediate, and hence persuasive; but instead they were attacked by conservative spokesmen of the upper and middle classes for subverting the traditional foundation of social order, the Christian religion. The Transcendentalist controversy (1836–40) was the catalyst which transformed revisionists of religious philosophy into radical social reformers. Their communitarian and family reforms of the 1840s are the heart of Transcendentalism as a social movement. Even so, by 1850 these reform activities all but ceased. Slavery did not consume their energies, as is often supposed, for as abolitionists the Transcendentalists were not especially active, though their younger followers were. Rather, the 1850s marked the rise of American Victorianism and a mood of acquiescence to the ills of industrial capitalism, mixed with pride in its visible achievements. Yet the transience of their reform commitment cannot detract from the Transcendentalists' passionate idealism and, perhaps more surprising, their social realism. They have commanded Americans' interest and admiration for generations, and rightly so.

My own interest in Transcendentalism, though of less impressive duration, is nevertheless nearly as old as my academic life and began in a seminar on the American Renaissance taught by Michael Colacurcio at Cornell University. The interdisciplinary emphasis of Cornell's English and history departments allowed me to explore American culture with unusual freedom, and I am especially indebted to the excellent teaching and encouragement of Robert Elias and Richard Polenberg.

The stimulating atmosphere of Yale University's American studies program, where this book began as a dissertation, has likewise been invaluable. A special note of thanks must be given to Myra Jehlen, who, as a visiting professor, labored with me through my first attempt to explain Emerson. Among those who read various drafts of the manuscript, I am especially grateful to Sydney Ahlstrom, David Brion Davis, Alan Trachtenberg, Bryan Wolf, Joel Bernard, Karen Halttunen, Jane Hunter, Chris Stansell, and Marta Wagner. David Davis has been consistently generous with his time and insights and at all stages has suggested exciting new questions to ask about Transcendentalism. Sydney Ahlstrom has sustained me over the years in innumerable ways. But what has been most important to me is the humanity he brings to the historian's craft. To understand that the historian writes about individual people, whose lives were of consequence to their contemporaries and still are to us, is an invaluable lesson from a fine teacher and good friend.

The manuscript has also profited from the intelligent criticism of my colleagues at California Institute of Technology, Dan Kevles and Morgan Kousser, as well as from frequent discussions on a host of issues with Karen Blair, David DeLeon, Nick Dirks, Will Jones, Terry McDonald, Randy Splitter, David Sundelson, and Alan Sweezy. I am also grateful to Dick Andrews and Margaret Rhodes, who once gave me the chance to learn women's history in the best possible way, by teaching it.

A number of libraries have facilitated my research, and I would like to thank their staffs: Sterling and Beinecke libraries, Yale University; Widener and Houghton libraries, Harvard University; Boston Public Library; Massachusetts Historical Society; Berg Collection, New York Public Library; Henry E. Huntington Library; the library of the University of California, Riverside; and Millikan Library, California Institute of Technology. Permission to quote from manuscripts in their possession has been granted by courtesy of Houghton Library, Harvard University; the Trustees of the Boston Public Library; the Massachusetts Historical Society; and the Henry W. and Albert A. Berg Collection, The New York Public Library, Astor, Lenox and Tilden foundations. I have quoted Lidian Emerson's letters by permission of the Ralph Waldo Emerson Memorial Association and those of Abigail Alcott by courtesy of Theresa W. Pratt.

I thank the National Endowment for the Humanities for the summer fellowship which supported my final research and revisions. I am also grateful to my typists—Kaylyn Gary, Poinka Wong, Lynne Schlinger, Mary Bennett, and Gail Peterson—whose technical expertise, common sense, and moral support have been indispensable. No less important was Chuck Grench at Yale University Press, whose unfailing patience with my nagging question was equaled only by his ingenious solutions. My thanks to Al Metro, too, for his conscientious and skillful editing.

My family knows that none of this would have been possible without their love and support. To my grandmother, Helen, my mother, Virginia, my mother- and father-in-law, Eugenia and Isaac, my husband, Adam, and my dogs, Maggie and Duffy, I can only say that this book belongs to you as much as to me.

1   Boston Unitarianism, 1790–1840

So heartily did Emerson strike out on more than one occasion against "corpse-cold Unitarianism," the "thin porridge or cold tea" of genteel Bostonians, that we commonly think of Transcendentalism as a rebellion against the class-bound rationalism of Unitarian culture.[1] Scholars have been no less immune to the seductive appeal of Emerson's metaphors than the casual reader. Perry Miller makes the most explicit case for the Transcendentalists as American Romantics, men and women who broke away from the formalism of the Enlightenment and united in a spontaneous "community of the heart."[2] Miller's picture is not without its truth, but it obscures as much about the Transcendentalists' relation to their immediate predecessors as it explains. We need a fresh look at Boston Unitarianism to begin to understand Transcendentalism as a social movement. For in the 1830s Unitarians were by no means as unemotional and unresponsive to social trends as Emerson implied, and Transcendentalism was not a revolt but the legitimate child of a culture in transition. Indeed, Transcendentalism appeared in the midst of a Unitarian revival.

The Unitarian awakening belonged to a specific place and time, the industrial city of the 1830s. In the earlier decades of the century, Boston and Unitarianism, the city's dominant religion, had grown up together in a comfortable interdependence. The cosmopolitan sophistication and stable social hierarchy of the prosperous seaport favored the Liberal Christians' emphasis on reason, toleration, and congregational self-rule. Conversely, Unitarianism provided a workable value system for a well-educated and peaceable people. But the industrialization of New England changed Boston society and created new religious problems. The experience of Joseph Tuckerman illustrates the nature of the dilemma.

When Tuckerman left his congregation in Chelsea in 1826 to become the first Unitarian minister at large to the poor, he found that nearly

1. Emerson, *Journals*, 9:381, 339.
2. Introduction, *The Transcendentalists: An Anthology* (Cambridge, Mass.: Harvard University Press, 1950), p. 8.

one-third of Boston's residents attended no church. Many of them had recently migrated from rural New England, many could not pay for pews, many more were too proud to be seen in the free seats reserved for the poor. But the institutional problem was insignificant in Tuckerman's eyes compared with the spiritual one. Cut off from the means of mental and moral culture, the poor turned to vice, intemperance, and crime. And the ethical failure of the rich sadly matched the immorality of the poor. For did God intend "that a few should enrich themselves by the toil of the many and live in luxury and at ease, while the many should not obtain a bare subsistence, and be considered as much below their employers in worth, as in outward circumstances?"[3] No less than the modern historian, Tuckerman was aware of many of the distinctive characteristics of the industrial city: geographic mobility, status aspirations, alienation, class division, and the power of market values.[4] Unitarian evangelicalism was the result of this consciousness.

There were no protracted meetings, impassioned sermons, or mass conversions, but the Unitarian revival exhibited two basic traits which make it part of the Second Great Awakening, that multidenominational religious movement which significantly shaped the society and values of antebellum America. The first was an emphasis on religious feeling. Unitarian preachers in the 1830s aimed to convert the whole person, not just the mind, but the heart as well. William Ellery Channing said that a religion "with power" was needed in a complex urban environment, and sentiment, to Unitarians as to other nineteenth-century Christians, was synonymous with moral force. But Tuckerman knew that preaching could not reach the people outside the churches without new practical measures. His *Principles and Results of the Ministry at Large* (1838) was an appeal for support of an itinerant ministry to the poor and, just as important, an attempt to arouse the sympathy of the rich who did not attend, in either sense, the Sunday sermon. Thus the second characteristic of the awakening was experimental activity, the use of books, magazines, lectures, and voluntary associations to adapt religion to a society where life no longer centered on the instituted church.[5]

3. Joseph Tuckerman, *The Principles and Results of the Ministry at Large, in Boston* (Boston: James Munroe, 1838), p. 323.

4. For clarity's sake, I should mention here that Boston did not industrialize in a technological sense, as I explain below. But the introduction of manufactures in surrounding towns spurred Boston's growth and occasioned the changes in behavior and attitudes I describe in this chapter. "Industrial city" refers to this new urban culture.

5. Historians who argue that the Second Great Awakening helped reorder a changing society are Donald G. Mathews, "The Second Great Awakening as an Organizing Process, 1780–1830: An Hypothesis," *American Quarterly* 21 (1969): 23–43; Paul E. Johnson, *A Shopkeepers's Millennium: Society and Revivals in Rochester, New York, 1815–1837* (New York: Hill and Wang, 1978); and Donald M. Scott, *From Office to Profession: The New*

One more preliminary word on "evangelical Unitarianism" is needed because of the dissonant sound of the concept. Technically, an evangelical is one who preaches the Gospel. So notorious were Unitarians as pioneers in rationalistic higher criticism of the Bible that their Orthodox contemporaries hardly saw Unitarian dedication to Christian truth (as opposed to literal scriptural doctrine) as evangelical; rather, Orthodox Christians regarded it as pernicious infidelity. Antebellum Unitarians never in fact dismissed the Bible altogether.[6] Be that as it may, however, I am using "evangelical Unitarianism" primarily to denote a social phenomenon. I have chosen the term to emphasize the connection between the Unitarian efforts of the 1830s and the Second Great Awakening as a movement, an aggressive campaign to seek heartfelt conversions as an antidote to the problems that came with socioeconomic change.[7]

England Ministry, 1750–1850 (Philadelphia: University of Pennsylvania Press, 1978), pp. 36–51. Perry Miller emphasized the importance of feeling in the epistemology of the Awakening in *The Life of the Mind in America: From the Revolution to The Civil War* (New York: Harcourt, Brace and World, 1965), pp. 3–95. For a more general discussion of experimental piety in the Puritan tradition, see Sydney E. Ahlstrom, *A Religious History of the American People* (New Haven: Yale University Press, 1972), pp. 124–34. Two excellent studies of the Awakening in antebellum cities are Timothy Smith, *Revivalism and Social Reform: American Protestantism on the Eve of the Civil War* (New York: Harcourt, Brace and World, 1965), and Carroll Smith Rosenberg, *Religion and the Rise of the American City: The New York City Mission Movement, 1812–1870* (Ithaca: Cornell University Press, 1971).

6. See Timothy Smith's discussion of Unitarians' increasing interest in scriptural and church tradition in the 1850s, which he very properly calls "evangelical Unitarianism," in *Revivalism*, pp. 95–102. Daniel Howe, on the other hand, applies the term more generally to an emotional style of preaching which struck a secondary note in the denomination from 1800 on, in *The Unitarian Conscience: Harvard Moral Philosophy, 1805–1860* (Cambridge, Mass.: Harvard University Press, 1970), pp. 160–66.

7. One should note that the Unitarians were not the only denomination in Boston to respond to the city's problems. Edward Taylor, for example, was a Methodist who began to preach to sailors in 1829, while E. M. P. Wells became the Episcopal city missionary in 1843 and ministered to the poor at St. Stephen's Chapel. See Gilbert Haven et al., *Life of Father Taylor: The Sailor Preacher* (Boston: Boston Port and Seamen's Aid Society, 1904), esp. pp. 102–27, 447–54, and Samuel W. Francis, *Memoir of the Life and Character of Rev. E. M. P. Wells* (Newport, R.I.: Charles E. Hammett, Jr., 1878). I have limited the present discussion to the Unitarians, however, because, first, they were the largest and most influential denomination in Boston, and second, the Transcendentalists began as Unitarians. Information on other religious groups is plentiful but scattered; two helpful sources are William G. McLoughlin, *New England Dissent, 1630–1833: The Baptists and the Separation of Church and State*, 2 vols. (Cambridge, Mass.: Harvard University Press, 1971), 2: esp. 1107–27, 1263–74, and James Mudge, *History of the New England Conference of the Methodist Episcopal Church, 1796–1910* (Boston: New England Conference, 1910), esp. pp. 87–113, 298–323.

RELIGION AND SOCIETY, 1790–1830

The development of Boston Unitarianism involves a paradox: Unitarians broke away from the Enlightenment tradition in the nineteenth century because of the rise of the industrial city, but they originally embraced rationalism in the eighteenth century because of the commercial growth of the seaport. Puritanism split into Liberal and Orthodox factions during the First Great Awakening of the 1740s. It was a division that reflected the increasing difference between city and country.

Liberal Christianity, as Unitarians commonly called their interpretation of the Puritan tradition, originated in the opposition of eastern Massachusetts congregations to the fervent revivalism of the Great Awakening. To Bostonians, whose livelihood increasingly depended on transatlantic trade, the unbridled passions of the predominantly rural revivals were an unwelcome sign of American provincialism. Charles Chauncy, minister of Boston's First Church, set the tone of Liberal criticism when he wrote in 1743 that "an *enlightened Mind,* and not *raised Affections,* ought always to be the guide of those who call themselves Men; and this, in the Affairs of Religion, as well as other Things: And it will be so, where GOD really works on their Hearts, by his SPIRIT."[8] Chauncy's concern with the supremacy of reason was matched by his allegiance to civic order, threatened, from his perspective in the midst of the Awakening, by the challenges of enthusiasts to established authority.[9] The value Liberals attached to rationality and order clearly served the interest of a commercial society in deliberate, routinized progress. Although the schism in Puritanism may with some justice be seen as the divorce of the Protestant ethic from its roots in Puritan piety, the Liberal revision is better viewed as the adaptation of religion to the preindustrial city.[10]

It was not until after the Revolution, however, that Liberal opinions gained the institutional support needed to mark out a well-defined Unitarian sphere of influence. On a congregational level, the Unitarian party gathered strength as Liberal majorities chose ministers of like opinions. In

8. "Seasonable Thoughts on the State of Religion," in Alan Heimert and Perry Miller, eds., *The Great Awakening: Documents Illustrating the Crisis and Its Consequences* (New York: Bobbs-Merrill, 1967), p. 298. The italics are Chauncy's. All italics within quotations are those of the writer in question unless otherwise noted.

9. Historians who emphasize the Awakening's challenge to authority and the Liberal commitment to order are Richard L. Bushman, *From Puritan to Yankee: Character and the Social Order in Connecticut, 1690–1760* (Cambridge, Mass.: Harvard University Press, 1967), and Alan Heimert, *Religion and the American Mind: From the Great Awakening to the Revolution* (Cambridge, Mass.: Harvard University Press, 1966).

10. The most recent critic to equate the rise of Liberal Christianity with a relaxation of spiritual and intellectual rigor is Ann Douglas, *The Feminization of American Culture* (New York: Knopf, 1977), pp. 121–64.

1820, the Dedham decision of the Massachusetts Supreme Court confirmed the right of the noncommuning, usually Unitarian, members of the congregation to control church property and elect the minister despite the vote of a minority of full communicants. By defending the prerogatives of pew owners and thus recognizing the church as a joint stock company, the court overturned the Puritan concept of rule by the elect and passed church power into the hands of the prosperous. Only one of the seven Congregational churches established in Boston prior to the Revolution, the Third Church or "Old South," adhered to Orthodoxy in 1820.[11]

The Unitarians also won control of Harvard College. Beginning with the election of Rev. Henry Ware as Hollis Professor of Divinity in 1805, they consolidated their power when Rev. John Thornton Kirkland became president in 1810. Kirkland worked hard to promote professional education for the ministry to replace informal study with a clergyman, thereby ensuring a steady supply of ministers with uniform opinions to the Liberal churches.[12] But the success of Unitarianism depended less, in the end, on judicial backing and education than on social structure.

Between 1790 and 1830, Boston society was notable for its increasingly self-conscious stratification but nevertheless remained relatively homogeneous and free of serious conflicts. The emerging Unitarian ethos corresponded to these trends. As wealth and a sense of corporate identity augmented the power of merchants and professionals in religious affairs, Unitarianism stressed the value of intellectual liberty and social harmony, thus reflecting the interests of well-educated people too committed to Enlightenment ideals to govern willingly by visible authority. But Uni-

11. See appendix A for a list of Boston churches with their dates of founding. Among the seven I have counted neither King's Chapel, which was originally Episcopalian, nor the Federal Street Church, which was originally Presbyterian. King's Chapel, however, was the first to become Unitarian in 1783. See Henry Wilder Foote, *Annals of King's Chapel*, 2 vols. (Boston: Little, Brown, 1896), 2:378–98. Other church histories useful for tracing the growth of Unitarianism are Arthur B. Ellis, *History of the First Church in Boston* (Boston: Hall and Whiting, 1881); Chandler Robbins, *A History of the Second Church* (Boston: Committee of the Society, 1852); Samuel Kirkland Lothrop, *A History of the Church in Brattle Street, Boston* (Boston: Wm. Crosby and H. P. Nichols, 1851); *The West Church and its Ministers* (Boston: Crosby, Nichols, 1856); [Ephraim Eliot], *Historical Notices of the New North Religious Society* (Boston: Phelps and Farnham, 1822). See Katherine G. Allen, ed., *Sketches of Some Historical Churches of Greater Boston* (Boston: Beacon Press, 1918), a collection of addresses on Unitarian churches which supplies details on congregations that lack church histories. The best modern study of early Unitarianism is Conrad Wright, *The Beginnings of Unitarianism in America* (Boston: Starr King Press, 1955). On Old South, see Hamilton Andrews Hill, *History of the Old South (Third Church), Boston, 1669–1884*, 2 vols. (Boston: Houghton Mifflin, 1890), 2:326–75.

12. On the divinity school, see Wright, *Unitarianism*, pp. 274–80; Conrad Wright, "The Early Period, 1811–1840," in George Huntson Williams, ed., *The Harvard Divinity School: Its Place in Harvard University and in American Culture* (Boston: Beacon Press, 1954), pp. 21–28; and Samuel Eliot Morison, *Three Centuries of Harvard* (Cambridge, Mass.: Harvard University Press, 1936), pp. 241–45.

tarianism in this period was not the exclusive religion of a class. Working people were committed to the social order and were involved in the cultural life of the city. Literate and progressive, they generally attended Unitarian churches and subscribed to the Liberal creed.

Prosperity was largely responsible for the character of Boston society at the turn of the nineteenth century. As early as 1770, expansion and specialization of the commercial economy had concentrated capital in the hands of a merchant elite and, at the other end of the social scale, encouraged growing numbers of apprentices to become independent wage earners instead. During the Napoleonic Wars, Boston's economy flourished as a result of the re-export trade, that is, transporting goods produced and consumed by the warring European nations. Moderate in-migration from eastern New England, particularly smaller seaports, followed the economic growth of the city. Geographic mobility was matched by moderate upward mobility.[13] But the period was also one in which social groups became aware of their separate identities.

Family ties and institutional affiliations both reflected and furthered the consolidation of the merchant and professional classes. The genealogy of Transcendentalist William Henry Channing (1810–84) provides a good example of how intermarriage among Boston merchants promoted common interests. Channing's mother, Susan, was the daughter of Stephen Higginson, a merchant who moved from Salem to Boston in 1778 to go into business with his relative Jonathan Jackson. By the first decade of the nineteenth century, the Higginsons were connected by marriage with the prominent Perkins family of Boston as well as with other post-Revolutionary emigrés from Essex County seaports—the Cabots, Clevelands, Lees, and Lowells. Some of these ties existed before in-migration among the merchant families of Salem, Beverly, and Newburyport. But in Boston, proximity reinforced kinship to create a tight-knit upper class.[14]

Intermarriage also united the merchant and professional elites. William Henry's father, Francis Dana Channing, was a lawyer, and his uncles were Boston professionals as well—William Ellery (a minister), Walter (a

---

13. For the colonial and revolutionary background, see James Henretta, "Economic Development and Social Structure in Colonial Boston," *William and Mary Quarterly,* 3d ser. 22 (1965): 75–92, and Allan Kulikoff, "The Progress of Inequality in Revolutionary Boston," *William and Mary Quarterly,* 3d ser. 28 (1971): 374–412. On economic, social, and demographic trends in early nineteenth-century Boston, see Douglass C. North, *The Economic Growth of the United States, 1790–1860* (Englewood Cliffs, N.J.: Prentice-Hall, 1961), esp. pp. 17–58; Samuel Eliot Morison, *The Maritime History of Massachusetts, 1783–1860* (Boston: Houghton Mifflin, 1921), pp. 1–224; and David Montgomery, "The Working Classes of the Pre-Industrial American City, 1780–1830," *Labor History* 9 (1968): 3–22.

14. Octavius Brooks Frothingham, *Memoir of William Henry Channing* (Boston: Houghton Mifflin, 1886), pp. 5–6. See also Morison, *Maritime History,* pp. 119–33, on the merchant class.

physician), and Edward (a scholar). The sons of a Rhode Island lawyer of moderate means, the four Channing brothers all attended Harvard between 1790 and 1810 and achieved coequal status with the merchant class. Harvard College served as a means of assimilation and a meeting ground for prominent Bostonians, as did cultural institutions such as the Boston Athenaeum, a corporately owned private library founded in 1807.[15] Bostonians' pride in their culture as well as their wealth encouraged such upward mobility as that which the Channings enjoyed because of their talent alone.

Churches served a social function similar to the one performed by the college and Athenaeum. The peaceable adoption of Liberal views, in contrast to the frequently contentious transition from Orthodoxy in the smaller towns, demonstrated the coherence of the upper class in religious as in secular affairs. But the churches were not the exclusive clubs of the influential, and although deference helped win the assent of less prosperous members to Liberal religion, the idea of rational progress must have had a general appeal. The absence of substantial dissent in Boston supports this conclusion. But some new denominations were established and indicate the existence of a distinct point of view among Boston's working population.

Under the provision for religious toleration in the Massachusetts Constitution of 1780, societies dissenting from both Liberal and Orthodox versions of Puritanism appeared in Boston after the Revolution.[16] Three Methodist, three Baptist, and two Universalist churches were founded between 1780 and 1820. Since the beliefs of many of these churches stood midway between Orthodoxy and Liberalism, retaining the doctrine of depravity but affirming human ability in conversion, the members were probably recent migrants from rural areas who were less prosperous, confident, and receptive to change than the Unitarian elite were. Their leaders conform to this profile. Hosea Ballou, a leading Universalist minister of the period, preached first in New Hampshire and then in Salem before moving to Boston. His associate editor at the *Universalist Magazine*, Thomas Whittemore, was a former bootmaker's apprentice. The Republican politics of Baptist preacher Thomas Baldwin, who was once a blacksmith, was another indication of the out-group constituency

15. Ronald Story, "Class and Culture in Boston: The Athenaeum, 1807–1860," *American Quarterly* 27 (1975): 178–99. On other elite institutions, see Wright, *Unitarianism*, pp. 259–69. For an excellent sketch of upper-class life, see J. P. Quincy, "Social Life in Boston: From the Adoption of the Federal Constitution to the Granting of the City Charter," in Justin Winsor, ed., *The Memorial History of Boston,* 4 vols. (Boston: James R. Osgood, 1881), 4:1–24.

16. On the legal status of dissenters during the Federalist period, see McLoughlin, *New England Dissent,* 2: passim, and John D. Cushing, "Notes on Disestablishment in Massachusetts, 1780–1833," *William and Mary Quarterly,* 3d ser. 26 (1969): 169–90.

of these churches in Federalist Boston. Foreigners were also prominent,
and two congregations, one Baptist and one Methodist, were composed of
free blacks. These societies were often small. There were only 619
Methodists in Boston in 1820, for example. But they nevertheless suggest a
feeling of separate interests among the working class.[17]

The beginning of trade unions during the same period supports this
conclusion. But in contrast to the other major seaports—New York,
Philadelphia, and Baltimore—where masters and journeymen formed
separate organizations and strikes were not uncommon, in Boston artisans
and the workers they employed belonged to the same unions as late as the
1830s.[18] Thus, like the new cultural societies of the elite, the trade unions
were evidence of a sense of class identity within, but not against, society at
large. In fact, craftsmen were most visible when demonstrating their pride
in their contribution to society. When peace was proclaimed in 1815,
workers paraded through the streets of Boston in anticipation of the
return of prosperity interrupted by the War of 1812. As one young woman
recorded in her diary:

> Representatives of all the trades were drawn on sleds, with appropriate
> insignia, and carrying their tools. The brick-layers were building a
> house; they broke their bricks and worked busily. The carpenters

17. See Winsor, *Memorial History,* for articles on the Baptists (3:421–32), Methodists
(3:433–46), and Universalists (3:483–508). Other city histories useful for compiling a
profile of denominations other than Unitarians are Caleb H. Snow, *A History of Boston,* 2d
ed. (Boston: Abel Brown, 1828), pp. 338–47, 382–85, and [I. S. Homans], *Sketches of
Boston, Past and Present* (Boston: Phillips, Sampson, 1851), pp. 66–129. See also the
denominational histories cited in n. 7. Not all of the members of these churches were artisans
and laborers. Amos Binney of the Second Methodist Church, for example, was a merchant
and agent of the U.S. Navy. But it is evident that most in this congregation were less
prosperous, since in an effort to redeem the society's debt in 1816 by finally selling its pews,
ten years after the building's construction, Binney offered to pay the equivalent in cash for
whatever labor or commodities the members could offer for pews. See Mudge, *New England
Conference,* pp. 82–83. There was a similar distribution of wealth at the Second Universalist
Society. Of the forty-two men and one woman who purchased 100-dollar shares to construct
the meetinghouse in 1816, thirty-four bought three shares or less, seven bought from four to
ten, and two took fifteen each. See A. A. Miner, "Historical Sketch," in *An Account of the
Celebration of the Seventy-Fifth Anniversary of the Second Universalist Society in Boston,
December 18, 1892* (Boston: Universalist Publishing House, 1893), p. 14. The suspicion
that all these subscribers were too wealthy to be working people is dispelled by the fact that
the church dedication in 1817 was postponed because of a conflict with a cattle show in
Brighton, a concession unimaginable (because unnecessary) in a Unitarian congregation. In
general, the contributing members of the non-Unitarian churches probably belonged to the
prosperous artisan elite described by Kulikoff in "Progress of Inequality," pp. 387–88, as
well as, less frequently, to a middle class of shopkeepers and small merchants.

18. Montgomery, "Working Classes," p. 6. See also "A Boston Mechanic's" rationale
for admitting masters to unions in the 1830s in John R. Commons et al., eds., *A Documentary History of American Industrial Society,* 10 vols. (Cleveland: Arthur H. Clark,
1910–11), 6:92–94.

were erecting a Temple of Peace. The printers struck off hand-bills announcing "Peace!" and threw them among the crowd. The bakers, hatters, paper-makers, and others each had their insignia.[19]

Working people clearly felt their importance as craftsmen in Boston's social hierarchy.

Although social differentiation was beginning to give Boston an urban character, in other ways the place was still an overgrown town. Three factors worked to perpetuate cohesion and stability in preindustrial Boston: geographic isolation, kinship ties between classes, and common institutions.

The continuing provincialism of Boston favored social homogeneity. Before 1830, the absence of good roads, canals, railroads, and steamships limited geographic mobility. New residents came primarily from the coastal towns of Massachusetts and, to a lesser extent, Rhode Island, New Hampshire, and southern Maine.[20] Most Bostonians therefore shared common traits as descendants of Puritan ancestors who were townspeople rather than farmers and who were raised, most likely, in churches with Harvard-educated ministers. Although the existence of the dissenting congregations and the founding of Orthodox Park Street Church in 1809 showed that opinion was not unanimous, Unitarianism was Boston's dominant value system. Regional isolation contributed to this cultural consensus.

In such a closed society, family relationships not only bound the elite but connected people of different ranks. Descendants of a common Puritan ancestor often followed a variety of callings, and the well-to-do recognized their obligation to their less prosperous kin. Substantial aid in business and education was not uncommon. Peter Chardon Brooks, one of Boston's wealthiest merchants, recorded gifts and loans to relatives no closer than "a kinswoman" in his diary. On one occasion, he loaned 20,000 dollars to a brother-in-law who owned a farm and distillery, and when the man failed to prosper, Brooks absolved him of 4,440 dollars in back interest "out of affection to him and his wife, and to encourage him in business."[21] Aid in education ranged from the year's preparation for Harvard that Rev. Samuel Ripley gave to his nephew George, the son of a tavernkeeper, to virtual adoption by a well-placed relation. President Kirkland of Harvard took his nephew Samuel Kirkland Lothrop into his home at age thirteen. The son of an impoverished New York State lawyer,

19. Quoted in Quincy, "Social Life," p. 21.
20. Kulikoff, "Progress of Inequality," p. 401; Morison, *Maritime History*, pp. 129–30. Other sources of population, according to Kulikoff, were nearby agricultural areas and foreign countries.
21. Quoted in Octavius Brooks Frothingham, *Boston Unitarianism, 1820–1850: A Study of the Life and Work of Nathaniel Langdon Frothingham* (1890; reprint ed., Hicksville, N.Y.: Regina Press, 1975), p. 109.

Lothrop became the minister of the Brattle Street Church in the 1830s, with Daniel Webster, former mayor Harrison Gray Otis, and Amos Lawrence, one of the wealthiest manufacturers of the period, as parishioners. In this case, family ties were the means of upward mobility which closed social distances altogether.[22]

Similarly, Unitarian churches promoted contact between classes more successfully than they would after 1830. Their economic organization was a decisive factor. Although Unitarian congregations were guaranteed tax support until 1833 as the established church of Massachusetts, Boston societies collected their income by the proprietary system. Pews were rented or sold at rates depending on their location in the meetinghouse. But for long-time residents of Boston, pews were virtually hereditary and involved no prohibitive expense. Prices were comparatively low, moreover, before increasing demand by an elite growing in numbers and wealth led to soaring costs. In 1836, prices as high as 500 dollars were cited, while as recently as 1824, seats in the new Twelfth Congregational Society sold for an average of 20 dollars.[23] Thus in preindustrial Boston the working class still worshiped with the well-to-do. As Joseph Tuckerman recalled: "The rich and the poor,—or in other words, those who had some capital, and those who had none,—met on terms of equality before the church door on Sunday, interchanged expressions of friendly greeting, and separated to pass into their own pews, or into free galleries, without the slightest feeling in either case, that distinction of condition was implied between them."[24]

22. *Some Reminiscences of the Life of Samuel Kirkland Lothrop,* ed. Thornton Kirkland Lothrop (Cambridge, Mass.: John Wilson and Son, 1888), pp. 3–95 and passim.

23. Lewis G. Pray, *Historical Sketch of the Twelfth Congregational Society* (Boston: Committee of the Society, 1863), p. 12. The 1836 figure is quoted in Orestes A. Brownson, *A Discourse on the Wants of the Times* (Boston: James Munroe, 1836), p. 7. McLoughlin states, in *New England Dissent* 1:118, that Boston Congregational churches, unlike other standing order churches in Massachusetts, were financed by pew sales rather than by taxes from the seventeenth century on because their wealth was sufficient to guarantee their security without compulsory measures. Other denominations in Boston conformed to this system, even when the denomination as a whole, most notably the Methodists, operated under ecclesiastical laws which prescribed free seats and voluntary offerings, as Mudge explains in *New England Conference,* p. 99. As the restrictive effect of the proprietary system became clear after 1830, there were movements in virtually every denomination to establish free churches. For an interesting case of an Episcopal free church which was high church in its ritual, see *A Sketch of the History of the Parish of the Advent in the City of Boston, 1844–1894* (Boston: Parish of the Advent, 1894). On the Transcendentalists' involvement in this aspect of church reform, see William R. Hutchison, *The Transcendentalist Ministers: Church Reform in the New England Renaissance* (New Haven: Yale University Press, 1959), pp. 137–89. Richard E. Sykes has documented the narrowing social base of Unitarian congregations outside Boston in "The Changing Class Structure of Unitarian Parishes in Massachusetts, 1780–1880," *Review of Religious Research* 12 (1970): 26–34.

24. *Ministry at Large,* p. 14.

Prosperous members of the congregation recognized their duty to the poor, moreover, by contributing to the minister's "poor purse." The recipients of these gifts were not "strangers," Tuckerman noted, but the "aged, enfeebled, impoverished" to whom the church was "endeared by associations even of very early life; and who, as a little band of much respected, and even endeared, dependents, are objects even of peculiar ministerial sympathy, interests, and care."[25] Lay people sometimes visited the poor to deliver alms as delegates of the congregation. At William Ellery Channing's Federal Street Church, two daughters of Stephen Higginson took on these responsibilities.[26] Thus the firm hold of religious values on the Unitarian conscience, as well as broad church membership, made the Liberal congregations a socially unifying influence.

Against this social background, Unitarianism developed between 1790 and 1830 from a critique of Orthodox revivalism into a coherent value system. Unitarians stressed the importance of reason, intellectual freedom, and moral duty. Their doctrine was well suited to a community where freethinking could safely be permitted because it was grounded in basic consensus and where reasoned acceptance of duties was sufficient because of general social stability.[27]

To early nineteenth-century Liberals, religion remained primarily an affair of the mind. By a "rational faith," Unitarians meant not only that Christianity concurred with reason but that conversion was the calm assent to clear propositions, followed by progressive enlightenment and conviction. They amended Charles Chauncy's position, however, by allowing reason to judge Scripture. As William Ellery Channing said in his definitive sermon on "Unitarian Christianity" in 1819:

> Our leading principle in interpreting Scripture is this, that the Bible is a book written for men, in the language of men, and that its meaning is to be sought in the same manner as that of other books. . . . With these views of the Bible, we feel it our bounden duty to exercise our reason upon it perpetually, to compare, to infer, to look beyond the letter to the spirit, to seek in the nature of the subject, and the aim of the writer, his true meaning; and, in general, to make use of what is known, for explaining what is difficult, and for discovering new truths.[28]

25. Ibid., pp. 138–39.

26. Elizabeth Palmer Peabody, *Reminiscences of Rev. William Ellery Channing* (Boston: Roberts Brothers, 1880), p. 41.

27. The best study of Unitarianism as an intellectual system is Daniel Walker Howe, *The Unitarian Conscience.* While Howe stresses the philosophical grounds of consensus in Scottish Common Sense principles, Conrad Wright's *Beginnings of Unitarianism* emphasizes theology and, although focusing on the formative phase of Liberalism in the late eighteenth century, complements Howe's work.

28. "Unitarian Christianity: Discourse at the Ordination of the Rev. Jared Sparks, Baltimore, 1819," in *The Works of William Ellery Channing* (Boston: American Unitarian Association, 1875), pp. 367–68.

This critical method introduced a measure of historical relativism into Christianity. The Bible no longer set the limits of thought but might itself be improved by general enlightenment. Unitarians did not dismiss Scripture. But their acceptance of rationalistic "higher criticism," by making room for the advancement of the secular mind, licensed the cosmopolitan interests of Bostonians aware of European literature and letters and intent on producing their own.

The Liberals' dedication to freedom logically followed, since liberty was the necessary condition of intellectual progress. Christian liberty was the individual's right to formulate truth for himself and, in church affairs, the independence of congregations from domination by a clerical hierarchy. Rev. Bernard Whitman stated the Unitarian ideal when he protested the Orthodox use of standardized creeds and meddling consociations in an open letter to Moses Stuart in 1830:

> When I hear a person declare his firm belief in the divine origin of Christianity, and see him take the Scriptures as his only infallible rule of faith and practice, and search them out with honesty and perseverance and devotion, and exhibit a holy temper and character, and manifest a willingness even to lay down his life in defense of his religious faith, my conscience compels me to grant him the Christian name, although he rejects some of the most precious articles of my belief.[29]

Clearly, liberty for Unitarians in predominantly Orthodox New England was foremost in Whitman's mind. But even his definition of terms restricted the meaning of freedom: one might vary Christian doctrines, but neither reject the Bible nor slight its moral guidelines. Such built-in controls helped make Unitarianism a viable value system.

Unitarians relied mainly on "character," however, to ensure peaceable social relations among freethinking people. Character formation was the gradual process of understanding, accepting, and acting on moral truths. The mind was the guide, but sentiment was the source of motive power to perform acknowledged duties. Although reason and order remained the twin Liberal commitments in the early nineteenth century, the system was refined and softened by the admission of feeling. Rational education now became the nurture of a well-proportioned character, and civic authority was replaced by voluntary obedience as the basis of order. Unlike their predecessors, moreover, Unitarians did not value order so much as the support of right religion, as they hoped Christianity would contribute to social harmony. We accept Unitarian Christianity, Channing said, "not

29. *Two Letters to the Reverend Moses Stuart; On the Subject of Religious Liberty* (Boston: Gray and Bowen, 1830), p. 66. On the Unitarian understanding of religious freedom, see also Wright, *Unitarianism*, pp. 223–40, and Peabody, *Reminiscences*, pp. 21–23.

merely because we believe it to be true, but because we regard it as purifying truth, as a doctrine according to godliness, as able to 'work mightily' and 'bring forth fruit' in them who believe."[30] A moral society had become as important as eternal salvation.

Despite these modifications, Liberals opposed the Second Great Awakening as vehemently as they had the First. As the Awakening gained momentum after 1800, Unitarians voiced their doubt of the lasting efficacy of emotional conversions without rational understanding, deplored the manipulative methods used by preachers to awaken sinners, criticized the demoralizing pessimism of the doctrine of total depravity, and denounced the competition for converts among evangelical sects as the antithesis of Christian toleration.[31] But when a revival began in 1822 in Boston's three Orthodox churches—Old South, Park Street, and the new Union Church—the Unitarian counteroffensive changed direction. Without renouncing their primary allegiance to reason, liberty, and moral practice, Liberals began to answer Orthodox evangelicals on their own terms. The evangelical possibilities Unitarians explored in the context of sectarian contention laid a basis for the revivalism of the 1830s, when their attention turned from the Orthodox threat to concrete social problems.[32]

An emphasis on experimental faith and a willingness to organize to propagate their views characterized Unitarians in the 1820s. Ministers insisted on the ability of Unitarian beliefs to inspire heartfelt conviction. In "Unitarian Christianity Favorable to Religious Zeal," Ezra Stiles Gannett described a personal religious experience much more akin to Orthodox conversion than the cultivated sensibility that earlier preachers such as Joseph Buckminster hoped to arouse.[33] Similarly, Channing called for strenuous preaching at the dedication of Harvard's Divinity Hall in 1826: "By the power of which I have spoken I mean that strong action of the understanding, conscience, and heart, on moral and religious truth, through which the preacher is quickened and qualified to awaken the same strong action in others."[34]

The construction of Divinity Hall to house an increasing number of theological students was one indication of the Liberals' intention to pro-

30. "Unitarian Christianity," in Channing, *Works,* pp. 382–83. On character, see also Howe, *Conscience,* pp. 116–20.

31. Whitman, *Letters,* pp. 3–100; Peabody, *Reminiscences,* pp. 44–50; Channing, "Unitarian Christianity," in *Works,* pp. 377–78.

32. On the Orthodox revival, see *The Autobiography of Lyman Beecher,* ed. Barbara Cross, 2 vols. (Cambridge, Mass.: Harvard University Press, 1961), 2: 33–206, and Hill, *Old South,* 2:465–89. The Unitarian response is well documented in William C. Gannett, *Ezra Stiles Gannett: Unitarian Minister in Boston, 1824–1871* (Boston: Roberts Brothers, 1875), pp. 107–11.

33. Gannett, *Gannett,* p. 115.

34. "The Christian Ministry," in Channing, *Works,* p. 257.

mote their opinions by practical measures. In 1825, the American Unitarian Association (AUA) was organized for similar ends. Even so, many Unitarians saw the AUA as an agency of sectarian control dangerous to religious liberty. Its officers were defensive in 1830 when they recommended the Association as a means of concerted action: "While it is founded on the principles of individual freedom and personal responsibleness in religious matters, it affords an opportunity for the culture of Christian sympathies and the exercise of a benevolent zeal, which ought not to be neglected without sufficient reason."[35] Since the AUA collected contributions in the 1820s that were minimal as compared with the wealth of the denomination, and its activity was virtually limited to the publication of tracts, this aspect of the Unitarian program was hardly successful.

Ad hoc efforts to extend Liberal religion were better supported. In 1822, prominent Unitarians associated to establish a new church in a growing middle-class neighborhood in west Boston. The building was funded by subscription, with shares valued at 100 dollars each, and was dedicated in 1824 as the Twelfth Congregational Society. Before the pews were sold to local residents, a standing committee of the subscribers chose Samuel Barrett, a recent Harvard Divinity School graduate, as the minister to make sure that Unitarian ideas would be preached. Here the voluntary basis of the temporary association was generally acceptable—and the abridged liberty of the future congregation passed without notice.[36]

Unitarian efforts effectively met the Orthodox challenge. Although six new Orthodox congregations were established in Boston between 1822 and 1830 to the Liberals' five, the Unitarians retained a numerical majority at the end of the decade, with fourteen churches to the Orthodox ten.[37] The revival proved a transient threat, moreover. Lyman Beecher, then minister of the Hanover Street Church and the leading Orthodox evangelical, was distracted by Orthodox infighting throughout his stay in Boston from 1826 to 1832. His controversies, on the one hand, with Charles

35. *Suggestions Respecting the Formation of Auxiliaries to the American Unitarian Association,* American Unitarian Association tracts, 2d ser., no. 6 (1830), p. 1. On the difficulties and activities of the AUA, see Gannett, *Gannett,* pp. 101–05.

36. Pray, *Twelfth Society,* pp. 3–19.

37. See appendix A for a list of the new churches. The Twelfth and Thirteenth Societies were middle-class churches formed with elite support. See Pray, *Twelfth Society,* 3–19, and, on the Thirteenth, or Purchase Street, Church, see Charles Crowe, *George Ripley: Transcendentalist and Utopian Socialist* (Athens: University of Georgia Press, 1967), pp. 42–44. The South Congregational Society separated from the Hollis Street Church when the meetinghouse of the latter became overcrowded (Allen, *Sketches of Churches,* p. 123). The Hawes Place Church, founded as an Orthodox congregation in 1819, became Unitarian in 1823 when the majority chose Lemuel Capen as minister (Homans, *Sketches,* p. 91). The Friend Street Chapel was constructed for Tuckerman's work with the poor. See Daniel T. McColgan, *Joseph Tuckerman: Pioneer in American Social Work* (Washington, D.C.: Catholic University Press, 1940), pp. 131–33.

Grandison Finney over Finney's "new measures" and, on the other, with conservative Congregationalists over Beecher's Arminian theology indicated serious divisions in Orthodoxy. The Boston revival showed the strain of these difficulties in the 1830s. While the number of Orthodox churches in the city increased by an impressive 150 percent in the 1820s, the growth rate fell to 30 percent in the next decade and declined to −6 percent just before the Civil War. But the Unitarians experienced similar setbacks. In the 1830s, the rate at which they established new churches decreased by almost half, dropping from 56 percent in the 1820s to only 29 percent. There was a temporary resurgence in the 1840s, when the number of Liberal congregations increased by 39 percent. But the Unitarians, like their Orthodox opponents, dramatically lost ground in the 1850s when enough churches disbanded to produce a −16 percent rate of change. Their problem was clearly more complex than a one-to-one contest with Orthodoxy, as they soon came to see.[38]

The growing strength of Methodists, Baptists, and Universalists in the 1830s and of Episcopalians and Catholics in the 1840s hastened the decline of both Orthodoxy and Liberalism. The success of the evangelical denominations was probably due to their ability to attract the in-migrants who flocked to Boston after 1830. The Orthodox disputes on free will and engineered revivals undoubtedly hurt their chances with the newcomers, as did the Unitarians' comparative lack of religious fervor and increasingly expensive, and hence exclusive, churches. The rise of Universalism, the rural counterpart of Unitarianism which likewise stressed reason in religion, supports the case that in-migration greatly changed the religious map of Boston.[39] By the 1840s, the Episcopal church profited by the taste for

38. See appendix B for growth rates of these and other denominations between 1820 and 1860. Geographically, I have based my calculations on an area including the peninsula of Boston proper, South Boston, and East Boston, since adjacent towns such as Roxbury were not annexed to the city until after the Civil War. I have relied primarily on the following sources: Winsor, *Memorial History*, 3:401–546; Snow, *History*, pp. 338–47, 382–85; Homans, *Sketches*, pp. 66–129; Thomas C. Simonds, *History of South Boston* (Boston: David Clapp, 1857), pp. 154–82; and William H. Sumner, *A History of East Boston* (Boston: J. E. Tilton, 1858), pp. 643–63.

39. One index of the extent to which these denominations grew because of in-migration is the proportion of their new churches located in South and East Boston, two areas of the city separated from the peninsula by water, which were developed after the War of 1812. The Universalists profited most by in-migration, owing 50 percent of their total growth between 1815 and 1860 to these outlying areas, while the Unitarians, at 16.7 percent, were among the least successful with the same population (only the Episcopalians, at 10 percent, fared worse). For other denominations, the proportions of new churches in South and East Boston during this period were: Orthodox, 29.4 percent; Catholic, 23.1 percent; Methodist, 21.4 percent; and Baptist, 20 percent. The relatively equal dependence of the three evangelical denominations on churches in these regions for their total growth suggests that they were competing for newcomers, and the overall decline of Orthodoxy, compared with the relatively steady rise of the Baptists and Methodists (see appendix B), indicates that the

ritual and benevolence, the twin components of the Oxford movement, of
the middle and upper classes. Even Unitarian congregations lost members
to a church more inherently patrician than their own relatively stark form
of worship.[40] Finally, the Catholic church owed its strength to the Irish
immigration. But the Unitarians' dilemma after 1830 had less to do with
the choice of religious alternatives by new urban groups than with the
declining influence of religion as Boston grew.

Between 1820 and 1860, the number of churches in Boston increased
from 27 to 102. Organized religion grew four times as much in just four
decades as it had in nearly two centuries since the establishment of the
First Church in 1630. But religious activity failed to keep pace with
population growth, and the 1830s, the first decade in which this became a
visible trend, were a turning point for Christianity in the city. In the 1820s,
church growth exceeded population growth by almost two to one, at 63
percent and 35 percent, respectively. But in the 1830s, the pace of establishing new congregations fell decisively to 48 percent and barely kept
ahead of the increasing population growth rate at 38 percent. There was a
slight revival of religious interest in the 1840s, with a growth rate of 50
percent, but population now outdistanced this gain at 61 percent. Urban
expansion slackened to 30 percent in the 1850s. But religious activity

---

latter groups profited at the former's expense. On the churches in the outlying areas, see
Simonds, South Boston, pp. 154–82, and Sumner, East Boston, pp. 643–63. The best
studies of the social geography of antebellum Boston are Walter Muir Whitehill, Boston: A
Topographical History (Cambridge, Mass.: Harvard University Press, 1963), pp. 47–139,
and Peter R. Knights, The Plain People of Boston, 1830–1860: A Study of City Growth
(New York: Oxford University Press, 1971), pp. 11–18, 71–74.

40. Though the rise of Episcopalianism is commonly, and in some measure correctly,
attributed to the status consciousness of aspiring groups, genuine religious commitments
figured largely in the Boston movement. Wealthy Unitarian converts such as Amos Lawrence, who left the Brattle Street Church for St. Paul's, and William Appleton, who built St.
Stephen's Chapel on Purchase Street for E. M. P. Wells's work with the poor, turned to
Episcopalianism because it combined charity with ecclesiastical formalism. On Appleton,
see Chandler Robbins, Memoir of Hon. William Appleton (Boston: John Wilson and Son,
1863). For an illuminating look at the piety which motivated one prominent Orthodox
convert, see The Journal of Richard Henry Dana, Jr., ed. Robert F. Lucid, 3 vols. (Cambridge, Mass.: Harvard University Press, 1968), 1: esp. 114–299. Dana, who was a lawyer,
along with several physicians and others was responsible for founding the Church of the
Advent in 1844, a free church in a relatively unfashionable area of west Boston which
adopted high church ritual. See Parish of the Advent, pp. 13–43. The strength of Episcopalianism among professionals in this instance conforms to William Manross's findings
on the social composition of the denomination as a whole, in The Episcopal Church in the
United States, 1800–1840 (1938; reprint ed., New York: AMS, 1969), pp. 180–85. For a
more general discussion of the Oxford movement in America, see William Stevens Perry, The
History of the American Episcopal Church, 1587–1883, 2 vols. (Boston: James R. Osgood,
1885), 2:269–76.

dropped even more precipitously to a mere 6 percent increase over the previous decade.[41]

It is possible to argue that large memberships of urban churches, compared with smaller rural congregations, make church growth rates a questionable indicator of religious vitality.[42] But the difficulties of Unitarian churches suggest that this is not the case. By the 1850s Liberal churches were plagued by embarrassingly small memberships. The historic First Church had fewer than eighty active families in 1853. Struggling congregations disbanded, as did the Twelfth and Thirteenth Congregational Societies in the early 1860s, or consolidated, or migrated to more prosperous neighborhoods in hopes of regaining support. Unable to pay its mortgage, the Second Church united with the Church of Our Savior in 1854 but continued to lose members and finally moved to Back Bay.[43] The conclusion is inescapable that Unitarianism, and religion in general, failed to command a broad urban following. The problem was already apparent to Tuckerman in 1838, when he estimated in his *Principles and Results of the Ministry at Large* that from one-quarter to one-third of Boston's inhabitants were unchurched.[44] He used this fact to startle his readers and, having gained their attention, turned to the subtler dilemma of religion in the city.

INFIDELITY

Unitarians were deeply worried in the 1830s by the problem of "infidelity." Many people were staying away from church, even more were indifferent to basic morals and ethics, and a few went so far as openly to ridicule the Christian religion. But in the largest sense in which they used the word, "infidelity" meant that life in Boston seriously violated the Liberals' idea of a Christian society.

In the 1830s Unitarians saw their community changed into a city of diverse and conflicting interests. As the industrialization of nearby towns made Boston the financial and commercial center for New England man-

41. Population growth rates are cited in Knights, *Plain People*, p. 20.

42. This might be one way to reconcile the rising church membership figures cited by some historians with my findings on the declining rate of church formation. Winthrop Hudson estimates that the ratio of church members to population nationwide rose from 1:15 to 1:8 between 1800 and 1835, in *Religion in America* (New York: Scribner's, 1965), p. 129. The evidence I cite below, however, does indicate that declining church growth rates reflect a real decline in religious interest, at least in Boston in the late antebellum period. See appendix A for a more detailed discussion of the uses and problems of church growth rates in urban religious history.

43. Ellis, *First Church*, p. 317; Pray, *Twelfth Society*, pp. 60–110; Robbins, *Second Church*, pp. 145–64; and George Eager, *Historical Sketch of the Second Church* (Boston: Robinson Printing, 1894), pp. 31–39.

44. *Ministry at Large*, p. 10.

ufacturing, three classes took shape in the city: a capitalist elite composed of the old merchant class with new interests in industry, banking, and transportation; an aspiring middle class ranging from small manufacturers to clerks and other white-collar workers; and a working class of skilled and unskilled laborers, now subject to the exploitation and fluctuations of a booming market economy. Social stratification was not new in Boston, but the distances between classes were. Each class possessed organizations and means of communication which formed the core of distinct subcultures. Most distressing, all three classes were learning to use these weapons to defend their status against intruders, that is, against each other. How far industrial Boston diverged from Unitarian reason, toleration, and ethical practice need not be said. When Unitarians set out to evangelize the city, their movement was based on a recognition that Liberal religion was no longer a value system commanding common allegiance but was at best a prescriptive solution to a cultural crisis.[45]

Economic change was at the root of these developments. In the middle decades of the antebellum period, industrial production replaced foreign trade as the base of Boston's economy. The merchant elite led the transformation. When embargoes and war disrupted foreign commerce between 1808 and 1815, merchants invested idle capital in domestic manufactures on an experimental scale. The first trial was at Waltham, Massachusetts, in 1813, where the power loom, factory system, and corporate organization were introduced into textile production. The investors —Patrick Jackson, Benjamin Gorham, and Uriah Cotting—were all Boston merchants and relatives of the project's prime mover, Francis Cabot Lowell. Although trade resumed after 1815, these men and others extended their industrial investments. The high price of Southern cotton on the English market generally stimulated the American economy. And westward migration and improved transportation promised an expanding domestic market for manufactured goods.[46]

Industrialization spurred urbanization in turn. The textile center of Lowell is a classic example. In 1822, Lowell was a village of twelve houses; by 1840, with a population of 20,796, it was the second largest city in Massachusetts. Inland cities grew rapidly as the textile industry stimulated

45. For an excellent analysis of a similar process of social diversification in Rochester, which preceded the revivals of the 1830s, see Johnson, *Shopkeeper's Millennium*, pp. 15–94. Also significant is Anthony F. C. Wallace's discussion of evangelicalism in *Rockdale: The Growth of an American Village in the Early Industrial Revolution* (New York: Knopf, 1972), pp. 243–349, although his argument that this was a "counterattack" on Enlightenment rationalism is only marginally applicable to the Boston experience.

46. On the transition from a mercantile to an industrial economy, see North, *Economic Growth*, pp. 156–76; Winsor, *Memorial History*, 4:69–178; George Rogers Taylor, *The Transportation Revolution, 1815–1860* (New York: Harper and Row, 1951); and Edward Kirkland, *Men, Cities, and Transportation*, 2 vols. (Cambridge, Mass.: Harvard University Press, 1948), 1: passim.

subsidiary production of consumer goods and machinery.[47] Boston itself did not industrialize because of the shortage of open land for factory construction on the already crowded peninsula and the lack of water power for mechanization. But the city profited nevertheless, and trade, banking, and custom production for the prosperous urban market expanded as a result of regional development. In-migrants and immigrants were attracted by the prospects for advancement and by 1845 represented 40 percent and 33 percent of Boston's population, respectively, while only 27 percent were native Bostonians.[48]

Bostonians were not altogether happy with their prosperity, however. In the shifting urban scene, with unprecedented geographic movement and social mobility up and down the scale, people were anxious, fearful for their positions, and ready to fend off possible threats. Paradoxically, the dramatic changes in Boston society in the 1830s were matched by a new cultural rigidity.

Of all social groups, Boston's upper class was least in danger of changing in composition. Wealth was concentrated in the same few hands after 1830, since the merchant elite financed industry, banking, and railroads. According to Peter Knights's study of Boston's "plain people," it became increasingly difficult to enter an income group of over 10,000 dollars a year between 1830 and 1860, and the average age of those who did belong became older as time went on.[49] There was little chance for the small investor to rise to equal status with this powerful—and static—capitalist class. Nevertheless, the elite deliberately closed its ranks against potential members in a way symbolic of its increasing insularity.

Marriage into the upper class no longer guaranteed assimilation, and here social attitudes rather than market forces defended its corporate identity. Charles Follen (1796–1840), a professor of law and philosophy in his native Germany, married Eliza Lee Cabot in 1828. Already a language instructor at Harvard at a menial salary, he was allowed to teach German literature only when his wife's friends contributed special funds. The money ran out in 1834, and since Follen's antislavery views had become generally known, the college refused to renew his contract. In her

---

47. North, *Economic Growth*, pp. 159–65. In most cases, urban growth in Boston's hinterland was more gradual than Lowell's and was not altogether the result of industrialization. See Richard D. Brown, "The Emergence of Urban Society in Rural Massachusetts, 1760–1820," *Journal of American History* 61 (1974): 29–51. Brown makes the important point that urbanization was neither a sudden nor a strictly quantitative process but involved less visible changes in social and individual life—heterogeneity, cosmopolitanism, increased communications, and choice. Still, industrial expansion did accelerate urban development between 1820 and 1840. See Jeffrey Williamson, "Antebellum Urbanization in the American Northeast," *Journal of Economic History* 25 (1965): 592–608.

48. Knights, *Plain People*, p. 33.

49. Ibid., p. 123. See also Morison, *Maritime History*, p. 241, on the continuing power of the merchant class.

bitter memoir of his life, his wife recorded the refusal of Unitarian congregations to settle him as a minister when he turned to preaching.[50] Eliza
Cabot Follen found she could not bring her husband into her circle of
friends but had married out of her class. When new arrivals in Boston were
no longer Unitarians from Salem but Germans infected with the idealism
of their homeland, the elite used its money, college, and churches to
protect itself from contamination.

In-migrants from rural New England often fared no better, despite
equal talents and propitious marriages. Transcendentalist Bronson Alcott
(1799–1888), the son of a Connecticut farmer, arrived in Boston in 1828
to conduct a school sponsored by a group of prominent women. Two years
later he married one of them, Abigail May. But even with his family
connections, wealthy patrons, and acquaintance with Liberal ministers, it
was not until 1835 that Alcott gained access to the Athenaeum library, "a
privilege," he wrote in his journal, "that I have sought since my return to
Boston but sought hitherto in vain."[51] Always an exclusive institution, the
Athenaeum was becoming an inner sanctum to which outsiders were
admitted only after long scrutiny. Nor was acceptance any more proof of
lasting loyalty than the limited subscription for Follen's professorship. In
1837, Alcott's religious opinions caused a furor in Boston and the elite
withdrew support from his school—as well as his Athenaeum privileges.[52]
With neither a steady income nor social status for much of the rest of her
life, Abigail May Alcott as much as Eliza Follen bore the consequences of
upper-class suspicion.

The defensive self-containment of the upper class sometimes worked
directly against its own too-independent members. When Lydia Maria
Child, the wife of lawyer David Lee Child, wrote her *Appeal in Favor of
that Class of Americans called Africans* in 1832, the Athenaeum revoked
her reading privileges. In a patrician society built on nuances, the
action—a symbolic slap on the hand to a presumptuous woman—was not
insignificant.[53] The elite was learning to use its institutions to discipline its

50. *The Works of Charles Follen, with a Memoir of his Life* [ed. Eliza Cabot Follen], 5
vols. (Boston: Hilliard, Gray, 1841), 1:330–581. See also his "Address to the People of the
United States on the Subject of Slavery" (1834), in *Works,* 5:254–313.

51. Alcott, *Journals,* p. 65.

52. Abigail May Alcott was related to the Quincys and Sewalls, and children of those
families were among those withdrawn from the school, dramatizing the failure of kinship
ties in the face of questionable opinions. Though no complete list of Alcott's patrons has
been made, probably because they changed from term to term, the best attempt is Josephine
E. Roberts, "Elizabeth Peabody and the Temple School," *New England Quarterly* 15
(1942): 501.

53. Kirk Jeffrey documents the social ostracism and financial losses Child suffered as a
result of her abolitionism, in "Marriage, Career, and Feminine Ideology in Nineteenth-
Century America: Reconstructing the Marital Experience of Lydia Maria Child, 1828
–1874," *Feminist Studies* 1 (1975): 113–30.

members and to enforce standardized opinions. Moreover, their resort to pressure showed awareness of divisive forces within their ranks as well as dangerous influences without. Unitarians no longer agreed on the bounds of reason, liberty, and moral duty. To Lydia Maria Child, it was a duty as well as a right to advocate the abolition of slavery. But to the trustees of the Athenaeum, liberty became license when it threatened prosperity and order. The dependence of New England's largest industry, the manufacture of textiles, on the cotton produced by Southern slaves made freethinking like Child's too risky to pass uncensured.

Dissent within the elite extended to the status of religion itself. Was Christianity the rule of life or merely a Sunday affair? James T. Austin, the attorney general of Massachusetts, implied the latter in his anonymous attack on Channing's *Slavery* in 1835. While Channing had argued that slavery violated Christian teachings and should be gradually abolished, Austin made his rebuttal on purely practical grounds. Southern opinion could not be altered, he said, and the Northern view, that "it is a breach of our highest political contract, and a violation of good faith and common honesty, to disturb the internal condition, and domestic arrangements of the Slave-holding states," was perfectly sound. Slavery was a political question, outside the legitimate sphere of ministers with their troublesome ideals and "assumption[s] of superior sanctity" and "I charge him," Austin concluded, "—in spite of his disclaimer—with *the doctrine of INSURRECTION.*"[54]

Channing thought Austin's reasoning as dangerous a species of freethinking, however, as Austin did Channing's. Such devotion to secular interests—reflected in rhetoric distressingly free of a higher point of reference—was the root not only of injustice but of disorder itself. "A spirit of rivalry, jealousy, selfish competition," Channing wrote in 1833, "supplants the spirit of mutual interest, respect, support, and aid, by which Christianity proposes to knit mankind into *universal brotherhood.*"[55] He protested the social irresponsibility of the upper class: "This spirit of exclusiveness triumphs over the spirit of Christianity, and, through its prevalence, the great work given to every human being, which is to improve his less favored fellow-being, is slighted." Channing held the rich most accountable for the negligence of religious duty in the city because of their superior education and wealth. But he knew that others were responsible as well.

The members of Boston's middle class, in the opinion of Transcendentalist Theodore Parker, were hungry for wealth, status, and culture, and despite this moralizing tone, he was not far from wrong:

54. *Remarks on Dr. Channing's Slavery* (Boston: Russell, Shattuck and John H. Eastburn, 1835), pp. 5, 14. Channing's *Slavery* (1835) is in his *Works*, pp. 688–743.
55. Quoted in William Henry Channing, *The Life of William Ellery Channing* (Boston: American Unitarian Association, 1880), p. 463.

Young men—the children of honest parents, who live by their manly
and toil-hardened hands, . . . are ashamed of their fathers' occupation,
and forsaking the plough, the chisel, or the forge seek a livelihood in
what is sometimes named a more respectable and genteel vocation;
that is a calling that demands less of the hands, and quite often less of
the head likewise, than their fathers' hardy craft; for that imbecility,
which drives men to those callings has its seat mostly in the higher
region than the hands.[56]

Many of the new bourgeoisie were young men from New England farms
and towns, but the ones who prospered most were Bostonians who
profited by the business of recent arrivals.[57] All whom I include in this
group were white-collar workers such as clerks, tavernkeepers, grocers,
and the owners of small manufactures. As a class, they were as conscious
of impressions and as eager to assimilate the signs of gentility as Parker
implied. But they remained at a distance from elite culture. Condescension
like Parker's (particularly ironic in light of his own rise to the ministry
from artisan origins) was an unwelcome reminder of their subordinate
status, and the patrician sensibility failed, in any case, to account for their
tastes. The popular literature they read was at times partisan and sardonic,
at times sentimental. Joseph T. Buckingham and Sarah Hale were two
writers who spoke successfully to the interests of their class.

Joseph Tinker Buckingham (1779–1861) owned and edited the
Boston Courier from its establishment in 1824 until his retirement in
1848. The newspaper, he wrote in his autobiography, was "the organ and
the advocate of what might be called, without reproach, 'the Middling
Interest.' "[58] Buckingham's politics are an indication of whom he meant.
Although he was a vocal partisan of the Whig party, he opposed both the
National Bank and railroad construction, a position which favored men

56. "Thoughts on Labor," *Dial* 1 (Apr. 1841): 498.
57. On the sources of Boston's population between 1830 and 1860, see Knights, *Plain
People,* pp. 33–47. Although my class analysis aims more at identifying groups who shared a
common outlook than at sociological precision, Knights's more detailed socioeconomic
categories (pp. 149–56) help locate the middle class. See also Karen Halttunen's suggestive
study of middle-class culture, "Confidence Men and Painted Women: The Problem of
Hypocrisy in Sentimental America, 1830–1870" (Ph.D. diss., Yale University, 1979).
58. Joseph T. Buckingham, *Personal Memoirs and Recollections of Editorial Life,* 2
vols. (Boston: Ticknor, Reed, and Fields, 1852), 2:217–18. Buckingham named some of his
supporters (2:5–8): Isaac C. Pray, originally from Maine, an importer later involved in
cotton manufacturing; Samuel Billings, merchant and member of the city's first board of
aldermen; George Hallett, who came to Boston from Barnstable on Cape Cod as a grocer's
apprentice; Charles Thacher, son of Peter Thacher, minister of the Brattle Street Church;
Joshua Clap, originally from Westfield, Mass., who owned a woolen factory from 1824
until 1832, when he went bankrupt; Jonas B. Brown, who came as an apprentice from New
Hampshire and eventually owned a woolen factory in Worcester County but also went
bankrupt because of Henry Clay's compromise on the import of British woolens in 1832.

with limited capital who were eager to exploit the local market. Similarly, the *Courier* was a staunch supporter of social order and attacked all reforms indiscriminately, but it so interpreted conservative interests as to hasten the rise of the middle class.

Buckingham's personal history matched the background of his supporters. The son of a Connecticut tavernkeeper, he worked as a farm hand, printer, traveling actor, teacher, and editor of short-lived magazines before he began the *Courier*. His status was marginal throughout his life: he declared bankruptcy during the War of 1812 and mortgaged the *Courier* after the Panic of 1837. A resident of Boston since 1804, he was known as much for his infamy as for his talent. In 1822, the Commonwealth of Massachusetts tried Buckingham for libel when he accused John Maffit, an Irish Methodist preacher, of atheism and sexual improprieties.[59] But there were no similar attempts to silence him in the 1830s. Buckingham's slanderous style was unchanged. Because he was backed by a growing constituency and protected by the elite's own doubts about the safety of dissent, however, he was free to be as insulting as he pleased.

It is little wonder that infidelity bothered concerned Unitarians with Buckingham in town. He championed a kind of social order based on demolishing opposing opinions by sarcasm and forcing consensus by manipulating anxieties for acceptability. Aggressive as he was in print, his attacks betrayed the uneasiness of a class with little power other than language to defend its interests. Buckingham was aware of his conflict with Unitarian standards and was not without hostility toward the upper class. When he turned his ridicule on Bronson Alcott, one of its weakest members, he so twisted the Liberal idea of toleration that he implicated the entire ethical system in his attack: "Mr. Alcott is a very honest and sincere Christian for aught we know; but if he be either honest or sincere, he must be insane or half-witted, and his friends ought to take care of him without delay."[60] Consistent with his conservatism, Buckingham advocated legal repression of dissent from Unitarianism. But he disdained the clergy's "somnific theology" and "warm-water insipidity of ethics" and left no record of church membership.[61]

Buckingham's readers could use methods more forcible than words, however, when religion conflicted with their interests. The most dramatic instance was the controversy in the Hollis Street Church over Rev. John Pierpont's temperance preaching. In the late 1830s, liquor distillers and retailers bought up pews in the church to silence Pierpont by voting his dismissal. Practical politics underwrote the conflict, since Pierpont helped draft the Massachusetts law of 1838 which forbade the sale of hard liquor

59. Ibid., 1:105–18.
60. Editorial footnote to "To Fathers and Mothers," *Boston Courier*, semiweekly ed., Mar. 30, 1837.
61. Buckingham, *Memoirs*, 2:35–36.

in quantities of less than fifteen gallons. When the first ecclesiastical trial in Unitarian history was called to mediate between Pierpont and the congregation, Buckingham supported the "traffickers in ardent spirits" in the press, while the clergy, acting as judges, vindicated their colleague. Even so, Buckingham was in fact the victor. In terms of style, the politics of contention had effectively won the day on Hollis Street against reasonable, peaceable religion.[62]

The conflict between middle-class values and Liberal religion was comparatively hidden in Sarah Hale's case but was nonetheless real. Deferential, decorous, and moralistic, Hale (1788–1879) dedicated her *Ladies' Magazine* to the modest goal of educating women, "not that they may usurp the station, or encroach on the prerogatives of man; but that each individual may lend her aid to the intellectual and moral character of those within her sphere."[63] But her promise to preserve sexual boundaries obscured the fact that she was counseling upwardly mobile women in attitudes essential to respectability. No one demonstrated the art of self-creation better than Sarah Hale herself.

Hale was the widow of a New Hampshire lawyer who was left with five children to support in 1822. An intelligent and ambitious woman, she wrote a novel, *Northwood; A Tale of New England,* which extolled New England virtue as the source—and moral justification—of national prosperity. The book was an immediate success, and as a result she was hired to edit the *Ladies' Magazine* in Boston. She moved to the city in 1828 and in 1838 moved on to Philadelphia, the national publishing center for family magazines, to edit *Godey's Lady's Book.*

It was a career that revealed all the ambiguities of image-making as a means of self-advancement. Hale was a businesswoman anxious for success, but she gained respectability by advising a domestic role for women. In print and in fact, she created a persona of devoted widowhood commensurate with her prescriptions, wearing mourning clothes every day of her life from her husband's death to her own, fifty-five years later. She made herself into a "lady," in short, by manners, fashion, and particularly language, the only weapons available to women in a society where

62. For the transcript of the trial, see Samuel K. Lothrop, *Proceedings of an Ecclesiastical Council, in the Case of the Proprietors of Hollis-Street Meeting-House and the Rev. John Pierpont, their Pastor* (Boston: W. W. Clapp and Son, 1841). Francis Jackson, the key witness for Pierpont, documented a concerted effort by distillers and retail merchants to buy a majority vote in the church, pp. 173–200. The data supplied provide an unusual look at the social composition and tensions of one Unitarian church. Buckingham was a representative to the Massachusetts House of Representatives in 1838 and 1839 and officially opposed temperance legislation. See Mass. General Court, Joint Special Committee on the Sale of Spiritous Liquors, "Minority Report," *Reports and Bills relating to the Sale of Spiritous Liquors,* House document no. 37, Mar. 6, 1839, pp. 23–25.

63. "Introduction," *Ladies' Magazine* 1 (1828): 2.

economic and political power was denied the sex.[64] To the extent that the condition of women matched that of the middle class in general, Hale's success was a lesson in the politics of insinuation. Rather than bully their way to status, men too might imitate patrician styles and move up through self-effacement. But in the process, religion became a trapping of gentility as impressions were substituted for facts.

Hale's religious affiliations mirrored her rising status. She became an Episcopalian in Philadelphia, and although there is little direct evidence for the earlier years, she appears to have given up Orthodoxy for Unitarianism in Boston.[65] But her theory of domesticity posed an even more serious threat to religion than her concern with outward show. By designating women at home the guardians of piety, Hale effectually exonerated men in the marketplace from moral responsibility. As she divorced piety from power, she sacrificed ethics to advancement, and in a Protestant society based on individual accountability, this was one step toward legitimate irreligion. Sarah Hale and Joseph Buckingham were strange bedfellows, but they were partners in a cause understandably jarring to the Unitarian conscience.

In contrast to the new bourgeoisie, Boston's working class was less anxious to gain status in the 1830s than afraid of losing it. Many skilled journeymen, Tuckerman wrote in his *Essay on the Wages Paid to Females,* would never be more than wage earners.[66] Concentrated capital, competition for work, and the beginning of mechanization all blocked advancement to master status. During recessions, unemployment was high, and wages were driven below subsistence level.[67] Workers acutely felt their subordination in the context of Boston's growing prosperity, and to Tuckerman, it was not surprising that they avoided churches which epitomized the power of wealth, since "poverty itself would have been less revolting to them than the free seats in our churches which are intended for the poor."[68] Nor was religion as relevant to their daily lives as the new trade unions were. As weapons of secular class interest, the labor organizations of the 1830s were one more sign, to Unitarians, of urban infidelity.

64. See William R. Taylor's discussion of Hale's image-making as the counterpart of her status aspirations in *Cavalier and Yankee: The Old South and American National Character* (New York: George Braziller, 1961), pp. 115–41. For an excellent and more general discussion of these tactics, see Douglas, *Feminization,* pp. 44–79.

65. Hale's biographer Ruth E. Finley mentions no religious affiliation in Boston but does note that Hale's sons attended Harvard, in *The Lady of Godey's: Sarah Josepha Hale* (Philadelphia: J. B. Lippincott, 1931), pp. 82–85.

66. *An Essay on the Wages Paid to Females for their Labour* (Philadelphia: Carey and Hart, 1830), p. 8.

67. Tuckerman estimated that a total of 1,500 journeymen printers, carpenters, and mechanics found only occasional work during the recession of 1829 and, more generally, that there were twice as many workers in Boston as jobs, in *Wages,* p. 13.

68. *Ministry at Large,* p. 17.

The New England Association of Farmers, Mechanics, and Other Working Men, begun in 1831, and the Boston Trades' Union, its successor in 1834, aimed to unite workers of all trades behind broad reform programs. Some of their goals were free public education, legal restraints on monopolies, and the abolition of imprisonment for debt. But the ten-hour day symbolized labor's demand for equal rights:

> We have too long been subjected to the odious, cruel, unjust, and tyrannical system which compels the operative Mechanic to exhaust his physical and mental powers by excessive toil, until he has no desire but to eat and sleep, and in many cases he has no power to do either from extreme debility. . . . No man or body of men who require such excessive labor can be friends to the country or the Rights of Man. We also say, that we have rights, and we have duties to perform as American Citizens and members of society, which forbid us to dispose of more than Ten Hours for a day's work.[69]

What is important here, in terms of measuring the distance of Boston's workers from Unitarian culture, is that labor spoke a language of its own. By insisting on their rights, liberties, and duties as citizens, workingmen adhered to the tradition of the secular Enlightenment and American Revolution. It was true that Unitarians had incorporated these values into their religious system, but now labor divorced them from Christianity and applied them to economic and political issues. Liberal religion itself was seen as the tool of class oppression—"Starve us to prevent us from getting drunk!" union leaders bitterly commented on the temperance argument for low wages, "Wonderful Wisdom! Refined Benevolence! Exalted Philanthropy!"—and the Rights of Man philosophy became the only source of justice for the working class.[70]

The case of Abner Kneeland is a fascinating example of the way one working-class spokesman used attacks on religion to discredit the social establishment. Kneeland (1774–1844) was a carpenter from Worcester County who first became a Baptist and then a Universalist preacher in 1803. In 1829, he renounced Christianity altogether and moved to Boston

---

69. Boston Trades Union, "Ten Hour Circular" (1835), in Commons, *Documentary History,* 6:94–95. On the labor movement in New England in the 1830s, see John R. Commons et al., *History of Labor in the United States,* 4 vols. (New York: Macmillan, 1918–35), 1:302–25. The best study of labor leaders is Edward Pessen, *Most Uncommon Jacksonians: The Radical Leaders of the Early Labor Movement* (Albany: State University of New York Press, 1967), esp. pp. 103–11.

70. "Ten Hour Circular," p. 98. Although arguments of temperance reformers were not usually so crude, their identification of intemperance as a working-class problem was offensive. See *A Letter to the Mechanics of Boston, respecting the Formation of a City Temperance Society* (Boston: Massachusetts Society for the Suppression of Intemperance, 1831).

to publish his gospel of free inquiry in his paper the *Boston Investigator*.[71] Equating freedom from religion with liberty, Kneeland counseled his readers to use reason to fight superstition and exploitation at once. He demonstrated the mind's liberating power in 1833 when he published an exposé of the virgin birth and a skeptical inquiry into the character of God, the first so off-color and the second so sarcastic that they seemed far from reasonable to Unitarians. It is not hard to imagine how thoroughly Kneeland offended Whiggish Boston when the *Investigator* compared God answering prayers to Andrew Jackson dispensing the spoils of office: "I think the old gentleman is more a subject of pity than General Jackson was during his late visit, his bowing and shaking was very arduous, but it was all one way, congratulatory and pleasing, and he had some occasional respite; but only think of God having no respite whatever; day or night."[72]

The Commonwealth of Massachusetts tried Kneeland for blasphemy in 1834, and through four years of court battles before his final conviction, he flaunted his "crown of martyrdom" to drive home the contradiction between Unitarian freedom and such obvious repression. The federal Constitution was Kneeland's Bible, and he highlighted the theocratic feudalism of Massachusetts's blasphemy statute against liberal provisions of the First Amendment. When he wrote his memoir of the trials in the Suffolk County jail, Kneeland indicted Liberal Christianity in his usual irreverent style:

> BOSTON JAIL—alias *Hades*—alias *Hell*, June 18, 1838. *Fellow Citizens! Countrymen!! and Lovers of Liberty!!!*—Sixty-three years ago a battle was fought on Bunker Hill, in plain sight of my window, where I now am, and to commemorate which event a Monument has been raised, or attempted to be raised, and the drums are now beating, and

71. Kneeland supplied his own biographical information in *A Review of the Trial, Conviction, and Final Imprisonment in the Common Jail of the County of Suffolk, of Abner Kneeland, for the Alleged Crime of Blasphemy* (Boston: George A. Chapman, 1838), pp. 71–74. See also Roderick S. French, "Liberation from Man and God in Boston: Abner Kneeland's Free Thought Campaign, 1830–1839," *American Quarterly* 32 (1980): 202–21, and Henry Steele Commager, "The Blasphemy of Abner Kneeland," *New England Quarterly* 8 (1935): 29–41. Kneeland was not a labor leader per se but a preacher to his Society of Free Enquirers, which included members of the working class. Orestes Brownson attributed his influence more to his democratic politics than to his religious opinions: "People do not go to hear him because he advocates atheistical or pantheistic doctrines; not because he denies Christianity, rejects the Bible, and indulges in various witticisms at the expense of members of the clerical profession; but because he opposes the aristocracy of our churches and vindicates the rights of the mind. He succeeds, not because he is an infidel, but because he has hitherto shown himself a democrat" (*Wants of the Times*, p. 10).

72. Quoted in Kneeland, *Review*, p. 18. Both articles were in fact reprinted from the *New York Enquirer*, and Kneeland was prosecuted merely for publishing them. A third article written by Kneeland was also cited in the case because of this alleged denial of God: "Universalists believe in a god which I do not; but believe that their god, with all his moral attributes; (aside from nature itself,) is nothing more than a chimera of their own imagination" (Kneeland, p. 20).

the guns were this morning firing, in honor of that glorious battle. But what was it all for? LIBERTY! And what am I here for? For the honest exercise of that very Liberty for which our fathers fought and bled. . . . If this can be done to a man against whom no man says aught, save on account of his religious sentiments, what will be done to those who are less discreet in this respect? Arouse, fellow citizens, for a liberty more precious, much more valuable than that for which your fathers fought and bled is at stake.[73]

Shrewd and adept at manipulating symbols, Kneeland was a new type of popular leader not unlike Buckingham and Hale. He was well aware that he had put Unitarianism on trial and, by means of the popular press, had won his case with the people.

The reasoning of Chief Justice Lemuel Shaw of the Massachusetts Supreme Court in the Kneeland case was a recognition of what had happened to Boston in the 1830s. Shaw argued that the blasphemy statute did not "prohibit the fullest inquiry, and the freest discussion, for all honest and fair purposes" but did proscribe "an intended design to calumniate and disparage the Supreme Being, and to destroy the veneration due to him."[74] Kneeland's crime, it turned out, was a matter of style, and society was implicated in the charge. Bostonians no longer communicated in the measured phrases of the Unitarian pulpit but in the jarring language of the marketplace, as all classes and their advocates, from Austin to Kneeland, violated the reasonableness, toleration, and social harmony taught by Liberal Christianity. Style, however, was just a sign of deeper problems that came with the rise of the industrial city—elitism, status seeking, exploitation, and above all, a self-interested spirit, rooted in fear, that took hold of all classes and pitted each one against the others. The goal of Unitarian evangelicals was to right these wrongs. It would not be an easy task.

EVANGELICAL UNITARIANISM

Evangelical Unitarianism was a movement to reform Boston society by new religious means. The infidelity of the 1830s consisted not of reasonable objections to Christian doctrine but of trends to ignore, to sneer, and to reduce religion to a shadow of its intended meaning. Here was a problem that Unitarian rationalism could not touch, and it offered the motive for the campaign to enlist the heart. Similarly, evangelicals fought fire with

73. Quoted in Kneeland, *Review*, pp. 46–47.
74. Majority ruling, Apr. 2, 1838, quoted in Octavius Pickering, *Reports of Cases argued and determined in the Supreme Judicial Court of Massachusetts*, 24 vols. (Boston: Little, Brown, 1854), 20:220. Transcripts of the previous trials are found in John D. Lawson, ed., *American State Trials*, 17 vols. (St. Louis: Thomas Law, 1921), 13:450–575.

fire when they adopted the means of the cultural marketplace, such as magazines, lectures, and voluntary associations, to advance their cause. But who, we must ask first, were Unitarian evangelicals in social terms?

The idea of an "evangelical party" introduces a social category at variance with the class structure I have just described and may, quite legitimately, be puzzling. Since all Unitarians belonged to some class (usually upper or middle), how is it possible that they were "infidels" and "evangelicals" at once? The difference between weekday and Sunday behavior must account for part of the answer. By definition, urban industrial society makes conflicting demands on an individual, and the tension between market and religious imperatives was especially acute in this period of nascent capitalism. But there is a more concrete answer to the problem of evangelical constituency. Although the program won broad support in the denomination, some Unitarians were more active than others. Roughly defined, these were ministers, divinity students, teachers, women, and people with other reform commitments such as antislavery.[75] Other Liberals paid their dues in terms of either money contributions or passive assent but harbored a latent skepticism about the wisdom of the movement. After 1836, their differences exploded in the Transcendentalist controversy, and the beginnings of this conflict are visible in the present discussion.

The most widely supported evangelical program was the missionary effort to the poor. Nine Unitarian churches united in 1834 as the Benevolent Fraternity of Christian Churches (BFCC) to sponsor the ministry at large. These ministers were expected to follow the method Joseph Tuckerman (1778–1840) had devised since 1826, first visiting the poor in their homes to offer religious counsel, then gathering them into new congregations. The project was quite successful. By 1838, the BFCC had constructed two chapels valued at 30,000 dollars, had employed four ministers, and had provided over 100 volunteer teachers to instruct both children and adults in skills such as reading and sewing as well as religion.[76]

The secular services provided by the new churches showed that the evangelicals had learned something, too: religious faith could not thrive alongside the problems created by poverty. Tuckerman became a leader of campaigns for free public education, penal reform, temperance, and the efficient organization of charity. In 1834, the same year the Unitarians

75. It is likely that the same divisions, psychological and social, existed in other denominations and social classes. Although the evidence for the growth of irreligion in Boston is irrefutable, one should keep in mind that new churches continued to be formed which supported evangelical activities.

76. On the Benevolent Fraternity, see Gannett, *Gannett*, pp. 136–38. The four ministers were Tuckerman, F. T. Gray, C. F. Barnard, and J. T. Sargent. On their work, see Tuckerman, *Ministry at Large*, pp. 146–50, and Samuel A. Eliot, *Heralds of a Liberal Faith*, 3 vols. (Boston: American Unitarian Association, 1910), 2:103–17.

formed the BFCC, Tuckerman organized the Association of Delegates from the Benevolent Societies of Boston. The purpose of the association was to coordinate the relief work of twenty-one secular and denominational charities.[77] The juxtaposition of these two events suggests that Unitarian organizations at their best did not insulate their members behind sectarian lines or restrict them to spiritual methods but promoted diverse social contacts and an eclectic approach to reform.

Individual Unitarian congregations organized auxiliaries to the BFCC to collect contributions and recruit lay visitors to the poor from among their members. The auxiliary of the Twelfth Congregational Society supplemented their own missionary groups—the Association of Gentlemen for Benevolent Purposes, the Female Benevolent Association, and the Book and Pamphlet Society for the distribution of tracts. While the men gathered information on charities and determined the distribution of funds, the women collected subscriptions, sewed clothing, and visited families without church affiliations.[78] The primary objective of these groups was not economic aid, but the moral improvement of the working class by personal contact with exemplary Christians and, as Tuckerman wrote in his introduction to an instruction manual for the lay person, *The Visitor of the Poor*, "a more extended Christian union of the rich with the poor, with a view of a greater extension of human virtue and happiness."[79] Thus the associations aimed to close class distances by benevolent activity and to stimulate the religious sensibility of all involved, including the evangelicals themselves.

Liberal congregations were well aware that their voluntary associations should be means of self-improvement as well as reformation of the poor. The Purchase Street Association for Mutual Religious Improvement stated this dual purpose in the preamble to its constitution:

> Members of the Congregational Society in Purchase Street, desirous of promoting a spirit of union & sympathy with each other—of encouraging the acquisition & wider diffusion of the knowledge, of facts, interesting to a Christian community—of awakening a deeper concern

---

77. See McColgan, *Tuckerman*, pp. 244–45, on the Association of Delegates, and pp. 135–203, on Tuckerman's reform activities. For a more general account of Boston charities, see George Silsbee Hale, "The Charities of Boston and Contributions to the Distressed in other Parts," in Winsor, *Memorial History*, 4:641–74.

78. Pray, *Twelfth Society*, pp. 25–39.

79. Introduction, Joseph Marie de Gerando, *The Visitor of the Poor; translated from the French of the Baron Degerando, by a Lady of Boston* [Elizabeth Peabody] (Boston: Hilliard, Gray, Little, and Wilkins, 1832), p. iv. For other statements of the theory behind the ministry to the poor, see William Ellery Channing, "Ministry for the Poor: Discourse delivered before the Benevolent Fraternity of Churches, Boston, April 9, 1835," in *Works*, pp. 73–88, and [Cyrus A. Bartol], "Ministry for the Poor," *Christian Examiner* 21 (1837): 335–54.

in some of the religious charities of the times & of contributing pecuniary aid, to their laudable objects, do hereby form ourselves into an Association, with the following articles for a constitution.[80]

Church groups designed to awaken the religious interest of specific portions of the congregation were a similar innovation of the 1830s. In addition to parish and children's libraries, the Twelfth Society had a Sunday school, Bible classes for young people, and Bible lectures for adults. It should be noted that the Twelfth and Thirteenth (Purchase Street) Unitarian churches were especially active organizers. As middle-class congregations established in the 1820s with the financial backing of the well-to-do, these churches were a focus for the social life of their members. The church was less important to the evangelicalism of the upper class.

Wealthy Unitarians often had the means to demonstrate their religious commitments on their own. After his retirement from the family textile business at Lowell, Amos Lawrence made a profession of visiting the poor and rode around Boston in his carriage each day to dispense charity from his personal fortune.[81] More commonly, the rich gave direct donations to denominational and secular benevolent societies and sat on their governing boards. But nearly all the Liberal churches at least belonged to the Benevolent Fraternity and conducted a Sunday school for the parish children in the 1830s.[82] At William Ellery Channing's Federal Street Church, moreover, the weekly meetings of the Sunday school teachers attracted a diverse group of lay people, many of them from outside the church, and became an informal mutual improvement association for prominent evangelicals. Tuckerman, Charles Follen, and Edward Taylor, a well-known Methodist who preached to seamen, were some of the participants. The group was especially receptive to new people and new ideas, and the discussions ranged from disputed points of theology to questions of social justice.[83] Its openness contrasted with the defensive mood of the upper class and demonstrated the ability of evangelical religion to counteract social pressures.

Reforms at Harvard Divinity School were another aspect of the evangelical program. In 1830, Henry Ware, Jr. (1794–1843) was appointed to the new professorship of "pulpit eloquence and pastoral care"

---

80. Constitution of the Purchase Street Association for Mutual Religious Improvement, Ripley Papers (Frothingham donation), MHS.

81. Frank W. Ballard, *The Stewardship of Wealth: A Lecture delivered before the New York Young Men's Christian Association, January 4, 1865*, 2d ed., (n.p., n.d.), p. 11.

82. On the organizations supported by one well-to-do congregation, see Foote, *King's Chapel*, 2:466–69.

83. Elizabeth Peabody, another participant, kept extensive notes of the meetings. See her *Reminiscences*, pp. 204–75.

to prepare young men to contend with the infidelity of the times. It was hoped that Ware, a popular preacher during his ministry at the Second Church, would give a more practical direction to the traditional curriculum of ancient languages, didactic theology, and biblical criticism, since Unitarian clergymen were reputedly too scholarly (they "smell too much of the lamp," as one Maine resident colloquially put it) to move the heart.[84] Thus he initiated exercises in extemporaneous preaching, followed by informal discussion of current topics "to promote personal religion" among the students. In 1831, the students took this innovation one step further when they formed the Philanthropic Society, "whose object it is," Ware noted, "to collect information respecting the various benevolent projects of the day, to excite an interest in their own minds respecting them, and to prepare themselves to act understandingly when they shall go out into the world."[85] They investigated prison discipline, the reformation of criminals, missions, the condition of sailors, and slavery. A few preached weekly sermons to the prisoners in the state penitentiary and county jail. The union of personal piety and reform activity that Ware encouraged was typical of the Unitarian evangelical movement. In practice, too, Henry Ware was a model for his students.

The broad social objectives of the evangelical movement cast Unitarian ministers into a variety of new roles. Besides his teaching, Ware was a member of the executive committees of the American Unitarian Association and Benevolent Fraternity of Christian Churches, posts which required executive skills hitherto unnecessary for a parish minister. Ware also belonged to three associations to promote specific social reforms, the Cambridge Anti-Slavery Society, the Massachusetts Temperance Society, and the Massachusetts Peace Society.[86] The lectures he gave for the Peace Society, such as "The Bearings of the Doctrines of Political Economy on the Subjects of Peace and War," suggest the familiarity with secular issues that came with the evangelicals' commitment to applied religion.

Parish ministers frequently added a number of extracurricular activities to their already crowded schedules. Ezra Stiles Gannett (1801–71), Channing's colleague at the Federal Street Church, was one of the busiest ministers of the decade. He belonged to all the denominationwide organizations and the Peace, Temperance, and Colonization societies and edited the *Scriptural Interpreter,* in addition to his regular church duties—supervising the Sunday school and benevolent associations, teaching Bible classes, visiting families, and preaching twice on most Sundays. The burden of work these evangelicals imposed upon themselves contributed

84. Quoted in Peabody, *Reminiscences,* p. 49. On the divinity school curriculum, see Wright, "Early Period," pp. 36–59.

85. Ware to Lant Carpenter, Nov. 12, 1831, quoted in John Ware, *Memoir of the Life of Henry Ware, Jr.,* 2 vols. (Boston: James Munroe, 1846), 2:107–08.

86. See Ware, *Memoir,* pp. 127–74, on these reform activities.

to their common ill health. Ware, who was chronically ill himself, warned Gannett against overdedication: "Want of method, late and irregular hours, neglect of regular exercise of body to balance every day fatigue of the mind, and sometimes violent exercise, as if to do up the thing by the job,—no constitution can stand such a life."[87] It was good advice, but Gannett had a nervous breakdown in 1836 nevertheless and sailed to Europe for two years' rest.

Some ministers became magazine editors in an attempt to reach people who never came within earshot of a Unitarian pulpit. Bernard Whitman's *Unitarian,* for example, was aimed at the working class. Less scholarly and more sharply political than the major Liberal monthly, the *Christian Examiner,* the *Unitarian* bid for leadership against labor organizers ("Condemn those incendiaries who would put one class in opposition to another," Whitman told one contributor) and too often sacrificed social justice to harmony in the process.[88] Generally evangelicals urged moral improvement and rejected labor's legitimate demands for economic reform. When he lectured to the Mechanic Apprentices' Library Association in 1840, William Ellery Channing told workers to develop their characters through their work, families, and cultural opportunities such as the Unitarian-sponsored Library Association itself rather than agitate for power as a class.[89] Yet this was not a simple ploy to control the masses. Many evangelicals clung to the preindustrial ideal of a corporate hierarchical society and believed that Christianity, "which has no respect of persons" in spiritual things, should inspire "mutual deference and mutual interest in all classes of society."[90] Not all evangelicals shared this static social vision, however.

Transcendentalist Orestes Brownson (1803–76) was one who combined the insights of the worker with evangelical religion. A workingman's advocate in New York state before he became a Boston preacher, Brownson dismissed Channing's easy solution to the problem of labor: "Cultivation to any considerable extent is compatible only with leisure and easy circumstances. Instead, then, of enjoining culture as the means of social amelioration, we should effect amelioration as the condition of culture."[91] In 1836, Brownson organized a free church for workers, which

87. Quoted in Gannett, *Gannett,* p. 149. Gannett's evangelical work is discussed on pp. 79–155.

88. Whitman to Orestes Brownson, Dec. 26, 1833, quoted in Henry F. Brownson, *Orestes A. Brownson's Early Life, Middle Life, and Latter Life,* 3 vols. (Detroit: H. F. Brownson, 1898–1900), 1:101.

89. "On the Elevation of the Laboring Classes," in Channing, *Works,* p. 47. Another series of public lectures for working people was the Franklin Lectures, which originated at the Twelfth Congregational Society in the late 1820s (Pray, *Twelfth Society,* p. 27).

90. W. E. Channing to workers at the Slaithwaite Mechanic Institute, Huddersfield, England, Mar. 1, 1841, quoted in W. H. Channing, *Channing,* p. 484.

91. "Brook Farm," *Democratic Review* 11 (1842): 484.

he called the Society for Christian Union and Progress, and preached a doctrine that made Christianity a weapon of class struggle.[92] Needless to say, Brownson was not a typical Unitarian evangelical. But the fact that an outsider with decidedly radical opinions was tolerated at all is an indication of the open-mindedness of the movement.

The experience of some of the younger ministers led them to conclusions similar to Brownson's. When William Henry Channing (William Ellery's nephew) worked as a minister at large in New York City in 1837, he found that a missionary had to take a political stand to win the trust of the working class. He could prove "his sincere respect for human rights; his love of equal justice; only by lending, openly, his aid to every plan of social reform, which rectitude and charity approve." Channing's position, in fact, was strikingly similar to that of organized labor:

> [The minister at large] cannot cease to hope for that progressive improvement in civil institutions, which by lessening the expenses of government, will lighten the tax on every consumer, which by destroying monopoly and restriction, will encourage universal enterprise; which will leave men ever more and more free to find the station for which providence intended them, and enjoy that respect which their measure of worth merits.[93]

The contrast between his uncle's belief in the sufficiency of moral improvement and Channing's own commitment to free social mobility as the condition of spiritual regeneration is dramatic indeed. Clearly, when evangelicals stepped outside the bounds of Unitarian institutions to evangelize the working class, they risked conversion by the objects of their benevolence.

But Channing's decision to go to New York in the first place was a sign of tension between the majority of Boston Unitarians and more zealous evangelicals. The vision of a Christian community the movement inspired was bound to be frustrated at some point by upper-class prudence. At first there were no specific points of conflict, but Channing sensed the limits of Unitarian fervor on an emotional level. In a letter to his fiancée in 1836, he worried that his dedication to the poor was no more than his lack of courage to preach to the rich:

> It is the oppressed outcast from the privileges and improving influences of life I feel most called upon to seek & save. I am not sure but that I

---

92. See, e.g., *Babylon is Falling: A Discourse Preached in the Masonic Temple, to the Society for Christian Union and Progress, on Sunday Morning, May 28, 1837* (Boston: I. R. Butts, 1837). On Brownson's radical church, see Hutchison, *Transcendentalist Ministers*, pp. 152–69, and H. F. Brownson, *Brownson's Life*, 1:138–60.

93. "The Ministry at Large," *Western Messenger* 4 (Sept. 1837): 42–43. Channing's experience in New York is discussed in Frothingham, *Memoir of Channing*, pp. 129–43.

should be doing more good—and good of a higher sort & in a more direct way by preaching weekday and Sunday to them than some refined set of critics who would forget my teachings in pleasure & care. I have Julia almost too little faith to preach to the fashionable & refined. I never feel that the heart is open to me.[94]

Channing avoided an uncomfortable situation by leaving Boston. But even when evangelicals moved farther afield, they were hemmed in by the same dilemma.

The experience of James Freeman Clarke in Louisville, Kentucky, demonstrates the limits one Unitarian congregation set on evangelical religion. A classmate of Channing at the divinity school in 1833, Clarke (1810–88) decided to go west because "I thought that here was real freedom of thought and opinion and that it was therefore a more favorable scene for the development of a mind which wished to have the power to express individual convictions."[95] Even so, Clarke followed the precedents of Eastern evangelicalism so closely at first that he hardly used his freedom. He tried out Henry Ware's lessons in extemporaneous preaching on his congregation, which was mainly composed of transplanted New England merchants. He organized a Sunday school, Bible class, and weekly conversation meeting for mutual improvement. He joined the local temperance, education, and antislavery societies and edited the *Western Messenger* to evangelize the scattered population of the West.[96] But in 1836, when Clarke took a stand in the *Messenger* on the slavery issue, his difficulties began.

Ironically, Clarke's moderation was the source of the problem. In his review of William Ellery Channing's *Slavery,* he said that since slaveholders had inherited an evil institution, they should be treated with charitable understanding and be offered a plan for gradual abolition. A radical abolitionist in Cincinnati replied with a demand for uncompromising, immediate abolition, and for the next two years, Clarke and his adversary debated the question.[97] It was their minister's involvement in a public

94. W. H. Channing to Julia Allen, Oct. 2, 1836, Houghton.

95. Clarke to Margaret Fuller, Dec. 15, 1834, *The Letters of James Freeman Clarke to Margaret Fuller,* ed. John Wesley Thomas (Hamburg, Germany: Cram, De Gruyter, 1957), p. 86.

96. On the social composition of his congregation and his activities, see Clarke, *Letters,* ed. Thomas, esp. pp. 56–63, 84–85, 91, and Arthur S. Bolster, Jr., *James Freeman Clarke: Disciple to Advancing Truth* (Boston: Beacon Press, 1954), pp. 72–93. On Unitarianism in the West in the 1830s, see Charles H. Lyttle, *Freedom Moves West: A History of the Western Unitarian Conference, 1852–1952* (Boston: Beacon Press, 1952), pp. 5–53. The Cincinnati congregation was founded in 1830, Louisville in 1830, St. Louis in 1835, Alton, Ill., in 1838, and Quincy, Ill., in 1839.

97. "Channing's Slavery," *Western Messenger* 1 (Apr. 1836): 614–28. Clarke's critic identified himself as "T. M." and replied in "Criticism of Article VI, April No.," *Messenger* 2 (Aug. 1836): 50–59. Others joined in the controversy, and the last letter from "T. M." did

controversy on an emotional subject (Kentucky, after all, was a slave state) that brought the official censure of his congregation. They criticized his lengthy visits to Boston, his neglect of pastoral duties to edit the *Messenger,* and his decision to substitute topical discussions for the traditional Sunday afternoon service. But the sum of their petty complaints, Clarke was well aware, was a critique of the evangelical commitments that took him beyond strictly religious issues and onto political ground:

> Neither do I feel as if my time was so exclusively at the command of my parish that I am not to be permitted to take part in any other & more general measures for the diffusion of truth and pure Christianity. Hampered by such restrictions, I should not be adequate even to the performance of my parochial duties. . . . Is it possible, I ask, for any one to effect any good in a situation when his hands are thus tied?[98]

Rather than temper his zeal, the conflict sharpened Clarke's reform convictions. When he left Louisville for good in 1840 to return to Boston, he confided to his future wife, "Every day I become more of an abolitionist."[99]

What had happened, in the course of the decade, was that the evangelical movement had taken some Unitarians far beyond traditional roles and commitments, leaving others behind. By 1840, William Ellery Channing (1780–1842), the most prestigious clergyman of the denomination, was more a reformer at large than a congregational minister. His ill health was an excuse, in part, for his withdrawal from parish duties at the Federal Street Church, and the congregation "will not be surprised," he told the standing committee, "if I should use the freedom which I shall enjoy in giving a somewhat different direction to my exertions in the cause of humanity and religion."[100] He found that lecturing to reform societies and writing on social issues gave him a liberty impossible in a church which had refused to lend its meetinghouse for Charles Follen's funeral. As might be expected, some people whispered that he had become a politician with "an eye on a seat in Congress," and "were he not such a mighty man of renown in our little Unitarian army," George Ripley observed, "many would turn their backs upon him at once,—thinking less of his agreement

---

not appear until Feb. 1838. The best account of Clarke's antislavery views is Samuel May, "Antislavery," in *James Freeman Clarke: Autobiography, Diary and Correspondence,* ed. Edward Everett Hale (Boston: Houghton Mifflin, 1891), pp. 213–24.

98. Clarke to the Committee of the Society, Clarke Papers, Houghton. Bolster discusses this incident in *Clarke,* pp. 109–11, and dates the letter fall 1837.

99. Clarke to Anna Huidekoper, Mar. 18, 1839, quoted in *Clarke,* ed. Hale, p. 129.

100. W. E. Channing to the Committee of the Federal Street Church, Jan. 9, 1838, quoted in W. H. Channing, *Channing,* p. 397.

with them in theology, than of his differences in spirit, in his ideas of society, of the ministry, and of the progress of the church."[101]

Ripley's list of "his differences" is instructive, and the key word is "progress." The cleavage in the evangelical movement was based on a combination of religious and social issues (how much change is admissible in the church and society?) and is best seen, therefore, as a conflict between progressive and conservative orientations. It is especially ironic, moreover, that Ripley identified the single remaining source of consensus as theology. For when the tension between these parties exploded, the issue was a misty theological heresy known as "transcendentalism."

101. GR to Clarke, Mar. 15, 1837, Clarke Papers.

2 Transcendentalism as an Intellectual Movement, 1830–1836

The Transcendentalists were the philosophers of evangelical Unitarianism who stopped to consider the intellectual issues raised by the movement itself. For example, if feeling was as important as reason in religion, was the heart qualified to judge the Bible by the same logic of "higher criticism" as the head? And what was the value of the Scriptures and church tradition anyway, if new means of communication and organization were more effective in modern society? The Transcendentalists' answers made the Liberal awakening as much an intellectual movement as it was an emotional and practical one. For when they said that there was an intuitive source of truth independent of the Bible, they authorized men and women to change the forms of religious expression to suit their needs, unhindered by the Christian tradition.

Thus Transcendentalism rationalized the innovations of evangelical Unitarianism—and subverted its doctrine. What the Transcendentalists advocated was no longer Christianity per se but simply religion. Paradoxically, they took this radical step precisely because they were conscientious evangelicals. Despite the new Liberal emphasis on preaching basic truths with feeling, philosophically, Unitarianism remained a complex religion. The Transcendentalists simplified the system in order to facilitate belief, and few initially realized, in fact, how revolutionary their revision was. They had hoped to save Christianity from historical oblivion and to give it personal immediacy by pointing out the identity of Gospel truth and intuition. But so broad a conception of Christianity collapses all useful distinctions. We must agree with their critics' analysis (if not their judgment), concluding that Transcendentalism was not Christianity, the familiar religion of the Bible and the church, but some subjective usurper, with no more than an analogous connection with the religion of Christ.

When we turn from the Transcendentalists' public motives to their private ones, we find that they shared a common discontent, which helps explain why they went as far intellectually as they did. All of the principal Transcendentalists experienced crises of faith. The crisis was an acute spiritual struggle in some cases, in others a protracted malaise. But each of them felt that Christianity interfered with their religious feelings, misrepresented their goals, and limited their practical options. It was as if Christianity were an ill-fitting suit of old clothes, to borrow Carlyle's metaphor from *Sartor Resartus,* and Transcendentalism religion retailored, made to the personal specifications of nineteenth-century men and women, with room to grow.

Since the Transcendentalists began their careers as reformers of religious philosophy, I concentrate here on their intellectual history from roughly 1830 to 1836. Socially, however, the Transcendentalists were not yet a party distinct from the Liberal evangelicals. Hence my title, "Transcendentalism as an Intellectual Movement."

MAKING A MODERN RELIGION

Boston Unitarians were Christians, despite the claims to the contrary by their Orthodox critics. They believed that the supernatural revelation of Christ recorded in the Bible and passed down through the church was the ultimate source of salvation. But the Liberals were also Enlightenment humanists who argued that reason had a light of its own, able to clarify the Christian tradition. It is little wonder that the Transcendentalists thought Liberal Christianity a cumbersome doctrine, too ambivalent in its allegiances to revelation and reason, church and society, and tradition and progress to be an effective instrument of conversion. Nor is it surprising that they declared the freedom of modern man from the Christian past as readily as they did.

How far Unitarians had already come from the Puritans' strict adherence to biblical Christianity can be seen in their attitude toward revealed religion. Although they still believed that the Bible contained the only full revelation of saving truth, they had doubts about the veracity of the literal words and borrowed interpretative methods pioneered by German theologians to separate the wheat from the chaff. The basic assumption of the "higher criticism" was that the Bible was a historical document produced by human authors in a less enlightened age. The substance of Christ's teaching was a direct revelation, but the received form reflected local culture and incorporated the prejudices of ancient writers, which were not only irrelevant but misleading to modern Christians. Close textual analysis was one way to extract the spirit of the Gospels. But the Germans insisted even more strongly that the scholar must thoroughly understand ancient society to distinguish the peculiarities of the times from revelation.[1] The result of this emphasis on history was ironic. Biblical criticism was designed to answer Enlightenment skeptics who dismissed the Bible as a superstitious old book. Yet the Christian apologists set the Scriptures in the remote past just as decisively, thereby diminishing the authority of revelation and highlighting the ability of modern thinkers to discover the truth instead.

The Unitarians' ideas on natural religion had the same problematic effect. Eighteenth-century Liberals hoped to lend supporting testimony to revealed religion when they contended that reason could discover basic truths by studying nature, for example, discovering the existence of God from the perfect design of the universe. In the nineteenth century, Unitarians adopted the Scottish Common Sense philosophy to provide an apologetic basis for their faith. According to the Common Sense thinkers, the mind had an innate grasp of a complete array of metaphysical and moral laws. Their intention was to refute the skepticism of the late Enlightenment, which had ended in Hume, by making a foundation for revealed religion in human psychology.[2] Needless to say, it was a dangerous step if the goal was to defend Christianity, for the sufficiency of nature was a tempting conclusion. But Boston Unitarians were moderate people little inclined to upset the delicate balance of their religion. Indeed, their painstaking efforts to prove the authenticity of the Gospels show how carefully they harnessed reason to the cause of tradition.

Ultimately, the Unitarians believed, man could not work out his own redemption without the supernatural light of Scripture, and thus they set out to validate Christianity's claim to a divine origin by rational proofs. They marshaled a variety of evidence to demonstrate that Christ was the chosen messenger of God and the Gospels the true revelation. The anomalous purity of Jesus' character in ancient society, the internal consistency of the accounts of his life, the reliability of the biblical authors, and the remarkable spread of Christianity all testified to the divine origin of the Christian religion. One last kind of evidence particularly concerned (and irked) the Transcendentalists. The Unitarians used the miracles

1. The best contemporary statement of Unitarian critical principles is William Ellery Channing, "Unitarian Christianity," in *The Works of William Ellery Channing* (Boston: American Unitarian Association, 1875), pp. 367–71. See also Jerry Wayne Brown, *The Rise of Biblical Criticism in America, 1800–1870* (Middletown, Conn.: Wesleyan University Press, 1969), pp. 10–44, 60–93.

2. On natural religion and Common Sense, see Conrad Wright, *The Beginnings of Unitarianism in America* (Boston: Starr King Press, 1955), pp. 135–60; Daniel Walker Howe, *The Unitarian Conscience* (Cambridge, Mass.: Harvard University Press, 1970), pp. 27–44, 69–92; and Sydney E. Ahlstrom, "The Scottish Philosophy and American Theology," *Church History* 24 (1955): 257–69. For a more general view of the impact of Common Sense principles on antebellum Protestant thought, see Theodore Dwight Bozeman, *Protestants in an Age of Science* (Chapel Hill: University of North Carolina Press, 1977).

Christ performed, such as changing water to wine for the wedding feast at Cana, healing the sick, and raising Lazarus from the dead, as evidence of his divine appointment. In short, Unitarians were willing to cite acts which defied the comprehension of reason as rational proofs of supernatural religion.[3]

To the Transcendentalists, the miraculous proofs epitomized the tortured results of the Liberals' moderation. Passing off unreason as reason was bad enough. But more important, how was it possible to build a lively spiritual faith on extraordinary manipulations of matter or to move the hearts of modern Bostonians by showing them a few incredible happenings of the distant past?[4] These were precisely the questions that had to be asked if evangelical Unitarianism were to have a popular impact. But in fairness to the Unitarians, it must be said that as evangelicals they deliberately ignored the fine distinctions of their system.

The call for heartfelt religion in the 1830s was essentially a matter of technique, not a challenge to the assumptions of Liberal philosophy. To be effective, the evangelical preacher must "forget the modes of address under which he was himself educated," William Ellery Channing said in 1834.

> He must find a new tongue. He must reach the understanding through the imagination and the heart. He must look, not upon his notes, but into the eyes of his hearers. He must appeal to the simple, universal principles of human nature.[5]

Channing himself was skilled at adapting his message to his audience. To a group of apprentice mechanics, he emphasized innate understanding (as explained by Common Sense principles), at the expense of the tradition of scholarship which supported revealed religion: "All theology, scattered as it is through countless volumes, is summed up in the idea of God; and let this truth shine bright and clear in the laborer's soul, and he has the essence of theological libraries, and a far higher light than has visited thousands of renowned divines." Nevertheless, "the chief and most sustaining [hope for the laborer] is the clearer development of the principles of Christianity."[6] For all the worker's said ability, Channing still looked back to Christ for a

---

3. Channing used all of these arguments in "The Evidences of Revealed Religion: Discourse before the University in Cambridge, at the Dudleian Lecture, 14th March, 1821," in *Works,* pp. 220–32. Channing argued that it was rational, that is, consistent with man's understanding of God's benevolent character, to believe that God interrupted natural processes by miracles for the purpose of human edification, pp. 223–24.

4. The best Transcendentalist critique of miracles is Ralph Waldo Emerson, "The Divinity School Address," in *Works,* 1:119–51. See also William Hutchison's excellent discussion in *The Transcendentalist Ministers* (New Haven: Yale University Press, 1959), pp. 52–97.

5. "On Preaching the Gospel to the Poor," in Channing, *Works,* pp. 89–90.

6. "On the Elevation of the Laboring Classes," in Channing, *Works,* p. 63.

ıplete revelation. He had reached the brink of a broad humanism—and ⌐ed there, clinging to what Perry Miller has so well named "Christian specificity."[7]

The Transcendentalists, in contrast, took the leap. They escaped the bonds of historical Christianity by translating the evangelicals' rhetoric of feeling into a new philosophical statement. It is "to the heart," George Ripley wrote, "or inward nature of man, in a state of purity or freedom from subjection to the lower passions, that the presence of God is manifested."[8] No special revelation was necessary. Ripley's use of such phrases as "intuitive perception," "intuitive reason," and "consciousness" suggests the Transcendentalists' debt to the moral optimism of the European (particularly French and German) Romantics:

> The power of the soul, by which it gains the intuitive perception of spiritual truth, is the original inspiration that forms the common endowment of human nature. This, we maintain, is established by the testimony of the absolute and intuitive reason in man. Our own consciousness assures us that a revelation of great spiritual truths is made to the soul.[9]

Despite these transatlantic connections, Transcendentalism was still the answer to two specific religious problems in the neighborhood of Boston, both of which had to do with history.

First, it was the Transcendentalists' firm belief that the Unitarians' continuing loyalty to Christianity as the unique revelation was a positive obstruction to faith. The preacher had to perform contortions to bridge the gap of nearly two millennia. Technically, he had to appeal to his listener's natural reason, then authenticate the Gospels by rational proofs, then interpret the language of Scripture—merely to explain the grounds of belief, not to mention inspire conviction. Furthermore, because suspicions about so old a book necessitated biblical criticism, scholars now had an unavoidable role in teaching religion, often taking years to amass, sift, and disseminate the truth in a final form too dry to appeal to the average person. No wonder the distance between the historical objects of faith and

7. *The Life of the Mind in America* (New York: Harcourt, Brace, and World, 1965), p. 3.

8. *Discourses on the Philosophy of Religion: Addressed to Doubters who Wish to Believe* (Boston: James Munroe, 1836), p. 70. Perry Miller emphasizes the heart-focus of Transcendentalism in his introduction to *The Transcendentalists* (Cambridge, Mass.: Harvard University Press, 1950), pp. 3–15.

9. "Martineau's Rationale of Religious Inquiry," *Christian Examiner* 21 (1836): 245. On the influence of European philosophy on the Transcendentalists, see Octavius Brooks Frothingham, *Transcendentalism in New England* (1876; reprint ed., New York: Harper and Row, 1959), pp. 1–104.

the people these were meant to convert seemed so vast to George Ripley.

> We are inclined to substitute a blind reliance on tradition, for a clear insight into divine truth, to confound the passive reception of ideas on foreign authority with their vital appropriation from personal experience; and in our zeal for the supremacy of the Father, or the divinity of the Son, not to know so much as whether there be any Holy Ghost.[10]

But there was indeed a Holy Ghost, the Transcendentalists argued, in the heart; and by a single stroke, they obviated the whole operose process of historical reconstruction.

It is by no means true, however, that the Transcendentalists had no sense of history, as scholars almost universally have claimed. Indeed, by identifying an original source of truth in the heart, the Transcendentalists liberated their generation from the precedents of a single tradition and prepared the way for a thoroughly dynamic religion. Orestes Brownson explains:

> Religious institutions are the forms with which man clothes his religious sentiment, the answer he gives to the question, What is the holy? Were he a stationary being, or could he take in the whole of truth at a single glance, the institution once adopted would be universal, unchangeable, and eternal. But neither is the fact. . . . All things change their forms. Literature, art, science, governments, change under the very eye of the spectator. Religious institutions are subject to the same universal law. . . . As the race itself does not die, as new generations crowd upon the departing to supply their places, so does the reproductive energy of religion survive all mutations of forms, and so do new institutions arise to gladden us with their youth and freshness, to carry us further onward in our progress, and upward nearer to that which "is the same yesterday, to-day, and forever."[11]

We saw in chapter 1 that evangelical Unitarianism had split the seams of the instituted church, spilling over into voluntary associations, lectures, magazines, and the like. Transcendentalism justified these changes and, more important, established a method for future reform by creating a usable past. Once the idea of intuition cut the Transcendentalists loose from the Christian tradition, they were free to draw on the achievements of all times and places to make a new religion. A contemporary school of French philosophers admired by some of the Transcendentalists called this

10. *The Claims of the Age on the Work of the Evangelist: A Sermon Preached at the Ordination of Mr. John Sullivan Dwight, as Pastor of the Second Congregational Church in Northampton, May 20, 1840* (Boston: Weeks, Jordan, 1840), pp. 19–20.

11. *New Views of Christianity, Society, and the Church* (1836), in Brownson, *Works,* 4:3–4.

"Eclecticism."[12] But whatever the name, it is clear that the Transcendentalists had transformed history from the burden it remained to the Liberal Christians into an instrument of progress.

THE TRANSCENDENTALISTS

To twentieth-century readers, the Transcendentalists' conclusions may seem so obvious that we are apt to forget that emotionally they were hard won. It was no small step to question the religious heritage of Western civilization. Nor would the Transcendentalists have done so, were it not for their deep, personal discontent with historical Christianity.

ORESTES BROWNSON (1803–1876)   The restlessness of Orestes Brownson's religious career was an unmistakable sign of his discomfort with the Christian tradition. By the time he arrived in Boston as a Unitarian minister in 1836, he had adopted and abandoned three different creeds already—Presbyterianism, Universalism, and Skepticism. In 1850, six years after Brownson rejected Transcendentalism for Catholicism, James Freeman Clarke made a joke in the *Christian Examiner* of what was in fact the religious nightmare of a rapidly changing society: "We hardly thought it worth our while to exert our ingenuity in exposing the fallacy of arguments, which, judging by experience, Mr. Brownson would himself be ready to confute in the course of a year or two."[13] Brownson finally embraced the ultratraditionalism of the Catholic church. But he came by such an untraditional route that we must admit that his Transcendentalist conclusion—that religious feelings express themselves in transient religious systems—better explains his own experience.

Brownson was born in Stockbridge, Vermont, in 1803.[14] After his father's death in 1809, he was raised on a farm in Royalton by a childless couple with more or less Orthodox beliefs but no church affiliation. There were five Protestant churches in Royalton (Orthodox, Methodist, Baptist, Universalist, and Christian) and for a child without parental guidance, the result was bewilderment and frustration. Looking back in 1857 in his autobiography, *The Convert*, Brownson reconstructed the desperation of a young man in a society which gave preeminent importance to salvation

12. Brownson was the warmest admirer of the Eclectics. See his "Cousin's Philosophy," *Christian Examiner* 21 (1836): 33–64. Ripley published a translation of the writings of some of these thinkers as *Philosophical Miscellanies, translated from the French of Cousin, Jouffroy, and Benjamin Constant* (Boston: Hilliard, Gray, 1838).
13. "Orestes A. Brownson's Argument for the Roman Church," *Christian Examiner* 48 (1850): 228.
14. The most complete biography of Brownson is Henry F. Brownson, *Orestes A. Brownson's Early Life, Middle Life, and Latter Life*, 3 vols. (Detroit: H. F. Brownson, 1898–1900).

yet offered conflicting means of attaining grace: "I have, said I, in my self-communing, done my best to find the truth, to experience religion, and to lead a religious life, yet here I am without faith, without hope, without love. I know not what to believe. I know not what to do."[15] What Brownson did, in fact, was become a Presbyterian during a revival in upstate New York in 1822.

But Brownson quit the Presbyterian church within two years of his conversion, when he rebelled against its strict adherence to the doctrine of total depravity. The sectarian diversity of the Second Great Awakening demanded independent thinking ("self-communing") such as Brownson had done. Presbyterian dogmatism might satisfy the anxieties, but not the self-reliance of the times.[16] Thus Brownson struck out again on his own. As he moved from one New York state town to another, working first as a printer and then as a teacher, he learned more about religious alternatives and converted to Universalism in 1825. He became a Universalist minister and preached to congregations in New Hampshire and New York for the next four years.

Universalism satisfied Brownson's desire to engage in free inquiry while still remaining a Christian. As the rural equivalent of Unitarianism, Universalism held that reason might judge Scripture in the interest of progress. Universalists commonly favored social reform, moreover, as a result of their humanism. These were precisely the aspects of the religion that made Brownson accept it—and reject it. Universalists lacked the sophisticated critical methods which enabled the Unitarians to place the Bible in historical perspective, and in consequence, they continually wrestled with conflicting texts to force their conformity to reason. As Brownson became more involved in public controversies on social issues, he found this an increasingly difficult process, and in 1829 he denied the authority of revelation in favor of reason.[17]

It was rationalism of a distinctly anti-Christian variety. Still living in upstate New York, Brownson became the corresponding editor of the *Free Enquirer,* published in New York City by Fanny Wright and Robert Dale Owen. Both of them natives of Scotland, Wright and Owen had rebelled against the Scottish Presbyterian establishment, had become fierce partisans of the Enlightenment, and were notorious unbelievers. They condemned Christianity as authoritarian, superstitious, and dogmatic, the

15. *The Convert; or, Leaves from my Experience,* in Brownson, *Works,* 5:10.
16. On the revivals, see Whitney Cross, *The Burned-over District: The Social and Intellectual History of Enthusiastic Religion in Western New York, 1800–1850* (Ithaca: Cornell University Press, 1950), and Paul E. Johnson, *A Shopkeeper's Millennium* (New York: Hill and Wang, 1978).
17. On Brownson's intellectual difficulties with Universalism, see *The Convert,* in Brownson, *Works,* 5:20–39. His reform activities are discussed in Arthur M. Schlesinger, Jr., *Orestes A. Brownson: A Pilgrim's Progress* (Boston: Little, Brown, 1939), pp. 14–21.

foremost enemy of human progress. Man was not the sinful debtor of divine grace but a free agent who could perfect himself by rational reforms. At the time of their association with Brownson, Wright and Owen were promoting the workingmen's parties which first appeared in the late 1820s.[18] But the political labor movement was as short-lived as Brownson's enthusiasm for this brand of rationalism. When the parties disbanded around 1830, in part because of the determined resistance of American Protestants to such shameless irreligion, Brownson concluded that the reform had failed because it was based on self-interest rather than on the selfless idealism of religion. In the end, he was no more comfortable with godlessness than his countrymen.

In 1831, Brownson found a religious alternative in William Ellery Channing's sermon "Likeness to God." Free from the Presbyterians' pessimism and the Universalists' tangles of Scripture, Channing argued that God perfected man by giving him a natural capacity for self-improvement.[19] Brownson embraced Unitarianism as a rational religion consistent with his social goals. He was ordained minister of the Unitarian church in Walpole, New Hampshire, in 1832 and in 1834 moved to the Liberal congregation at Canton, Massachusetts, south of Boston.

During his first year in Canton, Brownson wrote a fictional autobiography called *Letters to an Unbeliever* and first published in 1839 as *Charles Elwood; or, The Infidel Converted.*[20] His purpose was to convert skeptics by retracing his own steps from Orthodoxy to Liberalism. But the book went beyond Unitarian Christianity. It was the earliest major statement of Brownson's Transcendentalism.

Charles Elwood, Brownson's hero-prototype, begins as the village skeptic, the victim of the petty provincialism and narrow religion of a small country town. He is ostracized by the regenerate Christians, who fear that to tolerate Elwood would make their own sanctity suspect in their neighbors' eyes. He is just as hemmed in by the pessimism of Orthodox theology. In tedious arguments with local ministers (which make *Charles Elwood* as much a discourse as a novel), Elwood demonstrates the hopeless contradictions of their proof of revelation. They say that the Bible is indispensable because natural reason has no understanding of supernatural truth; but, Elwood rejoins, a mind without the vaguest prior notion of what divine truth is could not possibly distinguish a genuine revelation from a false one. Faith that Jesus was God's one chosen mes-

18. On Wright and Owen, see Edward Pessen, *Most Uncommon Jacksonians* (Albany: State University of New York Press, 1967), pp. 66–71.

19. Brownson acknowledged his debt to Channing in "The Mediatorial Life of Jesus: A Letter to Rev. William Ellery Channing, D.D., June, 1842," in *Works*, 4:140–71.

20. Brownson, *Works*, 4:173–316. The plot summary which follows refers to pp. 179–88, 241–51.

senger is just blind trust. It is better to rest with the skepticism required by the limitations of reason, Elwood concludes, than to renounce so basic an element of human dignity as thinking itself.

We cannot help but sympathize with Elwood's impeccable logic and brutal honesty, precisely the traits which make Brownson himself such a powerful figure. But in this case, Brownson shows us that Elwood's argument for skepticism is built on error. He is still tangled in the meshes of total depravity, for he accepts the ministers' assumption that reason is too limited to know absolute truth. Thus Brownson sets the stage for a Transcendentalist conclusion.

Brownson follows his hero from the country to the city. Without hope of seeing God, Elwood dedicates himself to reforming the world. But reason alone proves a cold instrument of humanitarian zeal. Not until he is invited home by Mr. Howard, a Christian philanthropist modeled on Channing, does Elwood feel the warmth of his fellow man—or rather, woman. A gentleman of leisure and cultivation, Howard himself is a feminine figure; but it is the kindness of Howard's wife and daughters which really converts Elwood from infidelity to religion. The peculiar mixture of argumentation and sentimentality in *Charles Elwood* is convincing evidence that Transcendentalism was indeed a philosophy of the heart. Just so, Brownson caps Elwood's sentimental conversion with an exposition of the reasons for faith.

Mr. Morton, the Howards' minister, presents the Transcendentalist case for the "inward Christ," a voice we can trust rationally as both the source and proof of religion:

> It is this, sometimes termed the inward Christ, because a spiritual Christ, and not a corporeal, that judges the Bible, interprets the Bible and vouches for its truth. This is the Master, the Bible is merely the disciple. This Christ is near unto every one of us, knocking ever at the door of our hearts and praying for admission, and we may all let him in and receive his instructions. Whomsoever he instructs is the equal of the Bible, the peer of Peter, James, or John; for Peter, James, and John had no means of knowing divine truth, which you and I, my brethren, have not also within our reach. [P. 262]

Here were the two principal themes of Transcendentalism: the persuasive immediacy of intuition (the Christ "knocking ever at the door of our hearts") and the equality, even superiority, of the present generation to "Peter, James, or John" of the Bible. It is significant, moreover, that Brownson portrayed Channing as a layman engaged in practic⁻¹ charity and left the theory to Mr. Morton, that is, to Brownson himself.   ⁻ⁿ obviously thought that evangelical Unitarianism could not staʳ philosophical scrutiny and saw himself as an apologist for thⁱ

Similarly, he was critical of Mr. Howard's individualistic philanthropy and in the next few years worked to give religion a new institutional foundation.

In 1836, Brownson moved from Canton to Boston to begin a working-class congregation, the Society for Christian Union and Progress. He wrote *New Views of Christianity, Society, and the Church* the same year to explain "the principles on which that society is founded, and the object it contemplates."[21] That object was no less than the millenium, and his working-class followers were the instrument of the transformation. We will see in chapter 3 how Brownson wed religious to social radicalism. For now, the *New Views* are important to illustrate Brownson's decisive departure from the Christian conception of history and hence his mature Transcendentalism.

Man, not Christ, was the center of Brownson's scheme of redemption. "Religion is natural to man" and the purpose of history was to create an outward religion which did justice to the twin demands of human nature, spiritual and material fulfillment. So far, history was a bitter dialectical struggle between the forces of spirit and matter. Catholicism, devoted exclusively to spiritual things, set the stage for a counterrevolutionary movement of materialism, and the result was the Reformation. But Protestantism, which Brownson as much as Weber associated with prosperity and the rise of humanism, destroyed itself even more quickly and savagely in the French Revolution.

It was a violent view of history, one that belonged to an age of industrial and political revolution. What is surprising is Brownson's profound optimism. Self-consciousness, he concluded, was the legacy of the past, and with that, modern man could reconcile these hitherto clashing elements and move on toward perfection:

> Man's destiny is illimitable progress; his end is everlasting growth, enlargement of his being. . . . This is his duty. Hitherto he has performed it, but blindly, without knowing and without admitting it. Humanity has but to-day, as it were, risen to self-consciousness, to a perception of its own capacity, to a glimpse of its inconceivably grand and holy destiny. [P. 54]

In the past, only Jesus had understood the duality of human nature. But now the insight was general, and action, in consequence, collective. "I was alone in the world, my heart found no companionship, and my affections withered and died. But I have found him, and he is my father, and mankind are my brothers, and I can love and reverence. . . . I labor to bring them

---

21. Brownson, *Works*, 4:2. Subsequent page citations in the text refer to this edition. On the Society for Christian Union and Progress, see Hutchison, *Transcendentalist Ministers*, pp. 152–69, and H. F. Brownson, *Brownson's Life*, 1:138–60.

together, and to make them feel and own that they are all of one blood" (p. 55). The distance Brownson had come from the lonely perplexity of his Vermont childhood to this clear sense of his mission fully justified his hope for the future. The means of his own progress, as we have seen, was Transcendentalist philosophy.

GEORGE RIPLEY (1802–1880) It is not difficult to imagine that the majority of Boston Unitarians looked askance at Orestes Brownson. With his checkered past, dubious plans for the future, and overpowering manner, Brownson was hardly a model of Liberal moderation. Thus George Ripley's reaction was exceptional. When he preached the sermon at Brownson's ordination in 1834, it was a gesture of respect for the man and his ideas and a sign of their growing friendship. Yet temperamentally, few men were more dissimilar. Where Brownson swung impatiently between extremes in his search for truth, Ripley was cautious to the point of conservatism. Indeed, Ripley was pushed into Transcendentalism by the deep moral seriousness he brought to the work of saving souls.

Ripley was born in the western Massachusetts town of Greenfield in 1802.[22] His father, Jerome, was a native of Hingham who owned the local tavern and, though a man of modest means by Boston standards, was prominent in Greenfield society. Orthodoxy was secure in Greenfield for most of Ripley's childhood. Only after the War of 1812 did a moderate Calvinist congregation secede from the original church; still later, in 1825, a Unitarian society was formed.

The town's resistance to new ideas left its mark on Ripley, to the point where the son was more Orthodox than the father. At sixteen, Ripley favored Yale College over Harvard, he explained in a letter to his father, because moral laxity was the inevitable fruit of Liberal theology.[23] But Jerome Ripley held Unitarian opinions, and the son went to Harvard. When he graduated in 1823, he was still suspicious of Liberalism and urged his father to send him to Orthodox Andover Seminary because of its pious atmosphere and thorough attention to Scripture. The result was the same as before.[24] Ripley entered Harvard Divinity School the same year.

But once Ripley accepted Liberal religion ("so simple, scriptural, and reasonable," he wrote to his mother in 1825), his former stubbornness turned into equally earnest zeal.[25] Whether in Boston, organizing the Association for Mutual Improvement at his own Purchase Street Church, or as far away as Washington, investigating the problems of struggling

22. Standard biographies of Ripley are Octavius Brooks Frothingham, *George Ripley* (Boston: Houghton Mifflin, 1882), and Charles Crowe, *George Ripley: Transcendentalist and Utopian Socialist* (Athens: University of Georgia Press, 1967).
23. July 10, 1818, quoted in Frothingham, *Ripley*, pp. 5–6.
24. June, 1823, quoted in ibid., p. 18.
25. May 4, 1825, quoted in ibid., p. 31.

congregations, Ripley was a thorough evangelical. Only his wry sense of humor eased the task of regeneration he took upon himself, as it would again during the difficult years at Brook Farm. Heaven send anyone, he wrote to Ezra Stiles Gannett from Greenfield in 1828, "a Calvinist, a fanatic, any thing [sic], to preach & pray & fight, against this worse than Brethian spirit, of making money, which seems to be here the premium mobile; first, last & midst, & without end."[26]

Ripley's development in the 1830s is a classic example of the way evangelical Unitarianism sowed the seeds of its own subversion. The more intensely he sought conversions, the more dissatisfied he became with Unitarianism as it was. He read widely in French and German philosophy to improve his own effectiveness and saw, in contrast, that the Liberals' standard British sources presented religion "in a form as little adapted to produce emotion, as if they were actually wrought out by the unconscious operations of a machine."[27] To his dismay, moreover, he found that few Unitarians were much concerned with religious philosophy. Even "our most highly educated men," he wrote in his review of Friedrich Schleiermacher's theology in the *Christian Examiner* in 1836, care so little for "profound speculation, that we are apt to imagine that all inquiries, which descend much below the surface, are not only dark and repulsive, but useless and even dangerous."[28] It was prejudice as much as intellectual commitment which kept the Liberal preacher to a thin line between orthodoxy and progress.

> He must take care not to speak too much of sin, or of the need of a new heart, not to use too frequently or too fervently the name of Christ or of the Holy Ghost, not to press too warmly the reality of religious experience, and the heights and depths of the Christian life, lest he should be suspected of some faint shadow of approach to the gloom and darkness of Orthodoxy. . . . [But if] he venture to differ much from his teachers, if he wishes to wipe off the dust of centuries from some dark nook of the Gothic temple of our faith, if he speak out from the fullness of his own heart and in the strength of severe conviction, in dissonance with the prevailing echoes of departed voices,—he will be certain to raise a cry, by no means musical against his presumption and independence.[29]

26. Aug. 25, 1828, Gannett Papers, Houghton. He reported the results of his visits to Baltimore and Washington to Gannett, then secretary of the AUA, in a letter from Washington, Oct. 27, 1829 (Gannett Papers), and nearly a decade later, when he was preaching in Cleveland, enthusiastically reported the prospects for evangelizing the West to John Sullivan Dwight, Aug. 14, 1838, Norcross Papers, MHS.
27. "Degerando on Self-education," *Christian Examiner* 9 (1830): 71.
28. "Schleiermacher as a Theologian," *Christian Examiner* 20 (1836): 1–2.
29. "Letter to a Theological Student" (1836), *Dial* 1 (Oct. 1840): 184–85.

Between his studies and his frustration, Ripley was well on his way to Transcendentalism, but his friendship with Brownson seems to have been the catalyst to a clear statement of his own "new views." "Jesus Christ, the Same Yesterday, To-Day, and Forever" was Ripley's ordination sermon at Canton. In it he said that religion was natural, not supernatural, and that the greatness of Christ was his recognition of the truth of the heart:

> The Immutability of our Savior consists in the Immutability of the religious truths which he taught. While everything else with which the human mind is conversant suffers decay and change, the great principles of religion to which Jesus Christ bore testimony are everlasting realities. Religion has always existed, and in its essential elements is always the same. Its ideas are inseparable from man. They grow out of the unchangeable nature of things.[30]

At the same time, Brownson changed Ripley's politics, or rather, gave his reform commitment a political dimension for the first time. To Brownson, the historical Jesus remained important as an exemplary "teacher of the masses" who preached a "Gospel of human brotherhood."[31] But he attributed Ripley's awakening to the egalitarian implications of the idea of intuition when he told George Bancroft that Ripley "has fairly philosophised himself into Democracy."[32] Ripley's correspondence with Bancroft, once a candidate for the Unitarian ministry, now turned Democratic politician, was itself evidence of his conversion, and he wrote in 1837, "I hope to see the time, when religion, philosophy, & politics will be united in a holy Trinity, for the redemption and [blessedness?] of our social institutions."[33] Thus politics gave Ripley a new incentive to reform religion. His review of James Martineau's *Rationale of Religious Inquiry* in the *Examiner* in 1836 was a justification of such revisions according to Transcendentalist principles.

"Martineau's Rationale" was a critique of Christianity for its failure to conform to the law of historical change. Ripley praised recent progress in science, economics, government, and society and took issue with theology as the single exception to the rule of growth.

> It seems to have been taken for granted, that this was a sphere of thought, on which no new light could fall, which was absolved from the great law of advancement that binds all other human affairs. The idea of infusing any fresh life into its aged veins has been deemed

---

30. "Jesus Christ," in Miller, *The Transcendentalists,* p. 290. The complete manuscript is in the Ripley Papers (Frothingham donation), MHS.
31. *A Discourse on the Wants of the Times* (Boston: James Munroe, 1836), p. 18.
32. Sept. 25, 1836, Bancroft Papers, MHS.
33. Sept. 20, 1837, Bancroft Papers.

chimerical; so that theology alone, in the midst of scientific progress, nay, of revolution, retains the withered form and rigid features of the past.[34]

Ripley proposed a method for modernizing religion which challenged the authority of the Christian revelation. He argued that everyone was naturally inspired with "the absolute ideas of reason." Some, like Christ, were unusually prescient, not because they had access to any special revelation, but simply because they were more than commonly sensitive to intuition, and when "the supremacy of these ideas transcends the ordinary, the natural effects of culture and reflection, we pronounce them supernatural" (p. 246). Nevertheless, the mass of men—indeed, the democratic majority—were the final arbiters in the determination of religious truth: "Every thing [sic] which claims to be of an immediate divine origin in history, must be brought to the test of that which is to be admitted to be of immediate divine origin in the facts of consciousness. The natural inspiration which is possessed by all must sit in judgment on the supernatural inspiration which is imparted to an elect few" (p. 247).

Thus Ripley's Transcendentalism undermined the authority of Christianity in the interest of perfecting religion. It was a radical position in the mid-nineteenth century, especially for one who began with such conservative inclinations as George Ripley.

ELIZABETH PEABODY (1804–1890)   Two women made original contributions to Transcendentalist thought, Elizabeth Peabody and Margaret Fuller. New opportunities for women in urban society, for education and public activity, help account for their ability to do so. Evangelical Unitarianism, moreover, invited the participation of women by moving religion out of the church and into the sphere of voluntary associations, literature, the school, and the home. Yet it is not surprising that Peabody and Fuller did not remain Unitarians but became Transcendentalists instead. The Bible's record of Eve's unhappy role in the Garden of Eden is but the first example of the masculine bias of the Christian tradition. Transcendentalism was a means to do justice to their sex.

Elizabeth Peabody was born in 1804 and grew up in Salem. Her father was a pioneering dentist who filled teeth rather than pulled them, and her mother kept school at home to help support the family.[35] Peabody inherited her social and intellectual ambitions from her mother, also named Elizabeth, an unusually well-educated woman frustrated that her husband was content to experiment with new dental techniques in obscurity with-

34. "Martineau's Rationale," p. 225. For the complete citation, see n. 9. Subsequent page citations in the text refer to this article.
35. The standard biography of Peabody is Louise Hall Tharp, *The Peabody Sisters of Salem* (Boston: Little, Brown, 1950).

out wanting to use his skill to rise in society. As the daughter of an old Salem family, Peabody had access to the homes of the local elite and their Boston relations. She used her chance for self-advancement well. When she visited Boston in 1817, she managed to meet William Ellery Channing and opened a school in the city in 1825 with his support. Much as she valued his help, however, she was more interested in his company, and they met for private weekly conversations throughout the late 1820s.[36]

Peabody's friendship with Channing was a sign of her commanding enthusiasm for religion, an interest so scholarly that she undoubtedly would have been a minister—and a good one—were it not for her sex. When she directed the education of her twelve-year-old sister Sophia in the early 1820s, she reminded Sophia that at the age of twelve she felt that life was an immensely serious matter, and she reviewed the course of instruction intended to awaken a similar awareness in the young girl: "I have recommended to you the cultivation of your intellect, your taste, and your heart, by literature & science, by the fine arts, and by those habits of pious meditation, charitable judgment, benevolent feeling and severe selfexamination [sic] which taken together constitute religion." But "theology, my dear Sophia, is the science of all others the most interesting, the most absorbing, and the most important," and she recommended Paley, Enfield, and Priestly to complete this moral education with a rational understanding of Christian evidence.[37] Peabody was impressed by the need for authority to support religion, but not (and here was the root of her Transcendentalism) overawed. She cautioned Sophia: "I will not tell you—after all this—to think for yourself—I think your mind is too independent & bold *not* to think for itself—but you must recollect that it is much more unformed & inferior to those, many of whom you will differ from."

The evangelical movement gave Peabody a chance to use her talent, if not in a single profession, at least in a variety of activities. By 1834, she had translated Joseph de Gerando's *Self-education* and *Visitor of the Poor* from the original French, taught Sunday school at the Friend Street Chapel, and was trying to convert Horace Mann from skepticism to faith in private sessions on Sunday evenings.[38] Weekdays, she kept school to earn her living and, in response to the new interest in self-culture, con-

36. For Peabody's recollections of her friendship with Channing, which continued until his death in 1842, see her *Reminiscences of Rev. William Ellery Channing* (Boston: Roberts Brothers, 1880).

37. Mar. 31, 1823, Berg, NYPL. She testified to her youthful seriousness in another letter to Sophia, June 23, 1822, located in the same collection.

38. Joseph Marie de Gerando, *Self-education; or, The Means and Art of Moral Progress, translated from the French of M. le Baron Degerando* (Boston: Carter and Hendee, 1832), and *The Visitor of the Poor* (Boston: Hilliard, Gray, Little, and Wilkins, 1832). For a discussion of Peabody's relation with Horace Mann, see chap. 5.

ducted an "historical class" for women where she aimed to teach moral truth by means of literature. Most important, she made her first attempt at religious philosophy in the *Christian Examiner*. Andrews Norton, the retired professor of sacred literature at Harvard, was so disturbed by her doctrine that he ordered publication suspended after only three of the six articles appeared. For just that reason, the "Spirit of the Hebrew Scriptures" is interesting to us.

Even Peabody's choice of subject was a hint that this was not conventional Unitarianism. For the New Testament, not the Old, usually claimed the attention of biblical scholars attempting to separate truth from superstition. But it was exactly Peabody's purpose to rescue pre-Christian revelation from the obscurity to which it was consigned by the "cold, logical analysis" of critics like Norton. She argued that they were so blinded by the theological errors of the text that they overlooked the poetic beauty of the language, which made the Old Testament a valuable means of winning conversions. She did not doubt the greater perfection of Christ's revelation, but her defense of older forms of truth led her to an evolutionary view of religion:

> Do those who make this objection [that the Old Testament is imperfect] take into consideration the determinate finiteness of man's nature; the *growing* character of his mind; and especially, the necessary reaction of his mind, upon that which passes through it? A full revelation, we say, has now been received;—but only into one mind. For though Jesus Christ has freely opened himself unto all men, do we suppose that Christianity, in all its length and breadth, in which it existed in his mind, has ever been received into the mind of any one of his followers? Must not men's knowledge of truth, after all sources of it are laid open, necessarily be in proportion to their own activity, and faithfulness, and freedom from other influences?[39]

If one can imagine Norton's horror at the thought that the Christianity of the Bible was not a complete revelation (he devoted most of his life to collecting Christian evidences), Peabody's proposal for improving religion must have been the final blow. The best revelation of God's intention for man, according to Peabody, was in the example of women at home:

> Where else but in a limited circle, could be developed the enduring patience of love,—its effects in softening and opening the heart of frozen humanity; where else could be found the uncalculating spirit of

39. "Spirit of the Hebrew Scriptures—No. I. The Creation," *Christian Examiner* 16 (1834): 179. Subsequent page citations in the text refer to this article. The other two articles were "Spirit of the Hebrew Scriptures—No. II. Temptation, Sin, and Punishment," *Examiner* 16 (1834): 305–20, and "Spirit of the Hebrew Scriptures—No. III. Public Worship: Social Crime, and its Retribution," *Examiner* 17 (1834): 78–92.

a mother's devotion, that revelation of the disinterestedness of which man is capable. . . . In short, may not the social relations be considered a miniature of the spiritual universe, and the reception of all their influences the best means of understanding and becoming associated with the Father of the universe? [Pp. 194–95]

The cult of domesticity, as scholars have called this antebellum doctrine of the piety and purity of women, was not incompatible with Christianity so long as its advocates did not suggest that the ministry of women replace revealed religion, church tradition, and clerical authority. But Peabody integrated domesticity into this distinctly antimasculine critique of Christian scholarship and hence challenged all three. Unlike Margaret Fuller, she was not a feminist. But Peabody was a radical in religion, indeed, a Transcendentalist.

Her philosophy was rather vague, however, until she borrowed the idea of intuition from Bronson Alcott. From 1834 to 1836, she worked as Alcott's assistant at his Temple School in Boston. His basic assumption, as we will see, was that the child is born with a pure intuition of truth which could be drawn out by Socratic instruction. He convinced Elizabeth Peabody. In her preface to his *Conversations with Children on the Gospels* in 1836, she called the book "a revelation of the Divinity in the soul of childhood," so bright a gospel that Alcott hoped "that, through their simple consciousness, the Divine Idea of Man, as Imaged in Jesus, yet almost lost to the world, might be revived in the minds of adults, who might thus be recalled into the spiritual kingdom."[40] To some extent, it is regrettable that what Peabody gained in intellectual clarity from Alcott was at the expense of her attention to women's role in religion. But although the child was the center of her most sophisticated statement of Transcendentalist philosophy, a review in the *Western Messenger* of Rev. Jacob Abbott's *The Way for a Child to be Saved*, Peabody also achieved a broadly humanist view of religion.

Superficially, the review was a rebuttal of the Orthodox doctrine that children were sinful by nature. More important, Peabody outlined a method to reform religion that was similar in effect to George Ripley's idea of majority rule in "Martineau's Rationale." Rather than force the child's character into conformity with speculative theology, as Peabody claimed Abbott advised, the truth of religious systems should be tested against the nature of children:

Should we have undertaken to find a test by which to try the various systems which have been set up and called Christianity, we could not have fallen on a better one than the title of this book suggests to us. Let

40. *Conversations with Children on the Gospels*, 2 vols. (Boston: James Munroe, 1836–37), 1:xiii.

every sect come forward and tell us "the way that a child may be saved," according to its doctrines, and the great controversy will begin to draw to a close, especially if every sect is as faithful as the writer of this book has been, to involve no principles in its practice for which its creed does not give it literal authority.[41]

With the perfection of children as an unambiguous standard of truth, free from sectarian squabbles over biblical meaning, progress could be made toward pure Christianity, "the religion of eternal childhood."

What is most significant about the review, however, is Peabody's view of the history of religion. Just as Brownson described history as the dialectical conflict of spirit and matter, Peabody could account for the transmission of religious feeling without reference to the Christian tradition:

> From the beginning of time, the action of human beings on each other, has been in proportion to the inspiring power of one party, meeting the sympathies and aspirations of the other. . . . All movement, progress, the spirit of every age, is but the result of it; and it is because the loftier souls of men have the power of waking up a spirit kindred to themselves, which otherwise lies slumbering, unconscious of itself, that they become the prophets of future times. [P. 643]

Like her fellow Transcendentalists, Peabody had a perspective on human affairs that was no longer bound by Christian assumptions—or, for that matter, by an equally confining domestic religion which made intuition the exclusive property of mothers and children. What she had done was to generalize her earlier conclusions and explain all of history in essentially domestic terms, as the growth of religious feeling through personal interaction. We admire the Transcendentalists for their attachment to boundless prospects. For Elizabeth Peabody, her affinity with women was a stepping-stone to such universal views.

MARGARET FULLER (1810–1850)   Margaret Fuller's imagination was so loosely bound by Unitarian doctrine that her ability to envision progress without Christianity required a struggle, not to escape tradition, but to achieve a historical consciousness at all. In contrast to the erudite Miss Peabody, Fuller's view of religion was essentially personal. "One day lives always in my memory," she wrote to a friend in 1838, "one chastest, heavenliest day of communion with the soul of things":

> It was Thanksgiving-day. I was free to be alone; in the meditative woods, by the choked-up fountain, I passed its hours, each of which

---

41. "The Way for a Child to be Saved," *Western Messenger* 1 (Apr. 1836): 630. Subsequent page citations in the text refer to this article.

contained ages of thought and emotion. . . . All the films seemed to drop from my existence, and I was sure that I should never starve in this desert world, but that manna would drop from Heaven, if I would but rise with every rising sun to gather it. In the evening I went to the church-yard; the moon sailed above the rosy clouds,—the crescent moon rose above the heavenward-pointed spire. . . . May my life be a church, full of devout thoughts and solemn music.[42]

Here was the subjective core of Transcendentalism, the individual religious experience not only outside the church, but as a natural alternative ("May my life be a church") to the Christian religion. All that was needed to change these feelings into a doctrine available for social use was a theoretical basis. It was Fuller's commitment to the freedom of women which made her a philosopher of religion.

Margaret Fuller was born in 1810 and was raised in Cambridge.[43] Although she was educated mainly at home by her father, Timothy, a prominent lawyer and politician, for a time she attended the Cambridge Grammar School along with the sons of Harvard professors. Her first lesson in the limits of woman's sphere occurred when they entered the university and she did not. She continued to meet the students in Cambridge society but now fit, however uncomfortably, into a feminine role. As a divinity student, James Freeman Clarke should have kept his attention on loftier matters, but his letters to Fuller were filled with news of his romantic intrigues, where she was playing the matchmaker.[44] With no intellectual or professional outlet for her ability, Fuller became an expert at social manipulation, so skilled in fact that Emerson remarked that she wore her friends "as a necklace of diamonds around her neck."[45]

But her social facility hid her real frustration. Her correspondence with Clarke took a serious turn when he took his first church in Louisville in 1833, where, removed from the pleasantries of Cambridge drawing rooms, he became a perfect audience for her thoughts on literature, philosophy, and religion. Sometimes she joked about religious issues with the defensiveness of an outsider: "And tell me how goes your Un-

42. MF to a young friend, Oct. 21, 1838, in *Woman in the Nineteenth Century, and Kindred Papers*, ed. Arthur B. Fuller (1874; reprint ed., New York: Greenwood Press, 1968), pp. 359–60.

43. The most complete biography of Fuller is William Henry Channing, James Freeman Clarke, and Ralph Waldo Emerson, *Memoirs of Margaret Fuller Ossoli*, 2 vols. (Boston: Phillips, Sampson, 1852). See also Ann Douglas's analysis of Fuller's life in *The Feminization of American Culture* (New York: Knopf, 1977), pp. 259–88, and Paula Blanchard's recent *Margaret Fuller: From Transcendentalism to Revolution* (New York: Delacorte Press/Seymour Lawrence, 1978).

44. See his letters to Fuller of Dec. 16, 1830, and Jan. 10, 1831, in *The Letters of James Freeman Clarke to Margaret Fuller*, ed. John Wesley Thomas (Hamburg, Germany: Cram, de Gruyter, 1957), pp. 29–30.

45. Emerson, "Visits to Concord," in *Memoirs of Fuller*, 1:213.

itarianism. Before you went to the west I remember you were grafting sundry notions of your own on that most rational system." But more often she showed a genuine curiosity about his work: "How many hours a day do you study and *what:* any thing [*sic*] except sermon writing [?] Do you feel more or less alone than when with us [?] Is the promised freedom joyous or joyless?"[46] Privately, she felt the inadequacies of her education and set out an ambitious reading course for herself in German metaphysics on "God, the universe, immortality."[47] But without opportunities for action, her accomplishments did little but increase her "sense of 'unemployed force.' "[48] Fuller's dilemma was a perfect example of the fallacy of the Unitarian notion of self-culture as a means of reform. Her belief in the need for change in the social condition of women began with her own experience.

When she went to work teaching school after her father's death in 1835, however, Fuller's ambitions were still quite conventional. "I am not without my dreams and hopes as to the education of women," she wrote to her friend William Henry Channing. But they are "not at all of the Martineau class," she added, disavowing Harriet Martineau's position on social freedom for women and calling her goals instead "such, I think, as you, or any spiritual however sober-minded thinker would sympathize in."[49] Nevertheless, Fuller's ideas on women's education are significant. At the Green Street School in Providence in 1837 and 1838, she tried to counteract the effects of sentimental education by training the students in logical thinking: "A journal of your life, and analyses of your thoughts, would teach you how to generalize,and give firmness to your conclusions. Do not write down merely that things are beautiful or the reverse; but *what* they are, and *why* they are beautiful or otherwise, and show these papers, at least at present, to nobody. Be your own judge and your own helper."[50]

To encourage rational thought was also a principal aim of the conversations for women Fuller began in Boston in the winter of 1839. She explained her purpose to George Ripley's wife, Sophia:

It is to pass in review the departments of thought and knowledge, and endeavor to place them in due relation to one another in our mind. To

46. Feb. 1, 1835, Clarke Papers, Houghton. Fuller's surviving letters to Clarke were all written after he went to Louisville (with one possible undated exception) and are located in the Clarke Papers.
47. Quoted in *Memoirs of Fuller,* 1:128.
48. MF to William Henry Channing, Mar. 22, 1840, Fuller Papers, BPL. The collection of Fuller Papers cited in subsequent references in this chapter is in the Boston Public Library There is also a collection of Fuller papers in Houghton Library.
49. Dec. 9, 1838, Fuller Papers.
50. MF to an unidentified correspondent, Oct. 7, 1838, in *Woman and Kindred Papers,* ed. Fuller, p. 346.

systematize thought and give precision and clearness in which our sex are so deficient, chiefly, I think, because they have so few inducements to test and classify what they receive. To ascertain what pursuits are best suited to us, in our time and state of society, and how we may make the best use of our means for building up the life of thought upon the life of action.[51]

Now, significantly, Fuller anticipated a new role for women to follow this intellectual exercise. The conversations themselves were evidence of her awareness that her personal frustration was part of a social problem, common to women, which it required solidarity to resolve. Thus the meetings were to provide "a point of union to well-educated and thinking women, in a city which, with great pretensions to mental refinement, boasts at present nothing of the kind."[52]

Woman in the Nineteenth Century, published in the *Dial* in 1842 and as a book in 1844, was a justification of the movement Fuller hoped to begin. But it was also a work about religion. For in order to establish the equality and rights of women on philosophical ground, she had to confront the Christian tradition. In the summer of 1840, Fuller had a religious experience which brought her to her intellectual maturity.

The reasons for Fuller's conversion were as complex as her many-sided, volatile personality, and we will see in chapter 5 that a rupture in several key friendships helped precipitate the crisis. But the meaning of the experience is clear: Fuller gained a firm hold on her identity, not only as a woman, but also as a person. She described her feeling to Emerson in terms of submission to a higher law: "All things I have given up to the Central Power, myself, you also; yet, I cannot forbear adding, dear friend. I am now so at home, I know not how again to wander & grope, seeking my place in another soul. I need to be recognized."[53] For the first time in her life, she had definite objectives and the means to pursue them and her sense of self expanded and took root under the influence of her hard-won power. For the first time, too, she talked about reforming religion, because she saw how much of the responsibility for women's condition had to be laid at the door of the Christian tradition: "I would preach the Holy Ghost as zealously as they [the Unitarians] have been preaching Man, and faith instead of the understanding and mysteries instead &cc."[54] With deliberate irony, Fuller dismissed the Liberal faith in "Man" and invoked the "Holy Ghost" as the inner source of truth possessed by both sexes which guaranteed their equality.

51. MF to SDR, 1840, quoted in Thomas Wentworth Higginson, *Margaret Fuller Ossoli* (Boston: Houghton Mifflin, 1884), p. 113.

52. Ibid., p. 113.

53. MF to RWE, Sept. 29, 1840, cited in Emerson, *Letters,* 2:341.

54. MF to W. H. Channing, Oct. 25–28, 1840, Fuller Papers.

It was because of this experience that Fuller was able to frame her commitment to women in a new theory of human redemption in *Woman in the Nineteenth Century*. The basic insight of her conversion—that women had an identity beyond their sex because of their independent relation to God—structured her argument. The spiritual equality of women justified their freedom: "What Woman needs is not as a woman to act or rule, but as a nature to grow, as an intellect to discern, as a soul to live freely and unimpeded, to unfold such powers as were given to her when we left our common home."[55] On a historical level, however, Fuller reintroduced gender distinctions. She showed that freedom was not only women's absolute right, but an essential condition for the perfection of the race. "Male and female represent the two sides of the great radical dualism" of human nature, she wrote. It is man's destiny "to ascertain and fulfill the law of his being," and thus men and women must be equally free to express their special capacities for energy or harmony, power or beauty, intellect or love.

> I believe that the development of the one cannot be effected without the other. My highest wish is that this truth should be distinctly and rationally apprehended, and the conditions of life and freedom recognized as the same for the daughters and the sons of time; twin exponents of a divine thought. [Pp. xiii–iv]

All social injustices, Fuller went on to say, to slaves, Indians, and the poor, would be cured as soon as the hegemony of masculine nature gave way to the harmonious growth of the sexes. She was sure that now was the time for the revolution to begin, and she predicted nothing short of the millennium.

If Fuller's far-reaching hopes for women's liberation seem unrealistic to the modern reader, we should not forget that her organic view of society was also responsible for her sensitivity to the wide range of problems she included under the title *Woman in the Nineteenth Century*. Too often Fuller and Peabody have been left off lists of major Transcendentalists.[56] But Transcendentalism was a philosophy of protest against Christianity as much because it was a social system as because it was an intellectual system. Women had good reason to protest, and when they did so by means of the idea of an intuitive revelation, they should be considered, with just as good cause, Transcendentalists.

BRONSON ALCOTT (1799–1888)   At one time or another, both Elizabeth Peabody and Margaret Fuller worked for Bronson Alcott at his

---

55. *Woman and Kindred Papers,* ed. Fuller, p. 38. Subsequent page citations in the text refer to this edition.

56. Among authors of major studies of Transcendentalism, only O. B. Frothingham devotes a chapter to Margaret Fuller, in *Transcendentalism in New England.*

Temple School. All three were teachers who shared in the spirit of evangelical Unitarianism. They saw their job not as a utilitarian matter of instilling facts and laws but as a task of spiritual awakening. But it was precisely because Alcott was a teacher of this sort that he quarreled with the Christian tradition. More interested in awakening the god in man than in delivering man to God, Alcott complained that the church was stiff, impractical, and weighed down by doctrine, better equipped "to teach men how to *die* rather than how to live."[57] For Alcott, Transcendentalism was a way to make religion as spontaneous as the nature of children.

Alcott was born in Wolcott, Connecticut, in 1799.[58] Thus he grew up in the predominantly Orthodox Connecticut River valley, as did Brownson and Ripley. But as a young man he showed neither Brownson's longing for conversion nor Ripley's pious attachment to his childhood religion. In fact, Christianity had little personal meaning for Alcott until he was nearly thirty years old. His parents' religion helps explain his lukewarm feelings. His mother, Anna, was raised in the Episcopal church, of which her brother, Tillotson Bronson, became a local bishop. A dissenting sect in Connecticut since the early eighteenth century, the Anglicans were known for their commitment to tradition and order rather than to piety. His father, Joseph, was a farmer with no firm religious beliefs for much of his adult life. He joined the Wolcott Episcopal church with his son in 1816.

Anna hoped to send her son to Yale to become an Episcopal priest. Not only was money a problem, however, but Alcott had a taste for more worldly things. From 1818 to 1823, he made annual trips to Virginia and the Carolinas peddling New England manufactures. He welcomed the escape from the dull farm routine, the excitement of travel, and the chance to meet wealthy planters. "For my part I can make pedling [*sic*] in Virginia as respectable as any other business," he wrote to his parents in 1820. "I take much pleasure in travelling, & in conversing with the Virginians, in observing their different habits, manners, & customs, &c & I am conscious that it is of great advantage to me in many points of view."[59] But stiff competition from other Yankees, economic recession, and illness cut short Alcott's career. Disillusioned by the risks of business and the dissipation of Southern aristocrats, Alcott was ready to appreciate more solid virtues.

In 1825, Alcott became master of the common school in Cheshire, Connecticut, and an "enthusiastick" advocate of education. He wrote to

57. Oct. 5, 1828, Alcott, *Journals*, p. 113.
58. Standard biographies of Alcott are F. B. Sanborn and William T. Harris, *A. Bronson Alcott: His Life and Philosophy*, 2 vols. (Boston: Roberts Brothers, 1893), and Odell Shepard, *Pedlar's Progress: The Life of Bronson Alcott* (Boston: Little, Brown, 1937).
59. Alcott, *Letters*, p. 2. I have omitted brackets where the editor (Richard L. Herrnstadt) guessed at torn or illegible words.

his cousin William Alcott, then a medical student at Yale and later a noted health reformer, that he had found his true vocation:

> While many others, perhaps most, of our youthful associates are still groping their way through the mists of ignorance, to the attainment of wealth, or the gratification of their passions: the Great Author of Good has raised us from the grovelling herd, and illumined our minds, if it be but feebly, with the beams of knowledge. . . . God, in his goodness, has placed me, though unworthy, in a sphere in which I can with his assistance be useful—can benefit a few of my fellow-travellers, young and inexperienced in the world, by example and instruction, and endeavor to lead them to usefulness and happiness.[60]

Alcott never lost his taste for inflated rhetoric—or his messianic self-image. But in 1827, his self-righteousness must have fueled the controversy over his teaching which caused him to lose his school.

Alcott's enthusiasm for education was the result of his adherence to Enlightenment principles, ideas which sat none too well with the parents of Orthodox children. He believed that the child was not depraved by nature but had an innate capacity for virtue. In the classroom, he spared the rod, relied instead on voluntary obedience, and encouraged his pupils to express their natural feelings. Needless to say, the schoolmaster was not to the liking of the townspeople of Cheshire (there was only one Unitarian church in all of Connecticut at the time, that of Samuel J. May, Alcott's future brother-in-law, at Brooklyn), and he was dismissed. Alcott's reaction was a forewarning of his later Transcendentalism. He condemned tradition in the name of progress: "The opinions of men are associated with their antiquity; we adopt old opinions for ours; we defend them because we have adopted them, and thus put shackles on our own minds which Time cannot unrivet."[61] Feeling as beleaguered by the dogged conservatism of rural New England as Brownson's Charles Elwood, Alcott followed the footsteps of this hero of fiction into the city.

With the help of Samuel May and his sister Abigail, Alcott secured a teaching position in Boston in 1828 and conducted various schools in the city until 1832. Intellectually, Boston was important to Alcott because he discovered Scottish Common Sense principles, which explained his conviction that children were born with a faculty for goodness. In his *Observations on the Principles of Infant Instruction* in 1830, he concluded that every child "is already in possession of the faculties and apparatus required for his instruction, and, that, by the law of his constitution, he uses these to a great extent himself; that the office of instruction is chiefly to facilitate this process, and to accompany the child in his prog-

60. Jan. 3, 1826, Alcott, *Letters,* pp. 9–11.
61. Journal, May 17, 1827, quoted in Sanborn, *Alcott,* 1:90.

ress, rather than to drive or even to lead him."[62] Alcott now saw education in religious terms, as a matter of moral nurture, and the teacher as a minister to children, whose mind must be "beautified and adorned by the cultivation of its moral attributes, and purified and elevated by the faith and hopes of Christianity" (p. 8).

The events which led Alcott from Unitarianism to Transcendentalism did not occur in Boston, interestingly enough, but in Philadelphia. Professionally, Boston had little to offer. Gathering and keeping schools was precarious business, and in 1832, now with a wife, one child, and another on the way, Alcott accepted an offer to teach in Germantown, Pennsylvania. The school soon closed. What happened next was typical of the crises which recurred in the Alcott family for the next ten years. Alcott's practical failure, leaving him discontented on the one hand and at leisure on the other, was a catalyst to more radical opinions.[63] He left Abigail, Anna, and now Louisa to fend for themselves in Germantown, rented a room in Philadelphia, and immersed himself in Plato, Swedenborg, Coleridge, and other philosophers, whose one common trait was the idea of immediate inspiration. Back home with his family, Alcott collected evidence to confirm this doctrine. He kept voluminous notes on his daughters' growth from infancy as proof of the manifestation of spirit in matter.[64]

Alcott seems to have realized that he had taken an intellectual leap, since he listed Boston's "freer toleration of variant opinions" as one reason for his return in 1834.[65] With Elizabeth Peabody's help, he engaged students and rented rooms over the Masonic Temple for the "Temple School." Together, they published a transcript of the classes in 1835, *Record of a School; Exemplifying the General Principles of Spiritual Culture.*

It was a Transcendentalist work, but largely by omission. Elizabeth Peabody, who supplied the statement of theory, gave no hint of an antipathy between spiritual culture and Christian education, but it was clear that Christianity was superfluous to a child enrolled in the Temple School.

> To contemplate Spirit in the Infinite Being, has ever been acknowledged to be the only ground of true Religion. To contemplate Spirit in External nature, is universally allowed to be the only true Science. To contemplate Spirit in ourselves, and in our fellow men, is obviously the only means of understanding social duty, and quickening within

62. *Observations on the Principles and Methods of Infant Instruction* (Boston: Carter and Hendee, 1830), pp. 26–27. Subsequent page citations in the text refer to this edition.

63. The same pattern of events led to his anarchist social philosophy and to the founding of the Fruitlands community between 1840 and 1844. See chap. 4.

64. See Charles Strickland, "A Transcendentalist Father: The Child-rearing Practices of Bronson Alcott," *Perspectives in American History* 3 (1967): 5–73.

65. Journal, 1833, quoted in Sanborn, *Alcott*, 1:167.

ourselves a wise Humanity,—In general terms, Contemplation of Spirit is the first principle of Human Culture; the foundation of Self-education.[66]

Although Alcott was a better speaker than a writer and apparently hoped to show his skill in the conversations with his pupils which formed the body of the book, it was a mistake to leave the exposition to Peabody. Her emphasis on passive reflection was misleading. In practice, Alcott tried to awaken the spirit by engaging the child in the teaching process. He used the Socratic method to lead the children from commonplace to spiritual meanings of words. "The word *rich* was defined," Peabody recorded during one class. "It was decided that there were internal as well as external riches. He asked one boy if he was dying, which should he prefer to have, a whole world, to carry with him, suppose he could carry it, or a mind full of good thoughts and feelings. The boy replied the latter" (p. 54).

A Christian minister could not have expected better results and in Alcott's opinion would have done worse. Spiritual culture was adapted to the nature of children. Based on the premise that the child had an intuition of spiritual things, the method used to bring this insight to consciousness was entirely experimental. Whatever worked to stimulate the child was right and proper. Thus Alcott did away with the disputed doctrines, formal style, and long hours of sitting on hard church benches that made boys and girls squirm all over New England.

But Alcott knew that adults were restless, too, and in *The Doctrine and Discipline of Human Culture* in 1836 presented spiritual culture as a new, or rather all-encompassing, form of religion. Education was no longer subordinate to Christian nurture, Christianity was simply one means of human culture:

> Human Culture is the art of revealing to a man the true Idea of his Being—his endowments—his possessions—and of fitting him to use these for the growth, renewal, and perfection of his Spirit. . . . It seeks to realize in the Soul the Image of the Creator.—Its end is a perfect man. Its aim, through every stage of influence and discipline, is self-renewal. The body, nature, and life are its instruments and materials. Jesus is its worthiest Ideal. Christianity its purest Organ. The Gospels its fullest Text-Book.[67]

Alcott admitted that Christ was the first to recognize man's potential. But Jesus himself was only "a glimpse of the Apotheosis of Humanity" (p. 5).

66. *Record of a School,* 2d ed. (Boston: Russell, Shattuck, 1836), p. iii. Subsequent page citations in the text refer to this edition.

67. *The Doctrine and Discipline of Human Culture* (Boston: James Munroe, 1836), pp. 3–4. Subsequent page citations in the text refer to this edition.

It was the function of education to awaken people to their destiny and to complete the process of redemption Christ began. Thus the teacher became the minister, indeed, one of the "coming Messiahs to meet the growing nature of Man" (p. 26).

It was a doctrine well suited to the substantial ego of Bronson Alcott. But it was based on his equally tremendous sense of what the future promised—and of the relative poverty of Christian institutions as the instruments of progress. As we have seen more than once, this was the feeling that underwrote Transcendentalism as an intellectual movement.

RALPH WALDO EMERSON (1803–1882)   No one was a less likely Transcendentalist than Ralph Waldo Emerson. Whereas the other five were all outsiders to Unitarian culture, in terms of place of origin, childhood religion, or sex and might therefore be expected to upset the delicate balance of Liberal religion, Emerson was born to the Unitarian purple. He was the son of a Boston minister and the descendant of five generations of New England clergymen in all. Nevertheless, in no other case does one feel so strongly that here was a Transcendentalist by nature. Emerson disliked Unitarianism almost as soon as he knew what it was and dismissed the ritual, the theology, indeed, the entire worldview of the Christian tradition more completely than any of his fellow reformers. His career was clear proof that Liberal Christianity contained the seeds of its own subversion.

Emerson was born in Boston in 1803.[68] His father, Rev. William Emerson, was a respected member of the Unitarian community as the chaplain of the state senate, an overseer of Harvard College, and a member of the Boston Athenaeum and of the Anthology, Philosophical, and Massachusetts Historical societies. His death in 1811 substantially reduced the family's finances, but not their social standing. Emerson still managed to graduate from Harvard in 1821, tutoring and teaching school during vacations to pay his way. Nor did he doubt that he would enter one of the professions—medicine, law, or the ministry. In 1824, after working in the interim as a teacher, Emerson decided that he was best qualified to become a preacher because of his "moral imagination."[69]

Unfortunately, Unitarianism was not an imaginative religion, and Emerson's career as a Liberal minister was like trying to fit the proverbial square peg in a round hole. His discomfort with rationalism was not entirely the result of his unusual sensitivity. Unitarians were not so far removed from Puritanism that they were unaware of the drama of salvation, and in Emerson's case, the strenuous piety of his Orthodox aunt, Mary Moody Emerson, made him feel that reason could not explain the

68. The best biographies of Emerson are James Elliot Cabot, *A Memoir of Ralph Waldo Emerson*, 2 vols. (Boston: Houghton Mifflin, 1887), and Ralph L. Rusk, *The Life of Ralph Waldo Emerson* (New York: Scribner's, 1949).
69. Journal, Apr. 24, 1824, quoted in Cabot, *Memoir*, 1:101.

fundamental mystery of the human condition. Thus he hesitated before he entered Harvard Divinity School in 1825. The school "is but a garnished sepulchre, where may be found some relics of the body of Jesus," he wrote in his journal, and considered two alternatives, private study with William Ellery Channing and Orthodox Andover Seminary.[70] But in the end, Emerson chose the conventional route to the Unitarian ministry because his Puritan heritage also left him with a strong sense of social duty:

> The difficulty is that we do not make a world of our own but fall into institutions already made & have to accommodate ourselves to them to be useful at all. & this accommodation is, I say, a loss of so much integrity & of course of so much power. But how shall the droning world get on if all its *beaux esprits* recalcitrate upon its approved forms & accepted institutions & quit them all in order to be single minded? The double refiners would produce at the other end the double damned.[71]

When Emerson became the minister of the Second Church in 1830, it must have been encouraging to find that there was a certain flexibility in the doctrine Unitarian congregations would allow. He preached "The Authority of Jesus" in 1830 and again in 1832 without incident, even though the sermon challenged the special authority of the historical Christ:

> He is our Savior or Redeemer not because oil was poured on his head, nor because he descended by his mother of the line of David, nor because prophets predicted him or miracles attended him nor for all of these reasons but because he declared for the first time fully and intelligibly those truths on which the welfare of the human soul depends . . . because in short they were so vitally his own that he has identified his own memory almost with the conscience of good men from that day to this. . . . [This] authority belonged to this truth and not to any person, so it is not confined to the pure and benevolent Founder of Christianity but may and must belong to all his disciples in that measure in which they possess themselves of the truth which was in him.[72]

It is less complimentary to Unitarians that they were more interested in preserving "relics" than theology. In 1832, Emerson asked the Second

70. Journal, about 1824, quoted in Cabot, *Memoir,* 1:107.
71. Jan. 10, 1832, Emerson, *Journals,* 3:318–19.
72. *Young Emerson Speaks: Unpublished Discourses on Many Subjects by Ralph Waldo Emerson,* ed. Arthur Cushman McGiffert, Jr. (1938; reprint ed., Port Washington, N.Y.: Kennikat Press, 1968), pp. 96–97. The text included in this collection is the second draft of the sermon dated Mar. 31, 1832, in which Emerson more explicitly stated the distinction between the authority of Jesus' teachings and that of his person. The first draft was dated May 30, 1830. Both manuscripts are in the Emerson Papers, Houghton.

Church to discontinue the use of bread and wine at Communion, hoping to make the ritual a free tribute to Jesus rather than an act of obedience to his special power. When the proprietors defeated the proposal, Emerson resigned.[73]

It is an error of historical hindsight, made in light of Emerson's later indifference and even disdain of the church, to conclude that the quarrel over bread and wine was just an excuse to leave the ministry, as James Elliot Cabot argues in his *Memoir* of Emerson.[74] His desire to be "useful" makes it more likely that he hoped to take his congregation with him on the road to reform. But there can be no doubt that Emerson's frustration was not limited to a few symbolic objects, the Communion service, or even Unitarianism. "The Lord's Supper," preached after his formal resignation, shows that the issue was the constraint historical Christianity placed on his "moral imagination":

> This mode of commemorating Christ [Communion] is not suitable to me. That is reason enough I should abandon it. If I believed it was enjoined by Jesus on his disciples, and that he even contemplated making permanent this mode of commemoration, every way agreeable to an Eastern mind, and yet on trial it was disagreeable to my own feelings, I should not adopt it. I should choose other ways which, as more effectual upon me, he would approve more.[75]

Nor is there any question that Emerson's resignation triggered a religious crisis. He did not lose his faith ("When I fail to find the reason, my faith is not less"), but he had no adequate way to explain or express his religious feelings. In lieu of alternatives he clung less than halfheartedly to Christianity. "I dare not speak lightly of the usages I omit," he wrote in his journal during his voyage home from Europe in September 1833: "And so, with this hollow obeisance to things I do not value, I go on, not pestering others with what I do [not] believe, and so I am open to the name of a very poor speculator, a faint, heartless supporter of a frigid and empty theism; a man of no vigor of manners, of no vigor of benevolence."[76]

The trip to Europe had been a search for answers. But Emerson generally was disappointed with the ability of European intellectuals to fashion a religion for the times: "Ah me! what hope of reform, what hope of communicating religious light to benighted Europe, if they who have what they call the light are so selfish and timid and cold, and their faith so unpractical, and, in their judgment, so unsuitable for the middling classes?"[77] Thomas Carlyle was an exception. Emerson had been im-

73. See Cabot, *Memoir*, 1:154–55.
74. Ibid., 1:159.
75. Emerson, *Works*, 11:19.
76. Journal, Sept. 8, 1833, quoted in Cabot, *Memoir*, 1:201.
77. Ibid., p. 201.

pressed with Carlyle's articles on German transcendentalism in the *Westminister Review*, even more by his philosophical novel *Sartor Resartus*. Where others were "selfish and timid and cold," Carlyle was unequivocal: the spirit was a pervasive presence in nature, and the individual had a duty to reform the actual world in conformity with the ideal. Without a doubt, it was precisely because Carlyle was as opinionated and overbearing as Emerson was reserved that their meeting in Scotland had the electrifying effect of a conversion for Emerson. Despite his reservations on shipboard, the Transcendental idea of intuition, he told his former congregation in Boston on his return, was the answer to all his questions: "Man begins to hear a voice in reply that fills the heavens and the earth, saying, that God is within him, that *there* is the celestial host. I find that this amazing revelation of my immediate relation to God, is the solution to all the doubts that oppressed me."[78]

It was not until 1836 that Emerson published a complete statement of his Transcendentalism in a short book called *Nature*. Perhaps he took so much time and care because he knew that this was a revolutionary doctrine. He never mentioned Christianity. But his very heedlessness of this logical point of reference made *Nature* even more of a wholesale revolt against historical revelation:

> Our age is retrospective. It builds the sepulchres of the fathers. It writes biographies, histories, and criticism. The foregoing generations beheld God and nature face to face; we, through their eyes. Why should we not also enjoy an original relation to the universe? Why should we not have a poetry and philosophy of insight and not tradition, and a religion by revelation to us, and not the history of theirs? Embosomed for a season in nature, whose floods of life stream around and through us, and invite us, by the powers they supply, to action proportioned to nature, why should we grope among the dry bones of the past, or put the living generation into masquerade out of its faded wardrobe? The sun shines today also. There is more wool and flax in the fields. There are new men, new lands, new thoughts. Let us demand our own works and laws and worship.[79]

What followed was a proof of nature's self-sufficiency, which freed his generation from reliance on the Christian tradition. Emerson conformed to the laws of nature by proceeding empirically, demonstrating that nature provided for all our needs, for material necessities, the desire for beauty, symbols for language, and experience for education. Most important, nature offered a philosophy and a religion.

The philosophy was idealism. In a way strangely similar to his own passage from Unitarianism, Emerson showed that empiricism was self-

78. "Religion and Society" (Oct. 27, 1833), in *Young Emerson,* ed. McGiffert, p. 199.
79. Emerson, *Works,* 1:3. Subsequent page citations in the text refer to this edition.

subverting. With one hand, he raised Hume's specter of total skepticism; with the other, he anticipated William James's early pragmatism in this argument for "some god," whether a maker of objects or images, in nature: "In my utter impotence to test the authenticity of the report of my senses, to know whether the impressions they make on me correspond with outlying objects, what difference does it make, whether Orion is up there in heaven, or some god paints the image in the firmament of the soul?" (p. 47). But Emerson was not a pragmatist and his idealism was more than a "hypothesis to account for nature." He was a Transcendentalist who heard "a voice" in consciousness which assured him that there was a spirit in nature corresponding to his own soul:

> But when, following the invisible steps of thought, we come to inquire, Whence is matter? and Whereto? many truths arise to us out of the recesses of consciousness. We learn that the highest is present to the soul of man; that the dread universal essence, which is not wisdom, or love, or beauty, or power, but all in one, and each entirely, is that for which all things exist, and that by which they are; that spirit creates; that behind nature, throughout nature, spirit is present; one and not compound it does not act upon us from without, that is, in space and time, but spiritually, or through ourselves: therefore that spirit, that is, the Supreme Being, does not build up nature around us, but puts forth through us, as the life of the tree puts forth new branches and leaves through the pores of the old. As the plant upon the earth, so a man rests upon the bosom of God; he is nourished by unfailing fountains, and draws at his need inexhaustible power. Who can set bounds to the possibilities of man? [Pp. 63–64]

Thus, with the faith supplied by consciousness, Emerson transformed idealism from a philosophy composed of rational postulates into a religion capable of moving men and women to action. This was the end at which all the Transcendentalists' thinking aimed.

But Emerson moved more deliberately than the rest. Impatient as the other Transcendentalists were with the Christian tradition and eager for progress, the conclusion is inescapable that they did not quite realize how thoroughly they subverted Christianity. When they borrowed the idea of intuition, either from European sources or each other, they offered it to the public as a reform on the Unitarian reform, to preserve the essence of Christianity in consciousness to be reworked in new outward forms. *Nature* was different. It was an altogether original, closely reasoned philosophical statement. Emerson was aware that this radically new view of religion needed such a painstaking defense. After 1836 the Transcendentalist controversy made the others realize that they, too, had taken a leap. And it made them all painfully conscious that no rational apology, no matter how well executed, could have quieted the public outcry against Transcendentalism.

3   The Transcendentalist Controversy, 1836–1840

The Transcendentalist controversy was so protracted and so one-sided —in short, so unlike our idea of a controversy as a sharp clash between opposing parties—that historians have just begun to understand its significance. William Hutchison made the first thorough study of the opposition to Transcendentalism in *The Transcendentalist Ministers* (1959).[1] Because his stated interest was "church reform in the New England Renaissance," Hutchison viewed the events as a struggle among Unitarians where the underlying issue was their commitment to toleration. As it turned out, the Liberal Christians were not liberal enough to find room for Transcendentalism, since they adopted a confession of faith in Christ in 1853. One cannot improve on Hutchison's account of the religious side of the conflict. But despite Theodore Parker's weeping at ministers' meetings, the Transcendentalist controversy was more than a denominational trauma. It was a dispute in which questions of values and power which affected the entire city of Boston were at stake.

The attack on Transcendentalism was part of a conservative effort to impose order on Boston society. In the 1830s, Bostonians had moved away from the Christian beliefs and institutions which had structured social life in the preindustrial city. This is true whether we look at the aggressive partisan spirit which the evangelicals called "infidelity" or at the practical innovations of the Unitarian awakening itself or at Transcendentalist philosophy. The result, to borrow a concept from sociology, was that cultural boundaries had become indistinct. Kai Erikson has shown that seventeenth-century Bostonians clarified the limits of acceptable thought and behavior by persecuting their "wayward" neighbors, Antinomians, Quakers, and witches, precisely those groups whose heresies matched the points at which the Puritan community was least sure

<hr />

1. *The Transcendentalist Ministers: Church Reform in the New England Renaissance* (New Haven: Yale University Press, 1959), pp. 52–136.

of its orthodoxy.[2] Just so, the Puritans' nineteenth-century descendants were fearful of change and attacked reformers. The commonwealth prosecuted Abner Kneeland for blasphemy in 1834, a mob of "gentlemen of property and standing" broke up an abolitionist meeting in 1835, and even Sylvester Graham, a health reformer, was forced to flee over back fences to escape a mob in 1837. Because Christianity was identified with tradition and order, the assaults on the Transcendentalists in the press were the next logical step.[3] No wonder Hester Prynne and Arthur Dimmesdale of Hawthorne's *Scarlet Letter* not only recall Antinomians Anne Hutchinson and John Cotton but are suspiciously like Hawthorne's Transcendentalist friends Margaret Fuller and Ralph Waldo Emerson.

In contrast to Puritan Boston, however, the industrial city of the 1830s was by no stretch of the imagination a community. It was this heterogeneity which gave the modern witch-hunt against the Transcendentalists its distinctive character. First, the advocates of order neither represented all Bostonians nor were even an established faction when the decade began. Instead, they formed a spontaneous coalition as a result of their opposition to a common enemy. Thus the conservatives' position was filled with contradictions. What they presented as a campaign for morality, decency, and even good taste, waged in the name of tradition for the public good, was in fact a means to create new partisan loyalties. Second, a play for power lurked just beneath the surface of the conservative movement. The Unitarian clergy were not the leaders of the coalition but reluctant followers. Thus it is tempting to see the controversy as a challenge to the evangelical ministers made by nonclerical spokesmen of the upper and middle classes who intended to substitute various forms of coercion for moral suasion as the means of social control. On some level, these lawyers, newspapermen, and writers blamed the evangelicals for the unprecedented changes of a decade which had produced Transcendentalism. As we have seen, they were not completely wrong.

Third, Boston was sufficiently pluralistic for its less prosperous classes to ignore the lesson in orthodoxy preached by the anti-Transcendentalist press. Methodists, Democrats, and other articulate groups showed little

2. *Wayward Puritans: A Study in the Sociology of Deviance* (New York: John Wiley and Son, 1966), esp. pp. 1–29.

3. In his important essay on similar antebellum campaigns, David Brion Davis has demonstrated how these helped forge a national identity, in "Some Themes of Counter-subversion: An Analysis of Anti-Masonic, Anti-Catholic, and Anti-Mormon Literature," *Mississippi Valley Historical Review* 47 (1960): 205–24. More recently, Donald Scott has offered a persuasive analysis of how the controversy over abolitionism among the clergy of orthodox denominations in the 1830s defined the limits of evangelicalism in the interest of social order, in *From Office to Profession* (Philadelphia: University of Pennsylvania Press, 1978), pp. 95–111. Though the issue for Unitarians was Transcendentalism, the function of the controversies was similar.

interest in the Transcendentalist controversy.[4] For us, however, it is the significance of this freedom for the Transcendentalists which is most important. In a city scapegoating does not necessarily result in categorical exclusion from social life. Urban society by definition offers people alternatives. Thus individuals banned from respectable society have the chance, if they choose to take it, to make a sphere of their own. This is precisely what the Transcendentalists did in the late 1830s. They did not renounce social responsibility, although their decision was a sign of their alienation. Instead, the Transcendentalists began to experiment with new social relationships among themselves, which led to their public reform activity of the 1840s.

Was the Transcendentalist controversy really a controversy? It was not if our definition requires the Transcendentalists to have answered their conservative critics directly. But it was in the sense that two parties took opposing sides on issues of great importance.

THE PARTY OF ORDER

The Transcendentalist controversy roughly coincided with the first depression in American history caused by unregulated economic growth. Between 1837 and 1843, widespread bankruptcies and high unemployment raised unanswered questions about the free market economy. The bewilderment of Rev. Samuel Kirkland Lothrop in the *Christian Examiner* in July 1837 was typical:

> We were in the midst of peace, apparent prosperity, and progress, when, after extensive individual failures, the astounding truth burst upon us like a thunderbolt, was proclaimed from city to city with the light of every day, that we were in appearance if not in fact, either

4. Little, if any, recognition of Transcendentalism and its critics can be found in the following periodicals, all published in Boston, between 1836 and 1840: *Zion's Herald* (Methodist), *Trumpet and Universalist Magazine* (Universalist), *Christian Watchman* (Baptist), *Christian Review* (Baptist), and *Boston Morning Post* (Democratic). Their lack of concern with Transcendentalism does not mean, however, that these groups were not involved in a similar process of self-definition by means of contention. Methodists attacked the supposed infidelity of the Universalists, for example, while Universalists responded with professions of faith in Christianity, all in an obvious effort to convert the same social constituency. See, e.g., the series against Universalism in *Zion's Herald* 7 (Nov. 1836) and replies in the *Trumpet* 18 (Dec. 3 and 10, 1836), 94, 98. Nor were these periodicals altogether silent on the Transcendentalists, at times defending them (see below on the Democrats) and at times criticizing, as the Baptists did in an assessment of Alcott's supposed Socinianism in the *Christian Review* 2 (1837): 305–07. But in no case did they see objections to Transcendentalism as part of a life-or-death struggle with social disorder. In general, these spokesmen of Boston's lower classes viewed Unitarianism as a "religion for the aristocracy," to quote the *Trumpet,* and judged the difficulty with Transcendentalism no vital concern of theirs (*Trumpet* 20 [Sept. 22, 1838], 56).

through the want of means or the inability to use our means, a nation of bankrupts, a bankrupt nation. Now if foreign aggression or injustice, if providential calamity or disaster, have not, as they certainly have not, produced this state of things, what has?[5]

Without economic explanations, some Bostonians reacted to the prospect of social disorder by exposing dangerous doctrines. Thus Lothrop concluded his article on "Existing Commercial Embarrassments" by condemning agitators who said that "the few who have wealth or learning are separated from the many who have not" and by lamenting that much "heart-burning and ill-will, much disorganizing speculation and unjust aspersion, have arisen from this idea."[6] Since labor agitation virtually disappeared during the depression, after a record number of strikes in 1835 and 1836, Lothrop's rebuke was a combination of fear based on experience and fabrication. But it effectively reinforced what was, from the point of view of the minister of the prosperous Brattle Street Church, the safer doctrine that all Bostonians shared common interests.[7]

Such aggressive tactics were not altogether new in Boston in 1837. As I explained in chapter 1, spokesmen for the various classes readily denounced anyone who seemed to jeopardize their position. J. T. Austin's rebuttal of Channing's *Slavery*, Joseph Buckingham's slander of any and all reformers, and Abner Kneeland's exposé of Unitarian "liberties" were common in a city where increasing class distances encouraged suspicion and measures for self-defense. But Lothrop's action was significant because he was a minister who had supported evangelical activities. It indicated the growing acceptability of exclusionary methods, seen no longer as partisan weapons but as legitimate means of social control. It meant too that the clergy were not Boston's undisputed social leaders, since Lothrop now followed the example of two of his parishioners who

5. "Existing Commercial Embarrassments," *Christian Examiner* 22 (1837): 398. While traditional interpretations of the depression such as Reginald McGrane, *The Panic of 1837* (1924; reprint ed., New York: Russell and Russell, 1965), emphasize the causal impact of Jackson's fiscal policies, Peter Temin, in *The Jacksonian Economy* (New York: Norton, 1969), has shown the importance of economic factors intrinsically related to American growth as reasons for deflation, specifically, declining British investments in the U.S. economy and slackening British demand for cotton at high prices after mid–1836. The economic analysis better matches the feeling of many contemporaries that something beyond the sphere of politics was wrong with the system. For contemporary reactions, see Samuel Rezneck, "The Social History of an American Depression, 1837–1843," *American Historical Review* 40 (1935): 662–87. For Unitarian responses, see Nathaniel L. Frothingham, *The Duties of Hard Times* (Boston: Munroe and Francis, 1837), and George Ripley, *The Temptations of the Times* (Boston: Hilliard, Gray, 1837).

6. "Embarrassments," p. 400.

7. On labor activity in the 1830s, see John R. Commons et al., *History of Labor in the United States,* 4 vols. (New York: Macmillan, 1918–35), 1:302–25, and Edward Pessen, *Most Uncommon Jacksonians* (Albany: State University of New York Press, 1967), pp. 34–51.

habitually used verbal and legal force against dissent, Attorney General James T. Austin and Whig publisher Nathan Hale.[8] The four blasphemy trials of Abner Kneeland between 1834 and 1838, in which both laymen were involved, were an important rallying point for conservatives who were impatient with the evangelicals even before 1837. But the depression cemented the conservative alliance and made the use of censure synonymous with protecting the common good.[9] Kneeland's final trial in 1838 demonstrates both developments and suggests what the Transcendentalists, too, were up against.

Kneeland and his secular democratic principles were tried in the name of Liberal Christianity, but the proceeding itself violated Unitarian values, and not by accident. Attorney General Austin (1784–1870), who argued the case before the state supreme court in 1838, was not only critical of evangelicals such as Channing who supported antislavery and other reforms but skeptical of the ability of spiritual methods to protect society at all. "A sermon, a tract, a review may abound in fine sentiments and pure morals and good discourse, but it deals with virtue and vice in the abstract," he told the Temperance Society in 1830: "But let the same thing be touched *practically* through the operation of law, let the force and power of its penalties be applied and you may see the vast difference between advice and authority. It stirs the hornet's nest, and every venomous insect

8. More generally too, Lothrop was probably simply conforming to the conservative mood of the most prestigious Unitarian congregation in Boston, which also included Daniel Webster, former mayor Harrison Gray Otis, and capitalist Amos Lawrence. For more on this important church during this period, as well as on its subsequent decline due to the movement of its members to the suburbs and conversions to Episcopalianism, see Samuel Kirkland Lothrop, *A History of the Church in Brattle Street, Boston* (Boston: Wm. Crosby and H. P. Nichols, 1851), pp. 193–217, and *Some Reminiscences of the Life of Samuel Kirkland Lothrop,* ed. Thornton Kirkland Lothrop (Cambridge, Mass.: John Wilson and Son, 1888), pp. 184–251.

9. Besides the examples I have cited of verbal and legal aggression before 1837, there were also mob incidents occasioned by the same social tensions, most important, the burning of the Catholic convent in Charlestown in 1834 and the antiabolitionist mob of 1835. Conservatives built up their own self-image as social guardians by censuring violence while simultaneously working by more respectable means for similar ends. For example, J. T. Austin commented on mobs soon after the antiabolitionist riot in Alton, Illinois, in 1837: "The blackened and battered walls of the Ursuline Convent will stand by the half-raised monument of Bunker Hill, 'Like a mildewed ear, Blasting his wholesome brother.' So long as it does stand, it will frown contemptuously on any attempt we may make to rebuke the violence of other people, or to admonish them to respect the sanctity of the law" (speech at Faneuil Hall, Dec. 7, 1837, quoted in James Spear Loring, *The Hundred Boston Orators appointed by the Municipal Authorities and other Public Bodies, from 1770 to 1852* [Boston: John P. Jewett, 1852], p. 476). For more on the mobs, see Leonard Richards, *"Gentlemen of Property and Standing": Anti-abolition Mobs in Jacksonian America* (New York: Oxford University Press, 1970), esp. pp. 131–55, and Ray Allen Billington, "The Burning of the Charlestown Convent," *New England Quarterly* 10 (1937): 4–24.

thrusts its sting."[10] By prosecuting Kneeland, Austin was taking the work of enforcing Christianity out of the clergy's hands. But Kneeland's defenders at the Democratic *Morning Post* rightly pointed out that the trial, by its very nature, sacrificed religion to order: "It is not, then, truth, but conformity, that the persecuting part of the community demand—they dare not trust to the power of truth in overcoming error."[11]

Newspaper backing for the prosecution came from Nathan Hale at the *Boston Daily Advertiser* and Joseph Buckingham at the *Boston Courier.* Upper- and middle-class spokesmen thus united against a man who symbolized the subversive potential of the working class. Nathan Hale (1784–1863) was the son of a minister from Westhampton, Massachusetts, who arrived in Boston six years after Buckingham in 1810. But unlike his colleague, he soon became successful and respected. The *Daily Advertiser,* begun in 1813, consistently voiced Federalist, and later Whig, opinions. Hale married a sister of Edward Everett, belonged to a number of scholarly and professional societies and, as president of the Boston and Worcester Railroad Corporation from its founding in 1831 to 1849, promoted manufacturing interests to his own advantage. He was a member, and eventually deacon, of the Brattle Street Church.[12] In deference to the refined tastes of his readers, Hale generally refrained in the *Advertiser* from Buckingham's crude sarcasm and offered sober commentary on current events. During the Kneeland trial, he made his coverage seem evenhanded by printing debates on the question of plea bargaining, which indirectly touched the issue of religious liberty. But he refused to confront the hard questions Kneeland raised on intellectual freedom and

10. *An Address delivered before the Massachusetts Society for the Suppression of Intemperance, May 27, 1830* (Boston: John H. Eastburn, 1830), p. 30. Though Austin was in most ways thoroughly identified with Boston's upper class—born in Boston, graduated from Harvard, and attorney of Suffolk County for twenty years before becoming Massachusetts attorney general in 1832—he was something of a political heretic himself, since he got his start in public life by his marriage to the daughter of renegade Federalist Elbridge Gerry, also Madison's vice-president. But neither Gerry's nor Austin's Republicanism strayed too far from Federalist assumptions of elite leadership to protect property and order. See, for example, Austin's *An Oration, delivered on the Fourth of July, 1829, at the Celebration of American Independence, in the City of Boston* (Boston: John H. Eastburn, 1829). For more on his life, see Loring, *Orators,* pp. 470–76.

11. Quoted in Abner Kneeland, *A Review of the Trial, Conviction, and Final Imprisonment in the Common Jail of the County of Suffolk, of Abner Kneeland, for the Alleged Crime of Blasphemy* (Boston: George A. Chapman, 1838), p. 92. Kneeland reprinted this article, perhaps the best contemporary analysis of the trial, in full in his *Review,* pp. 87–124. The transcript of the supreme court trial is in Octavius Pickering, *Reports of Cases argued and determined in the Supreme Judicial Court of Massachusetts,* 24 vols. (Boston: Little, Brown, 1854), 20:206–46.

12. Lothrop gave one of the few accounts of Hale's life in "Memoir of Hon. Nathan Hale, LL.D.," *Proceedings of the Massachusetts Historical Society* 18 (1880): 270–79.

social justice and left no doubt that Boston could not afford to tolerate full discussion but needed decisive action.[13]

Editorially, Buckingham took the same position. Yet he published Kneeland's steady supply of self-defenses to capitalize on the trial's potential for scandal and, perhaps, to give Kneeland a forum for his animosity toward the rich, a feeling which Buckingham shared but now repressed.[14] Thus heresy-hunting made strange companions in Hale and Buckingham. But broad support for the prosecution gave credence to the idea that "every believer in the Christian religion, and every friend of the decencies of society" should be, and indeed was, united against dissent.[15]

In reality, perhaps a majority of Bostonians opposed the prosecution of Kneeland. *Zion's Herald,* the Methodist weekly, called his views "blasphemous, filthy, and obscene" and capitalized on his slide from Universalism to skepticism in their ongoing contest with the Universalists; nonetheless, the editor doubted "the wisdom of a statute making Mr. Kneeland's misdemeanor a penal offense, and we hope the sentence will be as far as possible of a nominal character." For once, the Universalists agreed: "Our opinion has never altered on the subject—the prosecution, though legal, was unjust, tyrannical, and injudicious, and has been, we have no doubt, deeply lamented by nine tenths of the christians [*sic*] in

13. There was extensive commentary on the case in the *Advertiser* during and immediately after the trial, Mar. 8 to Apr. 2, 1838, and again in late June, when a group of clergymen and other Liberals circulated a petition for Kneeland's pardon. Hale's remarks on June 28 typified his editorial stand: "It is with reluctance that we occupy our columns on the subject of this man's disgusting libel of the Christian religion, and of the attempt of some of the ministers of that religion, to shield him from the punishment to which he has been sentenced after a fair and most dispassionate trial, by the judgment of our highest judicial tribunal." For an example of the debate over legal details, see the letters to the editor, June 28 and 30, 1838.

14. Buckingham had good reason to take secret pleasure when Kneeland jibed at his competitor Nathan Hale that if Hale thought his punishment as light as he said in the *Advertiser,* let him try sitting in the county jail and see if he changed his mind (*Boston Courier,* semiweekly ed., July 2, 1838.). Buckingham had been hit hard by the economic collapse: he was forced to mortgage the *Courier* to avoid bankruptcy in the spring of 1837 and continued as a salaried editor under the control of a board of trustees (*Personal Memoirs and Recollections of Editorial Life,* 2 vols. [Boston: Ticknor, Reed, and Fields, 1852], 2:105). There were deeper political differences between the two editors as well, based on the conflicting interests of their constituencies. While both, as Whigs, favored the recharter of the National Bank, Buckingham was responsible for contention within the party when he criticized some of the bank's fiscal policies which were unfavorable to small merchants and manufacturers. See his *Memoirs,* 2:99–100. Nevertheless, he still turned around to condemn Kneeland as vehemently as Hale: "He published a most infamous and disgraceful paper—an obscene, filthy, blasphemous libel,—and deserves to be punished for it" (*Courier,* semiweekly ed., June 25, 1838.).

15. "Abner Kneeland," *Advertiser,* June 28, 1838.

Massachusetts."[16] Indeed, to all appearances the Kneeland affair was nothing less than class warfare, as papers in the factory towns—the *Lowell Advertiser, Fall River Patriot,* and *Nashua Gazette*—all concurred that this was an outrage to liberty which made "one's blood boil with indignation."[17] Modern Americans cannot help but be swayed by their view. But in 1838, these spokesmen for the popular classes had to compete with the subtle logic of Samuel Kirkland Lothrop.

When Lothrop (1804–86) preached *The Nature and Extent of Religious Liberty* at the Brattle Street Church, he added the authority of religion to the case for the prosecution. He explained that religious liberty was "liberty to be religious, and to teach some kind of religion, not liberty to be irreligious, and teach irreligion."[18] Kneeland deserved punishment, since he forfeited his right to toleration by denying the common objects of faith: "He has no conscience, and his rights are only those of any other animal without a God and without a soul, and not those of an intelligent, moral agent" (p. 13). It was the duty of the state to suppress such opinions, not because religion needed protection ("Let this nation pursue the path of moral degeneracy, anarchy, and revolution, and its free institutions be buried beneath the reckless depravity of the people, Christianity will still survive"), but to guard society with the uncorrupted strength of religion (p. 10). By the time Lothrop finished, legal force seemed to be the only Christian response to any deviation from the sentimentalized version of the Protestant ethic he invoked in his conclusion: "I think of my wife and children, of the wives and children of my neighbors, and of all the good, honest, industrious, and peaceable citizens, whose nightly rest is more secure, whose life, person, rights, and property are made more safe and sure, by having upheld, in all their force and majesty, those laws, which restrain some, that they may protect and bless all" (p. 18).

Lothrop's alliance with a cause at odds with the spiritual methods of the Unitarian evangelicals was a deliberate defection. A group of Liberal ministers and laymen had signed a petition for Kneeland's pardon on the grounds that "religion needs no support from penal law, and is grossly dishonored by interpositions for its defense, which imply that it cannot be

16. "Morbid Sympathy," *Zion's Herald* 9 (July 4, 1838): 106; "The Connection of Universalism with Atheism," *Herald* 9 (Aug. 1, 1838): 121; "The Case of Blasphemy," *Herald* 9 (Apr. 11, 1838): 58; "Abner Kneeland's Sentence," *Trumpet and Universalist Magazine* 20 (June 30, 1838): 6.

17. These papers were quoted in "Kneeland's Sentence," *Trumpet* 20 (June 30, 1838): 6, and "Abner Kneeland," *Boston Morning Post,* June 25, 1838. The quotation appeared in the *Nashua Gazette.*

18. *The Nature and Extent of Religious Liberty: A Sermon preached at the Church in Brattle Square, on Sunday Morning, June 17, 1838* (Boston: I. R. Butts, 1838), p. 13. Subsequent page citations in the text refer to this sermon.

trusted to its own strength and to the weapons of reason and persuasion in the hands of its friends."[19] When Lothrop prefaced his sermon with a denial of his sympathy with the petitioners, he revealed the extent to which tensions between evangelicals and conservatives had grown into an open partisan struggle, forcing ministers to choose between Liberal principles and loyalty to their congregations. The fact that Lothrop turned away from a man as prestigious as William Ellery Channing, whose name headed the petition, indicates the strength of the rival party. They won the Kneeland case. Kneeland was convicted of blasphemy and was sentenced to two months in prison. Shortly thereafter, he left Boston, and he died in Iowa in 1844.

The Transcendentalists probably would have been targets of conservative attacks because of their religious ideas alone. But they made themselves even more vulnerable in the late 1830s by adding social criticism to radical religion. An incident related to the Kneeland trial illustrates this new development.

Kneeland took habitual pleasure in exposing the ironies of his position and on one occasion drew attention to the similarity between his philosophical naturalism, now branded atheism, and the Transcendentalist position. Writing from prison, he reported the visit of a Harvard student who regarded "consciousness," much as Kneeland considered observation and experience, as the final test of truth. He gladly published his visitor's admission that "all Unitarians were as liable to be prosecuted as I was" for their various degrees of humanism but took care to note the special affinity between the views of the student and those of "my friend Brownson."[20] "Friend" was in part sarcastic, since in 1836 Brownson had announced his intention to fight Kneeland's atheistic influence among the working class with a religion committed to progress.[21] But it is almost certain that by 1838 Kneeland also recognized Brownson as an ally in the struggle of labor against capital. The suffering of Boston's wage earners and the conservatism of the propertied classes after the financial panic in the spring of 1837 radicalized Brownson's views. In May, he preached *Babylon is Falling*. He predicted the destruction of capital—the party of "privilege, inequality, war"—and supported his rhetoric with incisive social analysis. Capital did not work "to produce, but to make what others

19. Quoted in William Henry Channing, *The Life of William Ellery Channing* (Boston: American Unitarian Association, 1880), p. 505. Channing included the entire petition on pp. 504–05. It was written by Ellis Gray Loring, a reformer and abolitionist, and was signed by 167 people. For an idea of how Lothrop's position had changed, consider this statement from his *Address delivered before the Massachusetts State Temperance Society, May 31, 1835* (Boston: John Ford, 1835): "In the further prosecution of this enterprise we must rely on moral means and not on the arm of the law or the authority of the civil power" (p. 29).

20. *Review*, pp. 53–54.

21. Brownson's sermon against Kneeland's infidelity was *A Discourse on the Wants of the Times* (Boston: James Munroe, 1836).

produce pass into their own possession."[22] Mechanization and upward mobility, flaunted as solutions to inequality, "merely facilitated the means by which a poor man, a producer, may pass into the class of the non-producers, from one of the ridden to be one of the riders" (p. 16). A violent conflict was inevitable, Brownson concluded, and God promised victory to the dispossessed—the party of "liberty, equality, peace."

The militancy of Brownson's reaction was not typical of the Transcendentalists, but it signaled a trend toward more critical social attitudes. While perhaps only Ripley was as disaffected as Brownson by the injustices the depression exposed, all the Transcendentalists rebelled against the narrowing sympathies and interests of other Bostonians. At first, their discontent appeared in their public statements only in the form of undertone and innuendo. But the Transcendentalists were attacked precisely because their ideas seemed vaguely menacing to conservatives and needed to be defined as "dangerous" to dispel any possible threat.

A brief dispute over Ripley's "Martineau's Rationale" in the *Examiner* opened the controversy in late 1836, but was strictly academic as compared with what was to come. Andrews Norton (1786–1853), the retired Harvard professor of biblical criticism, issued a warning that Ripley's view of miracles (that every man's consciousness better proves Christian truth than these historical evidences) threatened the very "happiness of man."[23] Norton was more than a scholar protecting his material. He firmly believed that Christianity was the backbone of social order, which, as an unconverted Federalist, he conceived as a hierarchy built on authority. Although his views would make him an important conservative spokesman as the Transcendentalist controversy progressed, for now the issue was dropped. Other Unitarian ministers failed to support his censure of one of their own members, and Norton seemed reluctant to jeopardize the prestige of the clergy by further exposing their internal conflicts. Nor did the newspapers take up the cause. While Norton's charge seconded fears of subversion, the theological issue was too narrow to be useful in marking out cultural boundaries.[24]

22. *Babylon is Falling* (Boston: I. R. Butts, 1837), p. 15. Subsequent page citations in the text refer to this sermon.

23. "To the Editor of the Boston Daily Advertiser," *Advertiser*, Nov. 5, 1836.

24. On the theological aspect of the Transcendentalist controversy, see Hutchison, *Transcendentalist Ministers*, pp. 52–97. Norton's letter and Ripley's reply (Nov. 9) first appeared in the *Advertiser* only because the editor of the Unitarian weekly, the *Christian Register*, refused to publish Norton's contentious statement, not because of Hale's interest in the issue. Later the letters were reprinted together in the *Register* 15 (Nov. 12, 1836) : 182. Though the formal issue was miracles, even at this early stage in the controversy there was a conflict over social attitudes as well. Thus Norton told Ripley that he should have submitted his manuscript to "those who are capable of judging [its] correctness," while Ripley argued that the people were the legitimate judges of religious truth.

Alcott's *Conversations with Children on the Gospels* was the perfect material for controversy, in contrast, because of its sprawling indefiniteness. It was the publication of the second volume in the spring of 1837 that fired the conservative imagination. The *Conversations* presented the contemporary reader with confusion of expectations, values, and even style. What promised to be another work on the moral education of children was in fact a lesson to adults on religion delivered by the young. Alcott did not disguise his belief that the child, uncorrupted by the world, better understood the Bible by the simple light of consciousness than the most learned scholar; in that faith, he published the 500-page transcript of his students' commentary on the Gospels.[25] As the schoolroom became the source of religious truth, the book raised an image of a topsy-turvy world contrary to right notions of authority. To make matters worse, the children preached on temperance, politics, slavery, and more, as well as religion. Out of the mouths of babes, though clearly by Alcott's coaxing, came social criticism as stinging as its source seemed innocent: "*Mr. Alcott*: Are there many idolators in Boston? *Augustine*: A great many. They worship money." Or again: "Do you think ministers put on a sober look? *Andrew*: Yes, I think they do. I have always thought so. *Augustine*: They don't feel as they look."[26] Not only did such talk cast suspicion on Alcott's loyalties, but it made him liable to the sensitive charge of corrupting the young. Conversations on the conception and birth of Jesus drove home his lack of taste, if not of morals. The *Conversations'* rambling, eclectic style and confusion of religious and sexual language (one chapter was entitled "Marriage of Spirit: Conjugal Relation") reinforced the overall impression of disorder. Yet Alcott's obvious intention was to promote religion and that, as much as the book's specific content, was why he was attacked. Here was a questionable work parading under a mask of piety, a work which, given its own incoherence and society's ill-defined standards, might be taken seriously. The *Conversations* lingered on the borders of respectability. But to the advocates of order, the work's marginal status made it a valuable lesson in what was beyond the pale.

Hale and Buckingham treated the *Conversations* in a manner calculated to awaken public opposition. Talk of mob action against Alcott, though it failed to materialize, testified to their success.[27] Hale betrayed

---

25. For example: "*Mr. Alcott:* What is meant by his 'turning the hearts of the fathers to the children'? *Franklin:* The children should turn the hearts of their fathers from idolatry by their goodness. *Mr. Alcott:* Perhaps some of you make your parents better. They go out into the world and are tempted, and when they come home and see you, who are not tempted, it makes them better perhaps." *Conversations with Children on the Gospels*, 2 vols. (Boston: James Munroe, 1836–37), 1:44, continued in a note on p. 219.

26. *Conversations*, 1:44; 2:114.

27. Alcott, *Journals*, p. 88.

the book's borderline status when he noted that Alcott innocently left its "two neatly printed volumes" at the *Advertiser* office for review. But he put on the solemn face of a public defender when he wrote that even without the author's invitation, "we do not know that we should have felt at liberty to withhold from our readers the opinion which we have formed" of Alcott's system "we will not say of instruction, but of amusement," of children. No doubt Hale was sincerely distressed by Alcott's method of teaching. But he must have known just as well that corrupting the young was an emotionally charged issue and a perfect rallying point for public feeling. Thus he conveyed the book's subversive potential by detailing its disruptive effect on children:

> . . . to impress on their minds many erroneous notions, to puzzle and perplex them with a thousand useless and inexplicable fancies, to accustom them to trifling and irreverent habits of reflection upon the most grave and solemn subjects, to excite them in a degree injurious to their bodily health, as well as to the proper and healthful exercise of their minds, and to impress them with a degree of self-esteem, quite unfavorable to the future development of their understanding, as well as the improvement of their manners.[28]

Hale went on to explain that Alcott threatened society at large by inviting children to voice "their crude and undigested thoughts" on Scripture, bringing contempt on "the fundamental truths of religion as recorded in the gospels of our Savior." The safekeeping of religion belonged to "mature minds," not to children—or to Alcott. If the *Conversations* were an example of the much-heralded new religious truths, Hale concluded, "we cannot recommend any longer perseverance in the experiment."

Buckingham trod a thin line between respectability and scandal with his usual skill. Perhaps because he sensed his questionable authority on moral subjects, he did not review the *Conversations* himself, but printed a letter of warning "To Fathers and Mothers" by "A Parent," liberally footnoted with his own opinions.[29] The parent worked the *Conversations'* vaguely sexual content into a symbol of indecency by reviewing the book together with Sylvester Graham's *Lecture to Young Men, on Chastity.* Graham's work was offensive on several counts. While his advice was thoroughly Victorian, warning that a young man risked insanity if he enjoyed sexual relations more than once a month, the book dealt explicitly with physiology and sexual habits, especially nocturnal emissions and masturbation. The *Lecture* offered a serious critique of bourgeois habits, moreover, by exposing the effects of excessive eating and drinking on health. Finally, Graham had the presumption to say that his "scientific"

28. *Advertiser*, Mar. 21, 1837.
29. *Courier*, semiweekly ed., Mar. 30, 1837.

evidence for chastity confirmed biblical teachings on marriage, as if Scripture needed such questionable support.[30] Earlier the same month the review appeared (March 1837), a mob of men had confronted Graham at a lecture he was giving to Boston women, and now to link Alcott with Graham was conviction in itself.[31] The parent stated the case: "If, on the one hand, the *Lecture* will diffuse its poison through the whole *moral* constitution of society, the *Conversations with Children,* on the other hand, will as surely sap the *religious sentiment* of the community to the foundation." Echoing Hale's distrust of experimentation, the writer proposed to do "away with such useful knowledge" and "go on in the old fashioned way of our fathers." Buckingham called for stronger action. Not even in the writings of Abner Kneeland, he said, was there so much "to bring Christianity into ridicule and contempt" as in the *Conversations,* and Alcott deserved the same fate as the old blasphemer himself: "Has the honorable Judge of our Municipal Court examined these 'Conversations?' We have a copy which we will lend him with pleasure."

The best defense of Alcott came, not from Boston, where Unitarians seemed at a loss to know how to answer charges that so grossly misrepresented a writer's intentions, but from James Freeman Clarke in Louisville. Four years' experience as a New England Liberal in an Orthodox slave state had taught Clarke something about the use of polemics, even violence, against dissent. He wrote to the Unitarian *Christian Register:* "As LYNCHING seems quite fashionable with you in the East as with us, I apprehend from the tone of authority in which some of the papers declared

---

30. *A Lecture to Young Men, on Chastity: Intended also for the Serious Consideration of Parents and Guardians,* 2d ed. (Boston: Light and Stearns, 1837). Graham (1794–1851), who began his reform career as a temperance lecturer in 1830, was more than a health reformer, since he backed up his advocacy of a vegetarian diet and abstinence from stimulants with theories of religion and society. Basically he believed that the nervous tenor of American life contributed to excessive sex drives and general moral degeneracy, and his dietary prescriptions aimed to restore moral purity. For more on Graham, see Richard H. Shryock, "Sylvester Graham and the Popular Health Movement, 1830–1870," *Mississippi Valley Historical Review* 18 (1931): 172–83. Graham was only one of a number of reformers with similar opinions. Alcott's cousin, William A. Alcott, was another, and the two favorable reviews of the *Conversations* in W. A. Alcott's *American Annals of Education,* the first by the editor and the second by an even more enthusiastic subscriber, probably did nothing to help Alcott's case with the public. See *Annals* 7 (1837): 143, 178–80. Bronson Alcott, moreover, agreed with these reformers and had been a vegetarian since 1835. One reason for the extensive discussion of the human body in the *Conversations* was that Alcott believed that purification of the body must precede spiritual rebirth. See, e.g., the conversation on John the Baptist's "ministry of temperance" in *Conversations,* 1:48–53. Alcott focused on birth in particular, since, applying his own typology to Scripture, he thought that birth "typifies the bringing forth of the spirit, by pain, and labor, and patience" (1:63).

31. See "Graham's Lectures," *Courier,* semiweekly ed., Mar. 6, 1837, and "Indecent Public Lectures," *Advertiser,* Mar. 3, 1837.

that the school must be put down, that it was their object to excite a mob against the unhappy perpetrator of this new plan of education. We boast ourselves of our toleration, and wonder at the persecutions of past times; but I am afraid we are, after all, the children of them which killed the prophets."[32] Clarke's charge of intolerance was calculated to remand Unitarians to their own Liberal principles. To be effective, however, religious liberty had to retain its once broad significance, and that was not the case. Just as Lothrop would twist Liberal values to fit conservative interests in the Kneeland affair, in 1837 a Harvard instructor named Francis Bowen acted as an apologist against Transcendentalism.

Though only twenty-six years old and a generation younger than the Transcendentalists' other critics, Bowen (1811–90) played a decisive role in the controversy. It was Bowen who first identified Transcendentalism as a "school of philosophy." What the public had seen of Ripley and Alcott, he implied, merely scratched the surface of a dangerous movement. His two articles in the *Examiner* in 1837, their publication itself a sign of the changing mood of Unitarians, gave the case against Transcendentalism the flavor of intellectual respectability and moral righteousness.[33] No doubt many Unitarians were deeply offended when they realized that Transcendentalism raised basic questions about the Christian religion; but if Bowen is at all typical, they responded with the same zeal to defeat the dangerous intruder as the newspaper press.

Bowen said that Transcendentalism was a philosophical rebellion against Locke in favor of Kant, thus altogether ignoring Common Sense principles which made Transcendentalism as much a native development as a foreign import. He offered an impressive array of arguments to support his position but really objected to Transcendentalism on simple moral grounds. Bowen compared the urbane, tolerant, and practical spirit of Locke with the elitism and obscurantism of the German transcendentalists. He blamed contention in Boston on the like temper of Kant's American followers:

> We judge the tree by its fruits, when we assert, that the study of such writings tends to heat the imagination, and blind the judgment—that it gives a dictatorial tone to the expression of opinion, and a harsh, imperious, and sometimes flippant manner to argumentative discussion—that it injures the generous and catholic spirit of speculative

32. *Christian Register* 16 (Apr. 29, 1837): 66. Other reviews and defenses of Alcott by Transcendentalists were Clarke's "Religious Education of Children," *Western Messenger* 3 (Mar. 1837): 540–45, and "Mr. Alcott's Book and the Objections made to It," *Messenger* 3 (May 1837): 678–83; Emerson's letter of protest to the *Courier*, Apr. 4, 1837; Elizabeth Peabody's "Mr. Alcott's Book and School," *Register* 16 (Apr. 29, 1837): 65; and Brownson's "Alcott on Human Culture," *Boston Quarterly Review* 1 (1838): 418–32.

33. "Transcendentalism," *Christian Examiner* 21 (Jan. 1837): 371–85, and "Locke and the Transcendentalists," *Examiner* 23 (Nov. 1837): 170–94.

philosophy by raising up a sect of such marked and distinctive character, that it can hold no fellowship either with former laborers in the cause, or with those, who, at the present time, in a different line of inquiry, are aiming at the same general objects. The difference in the mode of philosophizing between the old and new schools is radical. Either one party or the other is entirely in the wrong.[34]

Bowen had his cake and ate it. Since he made it appear that the Transcendentalists exiled themselves by their own pretensions, defenders of the "old school" became the champions of toleration.

Bowen was an unusual figure in a controversy where it is often easy to identify participants with specific constituencies, since beyond his professed loyalty to a fictitious school of orthodox Lockeans, he spoke for no one but himself. Born in Cambridge in 1811, Bowen had worked his way through Harvard. In 1835, two years after his graduation, he was hired back by the college as a tutor in Greek and in 1836 taught the senior class philosophy and political economy as well. Thus he stood near the center of academic power when Norton first contested Transcendentalist opinions, and he seized the opportunity to make a temporary teaching post into a profession. He did not tackle the real philosophical challenge that the idea of intuition posed to Common Sense assumptions. Instead he depicted the Transcendentalist appeal to consciousness as a threat to all reasonable thinking and distilled a canon of orthodoxy out of the Unitarians' hitherto eclectic interests, to be defended by caretakers like himself. He succeeded in making himself indispensable. After ten years as editor of the *North American Review*, he was appointed Alford Professor of Natural Religion, Moral Philosophy, and Civil Polity at Harvard in 1853.

Bowen became a creative philosopher in his later life, and despite his youthful pretensions, his polemic set the stage for his serious work as well. In contrast to Norton, who fought Transcendentalism for the scholarly traditions of Christian theology, Bowen moved the issue onto the new ground of secular philosophy.[35] Nothing better illustrates the shift in Boston culture that began in the late 1830s than the eventual displacement

34. "Locke," p. 183. See Brownson's excellent rebuttal of Bowen, "Locke and the Transcendentalists," *Boston Quarterly Review* 1 (Jan. 1838): 83–106. Brownson answered Bowen's charge of elitism with two arguments: first, that Locke's premise that the mind was a tabula rasa gave the people no credit for knowing anything without the instruction of scholars, and second, that to the degree philosophy answered religious doubts raised by speculation, it reunited the intellectual with the people (pp. 101–04). On Bowen's allegation that Transcendentalism was a European philosophy, it should be noted that many scholars have followed the same reasoning and have highlighted the movement's important transatlantic connections without accepting Bowen's conclusion that Transcendentalism was un-American and thus subversive. The first was Octavius Brooks Frothingham, *Transcendentalism in New England* (1876; reprint ed., New York: Harper and Brothers, 1959), esp. pp. 1–104.

35. See his *Critical Essays, on a Few Subjects Connected with the History and Present Condition of Speculative Philosophy* (Boston: H. B. Williams, 1842), a collection of articles

of Norton, a man of settled and indeed dogmatic convictions, by Bowen, who promised to defend tradition even while changing the terms of the argument.

Emerson's commencement address at Harvard Divinity School in July 1838 may have lent credibility to Bowen's specter of a Transcendentalist conspiracy. To an audience filled with ministers, he condemned the habit of preaching the mere facts of historical Christianity in Boston churches and, in terms bordering on personal censure, implied that the cause was the ministers' spiritual failure: "The spirit only can teach. Not any profane man, not any sensual, not any liar, not any slave can teach, but only he can give, who has; he only can create who is."[36] Not since Anne Hutchinson had the Boston clergy been so harshly rebuked by one of the supposed elect, and Emerson's doctrine indeed savored of Antinomianism: "If a man is at heart just, then so far is he God; the safety of God, the immortality of God, the majesty of God do enter into that man with justice" (p. 122). But the most striking feature of the address was its harsh, determined, almost belligerent tone. Faced with conservative resistance to Transcendentalism and, by implication, evangelical Unitarianism, Emerson conveyed his frustration with the moderation of the majority of ministers and his hope to rouse them from their lethargy.[37] But he succeeded mainly in making himself vulnerable to the charges Bowen had thrown out against Transcendentalists in general—pride, contentiousness, and obscure language, now hinting of pantheism or even atheism.

Before Emerson's address, the Unitarian clergy had worked hard to practice their ethic of toleration. In 1836, neither the *Christian Examiner*

---

originally published between 1837 and 1842, including the two on Transcendentalism. On Bowen's life, see Waldo Higginson, *Memorials of the Class of 1833 of Harvard College* (Cambridge, Mass.: John Wilson and Son, 1883), pp. 101–03. For a discussion of his later political and economic views—basically, that government should be controlled by an elite to protect property—see Daniel Walker Howe, *The Unitarian Conscience* (Cambridge, Mass.: Harvard University Press, 1970), pp. 208, 227–31. On his later work as a philosopher, see Bruce Kuklick, *The Rise of American Philosophy: Cambridge, Massachusetts 1860–1930* (New Haven: Yale University Press, 1977), pp. 28–45.

36. "An Address, delivered before the Senior Class of the Divinity College, Cambridge, July 15, 1838," in Emerson, *Works*, 1:135. Subsequent page citations in the text refer to this edition.

37. The best analysis of the motivation behind Emerson's address is Conrad Wright's "Emerson, Barzillai Frost, and the Divinity School Address," in his collection, *The Liberal Christians: Essays on American Unitarian History* (Boston: Beacon Press, 1970), pp. 41–61. Wright argues persuasively that Emerson's frustration with the thoroughly mediocre preaching of Barzillai Frost, who came from the divinity school to Concord in 1837 as associate pastor to Emerson's great uncle, Ezra Ripley, focused Emerson's long-standing discontent with the ministry in the year prior to his address. While I would add that the conservative mood of the late 1830s made Emerson unusually impatient with Frost's lack of force, it is very likely that Frost became a symbol to Emerson of the problems of the Liberal clergy.

nor the *Christian Register* accepted Norton's censure of Ripley, although the *Register* later relented at Ripley's request and reprinted Norton's letter from the *Advertiser* together with a reply from Ripley. In 1837, both journals tried to do justice to Alcott. The *Register* published defenses by Clarke and Elizabeth Peabody, and the *Examiner* printed a temperate review of the *Conversations* several months after the newspaper controversy died down. Privately, too, at an 1836 meeting to reassess *Examiner* policy after Norton condemned the editors for publishing Ripley's opinions, the ministers responsible for the periodical reaffirmed its commitment to free speech.[38] But the "Divinity School Address" tried their principles to the breaking point. First Emerson broke the rule of friendly discussion, that differences should be aired without reference to character, by linking the "famine in our churches" to the clergy's shallow spiritual life. Nowhere, moreover, had the Transcendentalist critique of historical Christianity been so clearly stated nor the temptation to deify the soul more clearly shown. Coming from a man still considered a Unitarian preacher, the ministers' shock at the degree of Emerson's defection was probably equaled only by the shock of recognition at the direction of their own evangelical drift.

Thus the clergy turned back toward more traditional Christianity and toward a new concern with their denominational and professional identity. In the 1840s they worried more about Theodore Parker's theism and claim to clerical fellowship than about evangelical preaching or urban poverty.[39] While the cost was high, the ministers' focus was to some extent a matter of necessity. Unitarians had to define their beliefs more carefully

38. For citations for the *Register*, see nn. 24 and 32. The unsigned review in the *Examiner* was "Alcott's *Conversations on the Gospels*," 23 (Nov. 1837): 252–61. It is attributed to Elizabeth Peabody in Dorothy McCuskey, *Bronson Alcott, Teacher* (New York: Macmillan, 1940), p. 204. But although the thesis conforms to Peabody's views—that the child must be encouraged freely to develop his religious nature—neither the style nor her own difficulties with the Unitarians (see below) support the conclusion that she was the author. The ministers' meeting was reported by Elizabeth Peabody in a letter to her sister, Mary. She said that all the ministers in the Boston area except Alexander Young at the New North Church and John Palfrey at the divinity school supported Ripley, though they did not "*believe* with him in regard to the question of *Inspiration*." The ministers felt strongly enough to consider leaving the *Examiner* in the hands of the conservatives and establishing a new periodical but finally decided against it, since there was "no sympathy with Mr. Norton in the community" (undated letter, probably Nov. 1836, Berg, NYPL).

39. Both the *Examiner* and the *Register* moved decisively in the fall of 1838 to deny that Emerson's opinions represented the Unitarian position. See editorials in the *Examiner* 25 (Nov. 1838): 266–67, and *Register* 17 (Sept. 29, 1838): 154–55. For the events concerning Parker that led in 1853 to the adoption of a Unitarian "declaration of opinion," for all intents and purposes a creed, see Hutchison, *Transcendentalist Ministers*, pp. 98–136. See also Perry Miller, "Theodore Parker: Apostasy within Liberalism," *Harvard Theological Review* 54 (1961): 275–96. Donald Scott demonstrates that the same process of professionalization was occurring simultaneously in other denominations, in *From Office to Profession*, pp. 95–155.

to retain any denominational coherence in an urban culture which favored the proliferation of new views, of which Transcendentalism might be but the first example. Judging by his rising prestige, Andrews Norton was one who had some answers.

In contrast to their silence in 1836, the ministers met Norton's polemic against "The New School in Literature and Religion" in August 1838 with cautious support, since within a year he was invited to address the first meeting of the new association of divinity school alumni. Norton's attack, published in the *Advertiser*, mainly repeated charges which had been made before. He echoed Bowen when he accused the Transcendentalists of subverting reason and good taste by importing "German barbarisms" and followed Buckingham when he discredited them by association with all manner of radicals, "that foolish woman, Miss Martineau," "that hyper-Germanized Englishman, Carlyle," the "atheist Shelley," and "pantheist Schleiermacher."[40] So undiscriminating were Norton's denunciations that lawyer Theophilus Parsons, though a critic of Emerson's doctrine of "self-love and self-pride," tried to salvage a moderate position in the *Advertiser* a few days later by typing Norton as an archconservative altogether hostile to change: "The writer seems to identify the school he attacks with all inquiry—all progress; when he objects to it that it is rhapsodical, incoherent, ignorant and presuming,—he seems to feel as if all this were expressed by calling it *new*."[41]

But the formation of the ministers' professional association was a sign that they were looking for stability, not further experimentation, and the traditional concepts of religion and society Norton proposed in July 1839 matched their feeling. "Your office," he instructed, "is to defend, explain, and enforce the truths of Christianity," understood in the classic Liberal terms of Enlightenment rationalism: "By a belief in Christianity, we mean that Christianity is a revelation by God of the truths of religion, and that the divine authority of him whom God commissioned to speak to us in his name was attested, in the only mode in which it could be, by miraculous displays of his power."[42] United behind this doctrine, a clerical elite, guided themselves by full-time scholars like Norton (though he failed to state this obvious corollary), would keep the faith of the people, since "that degree of learning, reflection, judgment, freedom from worldly influences, and independence of thought, necessary to ascertain for one's

40. "The New School in Literature and Religion," *Advertiser*, Aug. 27, 1838.
41. "The New School and its Opponents," *Advertiser*, Aug. 30, 1838. Norton replied in "On the Article in the Advertiser of Thursday concerning the New School," Sept. 1, 1838, and Parsons, writing as before under the signature "S. X.," wrote another letter on Sept. 3.
42. *A Discourse on the Latest Form of Infidelity; Delivered at the Request of the Association of the Alumni of the Cambridge Theological School, on the 19th of July, 1839* (Cambridge, Mass.: John Owen, 1839), pp. 4, 5. Subsequent page citations in the text refer to this address.

self the true character of Christianity, is to be expected from but few"
(p. 7). What the "new school" called "consciousness," a democratizing
faculty which challenged the authority of the educated class, was nothing,
Norton concluded, but "undefined and unintelligible feelings." Empirical
evidence collected by scholars was the only ground of faith. The people
must accept Christianity "on trust" or not at all.

George Ripley rightly argued in his pamphlet rebuttal to Norton that
to say Christianity could be proved only by miracles and guaranteed only
by clerical authority was hostile to the Liberal commitment to the right of
private judgment.[43] But Norton proposed an alternative with equal claims
to legitimacy based on Protestants' belief in an objective revelation and
historical church. The kind of clerical rule Norton envisioned might be
impossible in modern society, in light of the multiple contenders for
cultural leadership; but he still gave the ministers a clear self-image at-
tuned to the conservative temper of the times.

Other events which followed Emerson's address confirm the clergy's
conservatism. In September 1838, Henry Ware, Jr. preached *The Personality of the Deity* at the Harvard chapel. Here a leading evangelical
significantly turned from reform to theological issues and outlined a
cosmology based on the family. If Norton's combination of rationalism
and Federalism, despite its advantages, still seemed outmoded, Ware's
Victorian alternative incorporated the evangelical emphasis on feeling
into a system where the thrust was not individual awakening but collective
safety.

Order, in Ware's scheme, was built on affection. The authority of the
Father and obedience of the children depended on the belief that Chris-

---

43. *"The Latest Form of Infidelity" Examined: A Letter to Mr. Andrews Norton,
Occasioned by his Discourse before the Association of the Alumni of the Cambridge
Theological School, on the 19th of July, 1839* (Boston: James Munroe, 1839), pp. 23–43,
95–119, and passim. Even though Ripley charged Norton with avoiding the real issue of
religious belief in Boston by accusing the Transcendentalists instead of importing the
atheistic opinions of Spinoza, Hume, and other pre-nineteenth-century European
philosophers, he followed Norton down the garden path of philosophical dispute, and their
exchange continued at some length. Norton replied in *Remarks on a Pamphlet entitled "The
Latest Form of Infidelity Examined"* (Cambridge, Mass.: John Owen, 1839), and then
Ripley wrote *Defence of "The Latest Form of Infidelity" Examined: A Second Letter to Mr.
Andrews Norton* (Boston: James Munroe, 1840) and *Defence of "The Latest Form of
Infidelity" Examined: A Third Letter to Mr. Andrews Norton* (Boston: James Munroe,
1840). Other important reactions to Norton's address were Andrew P. Peabody, "Mr.
Norton's Discourse," *Examiner* 28 (Nov. 1839): 221–31, and Richard Hildreth, *A Letter to
Andrews Norton, on Miracles as the Foundation of Religious Faith* (Boston: Weeks, Jordan,
1840). Peabody, a Unitarian minister, tried to reconcile Norton's theology with evangelical
religion by arguing that tangible evidence such as miracles was necessary to convert the
unsophisticated masses. Hildreth, a religious skeptic and political economist, compared
Norton's dogmatism to the Inquisition and praised the Transcendentalists' subjective religion because it removed religious obstacles to scientific progress.

tianity was the revealed word of a loving parent who won voluntary compliance to his law by personally touching the heart. To view Christianity as the mere record of consciousness, as the Transcendentalists did, was to rob it of its affective power, jeopardizing social order and defrauding man of the personal happiness that Ware conveyed by the following sentimental image of a motherless child: "And so the filial spirit is mocked;—as if the little child, with its full heart, longing for the embrace of its absent mother, should be told, 'That mother is but an idea, not a person; you may think of her, but you can have no intercourse with her; be satisfied with this.' "[44] Like the newspaper charges that Alcott corrupted children, Ware's sermon pulled the heartstrings of Bostonians closed against the Transcendentalists pictured here as frustrating the spiritual gratifications of the cosmic home. Ware was nearly as short on charity, moreover, as the daily press. Despite his private reassurance to Emerson that the sermon meant no personal censure, Ware was doubtless thinking of him when he said that a person who confused the voice of conscience with the voice of God might be moral but was in no way a religious man: "To the pure all things are pure; and some men will dwell forever in the midst of abstraction and falsehood without being injuriously affected. Express infidelity is not vice, and may exist together with great integrity and purity of life. Atheism is not immorality, and may coexist with an unblemished character."[45] But such individuals were rare, he warned, and the effect of this doctrine would be devastating to the majority.

Not all Bostonians acquiesced in the new conservative mood. Among the dissidents were spokesmen for the popular classes about whom Ware was concerned. In August 1838, a defense of Emerson in the *Morning Post,* the voice of the Democratic party, made a stirring case for progress. Far from deploring Transcendentalist innovations, a "new school," the *Post* declared, "is certainly needed, from which may come forth a literature in perfect harmony with the higher nature of man and the democratic institutions of this country."[46] Emerson's personal "independence" was to be admired; but the *Post* valued Emerson more for exposing the divinity students' impatience with the "tyranny which custom, conventionalism have exercised over them," personified by their Harvard professors: "Their own insensibility to the free spirit of the age and country, is the

44. *The Personality of the Deity: A Sermon, Preached in the Chapel of Harvard University, Sept. 23, 1838* (Boston: James Munroe, 1838), p. 15. See also Ann Douglas's discussion of the domestication of American religion during this period, in *The Feminization of American Culture* (New York: Knopf, 1977), esp. pp. 121–64.

45. *Personality,* p. 22. For his Oct. 3, 1838, letter to Emerson, see John Ware, *Memoir of the Life of Henry Ware, Jr.,* 2 vols. (Boston: James Munroe, 1846), 2:186–87.

46. "An Address delivered before the Senior Class, in the Divinity College, Cambridge, Sunday Evening, 15th July, 1838, by Ralph Waldo Emerson," *Boston Morning Post,* Aug. 31, 1838. Subsequent quotations refer to the same article.

cause which leads the young men, committed to their care, to seek inspiration and instruction elsewhere." The Democrats' commitment to experimental thinking was no doubt sincere. But it is equally true that Transcendentalism had become a political football in the *Post*'s own struggle with elite institutions such as Harvard College.[47]

There were protests within the elite as well, though the man who stood most openly behind toleration lost his head in the controversy. Chandler Robbins (1810–82), a divinity school classmate of James Freeman Clarke and William Henry Channing in 1833 and Emerson's successor at the Second Church, resigned the editorship of the *Christian Register* in March 1839 after sustained criticism of his policy to make the journal the voice of "an unbigoted and anti-exclusive religion."[48] Even in his farewell editorial he struggled to be as just to the conservatives as he had been to the Transcendentalists, by commending their "zeal in behalf of the interests of piety and truth." Nor did he wholly capitulate to their pressure, since "I would not now erase one sentiment to which they objected from the columns which I have written." But he sounded like a man worn down into acquiescence when he wrote that "my strongest desire, as far as the *Register* is concerned, is to retire into silence—grateful, tranquilizing, thrice welcome Silence—and, having made up my account as an editor for the judgment of the great day, to hear concerning myself in that capacity, no more either of commendation or censure from the lips of man."[49] Thus reluctant conservatives were recruited either by being forced into retirement like Robbins or by being so intimidated that they never spoke up.[50]

It was Transcendentalist Orestes Brownson who forged a new kind of liberalism that could survive in a partisan society. His vehicle was the

47. Just how much Emerson became the pawn of partisan politics can be seen in the following instance. When he protested the removal of the Cherokee Indians to a reservation in a public letter to Van Buren the preceding June, the *Post* dismissed the "high priest of transcendentalism" as a "federal[ist] grumbler," only to become his champion as soon as he was censured by his supposed "whig friends." See "Mr. Emerson's Letter," *Post,* June 19, 1838, and "Mr. Emerson's Letter and the Cherokees," June 27, 1838. The incident is a necessary reminder that the alignments which took shape around the Transcendentalists could be neither stable nor simple and, as important, that the *Post*'s liberalism with regard to Emerson was not matched by a like concern for the Indians.

48. Editorial, *Register* 17 (Dec. 29, 1838): 206.

49. *Register* 18 (Mar. 30, 1839): 50.

50. Besides public opinion, other factors which deterred opposition to the conservatives by moderate Unitarian ministers were a temperamental dislike of controversy and an adherence to historical Christianity in some form, despite the interest of some in philosophical experimentation. Frederick Henry Hedge, minister to the Unitarian congregation of Bangor, Maine, exemplifies the reluctance even of close Transcendentalist sympathizers. See Emerson's comments on Hedge in a letter to Fuller, Mar. 30, 1840, *Letters,* 2:271. See also Ronald Vale Wells, *Three Christian Transcendentalists: James Marsh, Caleb Sprague Henry, and Frederick Henry Hedge* (New York: Columbia University Press, 1939), pp. 96–145, 202–16.

Boston Quarterly Review, which he began in 1838. Whereas Robbins's commitment to freedom had little more intellectual substance than the idea of toleration itself, Brownson built his policy of free speech on the solid base of his own religious and social principles. He set himself up as a party of one and then, in effect, invited others to join him in an alliance of independent thinkers by choosing their works for review. The criterion for membership was not agreement with Brownson but courage to defend one's own convictions. Thus although he admitted that theologically Andrews Norton sat "in a room with the shutters closed," he commended him for saying what other Liberals whispered: "He is almost the only one in this neighborhood, who has been willing to come out publicly in defense of the old school, and to give the advocates of the new an opportunity to speak out on their own behalf."[51] Nor did similar views mean uncritical acceptance of a writer's opinions. Brownson treated Emerson's address at the divinity school with the respect due a serious statement of belief. But because Brownson's own Transcendentalism was dualistic (he subordinàted God's revelation in the soul to God himself), he severely criticized Emerson's monism as "a system of Transcendental selfishness."[52] Brownson's idea of a party of thinkers, possibly with radically different opinions but held together by debate, allowed a degree of pluralism never envisioned by Boston Unitarians and indicated his grasp of the real direction of urban intellectual life. But attacks on his article "The Laboring Classes" in the summer of 1840 showed that most people were not prepared to sanction such freedom.

"The Laboring Classes" was the strongest example of how the Transcendentalists grafted social reform onto radical religion in the course of the Transcendentalist controversy. Spiritual awakening, Brownson boldly proposed, was but the first step toward social revolution. He explained precisely what he intended. First, the "priesthood" must be abolished. Brownson traced the root of all modern forms of oppression to a primitive class of priests who conned the people into subordination by claiming salaried servants of corporate wealth; but Brownson believed that religious sanctions given to patience and obedience were still the strongest ous sanctions given to patience and obedience were still the strongest barrier to working-class action. Second, government must repeal all laws unfavorable to labor, and although the state should protect the worker's right to the products of his industry, it should not encroach on the liberty of the people. Third, banks, the tools of wealth, must be destroyed, and fourth, the permanent concentration of capital should be blocked by

51. "Two Articles from the Princeton Review," *Boston Quarterly Review* 3 (1840): 269. Philosophically, Brownson's practice conformed to the premise of Victor Cousin's Eclecticism, that all statements represented a partial expression of truth. See his "Cousin's Philosophy," *Examiner* 21 (1837): 33–64.

52. "Mr. Emerson's Address," *Boston Quarterly Review* 1 (1838): 504.

prohibiting the inheritance of property. All this, Brownson predicted, must come about by revolution.[53]

The charges against Brownson fell into expected patterns—that he threatened Christianity, property, the family, and so forth. But these polemics were different from the others against the Transcendentalists because of the obvious lack of common ground among the critics. Precisely because the reaction was so explosive, this was the last episode in the Transcendentalist controversy as I have defined it.

The campaign against Transcendentalism succeeded in organizing the loyalties of Bostonians only so long as the self-proclaimed respectable society submerged its internal differences and maintained a convincing show of unity against dissent. Otherwise the distinction so carefully built up between the community and this dangerous faction fell apart once again. Until 1840, the impression of a solid phalanx held up surprisingly well. The rhetoric of Hale, Buckingham, Bowen, Norton, and Ware suggested a united front of all those of any social account in the Boston —upper class, middle class, Liberal clergy—all, moreover, Whigs and Unitarians of various sorts. But "The Laboring Classes" brought unsolicited allies with so little kinship to these Bostonians that merely to scratch the surface exposed the lie of consensus. In Washington, the Democratic party repudiated Brownson's radicalism. Since 1840 was an election year and Brownson was a prominent Democrat, "The Laboring Classes" made him a political liability, to be cut off rather than defended. In New York, the editor of the *Methodist Quarterly Review* expressed outrage at Brownson's views of Christianity and society, even fabricating evidence out of some of his ambiguous passages for his supposed denial of marriage. In Lowell, the women editors of the *Lowell Offering*, apparently more loyal to their wealthy patrons than the female operatives whose interests they claimed to represent, contested Brownson's statement that the domestic ideal of bourgeois society degraded working women.[54]

---

53. "The Laboring Classes," *Boston Quarterly Review* 3 (July 1840): 375.

54. For summaries of the controversy, see Henry F. Brownson, *Orestes A. Brownson's Early Life, Middle Life, and Latter Life*, 3 vols. (Detroit: H. F. Brownson, 1898–1900), 1:241–81, and, with special emphasis on the Democrats, Arthur M. Schlesinger, Jr., *Orestes A. Brownson* (Boston: Little, Brown, 1939), pp. 91–111. On the Lowell women and the controversy over factory conditions in which Brownson became involved, see Norman Ware, *The Industrial Worker, 1840–1860: The Reaction of American Industrial Society to the Advance of the Industrial Revolution* (Boston: Houghton Mifflin, 1924), pp. 80–95. The article in the *Methodist Quarterly Review*, "The Rich against the Poor," 23 (1841): 92–122, is particularly interesting, since the editor agreed that there were basic social injustices in American society, despite his criticism of Brownson's radical solution. Brownson answered the charges against him in a general way in a second article on "The Laboring Classes," *Boston Quarterly Review* 3 (Oct. 1840): 420–512. See also his "To the Editors of the Lowell Offering," *Boston Quarterly Review* 4 (1841): 261–64, and review of "Hereditary Property Justified," *Boston Quarterly Review* 4 (1841): 390–91.

The entry of these critics into the Transcendentalist controversy raised as many questions as it answered. Was allegiance to the party of order as universal as its spokesmen claimed all along, or was the conservative party itself no more than a collection of sects and factions held together by shared fears and shallow watchwords? Were conservative Bostonians the leaders of a national movement to preserve American traditions, or were they just one group among many, all defending their separate interests? If it was true that the Transcendentalists were simply another party in a pluralist society, not deviants from an orthodox standard, then the stigma attached to them lost much of its meaning. And if they were excluded by the local establishment, Boston's propertied classes did not control all, or even most, of the alternatives in a changing society. It was precisely the Transcendentalists' sense of the freedom, as well as the liabilities, of their position which enabled them to turn their energies in new directions.

THE BEGINNINGS OF TRANSCENDENTALISM AS A SOCIAL MOVEMENT

The most important result of the controversy was the Transcendentalists' interest in social reform by collective means. Writing to Emerson in 1840, George Ripley did not need to explain what he meant by "the 'city of God' which we shall try to build."[55] It would be the antithesis of the city of Boston. Alienated by a culture built on fear, the Transcendentalists took steps to establish social relations allowing freedom, growth, justice, and love.

Part of the reason for this new direction was the sense of social deformity nurtured by the conservative attacks. As religious reformers, the Transcendentalists put the question this way: how could a person once awakened to his spiritual power act according to conscience if society were hostile to the teachings of religion, not only in its spirit, but somehow in the structure of its relationships? "But if there is a divine principle in man, it has a right, and it is its duty to unfold itself from itself," Elizabeth Peabody wrote in 1840. "A social organization, which does not admit of this, which does not favor, and cherish, and act with main reference to promoting it, is inadequate, false, devilish."[56] The Transcendentalists began to realize that a revival could not regenerate society without concurrent social reforms. Peabody concluded: "The problem of the present age is human society, not as a rubric of abstract science, but as a practical matter and universal interest; an actual reconciliation of outward organization with the life of the individual souls who associate; and by virtue of whose immortality each of them transcends all arrangements" (p. 219).

55. GR to RWE, about Oct. 1840, Emerson Papers, Houghton.
56. "A Glimpse of Christ's Idea of Society," *Dial* 2 (Oct. 1841): 222. Subsequent page citations in the text refer to this article.

The new social orientation of the movement owed more, however, to the fact that the controversy changed the Transcendentalists' lives. Excluded from conventional society, they approached social relations in an experimental frame of mind. They neither followed nor formulated theories of social organization at first. They simply tried to live according to their convictions. Thus the late 1830s were years of transition for the Transcendentalists as they left off revising religious philosophy and turned toward social reform.

Bronson Alcott's history is a good introduction to these trends. Criticism of *Conversations with Children on the Gospels* forced him to close the Temple School. Although the parents of his students had to be more open to new ideas than were most Bostonians to patronize the school at all, within months of the newspaper attacks only six of thirty pupils remained.[57] Alcott saw that his unconventional thinking had contributed to public opposition ("My studies lead me aside from the thoroughfares of ordinary thought"); but he was still embittered and in self-pitying moods thought of himself as a martyred "exile": "I am self-subsistent, yet not from choice."[58] Other times he faced the practical problem of what to do. Since it was the parents who frustrated his plans, he considered a boarding school in a country town where, with the children "under my sole direction and discipline," he still hoped to prove "the doctrine of culture which I would settle to the acceptance of the community." He had Concord in particular in mind and in 1838 listed other advantages in his journal that made the plan appealing: healthier surroundings, leisure to think and write, friendly neighbors for his wife and daughters, and, for himself, "the society of my friend Mr. Emerson."[59]

The Alcott family did move to a small Concord farm in the spring of 1840. But by then Alcott's priorities had changed. He abandoned his plan for a school, in part because of continuing public disfavor but also because his approach to reform had become more immediate than education. Alcott now aimed wholly to reconstruct his life, including his work, his family relations, and his community ties, as the first step toward social regeneration.

The foundation of a religious life for Alcott was productive work. "Labor invests man with a primeval dignity," he wrote in July to his brother-in-law, Samuel May: "Let no man deem himself a servant of the divine Husbandman unless he labour in his vineyards for the wages of Peace."[60] Alcott found much to recommend farm work—tranquillity,

57. The best record of events which preceded the closing of his school in June 1839 is Alcott, *Journals*. See also F. B. Sanborn and William T. Harris, *A. Bronson Alcott*, 2 vols. (Boston: Roberts Brothers, 1893), 1:235–302.

58. Jan. 1838, Alcott, *Journals*, p. 98.

59. Mar. 1838, Alcott, *Journals*, p. 100.

60. July 29, 1840, Alcott, *Letters*, p. 51.

proximity to God in nature, and freedom from the competitive market economy. Concord also favored the integrated family life he described to his mother: "Abba does all her work and the children go to School in the village close by, and we are free to do all that farmers and farmers' wives find necessary in managing a household." When he added that he hoped to convert Bostonians "by this very pursuit of gardening in which I am now engaged," Alcott did not seem to mean so much that all city dwellers become farmers but that they too integrate their work with the teachings of conscience.[61] Far from feeling cut off from reform activity in Concord, Alcott believed that his experiment in subsistence farming tied him even more closely to others working for change. "A revolution of all human affairs is now in progress," he wrote that same summer, "we are in its midst; the issue we cannot doubt; but the crises are not without alarm: Brownson has sounded a note which must ring throughout the Land, in which that of Garrison will for a time be lost. For Slavery and war are but branches of a Tree whose root is selfishness, whose trunk is property, whose fruit is gold."[62]

Alcott came to Concord looking not only for work consistent with principle but also for good society. The long walks and conversations he enjoyed during his visits to Emerson in the late 1830s suggested that Concord offered a certain social space and relaxed rhythm of life that Boston clearly lacked. Here were conditions favorable to community feeling, it seemed to Alcott, and while the town was not quite the pastoral

61. June 21, 1840, Alcott, *Letters*, p. 48. Although a number of Transcendentalists besides Alcott left the city for Massachusetts towns and farms in the late 1830s and early 1840s, there was little rebellion against urban life per se. For the most part, they wanted to do away with the disadvantages of cities—competition, class division, social restraints—in order to accentuate their positive aspects, such as individual freedom, intellectual development, social diversity. Emerson wrote in his journal, Apr. 7, 1840: "It is not that commerce, law, & state employments are unfit for a man, but that these are now all so perverted & corrupt that no man can right himself in them, he is lost in them, *he* cannot move hand or foot in them. Nothing is left him but to begin the world anew, as he does who puts the spade into the ground for food. When many shall have done so, when the majority shall admit the necessity of reform, of health, of sanity in all these institutions, then the way will be open again to the great advantages that arise from division of labor & a man will be able to select employments fittest for him without losing his selfdirection [*sic*] & becoming a tool" (*Journals*, 7:342). Nevertheless, there was an undercurrent of antiurban feeling. Describing Brook Farm in "Plan of the West Roxbury Community," Peabody wrote: "On the other hand, what absurdity can be imagined greater than the institution of cities? They originated not in love, but in war. It was war that drove men together in multitudes, and compelled them to stand so close, and build walls around them. This crowded condition produces wants of an unnatural character, which resulted in occupations that regenerated evil, by creating artificial wants" (*Dial* 2 [Jan. 1842]: 361). Alcott stood somewhere between these two positions in 1840. For two instances where Alcott clearly favored rural life, see *Conversations with Children*, 1:229, and "Days from a Diary," *Dial* 2 (Apr. 1842): 409–37.

62. ABA to SJM, Aug. 10, 1840, Alcott, *Letters*, p. 53.

retreat he imagined, his experience as a Concord resident in fact broadened his idea of neighborliness beyond the intellectual kinship he anticipated with Emerson.[63]

Located fifteen miles west of Boston, Concord was growing slowly into a city in 1840 with a population of about 2,000. But its prospects were unpromising because of the lack of water power for industry. A single cotton mill employing forty workers was the town's largest manufacture. Two sawmills, two gristmills, a smithery, and other small workshops served the needs of local farmers, who were linked to the regional market, however, since they sold their surplus produce for cash. Like most Massachusetts towns, Concord had a social elite and was proud enough of its college graduates and professionals to list them all in the official town history published in 1835. Voluntary associations such as the Social Circle, a conversation club limited to twenty-five members, distinguished the residents with status from those without.[64] But despite these signs of commercial activity and class division, Alcott found that customs of cooperative labor remained intact. "Now is the prime of haying and tomorrow I enter the meadows with my neighbors," he observed with obvious pleasure.[65] Alcott had expected Emerson's companionship, cultivated in leisure and sustained by an exchange of ideas; now Concord showed a way to integrate work and friendship and to break down barriers that isolated intellectuals from other people.[66]

Emerson too valued Concord for the freedom to make friends outside the usual round of acquaintances of a Boston minister. His move to Concord in 1834 was not as deliberately experimental as Alcott's, and he

63. Alcott's first visit to Concord was in Oct. 1835 (see his *Journals,* pp. 68–69), and the value of his friendship with Emerson increased as they became "the butt of sectarian scandal": "All other men seem strange to me when I think of him; for no one knows me so well, and I value none so dearly. . . . My brother, we shall do and dare. God is on our side. We believe in the Real, and shall come off Victorious in our warfare against the seeming" (Mar. 23, 1839, *Journals,* pp. 120–21). But even before his move to Concord, Alcott suspected that Emerson was too much of an intellectual to satisfy his growing plans for social reform: "We agree, save in measures. He, faithful to his own Genius, asserts the supremacy of the scholar's pen. I plead the omnipotence of the prophet's spoken over the written word, and the sovereignty of epic action over both" (Aug. 5, 1839, *Journals,* p. 134).

64. On Concord, see Lemuel Shattuck, *A History of the Town of Concord* (Boston: Russell, Idiorne, 1835), esp. pp. 217–18, 227–32. For a thorough social history of eighteenth-century Concord, see Robert A. Gross, *The Minutemen and Their World* (New York: Hill and Wang, 1976).

65. ABA to SJM, July 29, 1840, Alcott, *Letters,* p. 51.

66. Although Brownson was most sensitive to the problem of the isolation of the intellectual, Alcott also felt the difficulty and had written in his journal (June 9, 1839) that he hoped his lack of a college education would give him "nearer access to the minds of the people" (*Journals,* p. 129). For Brownson's views, see "Locke and the Transcendentalists," *Boston Quarterly Review* 1 (1838): 101–04.

probably had little idea at first of what constituted the good society.[67] But over the years the diversity of people that Concord, unlike more rigidly segregated Boston, put within reach became an important condition. "At least I wish to hear the thoughts of men which differ widely in some important respect from my own," he wrote after a gathering of Transcendentalists in 1839, perhaps thinking of the company of his farmer friend Edmund Hosmer.[68]

The looser pattern of Emerson's days, when he wrote and walked and visited and gardened, also favored unusual chance acquaintances. Edward Palmer, an itinerant reformer and author of a pamphlet entitled A Letter to Those who Think, was one unexpected visitor in 1838. Emerson and Palmer agreed on first principles. Palmer believed that the divine potential in man must be freed from existing institutions to achieve the progress natural to man. But he came with a specific proposal that stretched Emerson's imagination, the abolition of money.

> The benevolent and fraternal, must take the place of the selfish and exclusive principle upon which the intercourse and business of Men is now conducted; and thus, if not a community of property, have a true community of interest; bringing into unity the clashing interests of the many, and superseding the faith-destroying and soul-perverting practice of giving and requiring bonds, notes, and metal pledges at every turn; as though no Man could confide in his fellow Man, precluding the confidence and love which would otherwise naturally exist, by continually forbidding its exercise; and enabling some to command the continual service of others, without rendering any actual service in return.[69]

Palmer practiced what he preached. He traveled through New England asking for free food and lodging to awaken the unselfish nature of the

67. Two months before he moved to Concord in Oct. 1834, Emerson did have the problem of society on his mind, however, when he wrote in his journal: "Carlyle says, Society is extinct. Be it so. Society existed in a clan; existed in Alaric & Attila's time, in the Crusades, in the Puritan Conventicles. Very well, I had rather be solitary as now, than social as then. Society exists now where there is love & faithful fellow working. Only the persons composing it are fewer—societies of two or three, instead of nations" (Aug. 9, 1834, Journals, 4:308).

68. Emerson appreciated the straightforward sincerity of Hosmer's perceptions: "I am afraid that the brilliant writers very rarely feel the deepest interest in truth itself. Even my noble Scotchman [Carlyle], I fancy, feels so strongly his vocation to produce, that he would not enter with half the unfeigned joy to a simple oracle in the woods that Hosmer or Hunt would find" (June 11, 1836, Journals, 5:173). Hosmer was not an unintelligent or uneducated man, however, as Emerson's account of a "teachers" meeting (probably Sunday school) where Hosmer stated his religious opinions showed (Feb. 11, 1838, Journals, 5:452).

69. A Letter to Those who Think (Worcester, 1840), p. 17.

people he met and offered his antimoney gospel in return. Emerson was sufficiently impressed to reflect on Palmer's exchange economy in his journal: "Why should not I if a man comes & asks me for a book give it to him? If he ask me to write a letter for him write it? If he ask me to write a poem or discourse which I can fitly write, why should I not? And if my neighbor is as skillful in making cloth, why should not all of us who have wool, send it to him to make for the common benefit, & when we want ten yards or twenty yards go to him & ask for so much & he like a gentleman give us exactly what we ask without hesitation?"[70] What Emerson admired most about Palmer, however, was his courage. Neither working for wages nor paying for goods, he lived by his principles in defiance of custom. It was precisely such people, whatever their ideas and perhaps the more unusual the better, that Emerson knew, as time went on, he would bring together in a perfect society.[71]

Even without deliberation, a community not unlike Emerson's model gathered in Concord as the controversy in Boston continued. Transcendentalists and a variety of other reformers from the city regularly visited Emerson's home and later that of Alcott, making a sort of society of reformers in rotation. The very proximity of people dissatisfied with Boston raised the question of something better.[72] But for Emerson the

70. Oct. 16, 1838, Emerson, *Journals,* 6:108. While little is known about Palmer except that he came from Belfast, Maine, he is an intriguing figure because his religious philosophy was nearly identical to Transcendentalism. See his *Letter,* passim. His ideas on money were similar to those of Josiah Warren, a member of Robert Owen's New Harmony community in Indiana in the 1820s and founder of a system of "equitable commerce" in the 1830s. Through an institution Warren called the "time store," labor rather than money was exchanged for goods and services. Although Warren did not come east until 1851, when he established the Modern Times community on Long Island, experiments imitating his exchange system were tried in Philadelphia and London. Palmer may have been familiar with these. On Warren, see John Humphrey Noyes, *History of American Socialisms* (1870; reprint ed., New York: Dover, 1966), pp. 93–99.

71. In the context of some reflections on Brook Farm in 1842, for example, Emerson described his own ideal community, composed of an eclectic group of Quaker acquaintances, a Methodist laborer, reformers, a philosopher, and characters in literature and art: "I have a company who travel with me in the world & one or other of whom I must still meet, whose office none can supply to me: Edward Stabler: my Methodist Tarbox, Wordsworth's Pedlar; Mary Rotch; Alcott; Manzoni's Fra Christoforo; Swedenborg; Mrs. Black; and now Greaves, & his disciple Lane" (Sept. 4, 1842, *Journals,* 7: 465).

72. The best sources on the social scene in Concord are Alcott's and Emerson's respective *Journals.* Plans for the Brook Farm community in particular were discussed at Emerson's house on Oct. 17, 1840 (Emerson, *Journals,* 7:407–08). But for some time before that, Emerson's journals suggest that there was talk of a community of some kind outside Boston. See entries beginning May 29, 1839, *Journals,* 7:204–05, 219–20, 238, 342, 348. Some Concord visitors and residents who went on to Brook Farm in the 1840s were George P. Bradford, Charles King Newcombe, John Sullivan Dwight, and Isaac Hecker. Henry Thoreau, a native of Concord, of course went on to his own social experiment at Walden Pond.

visits of Margaret Fuller especially brought up the problem of social relations.

The emotional demands and frustrations of the Fuller–Emerson relationship are part of Transcendentalist mythology, created in part by Emerson's confession in the 1852 memoir of Fuller that he could not warm sufficiently to the society of this "exotic" to satisfy her expectations.[73] But what is often overlooked is that there was a special seriousness on both sides, based on his desire, as much as hers, to get beyond the usual superficialities and constraints. For Emerson, friendship was a moral, indeed, a reform, issue, so that Fuller and the friends she introduced into the Concord circle symbolized society itself: "Since I have been an exile so long from the social world and a social world is now suddenly thrust upon me, I am determined by the help of heaven to suck this orange dry—no that cannot be—the expression is profane—the oranges of Olympus renew themselves as fast as the eater eats. But I will study to deserve my friends—I abandon myself to what is best in you all."[74] It is little wonder that such resolutions invariably turned into laments over the failure of social relations, since Emerson measured against an ideal too self-consciously pursued for spontaneous feeling: "We are armed all over with these subtle antagonisms which as soon as we meet begin to play, & translate all poetry into such stale prose!"[75] Nevertheless, the intimacy Emerson and Fuller did achieve during her frequent stays in Concord undoubtedly helped shape an idea of friendship which grew with experience, always putting satisfaction just so much farther out of reach.

As Transcendentalism gained momentum as a social movement, women became more involved in the group, and conversely the reformers became more sensitive to issues of women's status and family structure. From 1836 on, an informal association of Transcendentalists met periodically for discussion in various homes. No women attended at first because the men observed the usual custom of segregating reform societies by sex. But when the group met in Concord, it seemed natural to Emerson to invite the women who were part of the community of Concord reformers. "Will you not come & see me & inspire our reptile wits," he wrote to Fuller, clearly hoping she would bring a fresh point of view to men stuck in the narrow round of "Carlyle Cambridge Dr. Channing & the Reviews."[76] Other women who attended occasionally were Elizabeth Hoar,

73. See "Visits to Concord," in *Memoirs of Fuller,* 1: esp. 227–28, 308–11. On their relationship, see also Thomas Wentworth Higginson, *Margaret Fuller Ossoli* (Boston: Houghton Mifflin, 1884), pp. 62–68. The best source, however, is their correspondence, published largely in Emerson, *Letters,* vol. 2.

74. Sept. 13, 1840, Emerson, *Letters,* 2:332.

75. RWE to MF, Oct. 12, 1838, Emerson, *Letters,* 2:168.

76. May 8, 1840, and May 24, 1838, Emerson, *Letters,* 2:293, 135. Two facts demonstrate that initially there were no women in what is sometimes called the "Transcendentalist

the fiancée of Emerson's brother Charles before his death in 1836 and ever after considered a sister-in-law, and Sarah Alden Ripley of Waltham, Emerson's aunt. The inclusion of these women suggests how much Emerson's life in Concord conformed to the customs of woman's sphere where, in contrast to the working world of a Boston minister, family connections often determined social ties. By quitting the ministry and choosing literary work done largely at home, Emerson became a resident and not, like most men, a sojourner in the family. He spent much time with women and evidently came to value their companionship enough to try to incorporate the easy relations between kin of different sexes into a public association.[77]

The same set of circumstances contributed to Emerson's interest in child-rearing practices and the organization of household labor. Soon after the birth of their second child in 1837, Lidian Emerson wrote to Elizabeth Peabody that her husband was "a most attentive observer of nursery phenomena," well qualified to answer Peabody's questions on "the progress of our newest minister from the infinite."[78] He was bothered, moreover, by the system of domestic service which brought wage labor and social inequality into the home, and he invited his Irish cook to eat with the family, only to be frustrated by her conventional notion of status.[79] Nevertheless, Emerson was receiving a domestic education that broadened his perspective on social issues.

club." First, Alcott named no women in an early list of members in his journal in May 1837 (*Journals*, p. 92). Second, Emerson was quite self-conscious about the innovation when he first invited Fuller in 1837: "I will not certainly engage for them to break down any rule or expectations, but you shall gentilize their dinner with Mrs. Ripley if I can get her, and what can you not mould them into in an hour!" (Aug. 17, 1837, *Letters*, 2:95). The members of the club were mainly clergymen at first; but as the controversy progressed, more cautious ministers withdrew, and women were added. Throughout the late 1830s, the Transcendentalists held other conversations as well which were less formal than meetings of a voluntary association but more formal than simple talk. Both sexes participated in these, and the practice probably influenced the Transcendentalist club. See, e.g., Alcott, *Journals*, pp. 126–27, where he recorded a conversation meeting at Sarah Ripley's house in Waltham, a discussion with the Concord villagers led by Emerson, and a conversation at the home of Henry Thoreau's mother, all in the space of a four-day visit with Emerson, Apr. 30 to May 3, 1839.

77. For Emerson's opinion of Elizabeth Hoar and Sarah Ripley, see his *Journals*, 7:509–10 and 8:94.

78. Mar. 20, 1837, Emerson Papers, Houghton.

79. On Emerson's experiment in domestic labor, see Ralph L. Rusk, *The Life of Ralph Waldo Emerson* (New York: Scribner's, 1949), p. 289. For Emerson's understanding of the problem of wage labor, consider this journal entry, Apr. 7, 1840: "For see this wide society in which we walk of laboring men. We allow ourselves to be served by them. We pay them money & then turn our backs on them . . . . Thus we enact the part of the selfish noble & king from the foundation of the world . . . . In every household the peace of a pair is poisoned by malice, slyness, indolence, & alienation of domestics" (*Journals*, 7:343).

Closer relations among Transcendentalist women also emerged as the movement became a way of life, not just an intellectual reform. Particularly important were friendships between the wives of other Transcendentalists and the single women who, because of their work and writing, were already recognized as independent participants. By example and encouragement, Peabody and Fuller drew these women toward more active roles. When Emerson became engaged to Lydia Jackson of Plymouth in 1835, Peabody asked her for a statement of her religious views. The request was almost like a test of admission to a church, and perhaps Peabody meant to remind Lydia that she was marrying into a movement where convictions, as well as affections for one man, mattered. More likely, Peabody simply hoped to bring her into the group as a thinking individual, not just a wife. Although Lydia was an educated woman, Peabody's question was a challenge to her ability to think logically and write coherently—skills, as Margaret Fuller noted, that women were not encouraged to use. "I wish I could now see you, and talk instead of writing on these high matters," Lydia began. "Quickly and easily you know, the tongues of us 'womankind' can talk volumes,—and perhaps, no two women extant could more easily than you and myself—and in a shorter given time make a volume in this way."[80] But she did as she was asked and wrote a detailed account of the influence of Emanuel Swedenborg, the eighteenth-century philosopher, on her beliefs.

In the public sphere, Margaret Fuller's conversations in Boston gave all the women a voice outside the home. Transcendentalist wives, relatives, and friends attended the discussions, as well as women involved in other reforms such as abolitionist Lydia Maria Child. Soon men began to come as well, and Fuller's success demonstrates how the experimental tenor of the movement favored the rise of women to leadership roles.[81]

The choice of Fuller as editor of the *Dial*, the Transcendentalist magazine first issued in July 1840, exemplifies this trend. Part of the

80. July 28, 1835, Emerson Papers, Houghton. She changed her name from Lydia to Lidian when she married because Emerson preferred the sound of the latter together with "Emerson."

81. For a list of the women who attended, see *Memoirs of Fuller*, 1:338. For Peabody's notes on a few conversations, see "Conversations in Boston," *Memoirs*, 1:319–50. See also Caroline Dall's notes on a series in which men participated, which she dated 1841 but which actually took place in 1840, in *Margaret and her Friends; or, Conversations with Margaret Fuller upon the Mythology of the Greeks and its Expression in Art* (1895; reprint ed., New York: Arno Press, 1972). Dall gives the impression that the conversations were abstract and idealistic to the point of being rather silly. Although there is some truth to that view, all of these supposed "transcripts" are seriously flawed, since they omit everything relating to the personal lives of the participants. A comparison of Peabody's published notes and the originals in the Fuller Papers, Boston Public Library, reveals how much Emerson suppressed in his contribution to the *Memoirs*. Fuller's letters show, moreover, that she interrupted planned discussions to share important personal experiences with the group, such as her conversion experience in 1840. See her letter to William Henry Channing, Nov. 8, 1840, quoted in *Memoirs*, 1:340.

reason the men passed on this authority was their mood of rebellion against routine, responsibility, even intellectual work, all that they associated with their former Boston professions. "Have you heard of my pig," Emerson wrote to Fuller in 1838, deliberately turning discussion from ideas to the facts of country life. "I have planted forty four pine trees. What do you think my tax will be this year?—and never a word more of Goethe or Tennyson."[82] Fuller sensed, however, that for all their enthusiasm for practical living, the men failed to grasp social needs with a realism more natural to a woman in antebellum society and hoped the *Dial* under her editorial direction might help temper their still abstract idealism: "I believe, if they have opportunity to state and discuss their opinions, they will gradually sift them, ascertain their grounds and aims with clearness, and do the work this country needs."[83] How well, or rather how little, Fuller succeeded is another matter, and some men secretly blamed its woman editor for the *Dial*'s soft-spoken tone on reform issues.[84] Still, Fuller's editorship is a good indication that Transcendentalist women were being heard more than ever and, more important, were doing work that contributed to their political education.

Elizabeth Peabody, too, moved well beyond a conventional woman's role and in the process helped establish a Transcendentalist social circle in Boston. She had been forced to give up teaching because of her association with Alcott, and she needed a way to make a living independent of the patronage of the Boston establishment. Thus in 1840, just as "commerce seemed about to be *reformed out*" by critics of the market economy such as Alcott and Palmer, as she later recalled, Peabody opened a bookstore on West Street in Boston.[85]

"This was the original plan of my store," she wrote to a friend in 1841, "that I should keep one in which were to be found no *worthless books* —shadows of shadows—& nothing of any kind of a secondary na-

82. May 24, 1838, Emerson, *Letters*, 2:135.

83. Quoted in *Memoirs of Fuller*, 2:29.

84. Theodore Parker implied something to that effect when he said that the *Dial*, compared to Brownson's *Boston Quarterly Review*, was like "a band of men and maidens daintily arrayed in finery [in contrast] to a body of stout men in blue frocks, with great arms and hard hands and legs." When he began his *Massachusetts Quarterly Review* in 1847, he vowed to make it a " 'Dial' with a beard." Quoted in Sanborn, *Alcott*, 2:369, and Higginson, *Ossoli*, p. 161, respectively.

85. *Reminiscences of Rev. William Ellery Channing* (Boston: Roberts Brothers, 1880), p. 407. On Peabody's difficulties, which she encountered despite the fact that she left the Temple School before the *Conversations* were published, see Louise Hall Tharp, *The Peabody Sisters of Salem* (Boston: Little Brown, 1950), pp. 110–12. Part of the reason Peabody resigned was that she objected to the publication of the conversations on birth on simple grounds of propriety, as she wrote to Alcott on Aug. 7. 1836: "However, you as a man can say anything; but I am a woman, and have feelings which I dare not distrust, however little I understand them or give account of them" (quoted in Tharp, pp. 110–11).

ture."[86] Selling, lending, and soon publishing books appealed to Peabody because she was free to set her own standards, supported, of course, by a Transcendentalist clientele. The bookstore quickly became a meeting place for the Transcendentalists. Thinking along more conventional sexual lines, Dr. Channing had suggested that the shop be a "literary lounge" for Boston ladies.[87] But the Transcendentalist movement favored freer relations between the sexes, and the store attracted a mixed group interested in discussing meatier topics than literature. Transcendentalists who lived in Boston such as Ripley and Brownson stopped in regularly to read the foreign newspapers and journals Peabody imported. On designated evenings, more chairs were set up for Fuller's conversations. Thus, much like Concord, Peabody's bookstore was a place apart from ordinary proprieties, where the experience of more open male–female interaction doubtless contributed to the reform ideas discussed.

George Ripley's house was another Transcendentalist enclave in the city. Since Ripley remained in the ministry until 1840, his home attracted Harvard divinity students such as Theodore Parker and John Sullivan Dwight, who were looking for a middle ground between Norton's traditionalism and Emerson's decision to leave the church.[88] On paper, Ripley forged a concept of a democratic ministry to contest Norton's idea

86. EPP to Samuel Gray Ward, Sept. 13, 1841, Houghton. On the bookstore, see also her *Reminiscences*, pp. 407–14.

87. W. E. Channing to EPP, June 22, 1840, quoted in *Reminiscences*, p. 409.

88. The events of the late 1830s occasioned something of a crisis for young men entering the ministry, in which their doubts about the viability of the profession were exacerbated by tensions between ministers and congregations. Dwight, for example, preached on and off for four years after his graduation in 1836 before finding a congregation that would tolerate him and he them. Even then, he left after one year—and left the ministry itself. See George Willis Cooke, *John Sullivan Dwight: Brook-Farmer, Editor, and Critic of Music* (Boston: Small, Maynard, 1898). While Dwight's major problem was unsettled convictions, the example of another of Ripley's followers, George Frederick Simmons, demonstrates the difficulties which faced a young man with strong reform commitments when he was forced to flee Mobile, Alabama, for preaching *Two Sermons on the Kind Treatment and Emancipation of Slaves* (Boston: William Crosby, 1840). The remainder of Simmon's short life (1814–55) consisted of several ministries in New England that ended either because he wanted time to resolve his religious doubts or because of contention over his abolitionism. See Samuel A. Eliot, *Heralds of a Liberal Faith*, 3 vols. (Boston: American Unitarian Association, 1910), 2:173–74. Another sign of crisis was the plummeting enrollment in the divinity school classes that entered during the first two years of the Transcendentalist controversy in 1837 and 1838. While the average graduating class for the decade before the controversy (1827–37) was nearly ten a year, only four graduated in 1840 and three in 1841. See *Harvard University Quinquennial Catalogue of the Officers and Graduates, 1636–1930* (Cambridge, Mass.: Harvard University Press, 1930), pp. 1113–15. Although enrollments picked up, the school continued to have trouble attracting qualified students for much of the remainder of the nineteenth century. See Sydney E. Ahlstrom, "The Middle Period, 1840–1880," in George Huntson Williams, ed., *The Harvard Divinity School* (Boston: Beacon Press, 1954), esp. pp. 78–103.

of a scholar-preacher. He objected that Norton would "separate the pastor of a church from the sympathies of his people, confine him to a sphere of thought remote from their usual interests, and give an abstract and scholastic character to his services in the pulpit."[89] Instead, at Dwight's ordination in 1840 at Northampton, once the parish of Jonathan Edwards, Ripley called on "the evangelist" to preach for "the kingdom of God on earth": "Let the Evangelist then proclaim the dispensation of the spirit [and] the truth he sees, let it cut where it will; he will never wish to blunt the edge of the sword of the spirit which is the sword of God; and he will announce the whole counsel of his Master, whether men will hear, or whether they will forbear."[90]

There was a militancy in Ripley's tone after four years of controversy, and his image of the evangelist as the prophet of a revolution could scarcely be contained within any conceivable notion of a Boston ministry. Ripley recognized the conflict. While still in Northampton he sent a letter of resignation to his congregation:

> I cannot witness the glaring inequalities of condition, the hollow pretensions of pride, the scornful apathy with which many urge the prostration of man, the burning zeal with which they run the race of selfish competition, with no thought for the elevation of their brethren, without the sad conviction that the spirit of Christ has well-nigh disappeared from our churches, and that the fearful doom awaits us, "Inasmuch as ye have not done it unto the least of these, ye have not done it unto me."[91]

Thus Ripley set out on his own to find the true church: "The true followers of Jesus are a band of brothers; they compose one family; they attach no importance whatever to the petty distinctions of birth, wealth, and station; but feeling that they are one in the pursuit of truth, in the love of holiness, and in the hope of immortal life, they regard the common differences of the world, by which men are separated from each other, as lighter than the dust of the balance" (p. 73).

When Emerson praised Ripley's decision by saying that his friend now stood at the head of the "church militant," he knew on the basis of frequent conversations that Ripley's church would be, not a mere Sunday gathering, but a community of reformers.[92] By the time he left the ministry, Ripley already had plans for an experiment in Christian living. While his home had attracted men looking for solutions within the Unitarian church, it also became a point of contact between Transcendentalists and

---

89. *"Infidelity" Examined*, p. 95.

90. *Claims of the Age on the Work of the Evangelist* (Boston: Weeks, Jordan, 1840), pp. 20, 11–12.

91. Quoted in Octavius Brooks Frothingham, *George Ripley* (Boston: Houghton Mifflin, 1882), p. 74. Subsequent page citations in the text refer to this biography.

92. RWE to MF, May 27? and 29?, 1840, Emerson, *Letters*, 2:229.

more radical social critics, who not only helped channel Ripley's discontent into the idea of a community but because of their social distance from Unitarian culture made the meetings a preliminary lesson in Christian equality.

Adin Ballou was the most important of Ripley's new friends. A Universalist minister involved in multiple reform causes, including temperance, antislavery, and nonresistance, Ballou (1803–90) concluded that one comprehensive reform was not only the most practical solution but a moral duty. He later described the Hopedale community he founded in 1841 as a "church of Christ," a "miniature Christian republic," and a "universal religious, moral philanthropic, and social reform Association" combined.[93] Ballou and Ripley considered a joint experiment but finally separated on the question of whether to require pledges from the members to specific reform principles such as antislavery. Just free of the pressures of conservative Boston, Ripley was unwilling to accept the bonds of radical reformers and looked to the Transcendentalists for support. But his respect for the Universalists stayed with him. Rather than make his community a Transcendentalist retreat, Ripley was determined to bridge class distances at Brook Farm.

Ripley stated his goals in a letter to Emerson in late 1840:

> Our objects, as you know, are to ensure a more natural union between intellectual and manual labor than now exists; to combine the thinker and the worker, as far as possible, in the same individual; to guarantee the highest mental freedom, by providing all with labor, adapted to their tastes and talents, and securing to them the fruits of their industry; to do away with the necessity of menial services, by opening the benefits of education and the profits of labor to all; and thus to prepare a society of liberal, intelligent, and cultivated persons, whose relations with each other would permit a more simple and wholesome life, than can now be led amidst the pressures of our competitive institutions.[94]

Ripley's prospectus was a systematic statement of what all the Transcendentalists had been looking for: individual freedom and humane relation-

93. From an unidentified tract on Hopedale, 1851, quoted in Noyes, *Socialisms,* pp. 121–23. The son of a Rhode Island farmer, Ballou had been the minister of the First Church and Society of Mendon, Massachusetts, since 1831, where he was ordained by a joint council of Restorationist Universalists and Unitarians. Peabody recalled in her *Reminiscences* that Ripley met Ballou through the antislavery and temperance societies (pp. 413–14). Though he may have become acquainted with Ballou at their meetings, Ripley belonged to neither, however, since he told his congregation in his letter in 1840 that he was as unwilling to be constrained by the principles of a reform association as by the opinions of a church (Frothingham, *Ripley,* pp. 86–87). For more on Ballou, see Noyes, pp. 119–32; Eliot, *Heralds,* 2:297–300; and especially Lewis Perry, *Radical Abolitionism: Anarchy and the Government of God in Antislavery Thought* (Ithaca: Cornell University Press, 1973), pp. 129–57.

94. Nov. 9, 1840, quoted in Frothingham, *Ripley,* pp. 307–08.

ships established on a foundation of economic justice. But none of the Transcendentalists so far central to the movement joined Ripley. Emerson's reply suggests the reason why: "I am in many respects suitably placed, in an agreeable neighborhood, in a town which I have many reasons to love, & which has respected my freedom so far that I presume it will indulge me farther if I need it."[95] Emerson may not have found the good society by 1840, but he had a base from which to work. Concord provided the neighborliness and freedom Ripley promised at Brook Farm. More important, his home was only one link in an expanding Transcendentalist social network with multiple points of focus—Peabody's bookstore, Fuller's conversations, the *Dial,* Emerson's own lectures in Boston, and now Brook Farm. Within that sphere, Emerson could anticipate new friends, innovative thinking, and more chances for cooperative reform. Brook Farm would mean cutting himself off from means already at hand.

Thus Transcendentalism was well established as a social movement by 1840. The position of one Transcendentalist, Orestes Brownson, was ambiguous, however. Brownson's understanding of the need for structural social reform predated that of the other Transcendentalists. Perhaps for just that reason, he stood on the fringe of the movement itself. Paradoxically, the man most intent on securing social justice was also the most inveterate individualist.

As an active public reformer, Brownson was several steps ahead of the other Transcendentalists in the late 1830s. In January 1838 he began to publish the *Boston Quarterly Review* to bypass journals controlled by men afraid, he said in his introduction, of a really free thinker. "I must and will speak," he wrote, and committed himself to "the great Movement Party of mankind."[96] In his *Review,* he preached a twofold doctrine that gave voice to what all the Transcendentalists felt: no one had a right to call himself a Christian who did not work to institute the kingdom of God and this millennium would mean a fundamental reorganization of society.[97] In January 1840 Brownson allied himself to the Democratic party to secure these ends.

George Bancroft was a key figure in Brownson's commitment to party politics. The son of Aaron Bancroft, a Liberal minister from Worcester, Bancroft (1800–91) had "fairly philosophised himself into Democracy," as Brownson said of Ripley. He had encountered the transcendental idea of consciousness while studying in Germany in the early 1820s and, with opinions even more at odds with Unitarian rationalism than Transcenden-

95. Dec. 15, 1840, Emerson, *Letters,* 2: 369.

96. "Introductory Remarks," *Boston Quarterly Review* 1 (1838):3, 6.

97. See, e.g., "The Kingdom of God," *Boston Quarterly Review* 2 (1839): 326–50, and "Democracy of Christianity," 1 (1838): 444–73. See also Brownson's autobiography *The Convert* (1857), in *Works,* 5:99–108.

talism would be a decade later, abandoned plans for the ministry. When he turned to politics in the 1830s, his applied philosophy—that the voice of the people was the voice of God—made him a Democrat. To be a Democrat in Boston was even more suspect than to be a Transcendentalist, and thus Bancroft's association with the movement is not surprising. He was an important participant in Transcendentalist discussions because he proposed electoral politics as a means of reform.[98] But only Brownson was moved to action. Even before his pledge of support, he spoke at Democratic rallies as far away as New York; afterward, during the campaign of 1840, Brownson told Democrats that their party alone fought "privilege and monopoly," while the Whigs offered the people log cabins and cider not just as symbols, but as facts, all the while plotting to get "palaces and champaign [sic]" for themselves.[99]

Brownson's political involvement was more than an expedient to contend with the conservative backsliding of the Unitarians. It was a sign of his waning faith in the church as an institution and in spiritual methods of reform. Some new social agency must be found to prosecute what was ultimately a religious cause. For Brownson in 1840, that mechanism was government: "Now as the great work for the social reformer is to provide for the maintenance to each and every individual to his entire individuality, and as this can be done only by society, and by society through government, it follows that government, so far from being an obstacle to reform, a superfluous machine we should throw aside, is in fact the great and indispensable agent of reform."[100]

Brownson stood at a point of delicate balance common to the Transcendentalists as the Boston controversy died down. He still believed that

98. On Bancroft, see Russel B. Nye, *George Bancroft: Brahmin Rebel* (New York: Knopf, 1945), esp. pp. 3–136, and Arthur M. Schlesinger, Jr., *The Age of Jackson* (Boston: Little, Brown, 1945), esp. pp. 159–76. Ripley and Brownson first corresponded with Bancroft in 1836. Their letters are in the Bancroft Papers, MHS.

99. *An Oration before the Democracy of Worcester and Vicinity, delivered at Worcester, Massachusetts, July 4, 1840* (Boston: E. Littlefield, 1840), p. 28.

100. "Social Evils, and their Remedy," *Boston Quarterly Review* 4 (1841): 276. In religious terms, Brownson's emphasis on the state was linked to his growing skepticism about human ability. Though his disillusionment is sometimes attributed to the people's choice of Whigs over Democrats in the election of 1840, there was already a renewed emphasis on Christ as a mediator in the same article in Jan. 1840 where he announced his support of the Democrats. See "Introductory Statement," *Boston Quarterly Review* 3 (1840): 1–20. Thus it seems that his doubts were founded more on the self-interested conservatism he witnessed during the Transcendentalist controversy than on subsequent political developments, though these probably confirmed his feelings. For an important statement of his changing religious views, see "The Mediatorial Life of Jesus," in *Works*, 4:140–71. In politics, his distrust of the people made him a supporter of John C. Calhoun's theory of "concurrent majorities." On Brownson and Calhoun, see Schlesinger, *Jackson*, pp. 401–06.

religion must be the final source of principles in society; but he also saw that institutions must be changed to give conscience a chance to express itself in practice. The Transcendentalist controversy had been a lesson in the use, or rather abuse, of power. Now the Transcendentalists were beginning to see that to reach their original ends, they had to become social reformers.

4   Economy

From 1845 to 1847 Henry Thoreau conducted an experiment in living on Emerson's land at Walden Pond, and when he wrote up the results in *Walden,* he called the first chapter "Economy." Thoreau (1817–62) had been a Harvard undergraduate in the 1830s and had never actively participated in the Unitarian evangelical movement; but as a young man who aimed to live "deliberately," he must have known how decisively he departed from the usual religious assumptions about reform by beginning, not with the question of spiritual awakening, but with the way he supplied his material needs. His purpose was still religious. "Why has man rooted himself thus firmly in the earth," he asked, "but that he may rise in the same proportion into the heavens above?"[1] And he made "economy" ambiguous—meaning not only a system of production and consumption but also simple frugality—to show his connection to the Protestant past. But just as Thoreau intended to disprove suspicions that "there is no choice left" by his move to the woods, so his innovations in providing food, clothing, shelter, and fuel demonstrated that there were more ways than preaching to reform society.

Walden was the last of the Transcendentalist reform experiments, and Thoreau borrowed the lesson he taught from what the others had learned. In the 1840s, the Transcendentalists were less interested in saving souls than in radically altering social structure. Thus the priority of economics in *Walden* was typical of the Transcendentalist perspective, as was Thoreau's sense of "economy" as a humane discipline with far-reaching moral significance. But Thoreau was unrepresentative because he went to Walden alone. Living "free and uncommitted" is simply not social reform in the same sense that the Transcendentalist communities, Bronson Alcott's Fruitlands and George Ripley's Brook Farm, decidedly were. For

1. *Walden,* ed. J. Lyndon Shanley, *The Writings of Henry D. Thoreau,* vol. 1 (Princeton: Princeton University Press, 1971), p. 15.

that reason, I have concentrated on those cooperative efforts in this account of the Transcendentalists' struggle to institute a moral economy.[2]

THE PROBLEM OF A CALLING

The Transcendentalists' concern with economics can be traced to the Unitarian evangelical movement of the 1830s, since they followed the Liberal precedent when they judged society by the ethical standards of religion. The social consciousness of William Ellery Channing made him a model to the Transcendentalists, and it is useful to begin with his most important statement on economic relations, "On the Elevation of the Laboring Classes," to sketch the intellectual roots of Transcendentalist reform.

Channing presented his views to the Mechanic Apprentices' Library Association in 1840, and the occasion was indicative of the historical situation both he and the Transcendentalists confronted. Founded in 1820, the Library Association had become an agency of Unitarian benevolence aimed at the moral improvement of young men learning a trade. These were not industrial workers, nor were factory operatives the majority in New England in 1840. Only textile production was industrialized to a significant extent, since shoe manufacture, the second largest industry in the region, was still organized on the putting-out system, where workers finished shoes by hand at home or in workshops. But the craft tradition of which Channing's audience was a part was on the decline. The concentration of capital in all trades hurt an apprentice's chance to become a master one day and encouraged him to accept immediate employment in an increasing number of semiskilled jobs. The result was the beginning of a working class which economically and socially remained relatively unassimilated into the community. The Library Association represented an effort to bridge this distance by cultural means, a solution which Channing, despite his critique of the emerging economic system, finally endorsed.[3]

2. The most complete discussion of Thoreau's social attitudes is Leo Stoller, *After Walden: Thoreau's Changing Views on Economic Man* (Stanford: Stanford University Press, 1957), although I do not agree with his view that *Walden* should be read literally as an endorsement of a preindustrial subsistence economy; rather, I would argue that it is a demonstration of how to adapt any economy to human needs. More generally, the most stimulating recent study of Thoreau is Richard Lebeaux, *Young Man Thoreau* (Amherst: University of Massachusetts Press, 1977).

3. On the Mechanic Apprentices' Library Association, see Charles Bennett, *History of Manual and Industrial Education up to 1870* (Peoria, Ill.: Manual Arts Press, 1926), pp. 317–18. For a more general discussion of such institutes in the context of the breakdown of apprenticeship training, see David Montgomery, "The Working Classes of the Pre-Industrial American City, 1780–1830," *Labor History* 9 (1968): 6–9. On the changing condition of labor in the antebellum period, see Alan Dawley's excellent study of one city, *Class and Community: The Industrial Revolution in Lynn* (Cambridge, Mass.: Harvard

Channing measured the condition of the laboring classes against the Protestant ideal of a calling. Work was a religious activity to Channing, as it was to the Puritans before him. The settlers of New England saw labor in one's calling as a means of sanctification, the gradual growth in grace following conversion. Like election itself, there was a providential determinism in the choice of vocation and ethical imperatives bound up in its execution, making "the fulfillment of duty in worldly affairs," as Max Weber observed, "the highest form which the moral activity of the individual could assume."[4] Nineteenth-century Unitarians were distanced from Puritan theology by their humanism, and thus Channing valued labor as a means for the individual gradually to perfect himself. Even simple manual labor, he told the apprentices, could give "force to the will, efficiency, courage, the capacity for endurance, and of persevering devotion to far-reaching plans."[5] Most important, the worker would become aware of God's goodness and his own dignity, both innate ideas which the dialectic of work and reflection would bring to light. But Channing saw that labor fell far short of this ideal in contemporary society. A system "which leaves the mass of men to be crushed and famished in soul by excessive toils on matter is at war with God's designs, and turns into means of bondage what was meant to free and expand the soul" (p. 43). And he freely criticized the conditions which yielded this result: the long hours demanded by employers in a competitive market economy, the division of labor which confined the worker to "a monotonous, stupefying round of unthinking toil," and the reluctance of the rich to extend the means of culture to the laboring classes, for fear that education would produce discontent and rebellion in turn (pp. 39–40, 52–55).

University Press, 1976), as well as older and more general works, including Joseph Tuckerman, *An Essay on the Wages paid to Females for their Labour* (Philadelphia: Carey and Hart, 1830); Norman Ware, *The Industrial Worker, 1840–1860: The Reaction of American Industrial Society to the Advance of the Industrial Revolution* (Boston: Houghton Mifflin, 1924), esp. pp. 26–70; Caroline Ware, *The Early New England Cotton Manufacture* (Boston: Houghton Mifflin, 1931), pp. 198–298; and Blanche Hazard, *The Organization of the Boot and Shoe Industry in Massachusetts before 1875* (Cambridge, Mass.: Harvard University Press, 1921), esp. pp. 42–96. Stephan Thernstrom's study of unskilled workers in Newburyport between 1850 and 1880, *Poverty and Progress: Social Mobility in a Nineteenth Century City* (Cambridge, Mass.: Harvard University Press, 1964), is also useful to correct the impression created by some of the earlier histories that industrial workers were a majority in New England by the middle of the century.

4. *The Protestant Ethic and the Spirit of Capitalism,* trans. Talcott Parsons (New York: Scribner's, 1958), p. 80. For an example of the persistence of these attitudes in the nineteenth century, see Octavius Brooks Frothingham's portrait of his grandfather, merchant Peter Chardon Brooks (1766–1849), in *Boston Unitarianism, 1820–1850* (1890; reprint ed., Hicksville, N.Y.: Regina Press, 1975), pp. 93–126.

5. "On the Elevation of the Laboring Classes," in *The Works of William Ellery Channing* (Boston: American Unitarian Association, 1875), p. 39. Subsequent page citations in the text refer to this edition.

Sensitive to the practical problems of workers as Channing was, however, his remedy followed his primary concern with the spiritual dimension of labor. Thus he renounced any intention to change their outward
status and concluded, "I know but one elevation of a human being, and
that is elevation of soul" (p. 42). Channing encouraged the apprentices to
use the resources of institutions like the Library Association to sharpen
their thinking powers in their leisure time. Here he was forced to admit
that long hours and inevitable fatigue seemed calculated to block self-
improvement, but he contended nevertheless: "The people, as history
shows us, can accomplish miracles under the power of a great idea"
(p. 57). There was an unmistakable strain between Channing's clear perception of the force of economic circumstance and his moral prescriptions.
As if to salvage the possibility and thus the preeminent value of spiritual
means and ends, Channing finally blamed the worker for his own condition. The laboring classes suffered "not from outward necessity, not from
the irresistible obstacles abroad, but chiefly from the fault or ignorance of
the sufferers themselves"—intemperance, prodigality, sloth, ignorance of
health, and disorderly homes (p. 58).

Channing's conclusion struck a note of discord in a statement otherwise sympathetic to labor. But his religious convictions left him no alternative. Either to lay the blame on capital or to identify some impersonal
structural cause would release the worker from the sense of personal
responsibility Channing believed must be the moral foundation of any
lasting reform.[6] In the end, moreover, Channing did not doubt that the
individual had the ability to perform "miracles," as he said, to triumph
over circumstance by sheer force of will. Few of the younger generation
who grew up with the market economy were able to match Channing's
confidence in spiritual power.

Theodore Parker (1810–60) was one who could not. His "Thoughts
on Labor" in the Dial in 1841 was more sophisticated in its grasp of
market relations than Channing's "Laboring Classes"; but for just that
reason, Parker's spiritual solution crumbled under the extra burden he
imposed. Parker identified the relation between rich and poor as the
immediate source of worker's difficulty. "This aversion to labor, this
notion that it is a curse and a disgrace, this selfish desire to escape from the
general and natural lot of man, is the sacramental sin of 'the better classes'

6. Channing's views on individual moral responsibility are exemplified by his critique
of Transcendentalism's pantheistic tendencies. See Elizabeth Peabody, *Reminiscences of
Rev. William Ellery Channing* (Boston: Roberts Brothers, 1880), pp. 430–31. For other
important statements by Channing on economic issues, see the documents collected in
William Henry Channing, *The Life of William Ellery Channing* (Boston: American Unitarian Association, 1880), pp. 456–99, as well as his Franklin Lecture on "Self-Culture"
(1838), in *Works*, pp. 12–36, and "Discourse on the Life and Character of Rev. Joseph
Tuckerman" (1841), in *Works*, pp. 578–95.

in our great cities," he wrote, because their idleness passed the burden of production to the laboring classes.[7] Greed completed the process of exploitation. Because the owning class did not have "Christian but only selfish hearts beating in their bosoms," machinery at Parker's fictitious town of "Humdrum" did not set labor free but merely increased the output of operatives who still worked fourteen hours a day as before (p. 511).

As his description of the heartless employer suggests, economic problems remained moral ones for Parker. Manual labor was losing its dignity first because of the false gentility and excessive demands of the rich but also because the poor, if one reads closely enough, let themselves be morally degraded: "The wise men of Humdrum shut up in jail a large number:—a sacrifice to the spirit of modern cupidity; unfortunate wretches, who were the victims not the foes of society; men so weak in head or heart, that their bad character was formed FOR them, through circumstances far more than it was formed BY them, through their own free-will" (p. 512). Thus Parker was thinking of the sum of individual failings when he wrote that the "sin" belonged to "society at large." Yet the magnitude of the evil seemed to preclude reform by spiritual regeneration. "Who shall apply for us Christianity to social life?" he asked, and immediately continued:

> But God orders all things wisely. Perhaps it is best that man should toil on some centuries more before the race becomes of age, and capable of receiving its birthright. Every wrong must at last be righted, and he who has borne the burthen of society in this ephemeral life, and tasted none of its rewards, and he also, who has eaten its loaves and fishes and yet earned nothing, will no doubt find an equivalent at last in the scales of divine Justice. [Pp. 514–15]

The gap between Parker's social awareness and moral framework produced a disturbing crisis in his faith in man and a policy of inaction.[8]

Parker's "Thoughts" also raised a personal question which other Transcendentalists had to face as well, concerning the legitimacy of intellectual work. Parker was more self-conscious than Channing about his own vocation and was plainly uneasy about being a minister. There were two reasons to worry. First, since he viewed society in bifurcated terms, the more he condemned the idleness of a leisured class, the more he

7. "Thoughts on Labor," *Dial* 1 (Apr. 1841): 499. Subsequent page citations in the text refer to this article.

8. Parker did not become actively involved in social reform until he left his West Roxbury pulpit and began to preach in Boston in 1846. Even then he concentrated on moral reforms such as the reformation of criminals and prostitutes. See Henry Steele Commager, *Theodore Parker* (Boston: Beacon Press, 1947), pp. 151–95. He did, however, become a militant abolitionist, and I discuss this in chap. 6.

glorified manual labor. Work might be drudgery, but the laboring class still fulfilled one of the duties of a calling, productivity. Service, or improving God's gifts for the common good, was an aspect of labor as important to the Puritans as spiritual progress.[9] But if nineteenth-century workers performed their obligation twice over, where did that leave the ministry of the Word? Parker's dichotomy created the suspicion that the modern clergyman might be classed with the "indolent," especially—and this was the second cause for worry—since ministers seemed unable to remedy social problems and preached instead, as he did here, a doctrine of future promises and consolation. He was sure that Christianity contained the answers for a just economy but uncertain about how to translate ethics into action, and he suspected that preaching was not enough. But he silenced his doubts with a simple affirmation: "The productive classes of the world are those who bless it by their work or their thought. . . . They also, who teach men moral and religious truth, who give them dominion over the world; instruct them to think; to live together in peace, to love one another, and pass good lives enlightened by Wisdom, charmed by Goodness, and enchanted by Religion; they who build up a loftier population, making man more manly, are the greatest benefactors of the world" (p. 509).

In the final analysis, Parker's essay was an effort to come to terms with his calling in an even broader sense, as a choice of life. The son of a farmer-mechanic from Lexington, he had to think of himself when he reproached young men who were "ashamed of their fathers' occupation" and deserted the manual trades for a more "genteel vocation" (p. 498). Few ministers were better suited or more assiduous in their profession than Parker. But he must have wondered whether a desire for status was mixed with his promise to serve, how much his immense theological knowledge helped his effectiveness in society, and if the existence of a class of intellectuals was not one reason for the degradation of labor. The same questions troubled other Transcendentalists. For Emerson, the issue became a clear choice between intellectual and reformer.

What Henry Nash Smith has called Emerson's "problem of vocation," although an issue thoughout his early life, became more complicated around 1840, when Emerson weighed the claims of intellectual and manual labor and, at the same time, of moral and social reform.[10] Before the Transcendentalist controversy, Emerson never seriously doubted the importance of "man thinking," as he described the intellectual in his Phi Beta Kappa oration at Harvard 1837. As Smith suggests, he was concerned

9. Weber, *Protestant Ethic*, pp. 108–09 and passim.
10. "Emerson's Problem of Vocation: A Note on the American Scholar," in Brian M. Barbour, ed., *American Transcendentalism: An Anthology of Criticism* (Notre Dame, Ind.: University of Notre Dame Press, 1973), pp. 225–37.

about the passivity of the intellectual, a new social type without institutional ties who might fail by lack of means to serve society. But Emerson's impatience with the thinker's vocation increased as the contention with Boston conservatives heightened his sense of social deformity and his desire for immediate regeneration. The result, when in 1841 he composed a lecture from journal entries which began in 1839, was "Man the Reformer."

In general terms, the reformer was "a Re-maker of what man has made"—"social structure, the state, the school, religion, marriage, trade, science."[11] But Emerson was more interested, especially in the journals, in the reformer's personal duties, the most important of which was manual labor. He thought that some work with the hands, taken up in addition to intellectual pursuits, would build moral strength and at the same time correct the imbalance of labor and leisure in contemporary society. He sketched the revolution he expected to follow this change in work in his journal in 1839:

> But who takes hold of this great subject of reform in a generous spirit with the intent to lead a man's life, will find the farm a proper place. He must join with it simple diet, & the annihilation by one stroke of his will the whole nonsense of living for show; and he must take Ideas instead of Customs. . . . What a mountain of chagrins, inconveniences, diseases, & sins would sink into the sea with this one doctrine of Labor. Domestic hired service would go over the dam. Slavery would fall into the Pit. Dyspepsia would die out. Morning calls would end.[12]

The "reformer" was modeled on Emerson's experience. The farming he did on a small scale in Concord in the late 1830s made him feel the benefits of moderate physical labor. More important, the idea that society could be improved by practical measures grew out of his appreciation of how much simply changing his calling, leaving the Boston ministry and becoming Concord writer and farmer, had resolved his frustrations and conflicts.

For a brief moment in his career, social reform made sense to Emerson. What he could not accept was the prospect of changes in economic organization which might limit his private fulfillment. Emerson did not doubt that in the long run the interests of the individual and society were the same; but he sensed a new tension in modern society between the moral imperatives of calling, self-improvement and public service. If the issue were pressed, he was willing to sacrifice the "reformer" to the "man," as he did hypothetically in his journal in May 1840 when he

11. "Man the Reformer," in Emerson, Works, 1:248. Subsequent page citations in the text refer to this edition.
12. June 28, 1839, Emerson, Journals, 7:219–20.

appealed to the intellectual's higher usefulness: "If the doctrine of universal labor finds him in the midst of books whose use he understands & whose use other men wish to learn of him, shall he cast away this his skill & usefulness to go bungle with hoe & harrow with cow & swine which he understands not? should he not rather farm his books well & lose no hour of beneficient activity in that place where he now is?"[13] It is not surprising that Emerson declined Ripley's invitation to join Brook Farm the following November.

The decision against Brook Farm was still difficult ("I wished to be convinced, to be thawed, to be made nobly mad by the kindlings before my eye of a new dawn of human piety"), and when Emerson attempted to explain and justify himself, his claims for the efficacy of moral power became more extreme and his defense of the intellectual more unbending. When he delivered "Man the Reformer" in January 1841, he qualified his praise of the reformer pieced together from earlier journal entries with the thought that the "panacea of nature," after all, was the "sentiment of love" (p. 252). By 1842, Emerson defended "The Transcendentalist" in terms of which Channing would not have approved:

> But the thought which these few hermits strove to proclaim by silence as well as by speech, not only by what they did, but by what they forbore to do, shall abide in beauty and strength, to reorganize themselves in nature, to invest themselves anew in other, perhaps higher endowed and happier mixed clay than ours, in fuller union with the surrounding system.[14]

Paradoxically, in his return to an argument for spiritual power, Emerson subverted the classic concept of a calling by absolving the intellectual of any immediate social responsibility. At least for Emerson, the Puritan balance of self and society was no longer possible. To resolve his problem of vocation, he had to choose between extremes.

One curious aspect of "Man the Reformer," that it was presented to the Mechanic Apprentices' Library Association, requires a further comment because it highlights egalitarian and potentially anarchic strains in Emerson's thought. Channing had appropriately framed his remarks at the Library Association as a sermon to the laboring classes. Why, then, did Emerson describe the reformer, an ideal type more closely related to his own dilemma than to the concerns of young workingmen? The answer must be that Emerson believed his model had a universal application. Indeed, if one reads the lecture with his audience in mind, a quesion arises whether the reformer was an intellectual who took on practical labor or a worker aware of the significance of his work. This deliberate ambiguity reveals a mystical element in Emerson's approach to social reality and

13. May 9, 1840, Emerson, *Journals*, 7:348.
14. Emerson, *Works*, 1:359.

social reform. While the distance between leisured and laboring classes might be closed in practice by the intellectual's abdication of his privileged status and the worker's education, one feels even more that Emerson immediately dissolved social distinctions in language through the symbol of the reformer. This fiat of perception might easily become a license for inaction, if social justice is just a matter of consciousness. But there are also radical possibilities.

For example, because Emerson assumed the identity of thinkers and workers, he did not patronize this audience but started from the premise that they shared the discontent and critical eye that made the reformer. The current "inquest into abuses" began in the "bosom of society," he said, because young men found their advancement blocked by "ways of trade [which] are grown selfish to the borders of theft, and supple to the borders (if not beyond the borders) of fraud" (p. 230). Still looking beyond outward differences, Emerson was sensitive to the common oppression of work in a society where productivity and profit devalued spiritual goals. All classes were victims of the same circumstances when he wrote in 1837: "The tradesman scarcely ever gives an ideal worth to his work, but is ridden by the routine of his craft, and the soul is subject to dollars. The priest becomes a form; the attorney a statute book; the mechanic a machine; the sailor a rope of the ship."[15] This perspective might produce revivalism, the conversion of the world by an influx of the spirit; but it might also lead to anarchism, as Karl Mannheim uses the term in *Ideology and Utopia*. The anarchist, Mannheim writes, is one "who regards the existing order as one undifferentiated whole, and who, by according esteem only to revolution and utopia, sees in every topia (the present existing order) evil itself."[16] Precisely because spiritual equality and spiritual freedom were immanent possibilities to Emerson, standing just beyond and indeed condemning the divisions and bonds of society, he might, though impatient with the compromises of gradual reform, have been a revolutionist in a campaign which promised individual and social integrity at once. But Emerson was too practical to be a utopian and leaned toward mysticism instead. It was Bronson Alcott who carried what can be called "religious anarchism"—the judgment and renunciation of the world in the name of the spirit—into practice.

THE ECONOMICS OF ANARCHY

In the early 1840s, Bronson Alcott lived as if on the verge of the millennium, and his Fruitlands community in 1843 was not even a leap but a mere step toward perfection. The disjunction between the sinful world and

15. "The American Scholar," in Emerson, *Works*, 1:83–84.
16. *Ideology and Utopia: An Introduction to the Sociology of Knowledge,* trans. Louis Wirth and Edward Shils (1936; reprint ed., New York: Harcourt Brace and World, 1959), p. 197.

a state of grace was absolute in his eyes, but work could and indeed must be established now on divine principles. This conviction had a double impact on Alcott's attitude toward reform. First, the radical conflict Alcott perceived between actual and ideal made him sensitive to the internal (and for him evil) consistency of the present economy. Any critique of the devaluation of the individual calling expanded into questions on property, trade, and social structure. Thus the entire system had to be overthrown, in the second place, even for one individual to labor in the freedom of the spirit. Revolutionary as this sounds and in one sense was, the religious framework of Alcott's ideas did not make him a political activist, but a come-outer. Alcott simply took the idea of conversion to its literal conclusion when he envisioned a new society, outside entangling corruptions, built up by individual acts of self-renunciation and obedience to the spirit.

There was already an element of the come-outer's refusal to traffic with sin behind Alcott's move to Concord in 1840. He had taken up farming not only for the purifying discipline of manual labor but to disengage himself from an economy "whose root is selfishness, whose trunk is property, whose fruit is gold."[17] His association in the late 1830s with the Nonresistance Society, a radical offshoot of the abolitionist movement, was an important factor here, and Alcott's course of action should be seen in the context of the Nonresistants' leading principle, the systematic oppression of all human institutions opposed to divine law and the duty to withdraw immediately, leaving them to collapse under the burden of their own evil.[18] But in Concord Alcott discovered the flaws of this logic in practice. As he cut his ties with the oppressors, he fell into the ranks of the oppressed and found that poverty stifled the free workings of the spirit. Thus when farming failed to supply his family's needs, Alcott went to work for wages, chopping wood at a dollar a day. But hired labor, the most blatant form of economic bondage, was disturbing to his conscience, and it still did not keep him from falling more into debt than he already was to relatives, friends, and merchants.[19] Alcott had come to

17. ABA to SJM, Aug. 10, 1840, Alcott, *Letters,* p. 53.

18. I am indebted to Lewis Perry's discussion of Alcott's connection with contemporary forms of anarchism, in *Radical Abolitionism: Anarchy and the Government of God in Antislavery Thought* (Ithaca: Cornell University Press, 1973), pp. 81–88. Perry makes the important point that Alcott criticized the Nonresistants for focusing too narrowly on the constraints government placed on freedom. My discussion explores how Alcott applied his convictions to economic issues. But Alcott opposed the impositions of the state as well, as his refusal to pay the poll tax and his eventual arrest in Concord in Jan. 1843 show. See John C. Broderick, "Thoreau, Alcott, and the Poll Tax," *Studies in Philology* 53 (1956): 612–26.

19. For general accounts of Alcott's life in Concord and at Fruitlands, see F. B. Sanborn and William T. Harris, *A. Bronson Alcott,* 2 vols. (Boston: Roberts Brothers, 1893), 1:303–50 and 2:353–421, and Odell Shepard, *Pedlar's Progress* (Boston: Little, Brown, 1937), pp. 262–380. A noticeable shift in Alcott's concern—from disburdening himself of

Concord to experiment with a social alternative; now, more thoroughly entrapped than before, he had lost his chance for practical action.

The obvious conclusion, and the most disturbing to his principles, was that one needed money to be free. But Alcott did not meet his difficulties in a spirit of compromise. Instead, his rejection of an economy which resisted religious imperatives became complete, and his values became inverted, making anything opposed to the present system the only source of good. To the distress of his wife Abigail, who clearly saw that he "partakes of the wages of others" by borrowing money and tried to repay the loans, Alcott achieved a sublime indifference to his indebtedness, even reasoning that the charity of friends was a means to draw out their higher nature: "Persons, here and there, are taking us kindly by the hand, and, without complaints or misjudgments, ministering of their love, their confidence, their respect and substance to our needs."[20] In a similar reversal of common values, he made a virtue of failure in one's calling, arguing that "transcendent excellence is purchased through the obloquy of contemporaries; and shame is the gate of the temple of renown."[21] Most important, Alcott's economic philosophy now became more systematic and reflected his contempt for the status quo. He outlined a theory of "no property," the renunciation of both private and common ownership in favor of common stewardship, in the *Dial:* "But to property man has no moral claim whatsoever; use, not ownership of the planet and parts thereof, constitutes his sole inheritance; he is steward of God's estate, and commissary of heaven's stores to his brethren; nor rightfully hoards or appropriates the same to his own sole benefit."[22]

---

property to refusing to work for wages—tells the story of his progressive impoverishment. In 1840, Abigail Alcott inherited 3,100 dollars from her father's estate and approached her husband with a plan to invest it in property for their children. When he professed his "awful repugnance to the whole scheme of property," she resolved to "say as little on that account as is possible" in the future. (AMA to SJM, Apr. 26, 1840, Alcott Family Papers, Houghton). The question was academic, in any case, since the whole amount went to Alcott's creditors, after which he was still 3,400 dollars in debt (Shepard, p. 295). At the same time, his stand against hired labor became more adamant, and by early 1843 he was unwilling, Abigail wrote in her journal, to be employed "in the usual way" (Mar. 6, 1843, cited in Alcott, *Journals*, p. 152). This development suggests the way Alcott's economic critique grew in exact proportion to his declining fortunes.

20. ABA to Junius Alcott, Sept. 28, 1841, Alcott, *Letters*, p. 57. Although Abigail Alcott admired her husband's high-minded "faith clear as noon," her own, she wrote to her brother, was "yet as big as that grain of mustard seed they talk about," and as a "doubter" she understood the contradictions his convictions produced (June 21, [1839], Alcott Family Papers). Her letters and journals, in the Houghton Library at Harvard, are a remarkable commentary on his ideas. Selections from her journals, from Apr. 1, 1842, to July 14, 1844, are published in Alcott, *Journals*, pp. 141–58.

21. Journal, Mar. 12, 1841, in "Days from a Diary," *Dial* 2 (Apr. 1842): 424.

22. Aug. 12, 1841, in "Diary," p. 431.

It should not be surprising, to one used by this time to Alcott's ability to maneuver among paradoxes, that this psychological denial and intellectual devaluation of the world led to plans for another social experiment. With nothing to fall back on but the spirit during his troubles in Concord, Alcott came away with a renewed faith that a divine economy could be made to work, if not by one man (and perhaps this had been his problem), then by a community. Thus in 1841 Alcott began "to seek the members of that brotherhood whom God designs shall dwell together in his paradise."[23]

Alcott found his strongest support in England. In the summer of 1842, he went abroad to meet a group of reformers associated with a school they had named Alcott House after they had read and admired his *Record of a School* and *Conversations with Children of the Gospels*. James Greaves, the school's founder and Alcott's correspondent, died just before Alcott arrived. But his follower Charles Lane became Alcott's most important associate at Fruitlands.[24]

There was a remarkable similarity in the views of Alcott and the English reformers, although their ideas were formed for the most part independently against the background of the industrial revolution in the two countries. Like Alcott, they began as educators who aimed to bring out the potential perfection of the child's soul. But once they saw that society restrained individual development, they, too, became radical critics of institutions.[25] Thus at the convention Alcott attended at the school in July, they proposed an "integral" or total reform to change—among other things,

> questions publicly unmooted, or unfavorably regarded, such as (1) that of a reliance on Commercial Prosperity, (2) a belief in the value of the purest conceivable Respresentative Legislature, (3) the right of Man to inflict Pain on man, (4) the demand for a purer Generation in preference to a better Education, (5) the reign of Love in Man instead of human Opinions, (6) the restoration of all things to their primitive Owner, and hence the abrogation of Property, either individual or

23. June 12, 1841, in "Diary," p. 429. In the summer of 1841, Alcott traveled through Vermont conducting his "conversations" in hopes of winning converts and repeatedly urged his brother Junius to leave his farm in New York state and join him in a community. See, e.g., Sept. 28, 1841, *Letters*, p. 57.

24. On the reformers at Alcott House and their appreciation of Alcott, see R. W. Emerson, "English Reformers," *Dial* 3 (Oct. 1842): 227–55, and Charles Lane, "A. Bronson Alcott's Works," *Dial* 3 (Apr. 1843): 417–54.

25. The one intellectual connection between Alcott and the Englishmen was Heinrich Pestalozzi (1746–1827), a Swiss educator with whom Greaves studied for ten years. On the importance of Pestalozzi to Alcott and the Transcendentalists, see Dorothy McCuskey, *Bronson Alcott, Teacher* (New York: Macmillan, 1940), pp. 33–37, and George Ripley, "Pestalozzi," *Christian Examiner* 11 (Jan. 1832): 347–73.

collective, and (7) the Divine Sanction, instead of the Civil or Ecclesiastical authority, for marriage.[26]

To translate this and other of their statements into modern terms, the English reformers were communists in property (although technically they consigned all property to God, as did Alcott), anarchists in government, free lovers in marriage, vegetarians in diet and, going beyond education to biological means to redeem the race, early eugenicists. In everything, they aimed at perfect freedom from instituted authority.

There was a tension in the thinking of the English reformers, and of Alcott, too, that helped launch Fruitlands. While they insisted that regeneration must begin with individuals ("By reformed individuals only can reformed laws be enacted, or reformed plans effected"), the impatience of the perfectionist and the assurance that they, at least, were reformed enough already convinced them of the immediate possibility of a "new eden" and "Providence seems to have ordained the United States of America, more especially New England, as the field wherein this idea is to be realized in actual experience."[27] Emerson worried that Alcott, lately so disenchanted with his country, had misrepresented its possibilities.[28] But Charles Lane was enthusiastic when he wrote home to the *New Age* in March 1843, at least within such limits as his high standards and ethnocentricity would allow:

> It occurs to me continually that this is the land for the liberation of mankind, physically, socially, mentally, and morally. True it is that the people of this country are not free in all respects. There is much priestcraft, sensuality, and selfishness—a trinity generally found in unity. But facilities for freedom are great, perhaps beyond example in the world. At present the people do not value them at their fair estimate, but they are a teachable people.[29]

26. Emerson, "English Reformers," p. 242. Emerson included the proceedings of the convention held on July 6, pp. 241–47.

27. Ibid., pp. 243, 246.

28. How warmly Alcott pressed the idea of a community is uncertain. He left America discouraged at his prospects, since he wrote to his brother Junius on Feb. 19, "I seek sympathy, and possibly business in a foreign land" (*Letters*, p. 62). On June 12, he wrote to Abigail from England that he and Henry Wright, a teacher at Alcott House, might become "cooperaters" in a community, "whether here or in America, a few months will disclose" (p. 69). By June 17, he told Abigail that Wright hoped to make "our land the place of his grand experiment in human culture" (p. 72). Alcott undoubtedly had some role in focusing Wright's plans.

29. Letter dated Mar. 31, 1843, in the *New Age, and Concordium Gazette* 1 (May 13, 1843): 13 (this journal will hereafter be cited as *New Age*). Henry Wright shared Lane's reservations about America, without the same optimism. By Aug. 1, apparently without having joined Fruitlands, he had returned to England. "His sympathies are not at all in harmony with their democratical government," the *New Age* reported, "neither do the tone and character of the Americans generally so far please his taste as to induce him to remain in that country" (1:75).

For Alcott, his experience in England—where there was "no repose, no gentleness, nor grace"—renewed and intensified his love of New England. "I would dwell quiet with husbandmen, repose in gardens and tread fields unstained with blood," he wrote home to Abba, who had feared that the long awaited appreciation he found in England might turn his affections away from his family and friends.[30] Thus Alcott returned with precisely the sort of visionary radicalism which makes a utopian. And his hearty reception by the English reformers seemed to confirm him in the only calling equal to his millennial expectations, that of a redeemer.

The economy of Fruitlands was based on a single principle, abstinence from worldly activity. "Shall I become a hireling, or hire others?" Charles Lane asked halfway through the community's short life from June 1843 to January 1844: "Shall I subjugate cattle? Shall I trade? Shall I claim property in any created things? . . . To how many of these questions, could we ask them deeply enough, could they be heard as having relation to our eternal welfare, would the response be 'ABSTAIN?' 'Be not so active to do, as sincere TO BE.' "[31] Despite the reformer's intention simply "to be," however, and to follow the spontaneous dictates of the spirit instead of the calculations of social science, the result at Fruitlands was a tightly integrated system of property, trade, and labor.

Property was the easiest question to settle, since only Lane invested in the project. For 1,800 dollars he bought a ninety-acre farm in rural Harvard, Massachusetts, and explained the transaction in this way: "We do not recognize the purchase of land; but its redemption from the debasing state of *proprium*, or property, to divine uses, we clearly understand; where those whom the world esteems owners are found yielding their individual rights to the Supreme Owner."[32] Whatever willful blindness this logic required, there was a real selflessness behind Lane's action.

30. ABA to AMA, Aug. 2, 1842, Alcott, *Letters*, p. 87. "May he not love us less for having found those who deserve to be loved more," Abigail had written in her journal on July 8 (cited in Alcott, *Journals*, p. 144). Ultimately her fears were not unfounded, since Lane concluded as a result of his Fruitlands experience that the family, "the ground-work of the institution of property" used to justify "every glaring and cruel act of selfish acquisition," must be abolished (in "The True Life," *Present* 1 [Mar. 1, 1844]: 312–16).

31. Charles Lane, "The Consociate Family Life," *New Age* 1 (Nov. 1, 1843): 120. This article is the most complete exposition of the philosophy behind Fruitlands and also appeared in the *New York Weekly Tribune* on Sept. 2 and in abolitionist Nathaniel Rogers's *Herald of Freedom* on Sept. 8; it is quoted in full in Clara Endicott Sears, *Bronson Alcott's Fruitlands* (Boston: Houghton Mifflin, 1915), pp. 41–52. The title conveys an important tension in the philosophy, to be explored in chap. 5: while the reformers hoped to achieve freedom from worldly relationships by acts of individual renunciation and obedience to the spirit, these regenerate individuals were to come together finally in a universal family.

32. "Family Life," p. 118. Samuel May helped purchase the farm, since he lent Lane 300 dollars after Lane had used 300 dollars of his own money to pay Alcott's debts in Concord. See Lane to Isaac Hecker, Nov. 11, 1843, quoted in Walter Elliott, *The Life of Father Hecker*, 2d ed. (New York: Columbus Press, 1894), pp. 92–93.

Formerly editor of the *London Mercantile Price Current,* Lane sponsored the American community as part of a process of self-purification that left him "literally penniless," as he told a friend.[33] By this time Alcott was used to accepting the gifts of friends as contributions to the spirit. The identity of the owner of the land was insignificant to him beside the fact that its "free use" could be obtained for divine purposes.[34] A number of the nine other adults who eventually joined Fruitlands owned or had access to wealth; but they were required neither to relinquish their holdings nor to invest in the experiment, and none did so voluntarily. Here the anarchic impulse behind the community seems to have precluded binding rules, and the spiritual detachment everywhere in evidence allowed such contradictions in practice to be overlooked.[35]

There would have been more complications for people trying to abstain from ownership if the Fruitlands economy had been profitable. Not only did the community disband before the problem arose, however, but the reformers never intended to produce more than they needed. One reason for this policy was that a surplus of material goods would inhibit spiritual growth. But they were even more anxious to limit production to avoid entanglement in trade. Commerce epitomized the danger of worldly ensnarement, and Lane, acting in his usual role as publicist for the community, categorically condemned business as a "nursery for evil propensities" in the *New Age* and as "morally depressive" in the *Dial.*[36] Thus with a subsistence economy as the goal, the reformers hoped in the meantime to secure what they could not produce themselves "by friendly exchanges, and, as nearly as possible without the intervention of money."[37]

It was on one such trip to obtain seeds that they first visited the Shaker village nearby, a long established group of disciples of Ann Lee Stanley. Lane's description of the community in the *Dial* suggests another mechanism besides subsistence production by which he intended to minimize trade, limited consumption. Although Lane admired the Shakers' system of communal property and even more their abstinence from marriage, he was shocked that they did a cash business of 10,000 dollars a year in produce and textile manufactures. Skeptical that so much

33. Lane to William Oldham, June 28, 1843, quoted in Sears, *Fruitlands,* p. 28.
34. ABA to an unidentified correspondent, Feb. 15, 1843, Alcott, *Letters,* p. 99.
35. Joseph Palmer, for example, owned a large tract of unincorporated land called No Town and ran a butchering business in nearby Fitchburg. Apparently he was able to live with the contradiction between his reform principles and his commercial involvement, and he left Fruitlands periodically to tend his cattle. He bought Fruitlands after the community failed and operated a sort of refuge for transient reformers there for the next twenty years. See Sears, *Fruitlands,* pp. 53–67.
36. "Family Life," p. 118; "A Day with the Shakers," *Dial* 4 (Oct. 1843): 167.
37. "Family Life," p. 118.

commerce could be compatible with "a serene life," he traced the difficulty to what the Shakers ate—meat, milk, coffee, and tea—which forced them to look for a way to make money to purchase those goods on the market.[38] In trade as in property, Lane implied, abstinence was the key to spiritual freedom. True to their belief in "being," and "doing," the Fruitlands reformers were really less interested in developing an alternative system of subsistence production and friendly exchange than in eliminating economic activity altogether, as far as was humanly possible. Diet was given an economic function and was subjected to rigorous taboos. "Neither coffee, tea, molasses, nor rice tempts us beyond the bounds of indigenous productions," Lane wrote. "No animal substances, neither flesh, butter, cheese, eggs, nor milk pollute our tables, nor corrupt our bodies."[39] Living on fruit, vegetables, bread, and water, not only did they obviate trade, moreover, but they minimized labor.

The philosophy of abstinence clearly made a virtue of passivity and therefore tended to devalue work, even as a spiritual discipline. Neither Alcott nor Lane went so far as to denounce labor explicitly, but their ambivalence came out in their ideas about cattle. The strangest aspect of the Fruitlands economy was how much the reformers believed that spiritual freedom depended on dispensing with the labor of animals. Benevolence and disdain were both motives for the reform. They wanted to liberate cattle from the drudgery of farm work as well as from the ultimate degradation of being slaughtered for food; but they also meant to end the need for human contact with animals which, simply because they were animals, were revolting to the spirit. A city dweller all his life, Lane was vehement about the "debauchery" of cattle raising and denounced in graphic terms the use of their "filthy ordures" as fertilizer and the diseases they transmitted to man.[40] But eleven-year-old Anna Alcott concurred

---

38. "Shakers," p. 167. The Shaker village at Harvard, Massachusetts, was one of a number of Shaker communities in New England, New York, and the West. They believed that Ann Lee Stanley (1736–84), who had come from England with several followers in 1774, was a female incarnation of Christ whose advent had accomplished the Second Coming, thus making it a duty to withdraw from the world into the millennial church. Though the origins of the movement were European, subsequent followers were Americans converted during the Second Great Awakening. See Sydney E. Ahlstrom, *A Religious History of the American People* (New Haven: Yale University Press, 1972), pp. 492–94. While most communities of this type—begun by immigrants and bound by specific religious principles—were founded in the early decades of the nineteenth century, they were not altogether a thing of the past and occasionally allied themselves with American reformers in the 1840s. The Peace-Union settlement in Pennsylvania was composed of Austrian Catholics who emigrated in 1837 and in 1844 became involved, together with the Brook Farmers, in the Fourier movement. See the *Present* 1 (Mar. 1, 1844): 353–54. For a complete discussion of these communities, see Arthur E. Bestor, *Backwoods Utopias: The Sectarian Origins and Owenite Phase of Communitarian Socialism in America, 1663–1829*, 2d ed. (Philadelphia: University of Pennsylvania Press, 1970), pp. 20–37.

39. "Family Life," p. 119.

40. "Family Life," pp. 119–20.

when she wrote in her journal: "We have souls to think and feel with, and
they have not the same power of thinking, they should be allowed to live in
peace and not made to labour so hard and be eaten so much. Then to eat
them! eat what has life and feelings to make the body of the innocent
animals! . . . Besides flesh is not clean food, and when there is beautiful
juicy fruits who can be a flesh-eater?"[41]

When Lane went on to point out the multiple benefits of an economy
without cattle, the ideal society he described, despite all the reformers'
rebellion against the present system, was an urban culture dedicated to
leisure. Men would be relieved of the toil of growing food for animals, he
began, and women, no longer bound to "the servitude of the dairy and the
flesh-pots," could exercise their full moral influence in the family. Population density would increase to four times its present rate without the space
wasted on cattle, humanity would be reunited in purified cities, and the
land itself, "restored to its pristine fertility" by the exclusion of manure,
would stand as an outward symbol of the regenerate spirit.[42] Alcott had
gone to Concord in 1840 to find a vocation consistent with his conscience;
now, three years later, he was involved in a project which subverted the
traditional notion of a calling by sanctioning the unmistakable pattern of
an industrial society where workers commonly look to leisure for the
satisfaction denied in work. Efficient production, needed to secure free
time, was one of Lane's primary goals in eliminating cattle, and Alcott,
too, for the first time in his life, showed an interest in scientific agriculture
and manufacturing when he wrote to his brothers about plans for building
dams for irrigation and using water power for industry.[43] The impulse
behind these efforts to optimize resources and labor was still at odds with
a capitalist outlook, since the idea was to limit economic activity in the
interest of spiritual culture, not to increase productivity for the sake of
profit. But capital, labor, and technical skill were precisely what was
needed to make the Fruitlands economy work at all, and when the reformers had to choose between implementing practical measures for their
long-term success and living immediately in the spirit, they opted for the
latter—not at the farm, however, but in society, where economic man-
agement could be left to someone else.

The Fruitlands system was at first so primitive that it would have
subverted the reformers' desire for freedom had they not compromised
their principles instead. Labor became drudgery when they tried to plant
their crops without the help of animals. Although they kept up a regimen
of lessons for the children (Lane's son and Alcott's four daughters) and
uplifting conversations for themselves, Lane betrayed the effect of hard
work on culture when he apologized in a letter to Thoreau that "my usual

41. June 8, 1843, quoted in Sears, *Fruitlands*, p. 89.
42. "Family Life," p. 119.
43. ABA to Junius Alcott, June 18, 1843, and Chatfield Alcott, Aug. 4, 1843, Alcott,
Letters, pp. 102, 108.

handwriting is very greatly suspended" because of so much manual labor.[44] They solved the problem by acquiring an ox and a cow to pull the plow and also by taking vacations in society. Alcott and Lane developed a new interest in publicizing their views when faced with the reality of rural life and went on speaking tours as far away as New York.[45] With the men absent from Fruitlands, however, the usual division of labor that kept women from heavy outdoor work broke down: Abigail and the girls had to harvest the hay crop alone. Community life, as it was working out, merely accentuated the contrast in antebellum society between expanding opportunities for men and the menial work expected of homebound women. Dedicated to the principle of renunciation as Fruitlands was, the two women members agreed as to who was doing the sacrificing and who taking the credit. "Miss Page made a good remark, and as true as good," Abigail wrote in her journal, "that a woman may live a whole life of sacrifice, and at her death meekly says 'I die a woman.' But a man passes a few years in experiments of self-denial and simple life, and he says, 'Behold a God.' "[46]

Alcott's view of social structure was the source of further difficulties. To Alcott, socioeconomic inequalities were insignificant beside the question of personal purity. He had risen to near-professional status in Boston, had fallen close to pauperism in Concord, and found both stations in conflict with his desire to live according to conscience. Though increasingly alienated from his society, the moral criteria Alcott brought to his experience blunted his awareness of the special problems of any one group which might have produced a class-oriented radicalism such as Orestes Brownson's. Instead, his discontent was channeled into world-denying anarchism. The effect, however, was to replace social distinctions with spiritual ones just as damaging to freedom as the economic power of an owning class.

The membership of Fruitlands was composed, at least in theory, of a spiritual elite. "The entrance to paradise is still through the strait and

44. Lane to Thoreau, June 2, 1843, quoted in Sears, *Fruitlands*, p. 22.

45. It should be noted that one of the distinguishing (and paradoxical) features of nineteenth-century utopianism was the eager use reformers made of technological advances such as the steam packet, which carried Alcott and Lane to New York, and, more important, mass communications to publicize their views. Lane, for example, seemed to devote much less of his free time to self-culture than to turning out articles for the *Dial, New Age, New York Tribune, Present, Herald of Freedom*, and *Liberator*. The Fourier movement, as we will see, could not have gained a national following within approximately one year (1844) without a communications system of equal scope. This highlights the important fact that such protests against the status quo were inescapably part of a technologically sophisticated urban society.

46. Aug. 26, 1843, cited in Alcott, *Journals*, p. 155. The best single work on changing sex roles in the early nineteenth century is Nancy F. Cott, *The Bonds of Womanhood: "Woman's Sphere" in New England, 1780–1835* (New Haven: Yale University Press, 1977).

narrow gate of self-denial," Alcott wrote just before the community began: "Eden's avenue is yet guarded by the fiery-sworded cherubim, and humility and charity are the credentials for admission."[47] But as William Ellery Channing had argued in the early decades of the century against the Orthodox doctrine of election, the notion of special spiritual status led as easily to pride and intolerance as to selflessness and love. Charles Lane was far from charitable, for example, when he took special care to report to his English friends that the reformers at Brook Farm owned sixteen cows, sold milk in Boston, consumed 500 dollars' worth of butter a year, and were "playing away their youth and day-time in a miserably joyous frivolous manner."[48] His caricatured puritanism might have been amusing if it remained divorced from power. But he and Alcott exercised informal and thus dangerously unlimited authority at Fruitlands, and the results were not "miserably joyous" but plain repressive. "I am prone to indulge in occasional hilarity," Abigail Alcott confided to her journal, "but seem frowned down into still quiet and peace-less order" and "am almost suffocated in this atmosphere of restriction and form."[49] Though she concluded that this was an "invasion of my rights as a woman," some of the men complained about the two leaders as well. This suggests that outside the bounds of well-defined social relations, spiritual clitism led not just to sexual, but to multiple, forms of petty oppression.[50] No tension appeared along class lines, however, not so much because private property had been abolished and the former social position of members successfully overlooked as simply because most came from a similar background.

The gate of the spirit turned out to be as "strait and narrow" as Alcott predicted, since a total of only eleven adults joined Fruitlands and a good

47. ABA to an unidentified correspondent, Feb. 15, 1843, Alcott, *Letters,* p. 99.

48. Letter dated July 30, 1843, "American Correspondence," *New Age* 1 (Sept. 1, 1843): 90. More temperately, Lane said that people joined Brook Farm for any of three reasons—sociability, education, or freedom from economic anxiety—in "Brook Farm," *Dial* 4 (Jan. 1844): 351–57.

49. Nov. 29, 1842, cited in Alcott, *Journals*, pp. 148–49. Writing during a preliminary experiment in common housekeeping in Concord, immediately following Alcott and Lane's arrival from England in October 1842, Abigail felt that the months of "liberty and option" without her husband made her more intolerant of the new arrangement. "I hope the experiment will not bereave me of my mind," she wrote, and soon left home for a short visit to Boston.

50. Louisa May Alcott, in her short story about Fruitlands, "Transcendental Wild Oats" (1876), blamed the dictatorial tendencies at Fruitlands on Lane—"Timon Lion"—who made her father, "Abel Lamb," a victim along with the rest. But Lane told a correspondent in Sept. 1843 that Alcott set such strict standards of behavior that few members were willing to stay: "He also does not wish to keep a hospital, nor even a school, but to be surrounded by Masters—Masters of Art, of one grand art of human life" (To William Oldham, Sept. 29, quoted in Sears, *Fruitlands*, pp. 117–18). Probably both were at fault—and probably the others were especially sensitive to any infringement of their liberty, since they expected total freedom. "Transcendental Wild Oats" is reprinted in Sears, pp. 146–74.

number of them belonged to the commercial middle class. Four of the nine
men had been involved in the market either as white-collar workers or
owners of businesses: Lane edited the *Price Current,* Samuel Larned
worked in a countinghouse in Providence, Joseph Palmer owned a butchering business near Fruitlands, and Isaac Hecker was part owner of a New
York baking firm. The distinctive aspect in the experience of all four was
the conflict between their religion and their work. Each had undergone
an awakening of an unconventional sort. Lane was converted by James
Greaves, the founder of Alcott House, who, like Alcott, believed in the
possibility of perfection through education. The circumstances of
Palmer's awakening are unknown, but he was a temperance and an
antislavery advocate by the 1840s. Larned came from a circle of intellectuals in Providence who admired the Transcendentalists, and Hecker was
converted by Orestes Brownson.[51] Most is known about Hecker, since he
later became a prominent Catholic priest. The vocational crisis caused by
his religious experience suggests the kinds of problems they all hoped to
resolve at Fruitlands.

Hecker first heard Brownson preach his gospel of Christian democracy at a lecture in New York in 1841. What is striking about Hecker's
subsequent discontent is that he was affected relatively little by the social
ethic at the heart of Brownson's doctrine (though he did take steps to
improve conditions for his workers) and instead rebelled against the

51. Abigail Alcott recorded in her journal that Lane was "converted from infidelity" by
Greaves (July 8, 1842, cited in Alcott, *Journals,* p. 144). On Larned, see Charles R. Crowe,
"Transcendentalism and 'The Newness' in Rhode Island," *Rhode Island History* 14 (1955):
33–46. On Palmer, see Sears, *Fruitlands,* pp. 53–67. On Hecker, see Elliott, *Hecker,* esp. pp.
12–94, and Vincent F. Holden, *The Early Years of Isaac Thomas Hecker (1819–1844)*
(Washington, D.C.: Catholic University Press, 1939), esp. pp. 43–208. The other members
were Samuel Bower, another English reformer; Abraham Everett, a cooper; Christopher
Greene, a friend of Samuel Larned from Providence and probably from a similar social
background; Abram Wood, occupation unknown; and Anna Page, a teacher. My list is
based on Sears, though I have excluded Henry Wright, who, she argues, probably joined,
since he had arrived back in England by Aug. 1 (see n. 29). Counting all these people as
"members," however, introduces significant complications. There were no formal admission procedures or records of membership at Fruitlands, and when Abigail Alcott listed the
"friends" who had visited out of "curiosity" about "our new home," she included Palmer,
Bower, Larned, Hecker, and Wood (July 24, 1843, cited in Alcott, *Journals,* pp. 153–54).
Apparently she considered only Lane, his son, and her family as permanent members, and
not without reason. The term of residence for the others was sometimes extremely short.
Hecker, for example, came with intentions of staying for good but decided the community
did not answer his needs and left on July 25, two weeks after his arrival. Others came and
went at will, such as Joseph Palmer, who had left his wife and business in Fitchburg. Abigail's
evaluation may reflect her reluctance to sacrifice her own family for the sake of universal
reform, as Lane often complained, and the men seemed to take recruitment and membership
more seriously. See Alcott's letter to an unidentified correspondent, Feb. 15, 1843, *Letters,*
pp. 99–100. For my purposes, in any case, the type of person attracted to Fruitlands is more
important than the persistence of his or her commitment.

routine of commerce because it stifled his spiritual growth. He revealed his feelings when he warned his brother not to "get too engrossed in outward business" but "rather neglect a part of it for that which is immortal in its life, incomparable in its fulness."[52] All the Transcendentalists perceived the conflict between market labor and self-expression. But the issue was intensely personal to a man like Hecker, caught up in the daily grind of trade, and social reforms such as those which Brownson proposed seemed less pressing than an individual solution. Fruitlands matched Hecker's priorities. Built on a reform principle that was the exact antithesis of Brownson's—individual withdrawal from sin, not collective opposition to injustice—Fruitlands was much less an integrated community than a place for a person to realize his own potential. The anarchist's indiscriminate rejection of society, moreover, reflected the cataclysmic quality of a crisis like Hecker's. What began as impatience with his work mushroomed into an extreme inability to cope with the world. He had nervous fits, heard disembodied voices, and suffered from an unidentified sexual disorder for which others advised marriage but which convinced him always to remain celibate. The remedies he tried on his own were just as extreme. Taking rigorous measures for self-purification, he either fasted or restricted his diet to unleavened bread, fruit, and water and even expressed his wish, at one point, to do away with the digestive system entirely. Similarly, the lifestyles Hecker contemplated as alternatives to Fruitlands (either living alone in the woods or entering a European monastery) signaled the same utter denial of the world.[53] Thus on an emotional level the effect of radical religion on a man thoroughly involved in the trade nexus was just as extreme as the anarchistic theory of Fruitlands itself.

Ultraism such as Hecker's was common among the people who came to Fruitlands and reflected their middle-class backgrounds in another way as well. The fact that many favored symbolic protests over social reform betrays the basic conservatism of a group who, no matter how alienated from their own vocations or even society in general, were still afraid of widespread popular disruptions. Samuel Larned, for example, came from Rhode Island, the most feudal state in New England with its extremely restricted franchise and family system of factory labor. But Larned rebelled against the status quo by traveling through New England swearing at everyone he met, on the premise that profane language, uttered in a pure spirit, could be redeemed from vulgarity, even while men, women, and

52. Isaac Hecker to George Hecker, May 12, 1843, quoted in Elliott, *Hecker*, p. 43.

53. On Hecker's problems and remedies, see Elliott, *Hecker*, pp. 33–38, 101–10. Hecker's idea of a solitary life in the woods may have come from conversations with Thoreau while Hecker was studying in Concord after his residence at Fruitlands. Several letters they exchanged in the summer of 1844 appear in E. Harlow Russell, "A Bit of Unpublished Correspondence between Henry D. Thoreau and Isaac T. Hecker," *Proceedings of the American Antiquarian Society* 15 (1902): 58–69.

children clearly remained unredeemed in his native state.[54] Others at Fruitlands used similar methods to buck custom and establish their separate identities. A man named Abram Wood called himself "Wood Abram," Joseph Palmer wore a beard in an age of clean-shaven faces, and legend has it that one man left the community to experiment with nudism on his own when he concluded that clothing stifled the spirit. To some extent, these idiosyncratic protests were the result of the premises of religious anarchism; but the fact remains that there was an undeniable safety in these principles for the discontented of the middle class. A sojourn at Fruitlands made it possible to deny the world completely and yet leave society intact. Thus the behavior of these middle-class utopians might well be considered an evasion of their social responsibility. They felt that something was dreadfully wrong with the market economy but changed nothing except themselves.

Was Fruitlands itself an evasion, not only of constructive reform, but of economic and social reality? Alcott's anarchism was rooted in his bitter disappointment at his failure in Boston and Concord, and the doctrine of abstinence did to some extent legitimize a total withdrawal from the problems of urban industrial society. But to see only this side of the question cannot explain the reformers' hope at the outset. The power of the spirit was intensely real to Alcott. Why should he doubt that to live by conscience was an immediate possibility or that other people might follow him in a massive renunciation of evil? It is difficult for us to approve the come-outer's approach to reform because we cannot fully grasp the religious ideas and feelings that once made this type of anarchism a logical remedy to social problems. But Fruitlands was a natural, though extreme, result of antebellum religion and for that reason deserves a hearing as one attempt of a few men and women to cope with the difficulties of their time.

AN EXPERIMENT IN PRACTICAL CHRISTIANITY

Nothing suggests the difference between Fruitlands and Brook Farm better than the styles of ultraism at the two communities. While the people at Fruitlands adopted highly individualized forms of rebellion not only against society as it was but, as in the case of Hecker's fasting, against the world itself, the Brook Farmers showed a decided taste for social amuse-

54. On Larned's idea of profanity, see Crowe, "Transcendentalism in Rhode Island," p. 45. His tour of New England prior to his residence at Fruitlands in fact occurred in the midst of agitation over the franchise led by Thomas Dorr and a number of labor leaders in 1842. For an account of "Dorr's Rebellion," see Arthur M. Schlesinger, Jr., *The Age of Jackson* (Boston: Little, Brown, 1945), pp. 410–16. For a contemporary report of the conditions in Rhode Island factories, see the notes made by S. C. Hewitt in 1844, in Philip S. Foner, "Journal of an Early Labor Organizer," *Labor History* 10 (1969): 205–27. The instability of Larned's commitment to reform was further demonstrated when he subsequently became a Unitarian minister and married a slaveholder.

ments. In manners and morals, Boston was still a basically Puritan city where attending a lecture was about as far as one dared go in the direction of fun. But at Brook Farm, there was an almost insatiable desire for pleasure: music, dancing, cardplaying, charades, tableaux vivants, dramatic readings, plays, costume parties, picnics, sledding, and skating.[55] This drive to live as fully as possible is the simplest reason why Brook Farm changed in the course of its six-year history, from 1841 to 1847, beginning as an experiment in practical Christianity and becoming a center of reform activity to promote the social science of Charles Fourier. From the first, there was a serious purpose behind the Brook Farm amusements, to work out an economy that guaranteed everyone an equal chance for social, intellectual, and spiritual growth. By offering a structural solution to economic problems, which evangelical Protestantism with its emphasis on spiritual means and ends did not provide, Fourierism brought the Brook Farmers within reach of their goal.

Until 1844, Brook Farm conformed in many ways to reform principles derived from evangelical Christianity. The reformers' economic theory was simply applied Christian ethics, their method depended more on the goodwill of the members than on social reorganization, and their aim was first individual growth and only secondly institutional change. Freedom to live according to conscience was the most important condition of reform, and the farm in West Roxbury, nine miles from Boston, attracted Sophia Ripley as an ideal place for peaceful self-communion. "I am not at all disappointed in my expectations from seclusion," she wrote to John Dwight on a visit in 1840 before the community formally began. "For even my lonely hours have been bright ones, and in this tranquil retreat I have found that entire separation from worldly care and rest to the spirit which I knew was in waiting for me somewhere."[56] It was natural that George and Sophia Ripley, the organizers of Brook Farm, set their hopes for a better society mainly on the chance for personal integrity outside Boston. For although Ripley saw the need for changes in economic and social relations to facilitate moral development, his perspective was still more

55. Almost all the numerous reminiscences later written by members dwell on the light-hearted atmosphere, the best of which are John Codman, *Brook Farm: Historic and Personal Memoirs* (1894; reprint ed., New York: AMS Press, 1971), pp. 159–85; John Van Der Zee Sears, *My Friends at Brook Farm* (New York: Desmond Fitzgerald, 1912), pp. 81–104; and Amelia Russell, *Home Life of the Brook Farm Association* (Boston: Little, Brown, 1900), passim. For a contemporary view, see Marianne Dwight, *Letters from Brook Farm, 1844–1847*, ed. Amy L. Reed (Poughkeepsie, N.Y.: Vassar College, 1928), pp. 49, 59, 73–74, 82–84, 103, 161–62, and passim.
56. Aug. 1, 1840, quoted in Zoltan Haraszti, *The Idyll of Brook Farm as Revealed by Unpublished Letters in the Boston Public Library* (Boston: Trustees of the Public Library, 1937), pp. 12–13. The largest collection of letters relating to Brook Farm is in the Dwight Papers, BPL. Selections have been published in this work.

that of a minister than of a social reformer when he, Sophia, and several others moved to the farm in the spring of 1841.[57]

Thirty-two people in all became members of Brook Farm between 1841 and 1844, and while none was as active in evangelical Unitarianism or Transcendentalism as Ripley, a number were closely enough identified with these movements for us to assume they shared his priorities. Among those who signed the Articles of Association in September 1841, Minot Pratt was the printer of the *Christian Register* and Charles Anderson Dana was a former Harvard student. Three Unitarian ministers—Samuel D. Robbins, Lemuel Capen, and Warren Burton—signed the revised edition of the Articles in 1842. A majority of the members, moreover, came from social groups most likely to appreciate reform focusing on intellectual and moral development. Of the twenty-seven who can be identified with reasonable certainty, ten were ministers, teachers, writers, and their wives, and six were former students. The fact that only two were businessmen and nine were working people, five of whom were farmers and their wives, also suggests that Brook Farm steered a middle course between the spiritual anarchism of Fruitlands and trade unionists' demands for extensive economic and political change.[58] Ties of kinship and friendship made

57. For the events leading to the founding of Brook Farm, see chap. 3. The best accounts of Brook Farm in the pre-Fourier period are Octavius Brooks Frothingham, *George Ripley* (Boston: Houghton Mifflin, 1882), pp. 108–65, and Charles Crowe, *George Ripley* (Athens: University of Georgia Press, 1967), pp. 143–68.

58. See appendix C for a list of members, with the occupation, date of birth, place of birth, and date of admission to Brook Farm for each. I have used the following criteria for membership: signature of either edition of the Articles of Association (dated Sept. 29, 1841, and Feb. 17, 1842, respectively) or signature of the Constitution (dated Feb. 11, 1844) or admission recorded in the minutes of meetings. All these documents are located in the Massachusetts Historical Society. Some texts have been published independently and in the secondary works and periodicals which I cite below. A resolution was passed on Feb. 18, 1844, that each member must sign the Constitution and supply the biographical information about him or herself that I have included. Thus the record after that date is almost complete. Before 1844, members generally signed the official agreements without supplying biographical data. Thus my identifications of the pre–1844 group, as well as supplementary information about later members, are based on a survey of the literature on Transcendentalism and Fourierism. The most useful work is Lindsay Swift, *Brook Farm: Its Members, Scholars, and Visitors* (New York: Macmillan, 1900), esp. pp. 111–201. On the three Unitarian ministers, see Samuel A. Eliot, *Heralds of a Liberal Faith,* 3 vols. (Boston: American Unitarian Association, 1910), 2:106 (Burton), 2:6 (Capen), and 3:336 (Robbins). Newspapers and periodicals are also extremely helpful, including the *New York Tribune, Present, Phalanx,* and *Harbinger.* I have not attempted to impose a tight social classification system, since members do not always fit easily into standardized categories (such as the students in the Brook Farm school, who were admitted to membership when they came of age), and I generally use descriptive analysis instead. It should be noted, however, that in the "working-class" category, I count all those who earned their living by manual labor, including farmers and printers, and in the "business" or "commercial" group, white-collar workers and owners of businesses. Wives, who usually listed no occupation, have been classified with their husbands unless otherwise stated.

it possible to rely on voluntary allegiance to religious principles instead of on more formal methods of reform. George Ripley brought his sister into the community, for example, and Sophia Ripley her cousin and niece. Similarly, the social distance between Minot Pratt, the printer, and the Ripleys was minimized by their acquaintance since the early 1830s, when Ripley briefly edited, and Pratt compiled, the *Register*.

The number of Transcendentalists associated with Brook Farm, though not as members, reinforced the neighborly atmosphere of the community as well as the emphasis on spiritual means and ends. All of the Transcendentalists were frequent visitors in the first few years, and Margaret Fuller in particular used the farm as a retreat from the pressures of her increasingly active public life as editor of the *Dial* and leader of the Boston conversations. Transcendentalist children were some of the pupils in the school the Brook Farmers conducted—Fuller's brother, Lidian Emerson's nephew, and Orestes Brownson's son, to name the most important. The community also accepted paying boarders, and these were often friends of the Transcendentalists. Charles King Newcombe, a writer from Providence, was an acquaintance of Margaret Fuller, as was Almira Barlow, the estranged wife of an ex-Unitarian minister.[59]

Despite this initial informality, the Brook Farmers did introduce certain changes in social organization between 1841 and 1844, and we will look at three aspects of their economy: the plan for reuniting social classes, the voluntary system of labor, and the choice of agriculture as the principal industry. Consistent with the spiritual focus of the community in these years, the object of all these measures was to promote the free development of the individual. Ripley's statement of purpose to Emerson, although cited already in chapter 3, bears repeating here as the most concise expression of the reformers' original goals, against which we should measure, as undoubtedly they did, their success:

> Our objects, as you know, are to insure a more natural union between intellectual and manual labor than now exists; to combine the thinker and the worker, as far as possible, in the same individual; to guarantee the highest mental freedom, by providing all with labor, adapted to their tastes and talents, and securing them the fruits of their industry; to do away with the necessity of menial services, by opening the benefits of education and the profits of labor to all; and thus to prepare a society of liberal, intelligent, and cultivated persons, whose rela-

59. On the students and visitors, see Swift, *Brook Farm*, pp. 69–109, 203–60. On Fuller's relation to Brook Farm, see William Henry Channing's comments in *Memoirs of Fuller*, 2:72–80, and Thomas Wentworth Higginson, *Margaret Fuller Ossoli* (Boston: Houghton Mifflin, 1884), pp. 173–84. On Newcombe, see *The Journals of Charles King Newcombe*, ed. Judith Johnson (Providence: Brown University, 1946), esp. pp. 3–30, and his short story "Dolon," *Dial* 3 (July 1842): 112–23. On Barlow, see Haraszti, *Idyll*, pp. 19–22.

tions with each other would permit a more simple and whole-some life, than can be led amidst the pressure of our competitive institutions.[60]

It is clear that Ripley's first objective was to end the division of educated and laboring classes. This was not a simple act of benevolence but grew out of his understanding that both shared a common difficulty, that their work no longer met the standards of a calling. Channing had identified this as a working-class problem due to repetitive labor, lack of education, but finally, as we have seen, to the moral inability of the poor to transcend these obstacles. But the reformers knew by their own experience that strong convictions did not guarantee self-expression in one's voca-tion. Any independence in fact compounded the difficulty of finding a calling in a society that favored, as Emerson said, "safety, utility, de-corum." Ripley's frustration as a Transcendentalist in the Unitarian ministry was a case in point. Minot Pratt, the author of a moderate antislavery pamphlet in 1836, must have felt just as confined at the increasingly conservative *Register*, and Nathaniel Hawthorne, also one of the original members, described the stultifying routine at the Salem cus-tomhouse, where he earned his living in the late 1830s, in the preface to *The Scarlet Letter*.[61] Thus while Channing's solution was strictly cultural, to provide workers with preaching, lectures, and other aids to moral improvement, the Brook Farmers set up their economy so that work would not conflict with self-expression.

The idea was to share the manual labor on the farm in order to achieve economic self-sufficiency and thereby end "wage slavery." "Everyone must labor for the community in a reasonable degree, or not taste its benefits," Elizabeth Peabody reported in the *Dial* in 1842, after seeing the system in operation. On another trip she observed Charles Dana take time away from teaching Greek to care for the fruit trees and saw the ladies spend the morning doing the laundry.[62] "By the wide distribution of these

60. Nov. 9, 1840, quoted in Frothingham, *Ripley*, pp. 307–08.
61. Pratt's *A Friend of the South in Answer to Remarks on Dr. Channing's Slavery* (Boston: Otis, Broaders, 1836) was a rebuttal to J. T. Austin's attack on Channing's antislavery views, *Remarks on Dr. Channing's Slavery* (Boston: Russell, Shattuck and John H. Eastburn, 1835). Pratt defended Channing's position that individual Southerners were not responsible for slavery but that the institution itself was still immoral and should gradually be abolished. On Hawthorne, see "The Custom House," in *The Scarlet Letter* (Columbus: Ohio State University Press, 1962), pp. 3–45. Emerson's comment is in his *Journals*, Oct. 12, 1838, 7:104.
62. "Plan of the West Roxbury Community," *Dial* 2 (Jan. 1842): 364. The later report on the Brook Farm economy was sent to Orestes Brownson by a "highly esteemed friend and literary lady" and was published along with his own article on "Brook Farm" in the *Democratic Review* 1 (Nov. 1842): 481–96. Internal and external evidence suggest that the woman was Peabody. Like Brownson, Peabody became increasingly skeptical in the early 1840s of the ability of man to save himself without the supernatural intervention of Christ,

labors," she continued, "no one has any great weight in any one thing," which left plenty of leisure time for self-improvement. She told Orestes Brownson that some local mechanics ("carpenters, blacksmiths, shoemakers, tailors") "desired to join, and to forego some of the income they were already receiving from their trades, in order to have the enjoyment, the moral advantage, of a social life on principles so consistently democratic and Christian; and more especially, in order to have their children have every advantage of education to which their abilities can do justice."[63] But there is little indication, either in the minutes of meetings or in the lists of people who signed the Articles of Association, that these workers ever came, or if they did, that they became full-fledged members. The probable reason shows how Brook Farm was less "consistently democratic" than Peabody thought.

While Brook Farm guaranteed equality in labor and education, membership in the association depended upon the ownership of property. In financial terms, Brook Farm was organized as a joint stock company. The Articles of Association, signed in September 1841, fixed the price of a share at 500 dollars and defined the privileges of subscribers, the most important of which was the right to vote on community policies.[64] The reformers' religious convictions were responsible for this arrangement. Whereas Alcott believed that spiritual freedom demanded the renunciation of ownership, the Brook Farmers, though with much the same end in mind, concluded that individual integrity required private property for its material support. Any denial of property rights, Ripley wrote to a member of a reform community at Skaneateles, New York, which practiced communal ownership, "would so far destroy the independence of the individual as to interfere with the great object of all social reform; namely, the development of humanity, the substitution of a race of free, noble, holy men and women instead of the dwarfish and mutilated specimens who now cover the earth."[65]

---

and accordingly the author of the letter to Brownson said that even if all social ills were remedied, man would still "feel the whole opposition between the law of finite natures, and that Law of the Infinite God, which Christ mysteriously reveals to him as a glory to be had" (p. 493). For an idea of her changing views, compare "A Glimpse of Christ's Idea of Society," *Dial* 2 (Oct. 1841): 214–28, and "Fourierism," *Dial* 4 (Apr. 1844): 473–83. Peabody still believed that the social experiment at Brook Farm was of the utmost importance as a preliminary to regeneration, however, and criticized the Brook Farmers for failing to publicize the community, since "communication" is the "spirit of the day" ("Plan," p. 368). The fact that she took the role of publicist upon herself, supplying some of the best information available about the pre-Fourier period, also supports the conclusion that she was the author of the report to Brownson.

63. Peabody, in Brownson, "Brook Farm," p. 491.
64. This edition of the Articles is published in Frothingham, *Ripley*, pp. 112–14.
65. Undated letter, in ibid., p. 147.

Certain informal assumptions and subsequent revisions of the Articles did modify what might have been a system of elite control. In light of his statement to Emerson that he wanted to open "the profits of labor to all," Ripley probably expected workers to buy stock with the wages and share of the profits that the Articles guaranteed to everyone who labored, thus introducing mobility into the economy. Similarly, the second edition of the Articles, drawn up in February 1842, relaxed the property qualification by adding that a person might become a member simply by the vote of a majority of the associates. The reformers may have begun to see, perhaps because they had no way to assimilate mechanics such as those Peabody described, that inequalities in power based on wealth blocked the reconciliation of classes that they sought.[66] But it is not surprising that before the adoption of Fourierism, the workers who came were the ones who could afford to buy stock—a farmer and Minot Pratt, the printer, invested 1,500 dollars each—or that the flood of support from the working class came only after a provision that seemed to equate human dignity with ownership had been erased.[67]

The voluntary system of labor was another reform undertaken in the interest of individual freedom. But like the property qualification, the measure tended to cut the reformers off from the majority of the people, this time on moral grounds, since such strict standards of character had to be set to make the method work. Elizabeth Peabody gave an account of the elective system in 1842. "Everyone prescribes his own hours of labor, controlled only by his conscience," and she noted that the freer atmosphere also enhanced sociability. This lent pleasure to labor, on the one hand, since "the mind is active and elevated by noble sentiments," but it supplied an informal check on individual performance as well through the mutual influence of coworkers: "A drone would soon find himself iso-

66. Articles of Association, Feb. 17, 1842, MHS. Another function of the new procedure was to facilitate the admission of children to full membership, since the document also specified the age of majority as twenty years and made provisions for translating the labor a person did as a child into stock in the association when he reached that age.

67. There are no complete records of stockholders in Brook Farm. A list of the ten original stockholders and the number of shares each purchased was appended to the 1841 Articles of Association and is published in Frothingham, *Ripley*, p. 115. When Brook Farm disbanded in 1847, two meetings of stockholders and creditors were held on Mar. 4 and Aug. 18, and the minutes contained the names of seven people who subsequently joined Brook Farm and were not among the original investors (Frothingham, pp. 194–95). Three of the seven were working people. But the number seems insignificant compared with twenty-nine working-class families who joined after 1844, apparently without investing. Despite the importance attached to property as a guarantee of independence, moreover, Brook Farm was in debt from the beginning to the end of its existence. The reformers secured two mortgages on the farm in 1841 for a total of 11,000 dollars and arranged a third mortgage in 1843 and a fourth in 1845, bringing their total debt to 17,445 dollars in 1847. For details on these contracts, see Swift, *Brook Farm*, pp. 19–26.

lated and neglected, and could not live there."[68] More formally, the members voted general standards for work in 1841: 300 days was considered the equivalent of one year's labor, and ten hours in the summer and eight in the winter equal to a day's.[69] But there was still no authority behind these regulations to compel members unwilling to do their share.

The problem arose in the winter of 1842, and the response demonstrated the potential for moral elitism inherent in the system. The difficulty centered on the people recently accepted as members (some of them former students in the Brook Farm school who had come of age, as well as one farmer) who, judging by their prolonged absences from the farm the following summer, seemed to lack the founders' zeal.[70] The associates responded first by tightening internal organization. In January 1843, they passed a resolution that hours of labor, previously left to discretion, be officially recorded.[71] But at the same time, there was a trend toward greater selectivity in the admission of members, to avoid further restrictions on the liberty of those already there. In an effort to determine moral fitness, the Brook Farmers relied with surprising frequency on sexual conduct or opinions for evidence. In December 1842, they rejected Lydia Maria Child's appeal on behalf of the mother of an illegitimate child, "the victim," Child wrote, "of a false state of society."[72] They refused to take the daughter of sex reformer Mary Gove as a student the following year, especially, no doubt, since Gove offered to pay part of the tuition in the form of lectures at the farm. In another intriguing though

68. Peabody, in Brownson, "Brook Farm," p. 494.

69. Minutes of meetings, Oct. 30, 1841, cited in Frothingham, *Ripley*, pp. 116–17.

70. The absence of John Stillman Brown, for example, a farmer who became a member in Sept. 1842, was noted in the minutes of almost every meeting after Aug. 5, 1843. He seems to have deserted not only the community but also his family, since it was voted on Oct. 22 that they could stay through the winter without him at a charge of four dollars a week. Similarly, James Burrill Curtis, a former student who had been elected secretary of the Association for the year 1843, had formally withdrawn by Aug. 5. There also seem to have been discipline problems among the students generally, since a resolution passed on Jan. 28 prohibiting parties held in students' rooms. There were always those who were not ambitious workers. "The farm business, to-day, is to dig potatoes," Hawthorne wrote in his notebook on Oct. 8, 1841. "I worked a little at it." (*American Notebooks*, ed. Claude M. Simpson [Columbus: Ohio State University Press, 1972], p. 207). But the fact that the farm was not prospering by the winter of 1842 (a "retrenchment" program was adopted in Feb. 1843 which prohibited buying on credit and restricted purchases) made the productivity of workers a pressing issue. The minutes of these meetings are in the MHS.

71. Minutes of meetings, Jan. 7, 14, and 28, 1843, MHS. The fact that the resolution was debated throughout the month of Jan. suggests that it was a difficult decision.

72. Quoted in Haraszti, *Idyll*, p. 24. The woman was Caroline Henshaw, a German corsetmaker's apprentice, and the father of the child was John Colt, an accountant convicted of murder in a sensational New York trial who had finally married Henshaw but then committed suicide. Despite Lydia Maria Child's recommendation, it is not surprising the Brook Farmers were wary.

mysterious case in 1843, two full members, Abigail Morton and Manuel Diaz, left shortly after the directors asked "their intentions with respect to further residence at the Farm," as the official minutes stated. Since the couple later married, sexual misconduct may have had a part in the confrontation.[73]

It was not inconsistent with Alcott's perfectionism to say that the gate of the spirit was "strait and narrow," but this exclusivity at Brook Farm must have been disturbing to reformers who set up their community to facilitate moral growth. Following a policy that guaranteed freedom of labor seemed to require that Brook Farm be changed from a place for education to a retreat for the saints. Here was a second difficulty which Fourierism addressed, for in 1844 the Brook Farmers accepted new members almost as fast as they came.[74]

One final aspect of the Brook Farm economy, its agricultural basis, suggests the high priority initially given to spiritual interests. The Brook Farm Institute for Agriculture and Education was the name the reformers chose in 1841. While it referred on the one hand to their plan to unite labor and culture, it also designated the way they meant to earn their living, by farming and teaching. Making agriculture the principal industry was much less an economic decision than a moral one. The Transcendentalists generally saw farming as the occupation most favorable to personal growth because of its distance from the market, proximity to nature, and promise of a subsistence to protect moral independence. Fruitlands, whatever the ultimate dream of cities dedicated to leisure, was an extreme expression of this logic in its initial form. The Brook Farmers were more tolerant of market activity. They sold their milk, vegetables, and hay and kept their stock dividends low in order to have enough capital to expand production.[75] Operating what amounted to a boarding school where the students paid in cash unless they worked on the farm was further proof of the reformers' moderate stand on commerce, since in effect they were

73. The Gove decision was recorded in the minutes of meetings (MHS) for Sept. 24, 1843, and the Morton–Diaz action on Apr. 29, 1843. A probationary period was also established by Sept. 19, 1842, when Edward Appleton and his wife were admitted as residents with the "usual probation of two months." On Apr. 19 and Aug. 13, 1843, the Brook Farmers used the system to dismiss probationers whose "longer residence here is thought inexpedient."

74. That is not to say that the Brook Farmers did not follow standardized procedures for the admission of members. The following by-laws were passed on Feb. 7, 1844: (1) the associates had to be given twenty-four hours' notice before an application for admission could be voted on, (2) probation was two months, (3) probationers were required to work, (4) the directors had the authority to dismiss probationers (minutes, MHS). But other evidence suggests that they were eager to admit new members. On June 9, for example, two meetings were held on the same day to vote on applications. In several cases, the minutes note that letters were written to prospective members, encouraging them to apply. Finally, there were no records of dismissals.

75. See Swift, Brook Farm, pp. 40–42.

making money on culture. But there was something of Alcott's search for purity in Ripley's desire for a "simple and wholesome life," and Orestes Brownson came close to calling it escapism when he evaluated the "community system" in the *Democratic Review* in February 1843.

The critical error of all these social experiments, Brownson wrote, was to dismiss the laws of industrial development which should be used instead to create not only an ethical, but a viable, economic alternative to the present system. Rather than concentrate on subsistence farming, each of the growing number of reform communities should specialize in the one industry for which it was best equipped and should market that product on a mass scale. By his own admission, Brownson was willing to sacrifice the spiritual advantages of retired country life for the sake of social justice. "We are no great believers in the sinlessness of businessmen," but now wage earners "are unable to live a truly *human* life" and to send them back to the farm was no solution. We must do for labor, he concluded, "what our manufacturers are doing with respect to capital through corporations, and our businessmen with credit through banks, that is, *associate* it, and by association increase its relative power."[76]

By the time Brownson's article appeared, the Brook Farmers were already taking steps toward the goal he proposed. The second edition of the Articles in 1842 had modified the community's commitment to agriculture by stating that other industries might be introduced if it were thought desirable. But nothing was done until a cordwainer from New York named Lewis Ryckman made arrangements to manufacture shoes at the farm in early 1843. After his admission in January, Ryckman showed little inclination to conform to the usual routine of farm work and cultural activities and instead ordered materials for women's shoes from a Boston dealer to finish at the farm and sell in the city. The Brook Farmers' approval of Ryckman's initiative was a deliberate change in policy. On February 12, a "special meeting" was called "to consider the importance of more deliberation & accurate examination of facts before acting upon propositions, & after discussion of internal economic changes." Already in debt, they were worried about committing themselves too hastily to a new trade, but they soon advanced Ryckman nearly 100 dollars to begin the business. By November, the community was actively recruiting skilled shoemakers, accepting William Teel, for example, on the condition that he produce 4 dollars' worth of shoes a week.[77]

76. "The Community System," *Democratic Review* 12 (1843): 144.

77. Ryckman first proposed the scheme on Feb. 11, 1843, and by Feb. 19 had made a deal with a Mr. Kimball which the Brook Farmers approved: Kimball would supply the materials and pay twenty-two cents for each pair of shoes finished and six cents for binding. Ryckman received a stock worth 87.56 dollars for twenty-seven pairs on Feb. 25 arranged with another merchant to make and sell twenty-five pairs more. Teel, New York and probably a friend of Ryckman, was invited on Nov. 12 and became Apr. 11, 1843 (minutes, MHS).

What happened in the case of shoemaking shows the Brook Farmers' increasing interest in practical economics as a means to social justice in the year before they announced their allegiance to Fourierism. It is significant that Ryckman had been a member of the New York Fourier Society in 1842, thus making Fourierism itself a factor in their changing outlook.[78] But the fact remains that the new ideas would have had little appeal to the Brook Farmers had they not been ready to move in a different direction.

THE SCIENCE OF SOCIAL PERFECTION

On January 18, 1844, the Brook Farmers issued a constitution which made their community a more effective social alternative in an industrializing society. Labor as well as capital qualified a person for membership. Workers, now divided into agricultural, mechanical, and domestic groups with elected leaders, were sufficiently organized to accommodate the moral capacity of the average man or woman. Manufacturing was given equal status with farming, as the new name for the community implied, the Brook Farm Association for Industry and Education. The document showed the influence of Charles Fourier's ideas and indeed professed "an unqualified assent to that doctrine of universal unity that Fourier teaches, [while] our whole observation has shown us the truth of the practical arrangements which he deduces therefrom."[79]

The Brook Farmers were not alone in their admiration of Fourier. A convention had been held in Boston on December 27 and 28, 1843, "to take counsel together," as the "Call to the Friends of Social Reform" which appeared in various reform journals had stated, "that we may wisely, energetically, and efficiently aid the progress of Social Organization and Reform, in which all other reforms that we have so earnestly prayed for in times past are contained," made possible by the "TRUTHS of Social Science discovered by CHARLES FOURIER."[80] The meeting was the first public forum on the scale of conventions of the Antislavery Society, although the eclectic attendance and lack of a permanent supporting organization made it more closely resemble the Chardon Street conventions of 1840 and 1841, where reformers of every imaginable background deliberated on the sabbath, church, and ministry.[81] Indeed, the variety of

78. Ryckman was listed as a "vice-president" of the "Festival in Honor of Fourier," *New York Tribune*, Apr. 20, 1842.

79. *Phalanx* 1 (Mar. 1, 1844): 80–81.

80. *Phalanx* 1 (Dec. 5, 1843): 44. The call also appeared in William Henry Channing's magazine the *Present* 1 (Dec. 15, 1843): 207–08, and Horace Greeley's *Tribune*, Dec. 13, 1843.

81. "Madmen, madwomen, men with beards, Dunkers, Muggletonians, Comeouters, Groaners, Agrarians, Seventh-day Baptists, Quakers, Abolitionists, Calvinists, Unitarians, and Philosophers" attended this series of conventions, Emerson wrote, obviously taking pleasure in the diversity of individual viewpoints. See his "Chardon Street and Bible Conventions," *Dial* 3 (July 1842): 100–12.

people present in 1843 made it seem that Fourierism might be the panacea the call had promised: William Lloyd Garrison, Frederick Douglass, John Pierpont, Bronson Alcott, Orestes Brownson, Adin Ballou from the Hopedale community, and representatives from other communities founded by Boston reformers at Northampton, Massachusetts, and Skaneateles, New York.[82] For most of the participants, Fourierism was a restatement of their various goals—the abolition of "Repugnant Industry, Tyranny of Capital, Chattel Slavery" and the elevation of women—and a significant, though by no means authoritative, solution. But the twenty people who issued the call were committed to Fourierism beforehand and used the public support the convention drew to organize the New England Fourier Society.

Of the Brook Farmers, only Ryckman signed the notice. The convention in fact precipitated the conversion of Brook Farm to Fourierism, since the new constitution was not drafted until January 1844, after the meetings had been held.[83] But Fourierism was a familiar and serious matter for the other Brook Farmers as well.

Fourierism was introduced to the American public in 1840 when a New Yorker named Albert Brisbane published a compendium of Fourier's writings entitled *The Social Destiny of Man*. The son of a merchant, Charles Fourier (1772–1837) was deeply affected as a young man by the disorder in French society which exploded in the Revolution of 1789 but for which neither the revolution nor any subsequent political changes had an answer. He devoted his adult life to solving the problems of the market economy and by the early 1830s had attracted a small group of followers in Paris who published a journal called *La Reforme Industrielle*. Intellectually Fourierism was a product of the Enlightenment. Fourier believed that the cause of conflict and suffering was the perversion of natural human goodness by faulty social organization. But he was sure that reason could discover the laws of harmony and create perfect order by rearranging economic relationships. He devised a social blueprint with precise instructions for the size, layout, and industrial organization of each community or "phalanx" so perfect, in fact, that some American critics in the 1840s claimed that his "science" was hardly empirical but rather the idiosyncratic deductions of a crank philosopher.[84]

82. "Social Reform Convention at Boston," *Phalanx* 1 (Jan. 5, 1844): 46–47. The article was concluded in the *Phalanx* 1 (Mar. 1, 1844): 84–87. See also W. H. Channing's excellent evaluation of the significance of the convention in "Social Reform Convention at Boston," *Present* 1 (Jan. 15, 1844): 277–88. On the Hopedale, Northampton, and Skaneateles communities, see John Humphrey Noyes, *History of American Socialisms* (1870; reprint ed., New York: Dover, 1966), pp. 119–32, 154–60.

83. A committee to draft the Constitution composed of Ripley, Dana, and Ryckman was appointed Jan. 2, and it was approved by a vote of the associates on Jan. 7 (minutes, MHS).

84. The best modern abridged translation of Fourier's voluminous works—*Oeuvres Complètes de Charles Fourier*, 12 vols. (Paris: Editions Anthropos, 1966–68)—is *The Utopian Vision of Charles Fourier*, trans. and ed. Jonathan Beecher and Richard Bienvenu

Americans were even more doubtful about Fourier's religious ideas. God, Fourier said, was a "supreme economist" who had worked out a plan for a perfect society with human "happiness" the end and producing plenty of "riches" the principal means.[85] To Protestants raised on ideals of selfless virtue and temperate indulgence, these might easily seem low-minded, worldly goals; at least, they did to Elizabeth Peabody. "The first objection that strikes a spiritual or intellectual person, at the presentation of Fourierism," she wrote after the Boston convention, "is its captivating material aspect."[86] Orestes Brownson and James Freeman Clarke put the case in even more strenuous terms: Fourierism failed to take account of the soul. "Does society make man, or man society?" Brownson asked soon after his conversion to Catholicism in 1844, and despite his new faith (or rather because of it) agreed with the answer Clarke gave in the *Christian Examiner:* "This is the principal cause of social evil—*sin.*"[87] Man was more than an automaton created by circumstances, and only a change of heart could redeem society in a way consistent with the freedom and the dignity of the individual. "I am reading Brisbane's book on the reorganization of Society," Samuel Osgood, a young Unitarian minister and friend of

(Boston: Beacon Press, 1971). For an interesting discussion of Fourier in the context of European intellectual history, see Edmund Wilson, *To the Finland Station* (New York: Farrar, Straus, and Giroux, 1972), pp. 102–15. Although there is no study of Fourierism as a social movement in France in the 1830s and 1840s, one recent work which provides useful background information on French reform is Christopher Johnson, *Utopian Communism in France: Cabet and the Icarians, 1839–1851* (Ithaca: Cornell University Press, 1974), esp. pp. 62–108, 144–206. In *The Social Destiny of Man; or, Association and Reorganization of Industry* (Philadelphia: C. F. Stollmeyer, 1840), Brisbane alternated chapters translated from Fourier with summaries of Fourier's ideas and applications of these views to American conditions (he told the reader which chapters were which on p. xiv). This work was generally faithful to Fourier's thinking. On Brisbane (1809–90), see his reminiscences, published posthumously by his wife, *Albert Brisbane: A Mental Biography, with a Character Study by his wife Redelia Brisbane* (1893; reprint ed., New York: Burt Franklin, 1969), esp. pp. 47–266, and Arthur Bestor, "Albert Brisbane—Propagandist for Socialism in the 1840's," *New York History* 28 (1947): 128–58.
   85. Brisbane, *Social Destiny*, pp. 8, 21–23.
   86. "Fourierism," p. 480.
   87. "No Church, No Reform," *Brownson's Quarterly Review* 1 (Apr. 1844): 193; "Fourierism," *Christian Examiner* 37 (July 1844): 77. The lengthy replies to Brownson and Clarke in the *Phalanx*, the periodical begun in New York by Brisbane in Oct. 1843, show that the Fourierists saw the necessity of answering American Christians if their movement was to survive. In "Mr. Brownson's Notions of Fourier's Doctrine," the writer argued that Fourierism, much like Catholicism, aimed at universal unity, not individual happiness, and that social reorganization would supplement rather than supersede the church as a means of regeneration (*Phalanx* 1 [July 13, 1844]: 197–204, and 1 [July 27, 1844]: 213–20). "The Christian Examiner on the Doctrine of Fourier" claimed that Clarke's call for spiritual rebirth was an inadequate solution to economic problems—we have had "enough of the *sentiment*" and "parson-power" already—without comprehensive social reform (1 [Aug. 24, 1844]: 248–53). Even before Fourierism gained a popular following, Brisbane had begun to answer such objections. Brownson had argued that sin blocked efforts of human

the Brook Farmers had written in 1840: "I understand, however, that our new light Socialists eschew Brisbane's dictum."[88] More "new light" than "socialist" at the time, Osgood's impression was right. Why, then, did the Brook Farmers change, and how much?

The Brook Farmers adopted Fourierism because the progress they made under their original plan brought its shortcomings, practical and ethical, into vivid perspective. It has been relatively easy to measure the social impact of the Brook Farm economy, and we have seen that the reformers' devotion to individual development created various forms of elitism. Nevertheless, as a community dedicated to spiritual growth, Brook Farm surpassed their original expectations. George Ripley approached religious ecstasy when he wrote to Isaac Hecker in September 1843:

> Oh! that you would come as one of us, to work in the faith of a divine idea, to toil in loneliness and tears for the sake of the kingdom which God may build up by our hands. All here, that is, all our old central members, feel more and more the spirit of devotedness, the thirst to do or die, for the cause we have at heart. We do not distrust Providence. We cannot believe that what we have gained here of spiritual progress will be lost through want of material resources. . . . I long for action, which shall realize the prophecies, fulfil the Apocalypse, bring the new Jerusalem down from heaven to earth, and collect the faithful into a true and holy brotherhood.[89]

---

self-perfection, in "Social Evils, and their Remedy," *Boston Quarterly Review* 4 (July 1841): 265–91. Brisbane responded that Fourier's social science did in fact guarantee total reform, in "Mr. Fourier's Social System," *Boston Quarterly Review* 4 (Oct. 1841): 494–512. Emerson complained that Fourier treated man as "a plastic thing," in "Fourierism and the Socialists," *Dial* 3 (July 1842): 86–96, but lent Brisbane space in the same article to defend his views. See also Brisbane's argument for the compatibility of Fourierism and Christianity in the *Tribune*, May 26, 27, and 28, 1842. As the Fourier movement gained converts, such attacks became more frequent and came from a more diverse group of Protestants. See, for example, James H. Fairchild, "Fourierism," *Oberlin Quarterly Review* 1 (Nov. 1845): 224–45.

88. Osgood to John Sullivan Dwight, Nov. 21, 1840, quoted in Haraszti, *Idyll*, p. 14. As late as Dec. 1842, the Brook Farmers objected that Fourierism was opposed to individual freedom. Ripley expressed his disinclination to accept a science that "starts with definite rules for every possible case," in a letter to the *Tribune*, Aug. 13, 1842, and Ryckman, though already a Fourierist himself, confirmed Ripley's statement when he reported to the *Tribune* on Dec. 30 that Brook Farm was "not pledged to advocate or support his [Fourier's] or any other man's theories." These two brief statements are the only direct evidence of how the Brook Farmers felt about Fourierism before Jan. 1844. Obviously, they were aware of the theory, but 1843 seems to have been the critical year in which Fourier's ideas began to take hold.

89. Sept. 18, 1843, quoted in Elliott, *Hecker*, p. 91. Hecker had lived at Brook Farm in the spring of 1843 before moving on to Fruitlands.

The Brook Farmers looked to Fourierism as a science to implement this religious vision. The "ultimate design of Christianity," Charles Dana told the New England Fourier Society in 1845, "will be realized only when Science is brought to the service of Society, and a social order established, in whose form its divine principles can have their full action and effect."[90] They did not think that by accepting Fourierism they had to choose, as the critics implied, between spiritual regeneration and social organization as the means of reform. Ripley told Hecker that religious enthusiasm was still an essential component of change: "Oh, for men who feel this idea burning into their bones! When shall we see them? And without them, what will be phalanxes, groups and series, attractive industry, and all the sublime words of modern reforms?" And William Henry Channing, who became the religious leader of Fourierists in Boston and New York, in fact predicted that scientific reform would increase supernatural inspiration: "Religion tends naturally to form itself into Science, and through Science to embody itself in Society; and happy conditions of existence react upon our powers of intelligence, and prepare them for admitting purer influence from the Eternal world."[91] Far from dismissing religion, therefore, the Brook Farmers adopted social science to realize a religious ideal.

But they did turn away from a kind of religion that gave preeminent importance to the individual. "Out of idealism, and pantheism, and egoism," Channing wrote to John Sullivan Dwight at Brook Farm in 1846, "have we passed into realism, and mediation, and immortal communion."[92] In the 1830s, Transcendentalist philosophy had freed the individual from the Christian tradition in order to find a way to apply religious principles more effectively in modern society. But there were signs in the 1840s that some felt too much had been said about freedom and not enough about love, that the solitary individual had been glorified at the expense of man in society, and that Transcendentalism still lacked, in short, a social vision. Channing criticized Theodore Parker in 1842 for failing to preach "that the Race is inspired as well as the Individual; that Humanity is a growth from a Divine Life as well as Man; and indeed that the true advancement of the individual is dependent upon the advancement of a generation, and that the law of this is providential, the direct act of the Being of beings."[93] While Fourierism was neither a religious nor an ethical system in itself, Channing praised Fourier in 1843 for revealing "the means of *living* the law of love."[94]

90. "Convention of the New England Fourier Society," *Phalanx* 1 (Feb. 8, 1845): 312.

91. "Introduction," *Present* 1 (Sept. 15, 1843): 2.

92. Nov. 8, 1846, quoted in Octavius Brooks Frothingham, *Memoir of William Henry Channing* (Boston: Houghton Mifflin, 1886), p. 214.

93. Channing to Parker, June 9, 1842, quoted in ibid., p. 174.

94. "Social Reform Convention at Boston," *Present* 1 (Jan. 15, 1844): 283. William Henry Channing's career was one of the most troubled and interesting of all the Transcendentalists' and has been one of the least studied (Frothingham's 1886 *Memoir* is the only biography). Disturbed by the individualistic emphasis of Unitarianism from the time he

For the Brook Farmers too, their acceptance of Four̶ choice in favor of social involvement, not only with society at large. "The interests of Social Reform, w paramount to all others," the introduction to thei̶ *Harbinger,* stated in 1845: "We will suffer no attach taste for abstract discussion, no love of purely inteṉ̶ seduce us from our devotion to the cause of the oppressed, ṯ̶ trodden, the insulted and injured masses of our fellow men."[95] In all tḫ̶ areas of the Brook Farm economy we looked at before—class relations, labor, and industrial organization—Fourierism offered solutions that would break down the distance between the reformers and the world they lived in.

Whereas the Brook Farmers saw class division as the unequal distribution of work and education, Fourier defined the problem in terms of wealth and power. He argued that society was in a state of "commercial feudalism," a stage of historical development modern economists usually refer to as "merchant capitalism" where independent producers first experience market pressures. Merchants were the villains of Fourier's scheme, since they created none of the wealth of society but appropriated the profits of others' labor. Soldiers, lawyers, and politicians were just some of their servants who defended the property of these capitalists from

---

graduated from Harvard Divinity School in 1833, Channing was strongly attracted by the organic unity of Catholicism and almost converted in 1835 (Frothingham, p. 114), an experience which he described in his short story "Ernest the Seeker," *Dial* 1 (July 1840): 48–58, and 1 (Oct. 1840): 233–42. Instead he became a minister at large in New York in 1837 and subsequently the minister of the Unitarian congregation in Cincinnati between 1839 and 1841. He called for a restoration of the original unity of the church in "Christian Denominations," *Western Messenger* 7 (May 1839): 1–8, and as editor of that periodical made it a medium for various reformers to express their views on social reconciliation. See, e.g., "Christian Economy," 7 (Aug. 1839): 221–25; "Fraternal Community," 8 (Mar. 1841): 553–60; and "New England Non-Resistance Society," 8 (Sept. 1840): 193–201. By the fall of 1842, Channing had organized an independent congregation in Brooklyn, New York, with Horace Greeley and Henry James, Sr., both of whom became Fourierists, among the parishioners. He published the *Present* on his own in New York from Sept. 1843 to Mar. 1844. Though he never formally committed himself to Fourierism during that time, he used the periodical to develop an ethical and theological framework for scientific reform. See especially his series of articles on the "Call of the Present": "Social Reorganization," 1 (Oct. 15, 1843): 37–44; "Science of Unity," 1 (Nov. 15, 1843): 72–80; and "Oneness of God and Man," 1 (Dec. 15, 1843): 145–55. He was minister to the Religious Union of Associationists in Boston from 1847 to 1850, preaching what amounted to a coherent Fourierist religion. See *The Christian Church and Social Reform: A Discourse delivered before the Religious Union of Associationists* (Boston: Wm. Crosby and H. P. Nichols, 1848). His participation in the Fourier movement apparently branded him as a radical, and with pulpits closed to him in the United States, he left America in 1854 and preached in England for most of the rest of his life. Channing's letters and other documents relating to Fourierism, collected in Frothingham, pp. 144–252, are one of the most important sources on the movement.

95. "Introductory Notice," *Harbinger* 1 (June 14, 1845): 9.

h other and from the workers they defrauded. Poverty created more
ocial "parasites"—criminals, prisoners, prostitutes—though they were
victims of exploitation before they preyed on society in turn. But the real
victims were the laboring classes, farmers and craftsmen, who had to work
doubly hard to support these various nonproducers and then lost their fair
share of the profits.[96]

Fourierism probably made sense to the Brook Farmers because New
England was still in an early stage of the industrial revolution but especially because it matched their feeling of what Charles Dana called
"terrific confusion" in the present economy. Indeed, their relative isolation since 1841 accentuated their sense of the market as an alien and
hostile mechanism. I am glad "that you find so much in your own mind to
compensate for the evils of a city environment," Ripley wrote to Hecker in
New York, "and that your aspirations are not quenched by the huge
disorders that daily surround you"; but for himself, "I hardly dare to think
that my own faith or hope would be strong enough to reconcile me to a
return to common society" and "fear I should grow blind to the visions of
loveliness and glory which the future promises to humanity."[97] Under the
influence of Fourier's comprehensive and, despite its scientific claims,
melodramatic social analysis, the Brook Farmers' sensitivity to the ills of
the system grew to a point where in 1845 Dana saw all history as "the
epoch of one degradation, the triumph of depraved and furious passions,
innocence and wisdom overborne by cunning and violence, celestial
goodness slain by infernal hate" and "Fraud and Injustice everywhere
celebrating their impudent successes."[98]

Yet to remedy this radical disorder, Fourier offered a peaceable solution that left private property intact but still promised to do justice to labor
through a redistribution of wealth. Class relations were to be adjusted
scientifically within each phalanx of 1,800 members. Like the Brook
Farmers, Fourier expected everyone to work and the profits to be held as
private property. But he clarified their informal assumption of upward
mobility by guaranteeing labor the largest share of the wealth the community produced, 5/12 of the total, with 4/12 to capital and, reflecting the
value the Enlightenment placed on thought, 3/12 to theoretical or practical knowledge. When the Brook Farmers streamlined this system in the
1845 edition of their constitution, they gave a full 2/3 to labor and only
1/3 to capital. They also corrected the hidden flaw in Fourier's system. If
the rich lived in the community as Fourier planned, they had a chance to be

96. For this analysis, see Fourier's "Non-producing Classes of Civilization," translated
by Brisbane, in *Social Destiny*, pp. 58–74, and Brisbane's summary of Fourier's historical
analysis, pp. 277–339. See also *Vision of Fourier*, ed. Beecher and Bienvenu, pp. 103–21,
189–203.

97. Sept. 18, 1843, quoted in Elliott, *Hecker*, p. 91.

98. Address to the convention of the New England Fourier Society, Jan. 15, 1845, in
Phalanx 1 (Feb. 8, 1845): 311.

paid three times—for their wealth, their labor and, in all probability, their superior education. Now, the Brook Farmers decided that as an individual's capital stock increased, he would sacrifice his share of the allotment to labor in the same proportion.[99] Their willingness to amend Fourier's plan supports their contention that whatever their faith in his system, it was still only a tool in the cause of social justice.

Nevertheless, there is no question that Fourierism helped the reformers correct the shortcomings of their original experiment—among others, the problem of labor. With conscience the sole master in work, the result had been irresponsibility on the one hand and exclusivity on the other. Fourier, in contrast, proposed to make labor "attractive" by a system with enough internal controls to make it universally applicable. He planned to gather all the members of a community into productive units he called groups and series. A group was "a mass leagued together from identity of taste for the exercise of some branch of Industry, Science, or Art," and groups engaged in related occupations, such as various mechanical trades, formed one series, until finally all the series in the phalanx added up to about fifty altogether.[100] Free choice of labor was the first advantage of the system. Having computed the number of different personality types and then the number of jobs needed to satisfy the inclinations of all, Fourier reasoned that everyone could elect his work at will and everything vital to the community would be done. The perfect coordination of the whole, moreover, promised sociability. Fourier argued that work was now "repugnant" because of the monotony of isolated labor, a critique which logically followed his "merchant capitalist" model, where innumerable petty producers were competing for survival. Matching individual tastes to specific tasks in groups and series was simply a humane adaptation of the basic principle of industrial labor, specialization. To avoid monotony, moreover, Fourier recommended that everyone change his occupation every two hours and concentrate on several skills instead of just one. But the most important source of pleasure was the human contact made possible by industrial organization. Work in small groups of individuals with similar personalities clearly removed the drudgery of solitary labor, Fourier believed, and the system of rotation guarded against any friction that might result from insularity, as well as added variety to friendships, to give work the quality of a round of morning calls.[101]

99. On Fourier, see Brisbane, *Social Destiny*, p. 354. The Brook Farmers' constitution was dated May 20, 1845, and was published in the *Phalanx* 1 (May 28, 1845): 343–48. The document was extremely complex , and the Brook Farmers explained the new arrangement outlined in article 3 on pp. 347–48.

100. Brisbane, *Social Destiny*, p. 115.

101. On groups and series, see *Social Destiny*, pp. 115–42 (Brisbane's summary), and pp. 143–56 (translated from Fourier). For the critique of isolated industry, see pp. 190–205, and *Vision of Fourier*, ed. Beecher and Bienvenu, pp. 122–49. On the human passions and how they would be satisfied by this scheme of labor organization, see *Destiny*, pp. 157–89, 206–25, and *Vision*, pp. 205–32.

The introduction of groups and series at Brook Farm resulted in a democratic system of labor. Some method of organizing workers became imperative in 1844 when the reformers advertised in Brisbane's magazine the *Phalanx* for "men and women accustomed to labor, skilful, careful, in good health, and more than all imbued with the idea of Association, and ready to consecrate themselves without reserve to its realization."[102] As new members arrived, they were organized, according to their own skills and the community's needs, into groups of shoemakers, carpenters, seamstresses, printers, and domestic workers. The initiative for a new group sometimes came from the members rather than from the directors. The women formed a "fancy group," for example, to sew capes, caps, and collars for sale in Boston. All the groups handled their internal affairs such as work schedules in a democratic and relatively autonomous manner.[103] Discipline, absent in the former system except for informal controls, was now administered by coworkers, with the directors acting as a higher court of appeal, as an incident recorded by Marianne Dwight, John Dwight's sister, suggests: "Yesterday Mr. List and Mr. Reynolds were unanimously expelled from the carpenter's [*sic*] group in consequence of their being discordant elements,—so they went to the general direction requesting to be furnished with work, and that body sent them to work on the frame of the Phalanstery—so they are working right in the midst of the [carpenters'] group, doing just what they are told to do,—a sort of solitary labor and imprisonment."[104] Organization in groups gave workers self-determination and camaraderie that they should have been reluctant to lose; but if they abused their privilege, the reformers now had a method of discipline short of excluding people from the community.

The program of industrial expansion adopted in 1844 also helped remedy Brook Farm's exclusivity by making the community more appealing to the working class. Fourier prescribed both agriculture and manufacturing for his communities, making each one, in effect, a rural city that combined the peacefulness of country life with the amenities of a varied economy. Agriculture was the single largest industry, but Fourier projected a full range of manufactures to supply the community with necessities and luxuries—carpentry, shoemaking, printing, bookbinding, and even the making of candy and musical instruments, to name just a few.[105]

102. *Phalanx* 1 (Mar. 1, 1844): 81.

103. See Clarence Gohdes, "A Brook Farm Labor Record," *American Literature* 1 (1929): 297–303, for a discussion of the system. Gohdes included a list of everyone whose name appeared between May 1844 and May 1845 in manuscript records of the kind and hours of labor done. The records are now located in Houghton and the MHS. For an idea of how the groups functioned, see several letters Marianne Dwight wrote in 1844, in *Letters from Brook Farm*, pp. 24–27, 32–33.

104. MD to Frank Dwight, Sept. 19, 1844, Dwight, *Letters*, pp. 40–41.

105. Albert Brisbane, *A Concise Exposition of the Doctrine of Association, or Plan for a Re-Organization of Society, which will secure to the Human Race, Individually and Collec-*

If, however, this combination of farming and craft production had been as far as Fourier went, his scheme would have been nearly as poor an economic alternative in an industrializing society as the Brook Farmers' small-scale commercial farming. But his grasp of the fundamental principle of industrial organization, economy of scale, helped put his followers in touch with current trends.

Fourier was obsessed with the quantity of resources wasted in a system where the family remained the basic unit of production. Women's work was the worst example. Caring for the individual family required the needless duplication of storage space, fuel, utensils, and time spent cooking, washing, and cleaning in hundreds of isolated homes. His solution was to gather everyone into associations. In the case of housekeeping, all 1,800 members would live in a single building called a "phalanstery," where apartments were grouped around a common dining room, kitchen, and laundry. Besides the savings of combining many homes into one, Fourier expected women to work more efficiently, since the existence of a pool of workers allowed division of labor. The result would be the same for agriculture and manufacturing when both were established on a community scale.[106]

From the beginning, the Brook Farmers appreciated communal living and labor as ethical alternatives to the competitive system. It is difficult to know if they came to share Fourier's enthusiasm for efficiency, but the women in the fancy group certainly combined business sense and higher objectives. "Women must become producers of marketable articles" and "earn their support independently of man," Marianne Dwight wrote to her friend Anna Parsons in Boston: "By and by, when funds accumulate (!) we may start other branches of business, so that all our proceeds must be applied to the elevation of woman forever." Within months of her prediction, Dwight was using her "passional attraction for painting" in the new business of decorating lampshades for sale in Boston and had more orders than she could handle.[107] The community in general was just as committed to industrial expansion. To attract more shoemakers for Ryckman's enterprise, as well as other skilled craftsmen, the reformers advertised their new workshop in the *Phalanx*. By the summer of 1844, with the arrival of a number of carpenters, they began to construct a phalanstery to replace

---

tively, their *Happiness and Elevation (Based on Fourier's Theory of Domestic and Industrial Association)* (New York: J. S. Redfield, 1844), p. 53. The greater emphasis on manufacturing in this 1844 work, as compared with the *Social Destiny of Man* (1840), shows how Brisbane adapted Fourierism to the American situation in the 1840s, though manufactures were part of Fourier's original plan.

106. On the "economies" of life in an association, see Brisbane, *Social Destiny*, pp. 32–92.

107. MD to AP, Aug. 30, [1844], and Feb. 27, 1845, Dwight, *Letters*: pp. 32–33, 81.

the scattered houses in which they were living. The overall results were promising. The year 1844 was the first in which Brook Farm returned a profit, though it was still a small 1,160 dollars.[108] But this initial success was due much less to the effectiveness of Fourier's industrial program than to the outside support the community drew.

ORGANIZING FOR THE MILLENNIUM

The year 1844 was the annus mirabilis for Fourierism in America. As a result, the Brook Farmers were swept up and indeed took leading roles in two popular movements, the campaign for Fourierism on a national scale and the organization of labor in New England. They threw themselves into both movements in the faith that a millennium to make "Mankind thus once more at one with themselves" was at hand.[109]

The popularity of Fourierism was as sudden as it was substantial. Brisbane had reached a wide audience through the column he published in Horace Greeley's *New York Tribune* since March 1842. As economic conditions steadily improved for the first time since 1837, people who had experienced a major depression had the means as well as the motive to act on Fourier's directions. The Sylvania Association in Pennsylvania was the first phalanx established in May 1843 and conformed almost perfectly to Fourier's plan for class cooperation. Financed by wealthy backers from Albany and New York City (probably Greeley's Whig political associates, since he was treasurer of the project), Sylvania was settled by mechanics from those cities, the one flaw being the absenteeism of the investors.[110]

108. On these projects, see the *Phalanx* 1 (Dec. 9, 1844): 305, and Swift, *Brook Farm*, pp. 43–44. See also the annual financial report submitted Oct. 21, 1844, in Frothingham, *Ripley*, p. 158.

109. "General Convention of the Friends of Association in the United States," *Phalanx* 1 (Apr. 20, 1844): 105.

110. On Sylvania, see "Spread of the Doctrine of Association and Practical Trials," *Phalanx* 1 (Oct. 5, 1843): 15–16. Brisbane initially encouraged the establishment of communities and had stated in the *Tribune* on May 3, 1842, that he hoped a practical trial could be made the following spring. But as the phalanxes began to run into problems, usually because of bad planning and lack of capital (Sylvania was located far from markets on infertile soil, for example, and was disbanded in Aug. 1844), the spokesmen for the movement in New York discouraged rash attempts that might discredit Fourier's principles and urged the gradual dissemination of his ideas as an alternative course of action. See "A Word of Caution," *Phalanx* 1 (June 1, 1844): 161–62, as the earliest statement to that effect. For Horace Greeley's own account of his role in the movement, see his *Recollections of a Busy Life* (New York: J. B. Ford, 1868), esp. pp. 144–58. Because of his presidential aspirations at the time he wrote his autobiography, Greeley (1811–72) downplayed his reform activities, and even in the 1840s, as an ambitious Whig, he privately organized support for the movement without playing a prominent public role. Many of his readers probably agreed with the correspondent who wrote to the *Tribune* on July 26, 1842, that he took the paper because he was a Whig but thought Fourierist ideas the "vagaries of disordered brains."

Subsequent communities were usually formed after a convention similar to Boston's. Even west of the Alleghenies the origins of the movement were urban, since as early as September 1843 men of "high standing, superior talents, and indefatigable energy"—very often lawyers—held meetings in Pittsburgh, Cincinnati, and Ann Arbor. But in contrast to the East, in the West farmers instead of craftsmen were the majority of subsequent recruits.[111]

Religion was as important a moving force in the West as it was at Brook Farm, despite these social differences. At the Trumbull Phalanx in Ohio, most of the members were Disciples of Christ, a group which undoubtedly saw Fourierism as the means to effect their leading principle, the reunion of Christians in one universal church; the second largest group were Universalists.[112] Methodists and Presbyterians were also represented at Trumbull, and there was a common feeling, there and throughout the West, "that the genius of CHARLES FOURIER, directed in obedience to the 'commandment of the Word,' by diligently seeking the welfare of his fellow man, was blessed with a fulfillment of the Divine promise," as the Western Fourier Association professed.[113]

The regional distribution of the communities was another indication that Fourierism drew its strength from the aspirations of American Protestantism. During the time Brisbane published the *Phalanx,* from October 1843 to May 1845, he corresponded with twenty-six Fourier communities: ten in upstate New York, four in Ohio, four in eastern Pennsylvania, two in Illinois, and one each in Iowa, Michigan, Indiana, Wisconsin, New Jersey, and Massachusetts. Thus more than half were located where the most recent revivals took place, in New York's burned-over district and in the western reserve of Ohio.[114] Along the Erie Canal, the

111. On the Pittsburgh, Cincinnati, and Ann Arbor conventions, respectively, see the *Phalanx* 1 (Nov. 4, 1843): 19–21; 1 (Apr. 1, 1844): 98; and 1 (Mar. 1, 1844): 83. In most cases, the organizers were simply described as leading citizens; but a lawyer named Thornburgh was a leader of the movement in Pittsburgh (*Phalanx,* 1 [May 18, 1844]: 148), and the president of the Clermont Phalanx in Ohio was Judge Loofbourrow (*Phalanx* 1 [June 1, 1844]: 161). For evidence that farmers populated the western communities, see the *Phalanx* 1 (Feb. 5, 1844): 70, and 1 (June 29, 1844): 194.

112. *Harbinger* 1 (July 26, 1845): 98.

113. Letter to the "General Convention of the Friends of Association in the United States," *Phalanx* 1 (Apr. 20, 1844): 103.

114. The New York state phalanxes mentioned in the *Phalanx* were: Jefferson County Industrial Association, Moorehouse Union, Western New York Industrial Association, Ontario Phalanx, Ontario Union, Sodus Bay Phalanx, Bloomfield Union Association, Clarkson Association, Port Richmond Association, and Rush Industrial Union. In Ohio: Ohio Phalanx, Trumbull Phalanx, Columbian Phalanx, and Clermont Phalanx. In Pennsylvania: Sylvania Association, Leraysville Phalanx, Peace-Union Settlement, and the Social Unity community. In Illinois: Sangamon Association and Integral Phalanx. In Iowa: Iowa Pioneer Phalanx. In Michigan: Alphadelphia Association. In Indiana: Lagrange Phalanx. In Wisconsin: Wisconsin Phalanx. In New Jersey: North American Phalanx. In Massachusetts:

social composition of the movement reflected the region's relatively urban character with respect to the West. In his pioneering study of Fourierism in the Rochester area, where five communities were established, Arthur Bestor could identify one-third of the people involved in the movement through city directories. Half of them were "middle class" (merchants, manufacturers, doctors, ministers, and so on) and half "working class" (shoemakers, carpenters, tailors, masons), while the leaders were prominent businessmen.[115]

In New England, Fourierism gained most of its support in eastern Massachusetts, and the constituency of the movement showed that this was the most industrialized section of the country. While almost no farmers participated, neither did leading merchants, manufacturers, or professionals. Economic interests and social traditions were too entrenched to make Fourier's peaceable revolution appealing to the upper class. Fourierism in New England was an alliance between reformers and workers.

Sixty-seven men and women became members of Brook Farm in 1844, more than twice the number who joined during the first two and a half years of the community's existence. A resolution was passed in February that required members to give their date and place of birth and their occupation when they signed the Constitution. In the following discussion, I have used the membership data for 1844 only. Not only does the list

---

Brook Farm. Not all of the communities originated in the states where they were eventually located. The Integral Phalanx (Ill.) was organized in Ohio and moved west in search of land, as did the Iowa Pioneer Phalanx, which was begun in Watertown, New York, for the purpose of emigrating en masse. On the Integral, see *Phalanx* 1 (Feb. 8, 1844): 320, and *Harbinger* 1 (Dec. 6, 1845): 406–07, and on the Iowa, *Phalanx* 1 (Dec. 5, 1843): notices opposite p. 31. The Sylvania Association (Pa.) and the North American Phalanx (N.J.) both drew support from Albany and New York City, and the Social Unity community (Pa.) was established by mechanics from New York City and Brooklyn. On all of these communities, see *Phalanx* 1 (Oct. 5, 1843): 15–16. Finally, the Peace-Union Settlement (Pa.) was a religious community of European origin (see n. 38). See Bestor, *Backwoods Utopias*, pp. 280–82, for a list and brief description of Fourier communities. He included five more phalanxes established in the 1840s, one in New York and four in the West, which I have not seen listed by name in either the *Phalanx* or the *Harbinger*, and three founded in the 1850s. For a discussion of the relation to Fourierism of the revivals in New York state in the 1820s and 1830s, see Whitney Cross, *The Burned-over District* (Ithaca: Cornell University Press, 1950), pp. 322–40.

115. Arthur Bestor, "American Phalanxes: A Study of Fourierist Socialism in the United States (with Special Reference to the Movement in Western New York)" (Ph.D. diss., Yale University, 1938), pp. 42–60. Bestor assumes that the people he could not identify in Rochester city directories were farmers from surrounding areas (p. 218). Many probably were; but geographic mobility may also account for the absence of the names of others of urban backgrounds. While Rochester was one of the strongholds of Fourierism, the city also produced one of the most scathing attacks on the movement by Donald C. M'Laren, *Boa Constrictor; or, Fourier Association Self-Exposed as to its Principles and Aims* (Rochester: Canfield and Warren, 1844).

end in April 1845, but enrollment dropped precipitously in the latter year, with only three new names added after January. The record of 1844 is a good indication, therefore, of the people attracted to Brook Farm as a Fourier community.[116]

The social composition of the 1844 group reversed the earlier pattern and testified to the fact that now Brook Farm was dedicated much less to moral progress than to social reform. Where ministers, teachers, and students had been the majority before, the new members, counting wives and relatives with their heads of families when they listed no occupation themselves, included seven professionals, six business people, and forty-three workers, only four of whom were farmers. Only a few of the pre–1844 group ("our old central members," Ripley called them) still remained: George and Sophia Ripley, George's sister Marianne Ripley, Charles Dana, a teacher named Amelia Russell, Minot and Maria Pratt, and Lewis and Jane Ryckman. By no means all of those who had left did so because they objected to Fourierism, as a number of historians have suggested.[117] The people attracted to Brook Farm throughout its history were in most cases unsettled in either their convictions or their vocations. Thus it is not surprising that Samuel Robbins, a Unitarian minister with Transcendentalist sympathies, signed the Articles of Association in 1842 with an intention to join, only to change his mind, or that David Mack did the same but decided almost immediately to become a member of the Northampton Association instead. Nevertheless, the fact that there were no more converts like Nathaniel Hawthorne, now living and writing in Concord, is a clear indication of the community's preeminent social commitments.

A number of the new members in fact had prior reform experience. This was especially true of those with professional or commercial backgrounds. The antislavery movement contributed the most zealous converts. It was no accident that the call to the 1843 convention predicted that Fourierism would end "Chattel Slavery": at least three antislavery advocates signed the document, one former member and two future members of Brook Farm. The logic of their conversion to Fourierism, as the call itself stated, was that this was the one reform "in which all other

116. See appendix C for the membership records. See n. 58 for a discussion of these data.

117. Late nineteenth-century writers who remembered Brook Farm as a happy refuge from the problems of an industrial society tended to resent Fourierism as an intrusion that ended the "golden age," as Lindsay Swift characterized the earlier period in *Brook Farm*, p. 115. He emphasized the number who left the community on account of the new doctrine. But this seems to have been true mainly in the case of the former students and others admitted toward the end of 1842 and may have been one reason for their prolonged absences in 1843 (see n. 70). The minutes of meetings and a comparison of those who signed the successive Articles of Association in 1841 and 1842 show that many—Sarah Stearns, Charles Whitmore, Hawthorne, Icabod Morton—left within months of their arrival simply because community life did not suit them.

reforms that we have so earnestly prayed for in past times are contained."[118] George Leach was already committed to more than one cause when he left Brook Farm in 1843 to open a hotel run according to Sylvester Graham's dietary theory in Boston, where he later harbored runaway slaves. His brother-in-law, John Allen, had quit the Universalist ministry because of his antislavery principles. He lived at Brook Farm for a time after 1844. Frederick Cabot, the third signer of the call, had been the bookkeeper of the Massachusetts Antislavery Society. He joined the community in 1844, as did John Orvis, a young man who listed his occupation as "farmer" but who had attended Oberlin, had been converted to antislavery, and had lived at the community formed by radical abolitionists at Skaneateles, New York.[119]

The idea of calling a convention to organize the Fourier movement was an example of the kind of public initiative exercised by these reformers. Leach, Allen, and Cabot were all elected to the executive committee of the New England Fourier Society (NEFS) in 1845, and Allen and Orvis traveled extensively as lecturers. But the support of people who were nearly "professional reformers" brought problems as well. The same year they led the Fourier Society, none served on Brook Farm's committee of directors, and only two were full members of what was, after all, the only Fourier association in New England.[120] Apparently they had less patience with the day-to-day work of community building than with public campaigning. Just as antislavery led to Fourierism, moreover, so Fourierism led to other reforms that limited their effectiveness in any one. In June 1846, Allen became editor of a labor paper in Lowell called the *Voice of Industry*; but he resigned in a matter of months because of his demanding schedule of Fourier lectures.[121]

The leaders of Brook Farm were caught up in the same enthusiasm for public activity. In addition to his duties as chairman of Brook Farm's board of directors, George Ripley was president of the New England Fourier Society in 1845 and on the executive committee of the national organization which had been formed in New York. Similarly, Charles Dana took an active role in the national society's attempt to establish a

118. "Call to the Friends of Social Reform in New England," *Phalanx* 1 (Dec. 5, 1843): 44. The names of those who took responsibility for the convention were listed at the end of the notice.

119. On Orvis, Allen, and Leach, see Swift, *Brook Farm*, pp. 175–84. Marianne Dwight took a romantic interest in Cabot and eventually married Orvis, and both are mentioned in her *Letters*.

120. Officers of the NEFS were listed in the *Phalanx* 1 (Feb. 8, 1845): 309. Directors of Brook Farm were recorded in the minutes for Jan. 7, 1845. For an account of the lecture tour of New England that Allen made in the summer and fall of 1843, see *Phalanx* 1 (Jan. 5, 1844): 58. John Orvis wrote to John Sullivan Dwight about his experience lecturing in Vermont on Dec. 9, 1846, quoted in Haraszti, *Idyll*, 44–45.

121. Ware, *Industrial Worker*, p. 213.

central agency for coordinating the industrial and financial programs of communities across the country and attended regional conventions as far away as Rochester to marshal support. John Sullivan Dwight, who finally joined Brook Farm in early 1844 after prolonged indecision about whether to stay in the ministry, lectured on Fourier in Boston and New York. The demand for his services highlights the fact that the education of these Harvard men made them especially valuable in reaching sophisticated urban audiences.[122]

Working-class interest in Fourier, on the other hand, arose more or less independently and was fueled by the labor press. When the Mechanics' Association of Fall River, a textile center south of Boston, began to publish the *Mechanic* in 1844, S. C. Hewitt of nearby Dighton contributed a series of articles on Fourier. The purpose of the *Mechanic* was to organize workers throughout New England after the decline of labor activity during the depression, and the Fall River mechanics were apparently pleased enough with Hewitt's ideas to hire him as a lecturer in July. Thereafter he spoke in eastern Massachusetts, Rhode Island, and Connecticut on labor organization as an immediate need but Fourierism as the ultimate goal. Independent of Hewitt, workers' associations in Boston and Lynn issued the *Laborer* and *Awl,* respectively. The interest New England workers showed in cooperative production at their convention in October, when they passed a resolution in favor of "the formation of practical associations, in which workingmen can use their own capital, work their own stock, establish their own hours, and have their own price," is suggestive evidence that these publications carried information on the Fourier movement as well. Reformers from Brook Farm and New York who attended the convention were "highly gratified with the evident tendency toward *associative* principles." They formally combined with labor the following year.[123]

Too little is known about Lewis Ryckman's election as the first president of the New England Workingmen's Association (NEWA) in March

---

122. On Dana's participation in the Rochester convention held on Oct. 17, 1844, see *Phalanx* 1 (Dec. 9, 1844): 294–95. A constitution for a national Union of Associationists with broad regulatory powers had been presented in the *Phalanx* 1 (June 1, 1844): 167–69. There was little support, however, for a plan that seemed to mean greater control by an eastern elite, and by the time the American Union of Associationists was established in May 1846, it was little more than a paper organization. On Dwight's involvement in Brook Farm, see George Willis Cooke, *John Sullivan Dwight* (Boston: Maynard, 1898), pp. 31–145. Dwight's "A Lecture on Association, in its Connection with Education" and Dana's "A Lecture on Association, in its Connection with Religion" were published together as *Association, in its Connection with Education and Religion: Two Lectures delivered before the New England Fourier Society, in Boston, February 29th and March 7th, 1844* (Boston: Benjamin H. Greene, 1844).

123. "Workingmen's Convention," *Phalanx* 1 (Dec. 9, 1844): 302, 304. Hewitt kept a journal of his tour which was published in the *Mechanic* and appears in Philip S. Foner, "Journal of an Early Labor Organizer," *Labor History* 10 (1969): 205–27.

1845 to support Norman Ware's conclusion in *The Industrial Worker* that this was an attempt to co-opt a grass-roots movement.[124] More likely the Brook Farmers' zeal to propagate Fourierism and the workers' cooperative ideas together produced the alliance. Ryckman was the perfect intermediary, in any case, because he was a workingman with reform experience. He was sufficiently prominent in the New York Fourier Society to be elected vice-president of their convention in 1842, and in 1843, when he was living at Brook Farm, he delivered the Fourth of July oration at the Sylvania Association, the Pennsylvania community composed of workers from New York like himself. In his address, he described Fourierism as the means to achieve the liberties promised by the Declaration of Independence.[125] These were more than occasional remarks for the Fourth of July. The first resolution he presented to the New England Workingmen's Association was a proposal for an "industrial congress" like the pre-Revolutionary Continental Congresses, to organize labor politically for a class revolution to be won by suffrage.[126] His emphasis on economic rights matched the principles of labor unions in the 1830s, and his advocacy of political means might even date his activism back to the workingmen's parties of the late 1820s, which, since he was born in 1796, is entirely possible.

Two things are certain, however. First, Ryckman's resolution altered Fourier's plan for social reorganization in small communities almost beyond recognition. Second, its radical tone seemed both irrelevant and frightening to workers who voted, at the same convention, for such immediate measures as a ten-hour day, labor representation in government, and free public education. The idea of an industrial congress was consistent with what Fourierism had become as a public movement; but it contradicted the feeling of moderation Fourier had managed to build into

124. "Unfortunately for the working-class movements of the forties," Ware writes, "the intellectuals were always attempting to use them to advance their own plans" (p. 178). No evidence I have seen supports this conclusion, and in fact, the events that led to Ryckman's election are rather obscure. We know only that the Brook Farmers had attended the labor convention in Oct. 1844 and that articles supporting workers appeared in the *Phalanx* with increasing frequency. Ware's conclusion is based largely on the assumption that workers' interest in cooperative ventures was peripheral to more substantive issues such as a ten-hour day and that these ideas were imposed on them by the reformers (p. 178). Edwin Rozwenc shows, however, in *Cooperatives Come to America: The History of the Protective Union Store Movement, 1845–1867* (1941; reprint ed., Philadelphia: Porcupine Press, 1975), that between 1839 and 1842 farmers and mechanics in Vermont and New Hampshire had established cooperative stores to circumvent local merchants and, more generally, that cooperation in production and consumption was a natural alternative for workers in an economy just then being converted from a handicraft to an industrial basis.

125. "Fourth of July at Sylvania," *Tribune*, July 8, 1843.

126. "The New England Convention at Lowell, Mass.," *Phalanx* 1 (May 3, 1845): 334–35. On the industrial congresses eventually held, see Ware, *Industrial Worker*, pp. 208–09, 222–26.

his vision of social revolution, a quality that had attracted not only the Brook Farmers but the working people who joined them.

In July 1845, William Young, a mechanic from Fitchburg then editing the *Voice of Industry* in that city, complained that by introducing "strong measures" like the industrial congress, the Fourier advocates were in effect asking organized labor to "cut ourselves loose from many good and honest workingmen, who are willing to go with us as fast as they can see and understand."[127] The workers who came to Brook Farm in 1844, who unlike Ryckman left no evidence of labor activity during their stay at the community, seem almost exactly the kind of people Young had in mind. Generally they were skilled craftsmen from small New England cities and towns. Thirty-one men and three single women listed the following trades when they signed the Constitution (wives gave no occupation and have not been included): eight shoemakers, five carpenters, four farmers, three printers, three seamstresses, two cabinetmakers, two mechanics, and a domestic servant, a tallow chandler, a baker, a pewterer, a bricklayer, a gardener, and a carriage maker. Twenty-one came from Massachusetts, while seven were from other New England states, two from New York, and four from Europe. Although slightly more than half of the thirty-four were from urban places, less than one-third came from major cities, eight from Boston and one from New York, and not one from growing industrial centers such as Lowell, Lynn, and Fall River.[128]

127. Quoted in the *Harbinger* 1 (July 12, 1845): 78.
128. See appendix D for a demographic classification of the working people. My division of workers into rural and urban groups is not definitive, since in most cases only the birthplace is known. In only five of the forty-three cases do the minutes of meetings list a current place of residence to supplement the information recorded on the Constitution (see appendix C). In one case, Thomas Blake, a printer from Hallowell, Maine, there was no mobility. The other four instances did indicate mobility from a smaller to a larger city: Nathaniel Colson and his wife Hannah had moved from Abington, Massachusetts, to Boston; Alex Murray from St. Johns, New Brunswick, to Boston; and William Teel from Jersey City, New Jersey, to New York City. It seems safe to assume that others not living in their birthplace in 1844 also would have moved from a smaller to a larger place. But there is indirect evidence to suggest that if they were mobile, most had not moved to large cities such as Boston, Providence, and New York, or to the industrial centers of New England such as Lowell, Lynn, and Fall River. The minutes of meetings list a current residence for thirty-five people who applied for membership in 1844, most of whom did not subsequently join. Nine applications were from Boston and two from Providence, and the remainder from smaller cities and towns. This may suggest that mobility for the working group was within a range of cities about the same size or slightly larger than their home towns. In general, I have used the following procedures for compiling the rural–urban list in appendix D: (1) I have used the U.S. Census for 1840 to determine the size of the place of birth/residence that new members recorded on the Constitution of 1844; (2) if the husband and wife listed different birthplaces, I have counted them as residing together in the larger of the two cities; (3) I have excluded the five workers born abroad (with the exception of Alex Murray, who was currently in Boston), although they were probably living in New England cities in 1844. One study useful in suggesting possible mobility patterns is Peter Knights, *The Plain People of Boston* (New York: Oxford University Press, 1971), esp. pp. 33–77, 103–18.

These facts suggest two conclusions: the Brook Farm workers had
been affected only marginally by industrialization and their contact with
the labor movement was equally minimal. None of the shoemakers, for
example, came from the center of the women's shoe industry at Lynn,
where, with the return of prosperity, manufacturers were replacing the
putting-out system with factories. The Lynn shoemakers were the first
local association to support the call for a general convention issued in the
spring by the Fall River mechanics, most of whom were textile workers in
a similar situation. Boston workingmen, the leaders of New England
workers in the past but now less pressured by factory expansion than
workers in surrounding towns, were the last major group to respond to the
call in August.[129] For all these workers, who formed the core of the New
England Workingmen's Association, any interest in Fourier remained
subordinate to the need for a regional organization to agitate for better
wages and hours. In contrast, the Brook Farm workers were still
sufficiently free from the control of large manufacturers to make their
priorities reversed. Building up the collective strength of labor evidently
made less sense to them than joining a community which promised to
protect the autonomy and working conditions they were just beginning to
lose.

For despite the forward-looking elements of Fourier's economics, his
communities largely preserved craft traditions. The plan for profit sharing
promised the dignity of private ownership. Though the arrangement required an alliance with capital, this was probably less objectionable to
workers from places where the "capitalist" was a master craftsman or
local merchant rather than a wealthy manufacturer. At least three of the
workers—a shoemaker, a gardener, and a printer—were prosperous
enough to buy shares in Brook Farm, now 100 dollars each, and for them
the community was the next best thing to self-employment.[130] Labor in

129. On changing conditions in the shoe industry, see Dawley, *Class and Community*,
pp. 62–66; Ware, *Industrial Worker*, pp. 38–48; and Hazard, *Boot and Shoe Industry*, pp.
65–96. The Lynn shoemakers, besides answering the call of the Fall River Mechanics'
Association (*Phalanx* 1 [June 29, 1844]: 190–91) in July, sent out their own agents in the
summer of 1844 to organize a convention and a strike by shoemakers, neither of which took
place, however (Ware, p. 44). The reply of the Boston workers may have been delayed by a
tailors' strike in July. But in contrast to the angry tone of the Fall River mechanics—"The
riches of the affluent in Great Britain, are no more 'corrupted' in proportion to their power
over the working classes, than the riches of the wealthy among us, in proportion to *their*
power over the laboring communities in which *we* reside"—the statement issued by Boston
workingmen on Aug. 19 was mild; part of it read: "*Resolved*, That while we contend for
rights of labor, we show no hostility to *capital;* seeking merely the peaceable possession of
the one, and determined only to resist the aggressions of the other, and conceding willingly
to ALL the rights we would claim for ourselves" (*Phalanx* 1 [Sept. 7, 1844]: 276).
130. The following names of workers appeared in the minutes of meetings of Brook
Farm's stockholders and creditors, Mar. 4, 1847, and Aug. 18, 1847, in Frothingham,
Ripley, p. 194: Nathaniel Colson, shoemaker; Peter Kleinstrup, gardener; and Jonathan
Butterfield, printer.

groups and series, finally, duplicated conditions in small workshops. Fourierism compromised the ideal of an independent artisan in the sense that the price of private ownership and self-determination was coopera- tion. But since the solitary craftsman could not compete in an industrializ- ing society, these workers apparently were willing to accept a middle ground.

Practical considerations, much more than religious idealism like that of the reformers, motivated the Brook Farm workers. Their pragmatism was evident when many, including Ryckman, left immediately after the half-finished phalanstery burned in March 1846, a serious financial blow that jeopardized the community's future. Some, moreover, seem to have scoffed at the reformers' religious enthusiasm, since Marianne Dwight noted that the people who wanted to hear William Henry Channing preach had to meet privately to avoid "ridicule."[131] But there is some evidence that religion was a factor in their support of Fourierism as well. Six workers were among those who signed a pledge in January 1846 to sponsor the services Channing conducted. These six did not conform to the usual worker profile, since they were older than the approximately thirty-year average, were from rural backgrounds, or were among the prosperous few who invested in Brook Farm.[132] Nevertheless, the younger urban workers, too, may have been influenced by religion, specifically, by the evangelical activities of the 1830s.

In a recent study of Lynn, Paul Faler argues that the Society for Industry, Frugality, and Temperance, begun in 1826 by manufacturers for the moral improvement of their employees, inadvertently contributed to the resistance workers later made to policies that threatened the dignity of their work, precisely what the society encouraged them to value.[133] While the trade unionism of the 1830s demonstrates that many workers did not need to be taught by such agencies to respect their crafts, the labor movement of the 1840s does reveal the impact of the religious awakening of the previous decade. Mutual benefit associations begun in Lynn and Boston by the same workers who supported the New England Workingmen's Association required evidence of good character and tem- perance for admission.[134] Moreover, New England workers in the 1840s

131. MD to AP, Apr. 19, 1846, and Oct. 19, 1845, Dwight, *Letters*, pp. 164–65, 122–25.

132. Notes on a meeting to form the Religious Union of Associationists, Jan. 4, 1846, Fisher Papers, MHS. The six were: John Codman, a fifty-year-old machinist from Boston; Peter Baldwin, a thirty-eight-year-old baker from Boston; Charles Salisbury, a farmer from New Hampshire; Catharine Sloan, a seamstress from rural Dunstable, Massachusetts; Nathaniel Colson, a shoemaker and investor in Brook Farm; and Henry Trask, a twenty- four-year-old carriage maker from Cambridgeport.

133. "Cultural Aspects of the Industrial Revolution: Lynn, Massachusetts, Shoemakers and Industrial Morality, 1826–1860," *Labor History* 15 (1974): 367–94.

134. On the Journeymen Cordwainers Society established in Mar. 1844, see Faler, p. 392, and on the Working Men's Protective Union in Boston, see Rozwenc, *Cooperatives*, p.

deemphasized class conflict and, thinking in more pacific, and indeed Christian, terms, viewed labor organization as a means for mutual protection. "I have always endeavored to show that the *true* interests of all parties are most intimately connected," S. C. Hewitt, who was in fact a Universalist preacher, wrote during his lecture tour in 1844, "that to separate them is to essentially injure the whole social body and produce chaos and confusion in social life."[135] The majority of working people at Brook Farm were of just such an age—nearing thirty in 1844—that the evangelical activities of the 1830s may have been a decisive influence in their lives. If so, then Fourierism proved to be a social equivalent for these religious values, enabling reformers and working people to meet, at least for a time.

There was always a distance between these two groups at Brook Farm in spite of good intentions. Marianne Dwight, for one, did her best to live according to principle when in 1846, although ill, she made a point to attend a party given by one of the carpenters who "has always looked with a jealous eye upon the aristocratic element." She was so encouraged by the spirit of the gathering that she concluded enthusiastically, "In truth, we *are a Phalanx.*" But less than a month later, as more and more left after the fire, she was ready to concede that feelings, as well as ideals, should have been consulted as guides to action: "We feel too, our brotherhood with those who have gone,—but it always seemed to me a great mistake to admit coarse people upon the place."[136] Whatever snobbery her judgment betrayed, Dwight's conclusion was part of her growing feeling that somehow, in the rush toward social perfection, Brook Farm had ignored a range of experience that it was beyond the power of economic reform to correct. The destruction of the phalanstery was a symbol, a divine judgment on their presumption. "I was calm," Dwight wrote, "felt that it was the work of Heaven and was good; and not for one instant did I feel otherwise."[137]

33. Workers involved in these associations were the same ones active in the labor movement. The Cordwainers Society in Lynn, for example, published the *Awl* (Ware, *Industrial Worker*, p. 41), and John Kaulback, a Boston tailor responsible for transforming the Boston Mutual Benefit Association into the Protective Union to support cooperatives, had participated in the Sept. 1845 convention of the NEWA (*Harbinger* 1 [Sept. 27, 1845]: 255).

135. "They call me a minister, clergyman, preacher, &c," Hewitt wrote in the *Mechanic* in May 1844, but I am also a "mechanic": "I have not yet arrived at that sickly state of mind that would make me view Labor as the exclusive birth-right of serfs and slaves" (Foner, "Journal," p. 206). Hewitt's home town of Dighton, Massachusetts, was a small place near Fall River, and he may have combined preaching with a trade, a practice once fairly common but increasingly rare with the advent of theological schools, ministers' associations, and other developments making the ministry into a profession. His claims as a mechanic, however, may also have been strictly metaphorical. On his religious affiliation, see Russell E. Miller, *The Larger Hope: The First Century of the Universalist Church in America, 1770–1870* (Boston: Unitarian Universalist Association, 1979), p. 228.

136. MD to AP, Mar. 22, 1846, and Apr. 19, 1846, Dwight, *Letters*, pp. 162, 165.

137. MD to AP, Mar. 4, 1846, Dwight, *Letters*, p. 146.

Sophia Ripley concurred when, alluding to financial difficulties that had forced the community to cut back its industrial program even before the fire, she saw "a providential guidance in our all being led back to our primitive occupations & having somewhat collected our scattered forces & brought them to bear on definite objects of real value, before we were thrown into dismay by our calamity."[138]

But the Brook Farmers did not return to their "primitive occupations" for long. By the end of 1847, the community had been disbanded and the farm sold. They had moved too quickly from spiritual to social reform to feel comfortable with the new idea. All their experience before 1844 had made them ripe for a conversion. But it was a millennium of the head, not of the heart. Deep down, they were still the children of evangelical Protestantism who could not help seeing signs of divine judgment on their presumption to redeem the world by themselves. Yet even more tragically, they had seen the logic of social reform too clearly to turn back. The failure of Brook Farm was the result of this division of head and heart. The Brook Farmers had to relinquish their "visions of loveliness and glory" because they did not know how to attain what they most desired.

138. SDR to John Sullivan Dwight, Mar. 14, [1846], Dwight Papers, BPL.

5   Men, Women, and Families

The "most rabid radical," Emerson wrote in his journal in 1841, "is a good Whig in relation to the theory of Marriage."[1] Although this was an overstatement of the Transcendentalists' case, a decided conservatism tempered reform in Transcendentalist families.

It was just as natural that the Transcendentalists tried to improve domestic relations as it was that they stopped short of major innovations in family structure. In contrast to an issue-oriented movement such as antislavery, Transcendentalism in the 1840s began as a private search for ethical social relationships, a process in which entire families were involved. Wives participated in planning and decision making. Women, both single and married, were accepted more easily as equals of men, moreover, precisely because the Transcendentalists did not engage in public agitation, in effect domesticating the movement as a whole.[2] With more formal organization, the family became a basic social resource to reformers cut off from instituted power. Thus Orestes Brownson astutely praised Brook Farm in 1842 as an extended family, broadening the range of domestic affections without disrupting church or state; but he did not estimate how much public hostility to Transcendentalism had thrown the Brook Farmers back, by necessity, on the family as the most accessible

1. Emerson, *Journals*, 8:95.
2. Although the informal character of the Transcendentalist movement was an important source of domestic reform, it should not be forgotten that the issue of women's rights split the antislavery movement in 1839, as Aileen S. Kraditor explains in *Means and Ends in American Abolitionism: Garrison and His Critics on Strategy and Tactics, 1834–1850* (New York: Random House, 1967), pp. 39–77. But the relatively conventional marriage of Angelina Grimké, whose public speaking sparked the controversy, to Theodore Weld suggests that the women's issue had little immediate effect on abolitionist families. See Gerda Lerner, *The Grimké Sisters from South Carolina* (New York: Schocken Books, 1967), pp. 228–93. In general, there have been almost no studies of the impact of reform movements on the families of participants. One good exception is Kirk Jeffrey's discussion of abolitionists Lydia Maria and David Child, "Marriage, Career, and Feminine Ideology in Nineteenth Century America: Reconstructing the Marital Experience of Lydia Maria Child, 1828–1847," *Feminist Studies* 2 (1975): 113–30.

means of immediate action.[3] Finally, the high priority the Transcendentalists set on individual freedom in response to the challenge to their
liberty in Boston translated to some extent into self-conscious feminism.
Nevertheless, all these factors together changed the family much less than
might be expected.

The same conditions which encouraged reform in Transcendentalist
families guaranteed a fundamental conservatism. As the movement unsettled their lives, the home became more precious as a source of emotional
stability. "The world of want is all before us where to choose," Abigail
Alcott wrote from Concord in 1840, but the "claims of my children keep
me from despair."[4] The special relevance of contemporary domestic ideals
to the Transcendentalists seconded this attachment to the home. Since the
late eighteenth century, the family, bound together by the love and moral
authority of the mother, had been held up as a standard of perfection to an
increasingly competitive society in the works of the ministers, women
writers, and others who built a value system on domesticity. Thus if the
Transcendentalists questioned urban society on ethical grounds, was it
not more likely that they would embrace the family than reject it? While
the social critique implicit in the cult of domesticity was commonly swal-
lowed up by its conservative promise simply to keep the family inviolate
against the effects on ongoing progress, moreover, Transcendentalist discontent was the condition that transformed such "feminine" values as
purity, charity, and love into an alternative social ethic. It was no accident
that Fruitlands, absolutely opposed to the free market system, was conceived as a "consociate family." But whether Alcott's idea also challenged
established notions of women's status and family order or simply
reaffirmed domesticity in extreme terms is a question for which there are
no easy answers.[5]

3. "Brook Farm," *Democratic Review* 11 (1842): 489.
4. AMA to SJM, Aug. 30, 1840, Alcott Family Papers, Houghton. All of Abigail's
letters quoted in this chapter are located in this collection.
5. On the eighteenth-century origins of domesticity, see Nancy F. Cott, *The Bonds of
Womanhood: "Woman's Sphere" in New England, 1780–1835* (New Haven: Yale University Press, 1977), and on the men and women who wrote popular domestic literature in the
early nineteenth century, see Ann Douglas, *The Feminization of American Culture* (New
York: Knopf, 1977), esp. pp. 17–117. Although Cott emphasizes domesticity's positive
effects—the sense of identity and kinship these ideals gave women—she notes (pp. 69–70)
that the ethic vitiated its potential as a social critique by positing a sharp division between
home and society. Surprisingly, few historians have investigated the connection between
domestic ideals and utopian communities, either to explain how reformers transformed
domestic values into a critical social philosophy or to examine the role of families in the
experiments. One exception is Lewis Perry's discussion of the free-love ideas of the Modern
Times community in the 1850s, in *Radical Abolitionism* (Ithaca: Cornell University Press,
1973), pp. 208–16. From a different perspective, Kirk Jeffrey argues that the nineteenth-
century family was like a utopian community in its separation from society and expectation
of perfection, in "The Family as a Utopian Retreat from the City: The Nineteenth Century
Contribution," in Sallie TeSelle, ed., *The Family, Communes, and Utopian Societies* (New
York: Harper and Row, 1971), pp. 21–41.

How much did the Transcendentalists admit their social revolution in economy into the private sphere of men, women, and families? Just enough, as the following examples show, to demonstrate that while deliberation and circumstance produced some significant change, the family, conventionally ordered, was a remarkably resilient institution.[6]

A TRANSCENDENTALIST MARRIAGE

Ralph Waldo Emerson and Lydia Jackson (1802–92) were married on September 14, 1835. Both were thirty-two years old. It was Lydia's first marriage and Waldo's second, his first wife, Ellen Tucker of Concord, New Hampshire, having died at nineteen (in 1831) of consumption. When Emerson told his brother William about the engagement, he noted his "very different feeling from that with which I entered my first connexion" to his "wife-child," as a friend had called Ellen: "This is a very sober joy."[7] The absence this time of mutually exchanged love sonnets and of female relatives who lived with the ailing Ellen and her husband after their marriage was probably, as much as anything, a relief. Not only was Emerson just beginning his career as a lecturer and so busy in fact that he repeatedly postponed visits to Lydia to finish his notes, but he was in the process of working out his own philosophy, since *Nature* was published in 1836. Thus it was a welcome discovery to find "a quite unexpected community of sentiment & speculation" in this well-read, thoughtful, indeed "most philosophical Lidian." In the early years of their courtship and marriage, both had occasion to express their views on the family, and while there were similarities in their thinking, the relation better fit Lidian's conjugal ideal, "diversities of gifts but the same Spirit."[8]

The "infinitude of the private man," Emerson wrote in his journal, was the true theme of all his lectures. With this idea, Emerson translated the first principle of Transcendentalist philosophy—each person's immediate access to spiritual truth—into a social ethic in defense of unim-

6. In the interest of clarity, I should note that occasionally I discuss the personal relationships of people who were not kin, and hence my title, "Men, Women, and Families." The phrase also makes the important point that the women had identities apart from their family roles. However, since my intention here is to look at the Transcendentalists' private lives, I do not focus on the achievement of the two women who made substantial public contributions, Elizabeth Peabody and Margaret Fuller, and refer the reader to chap. 2 for such a discussion.

7. RWE to William Emerson, Feb. 5, 1835, Emerson, *Letters*, 1:436. On Emerson's marriage to Ellen Tucker, see Henry Pommer, *Emerson's First Marriage* (Carbondale: Southern Illinois University Press, 1967), and Ralph L. Rusk, *The Life of Ralph Waldo Emerson* (New York: Scribner's, 1949), pp. 131–50. Both historians stress the greater happiness of Emerson's first marriage, and the romantic love ideal which shaped their judgment has also discouraged a full consideration of the second marriage.

8. LJE to EPP, July 28, 1835, Emerson Papers, Houghton. All of Lidian Emerson's letters cited in this chapter are located in this collection.

peded individual growth. The doctrine raised two questions with respect to the family: how could such freedom be reconciled with the inevitable restraints of domestic ties, and was the infinitude of woman an analogous proposal? Emerson addressed these issues in several lectures delivered in Boston in 1838.

"Home" was Emerson's subject on December 12. At first he showed an orthodox respect for the home when he said that the mind's "inward sense of stability and repose" neeeded a corresponding outward type: "To the infant—the mother, the bed, the furniture of the chamber, the walls supply this office."[9] But the tension between the individual and the family quickly came to the surface. The disruption of the home by historical change (the "brothers have scattered" and "the father, the mother have grown old, and are dead") was not a tragic loss but an opportunity for growth, since "the man meantime has transferred his affection to his cause; to his trade and profession; to his connexion in society; to his political, religious, literary parties" (p. 26). More important, this was a lesson in the transience of nature and integrity of the soul. The individual learned to "discern stability at the heart of agitation" until he saw that the world at large simply reflected the truth in himself and could say, "Where I am, there I am at home" (pp. 28, 27). The family as a social institution might not be incompatible with spiritual freedom; but Emerson's logic belittled domestic life and deflated contemporary claims that the home could redeem society by its purifying "influence." Speaking six months after his "Divinity School Address," he was treading once more on dangerous ground, since the family was second only to Christianity itself in the conservatives' canon, as criticism of Alcott's *Conversations with Children* clearly showed. But three weeks into the series, Emerson tempered his doctrine.

Either Emerson was too sentimental to take the "high ground of absolute science" on the theme of "Love" on December 26, or someone had criticized his earlier lecture, but now he was tempted "to unsay as treasonable to nature aught derogatory of the social instincts."[10] Rather than make the family a stepping-stone for individual progress, Emerson gave his audience the familiar world of masculine and feminine spheres:

> Man represents Intellect whose object is Truth, Woman Love whose object is goodness. Man loves Reality, woman order; man power, woman grace. Man goes abroad into the world and works and acquires. Woman stays at home to make the house beautiful. [P. 62]

Marriage, he naturally concluded from his premises, "unites the severed halves and joins characters which are complements to each other." It might be argued that when "love" brought women into the discussion

9. *The Early Lectures of Ralph Waldo Emerson*, ed. Robert E. Spiller, Stephen E. Whicher, and Wallace E. Williams, 3 vols. (Cambridge, Mass.: Harvard University Press, 1972), 3:26. Subsequent page citations in the text refer to this edition.

10. Ibid., 3:56. Subsequent page citations in the text refer to this edition.

almost by necessity, Emerson took a dualistic perspective on the family simply because he could not envision the individuality of a woman. Capitalizing "Truth" but not "goodness," "Reality" and not "order," supports the case. Other evidence suggests a different conclusion, however. Not only did he take issue with the idea that "marriage is nothing but housekeeping and that woman's life has no other aim," but rising above "these trite ethics of society" (though not denying their truth in their place), he described marriage as a process of mutual education: "By the strictest dependence they rear each other to independence" (p. 67). In "Love," then, Emerson managed to contain his individualism within family bonds and to share its promises with a woman.

"Love" was not Emerson's final word on marriage, and it is useful to look at his critique of Emanuel Swedenborg's *Conjugial Love,* first presented in a lecture in 1846 and included as "Swedenborg; or, The Mystic" in *Representative Men* in 1850, since much of the Emersons' "community of sentiment & speculation" depended on this eighteenth-century Swedish philospher. Emerson's interest in Swedenborg began while he was still at Harvard, and he subscribed to the *New Jerusalem Magazine* published by the tiny group of Swedenborgians in Boston who had organized a congregation of the "New Church" in 1818. Lidian told Elizabeth Peabody in 1835 that her debt to Swedenborg's teachings was second only to those of Christ. "Not that I am a Swedenborgian," she wrote at the time; but by 1839 she referred to "we of the New Church," and her son Waldo, just learning to talk, confirmed her profession when he said "that is *mama's* book . . . when the New Jerusalem Magazine had accidentally strayed to the quartette table of grandmama—to whom the said magazine is an abomination."[11] From a philosophical standpoint, Swedenborg attracted the Emersons because of his doctrine of correspondence, that the natural and spiritual worlds were exact duplicates, or "Nature is the symbol of spirit," as Emerson wrote in *Nature.*[12] *The Delights of Wisdom Pertaining to Conjugial Love* (1768) applied this idea in a way that made marriage the symbol for their reconciliation.

To Swedenborg, marriage was a process of mutual regeneration, much as it was for Emerson, though the former retained an orthodox theology, since only "with those who become spiritual from the Lord [is] conjugial

11. LJE to EPP, July 28, 1835, and Jan. 20, 1839; LJE to LB, Oct. 1838. On Emerson's early interest in Swedenborg, see Rusk, *Life,* p. 87, and Pommer, *First Marriage,* p. 35. On the Swedenborgians in Boston, see Marguerite Beck Block, *The New Church in the New World* (1932; reprint ed., New York: Octagon Books, 1968), pp. 100–11.

12. Catherine L. Albanese has pointed out the importance of the idea of correspondence (by no means derived exclusively from Swedenborg) to all the Transcendentalists in *Corresponding Motion: Transcendental Religion and the New America* (Philadelphia: Temple University Press, 1977).

love purified more and more and becomes chaste."[13] Purification through marriage continued after death, Swedenborg reported on the basis of his special revelations of life in heaven. Indeed, if the right partner had not been chosen on earth, the couple was free to separate and find their true mates (pp. 58–62). Although the importance of the spiritual function of marriage led Swedenborgian Henry James, Sr., a close friend of Emerson in the 1840s, to a radical (though in his case still equivocal) stand in favor of divorce of unhappy unions, the general tendency of *Conjugial Love* was to confirm the duty to marry as the indispensable condition of salvation, not only on earth, but for all eternity.[14] Moreover, Swedenborg's system of correspondences made marriage the symbol of the restoration of universal order. The bond of man and woman was the type of the perfect union of divine attributes, wisdom and love, and of the reconciliation of Christ with the church, the means of redemption, though in the latter case, the couple together represented the church and Christ figured as the regenerating spirit governing their relationship (pp. 73–75).

It was against this identification of marriage with the fundamental condition of the universe that Emerson rebelled. It is "a child's clinging to his toy," he protested in "Swedenborg," returning to his original view of

13. *The Delights of Wisdom pertaining to Conjugial Love after which follow the Pleasures of Insanity pertaining to Scortatory Love*, trans. Samuel Warren (New York: Swedenborg Foundation, 1943), p. 158. Subsequent page citations in the text refer to this edition. Swedenborg gave a distinctive spelling to "conjugial" love to distinguish this spiritual affection from simple conjugal love.

14. See James's contribution to a debate with Stephen Pearl Andrews, who favored unrestricted free love, and Horace Greeley, who argued on biblical grounds that divorce should be limited to cases of adultery, carried on in the *New York Tribune* from Nov. 1852 to Feb. 1853 and reprinted as *Love, Marriage, and Divorce and the Sovereignty of the Individual*, ed. Stephen Pearl Andrews (1853; reprint ed., New York: Source Books Press, 1972), esp. pp. 38–45. On James's friendship with Emerson, see Austin Warren, *The Elder Henry James* (New York: Macmillan, 1934), pp. 39–54. Although biographers of the James family generally conclude that the father discovered Swedenborg in England in 1844 (see, for example, Leon Edel, *Henry James: The Untried Years, 1843–1870* [Philadelphia: J. B. Lippincott, 1953], pp. 29–34), James must have been familiar with Swedenborg before, not only through Emerson, but because he attended religious services conducted by William Henry Channing in New York in 1843, as O. B. Frothingham noted in *Memoir of William Henry Channing* (Boston: Houghton Mifflin, 1886), p. 185. Channing was much interested in Swedenborg at the time and subsequently printed three articles on the philosopher by one-time English Unitarian minister Phillip Harwood in the *Present* 1 (Jan. 15, 1844): 252–60; 1 (Mar. 1, 1844): 329–37; and 1 (Apr. 1, 1844): 386–98. Channing's example, moreover, highlights the connection between Swedenborgianism and Fourierism, specifically, the coincidence of Swedenborg's idea of universal marriage with Fourier's of universal unity. Not only was there a certain rapprochement between Swedenborgians and Fourierists (see n. 87 below), but Henry James and Lidian Emerson were both attracted to Fourierism in the late 1840s. Thus the Emersons were not alone in their interest in Swedenborg and the marital ethic he proposed.

the home as a preliminary to individual development, "an attempt to eternize the fireside and nuptial chamber; to keep the picture-alphabet through which our first lessons are prettily conveyed."[15] Rather, the "Eden of God is bare and grand," not "the pairing of two, but the communion of all souls" in constantly changing relations: "Of progressive souls, all loves and friendships are momentary." But there was a difference between this critique of the family and that in "Home" eight years before. If there was still something "grand" about the "infinitude of private man," his life was also a little "bare." The Transcendentalist movement had offered Emerson close relationships outside the family, as we will see. But by 1846, love among them was impossible by Emerson's standard—"Do you see the same truth?"—and he was left with a social vision at once more humane and more tragic than the one with which he began.[16]

Lidian Emerson derived a more interesting idea of marriage from her reading of Swedenborg than either her husband or Swedenborg imagined—common progress through the creative tension guaranteed by individual differences. Swedenborg himself assumed the subordination of wife to husband: "The male is born into the affection of knowing, understanding, and of growing wise, and the female into the love of conjoining herself with that affection in the male" (p. 41). The woman's role was critical because her love inspired the union; but the result was the gradual obliteration of the wife's identity as she "receives into herself the image of her husband, and thence perceives, sees, and feels his affections" (pp. 179, 186). In heaven, the couple was "not two but one angel"—"man *(homo)*" (p. 62). Thus the more egalitarian ideal Lidian outlined during her engagement in a long letter to Elizabeth Peabody was not taken from *Conjugial Love* but was her own adaptation of the theory of correspondence.

If every person is the type of every other, she reasoned, "each individual should consider himself as but a part of a great whole;—as bearing a relation, more or less near—more or less complex, to every other being—and also, that each one has some peculiarity of nature which fits him for his place, and some peculiar sphere of Duty, . . . some particular use, to his neighbor and to the whole as no other being is fitted." Whereas in his lecture on the "Home" Emerson used the idea of correspondence to prove that one man equaled the whole, it is a significant commentary on the education of nineteenth-century women that Lidian's thinking ran from individuality to community, from distinctive personal traits to their possible social use. Nor is it surprising that after describing the discovery of one's "vocation" as a "great attainment," she immediately turned to

15. Emerson, *Works*, 4:128.
16. Ibid., 4:128.

the family as implicitly providing her calling as a woman: "Each family circle is perhaps, or was intended to be, a harmonious whole—each member having his own part to perform in it that the harmony may be perfect."[17]

Lidian Emerson did not dismiss domestic conventions. Past thirty when she wrote this letter and fairly well-to-do, she had spent her time outside the home in literary and charitable associations, the acceptable activities for single women of her class, and had no career ambitions.[18] But her opinions were unusual precisely because she approached the subject philosophically, thinking in abstract rather than specifically sexual terms. As a result, she stressed the individuality and social obligation of both partners and, quite unconventionally, the personal identity of women and the social duty of men. Her letter of July 28, 1835, shows that her marital ideal logically followed:

> I think that the most perfect marriage, in which, with peculiar sympathy in some departments of their nature—in intellectual tastes—for instance—there is yet as marked a contrast in other points; opposite characteristics—opposite temperaments in their beings thus united. If to these conditions those of true affection and firm principle be added—the union will be strong—happy—more than if the parties were in all respects similar.

Waldo Emerson's ambivalence about the family depended on his feeling that marriage, at best, was all sweetness and light of mutual improvement. But Lidian, undoubtedly because she was a woman who sensed her own potential, believed that there would be two personalities and hence vitality in the home. In the early years of their marriage, however, neither acted on the more interesting implications of his or her ideas.

Emerson's marriage to Lidian was part of a larger effort to bring security to his private life, a scheme in which renewing his ties to his extended family also had a role. His intentions came out in the debate during their engagement about where they would settle down. Lidian favored Plymouth, her native town and current residence; Waldo preferred Concord, where he and his mother had rented rooms in September 1834. In contrast to the medium-sized seaport of Plymouth, Concord was wilderness to Lidian ("We live several miles *on this side* the Ohio," Emerson said reassuringly); but it was just this retirement he preferred: "A sunset, a forest, a snow storm, a certain river-view, are more to me than many friends & do ordinarily divide my days with my books." To be sure, Concord encouraged expanding thoughts: "Plymouth is streets; I live in

17. LJE to EPP, July 28, 1835.
18. Rusk includes biographical information on Lidian in his *Life of Emerson*, pp. 215–21.

the wide champaign." But for a home, the proximity of the Concord
river's "childish murmuring" appealed to Emerson more than the "sea's
surly roar."[19]

Concord also meant family. Emerson's mother was there, and his
brother Charles was engaged to Elizabeth Hoar, the daughter of a local
lawyer. The couples planned to share a house before Charles died in 1836.
"I determined to live in Concord, as you know, because he was there,"
Waldo told Lidian after the funeral, but now "I feel not only unfastened
there and adrift but a sort of shame at living at all."[20] Concord still offered
a family community in the form of continuity with the past. Five generations of Emerson's kin, from Peter Buckeley in 1635 to Ezra Ripley in
1835, had been Concord ministers, and thus the research he did for his
address at the town's bicentennial celebration in 1835 was, quite literally,
family history. It is the "dear old odious haunt of the race," he wrote to his
aunt Mary in Maine, urging her to return.[21] If Emerson felt constrained by
the family, there were evidently compensatory feelings. After living as a
child in successive boardinghouses his widowed mother kept in Boston
and then boarding again with Ellen, to set up housekeeping with Lidian in
Concord clearly meant coming home.

Lidian's concession to Concord was a sign of her practical assumptions about the duties of a wife and reflected the different expectations for
the behavior of single and married women in antebellum society. After the
wedding, the relative freedom that she felt she could legitimately exercise
in charity and in her own education gave way, by voluntary sacrifice, to
dedication to the family. She considered teaching Sunday school in 1836,
but only, she reassured her husband, if the work did not conflict with her
tasks at home, and she concluded with this really tragic vow: "I seek only
to improve my character—in doing which intellect will of course make
some progress—but I shall never again as I formerly did make mental
cultivation of a chief aim. God help me to have no aim in the future but to
do his will in seeking the happiness of others—forgetting my own."[22] Not
surprisingly, the balance of self and society she derived from Swedenborg
was replaced by a view that might have been copied from *Conjugial Love*.

19. RWE to LJE, Feb. 13, 1835, Feb. 1, 1835, and Mar. c. 4, 1835, Emerson, *Letters*,
1:437, 435, 440.

20. RWE to LJE, May 12, 1836, Emerson, *Letters*, 2:20. On the plan to live with
Charles and Elizabeth, see Rusk, *Life*, p. 230.

21. RWE to Mary Moody Emerson, Dec. 22, 1839, Emerson, *Letters*, 2:243. Emerson's
relatives who served as ministers in Concord were Peter Buckeley, from 1635 to 1639;
Edward Buckeley, 1659 to 1696; Daniel Bliss, 1739 to 1764; William Emerson, 1766 to
1776; and Ezra Ripley, 1778 to 1841. For sketches of these men, see Rusk, *Life*, pp. 43–48.

22. LJE to RWE, [Apr. 1836]. Cott discusses the difficult transition from the relative
freedom of girlhood (or spinsterhood) to marriage, in *Womanhood*, pp. 74–84.

Emerson's "love and the hope of being conformed to his Holiness are more to me," she told her sister Lucy, "than my great earthly blessings."[23]

Transcendentalism in some ways reinforced Lidian's domesticity. Emerson had a reputation as a renegade after he resigned from the Second Church in 1832, which translated, in the nineteenth-century mind, into suspicions of his fitness as a husband. Thus Lidian was delighted and relieved to find evidence to the contrary. "Little did they know Waldo Emerson who believed he could be content to pass through life without domestic happiness," she wrote to Lucy a week after the wedding, and for reassurance she went out of her way to include him in the domestic routine by instructing him "to stop at the grocers in his morning expedition, and ask him to send home some eggs & ginger;—and to inquire the price of molasses & rinsing tubs."[24] As late as 1841, when she was a mother of two, Lidian was grateful that "whatever high doctrine you may have announced concerning the other relations of life" you "never boasted of uncommon philosophy respecting the children."[25] Thus the social discontent and intellectual dissent of Transcendentalism made Lidian value the family's immunity from change all the more.

The movement did affect the Emersons, however, most practically by increasing the number of their guests and in consequence Lidian's duties as a hostess. She was incredulous at first that the "transcendentals"—"these wonderful beings"—actually ate at all, finding it "*so strange*" to be "turning out coffee for them and helping them to pie!"[26] But they dined well (only Alcott was a vegetarian in the 1830s): at one meal she served ham, tongue, mutton, and beef. She acquiesced cheerfully to the new developments. "O no," she wrote, answering the question she posed herself in a letter to Lucy on whether she minded this sociability. "When I turn my attention from high discourse to Martha-like care of wine and custards—I am happy knowing how much blessed satisfaction others are receiving, though I must give up a part of my portion of it."[27]

But Transcendentalism also helped free Lidian from a strictly domestic role by providing a circle of friends and activities outside the family. Emerson encouraged her involvement. Even during their engagement he quarreled with Lidian's self-abnegating posture, when he asked her not to call him "Mr. E" or to address her letters to "Rev.": "Have I not told you, dear Lidian, that I meet with much more reverence than I know what to do with?"[28] Thus it was consistent for him to press her to explain her

23. LJE to LB, Sept. 22, 1835.
24. LJE to LB, Sept. 22, 1835; Sept. 30, 1835.
25. LJE to RWE, July 15, [1841].
26. LJE to LB, Sept. 30, 1835.
27. LJE to LB, Oct. 6, 1837.
28. RWE to LJE, Mar. c. 4, 1835, Emerson, *Letters*, 1:441.

Swedenborgian views—"the sentiments which make my individuality" she called them when she recounted the incident to Elizabeth Peabody—to Peabody's friend Horace Mann in 1837. "You know it is the tendency of opposition to drive one to extreme statement," she wrote referring to Mann's religious skepticism: "I made the *extremest* to Mr. Mann of my views of God's agency in human affairs. And Mr. Emerson was quite wicked in drawing it out of me—and exposing all I kept back—I did not know before *how* charitably disposed he was to his wife's fancies."[29]

Her embarrassed reluctance to engage in friendly contention disappeared as such conversations became more frequent. When Alcott and Lane held a meeting in Concord in 1843, Emerson was in New York, and Lidian attended alone. Only she and Edmund Hosmer, a local farmer, spoke for "the common sense side" against the reformers. "Mr. Alcott was descanting on the iniquity of formal exchange—'brother should be free to take whatever he wanted of brother whenever he could find it' & I answered 'that might be, when & if there were but two people in the world,' " to which Lane replied, " 'there are but two people in the world the me and the not me.' " Not easily silenced, Lidian next put her knowledge of housework to critical use. How could Alcott expect a "life of ease," she wondered, if he planned to build chairs with linen seats, concluding "with a sigh that I would rather be excused from washing those linen covers preferring to dust common painted chairs."[30]

Lidian's interest in reform was not limited to good-natured debunking, however, a stance which after all worked in defense of the conventional home. In 1848 she wrote to her husband, then lecturing in Europe, that she had been converted to Fourierism by the women Associationists in Boston:

> It seems to me that this cause of Humanity-in-general as undertaken by the Associationists, is the one cause to which we need not fear giving too large a share of our attention or aid; and besides that the cause is so good the spirit in which it is considered seems to me, as far as I have seen its manifestations to be the true "spirit of love and of a sound mind" for which we have looked in vain in the advocates of other good causes—and which must of course be a spirit of "power."[31]

"I shall feel bound to do all to promote the success of this blessed movement," she added with a final qualification, "that my husband will sanction." Fourierism was not mentioned again in the Emersons' correspondence. Nor is there any indication that Lidian participated with any regularity in the Women's Associative Union established in 1847.

29. LJE to EPP, Dec. 4, 1837.
30. LJE to RWE, Jan. 10, 1843.
31. LJE to RWE, June 4–13, 1848.

Emerson's lack of sympathy for Fourierism probably decided the issue.[32] The broader social and intellectual contacts encouraged by Transcendentalism had introduced such individual differences into her marriage as Lidian once thought would stimulate mutual progress. But traditional attitudes of deference still blocked substantial change.

The movement affected Emerson even more peripherally in his role as a husband than it did Lidian as a wife. Without a regular profession, he was at home more than most men and took an interest in such domestic events as the birth of his daughter Ellen in 1837.[33] But he reserved the right to insulate himself from the family for the sake of his work and spent the mornings in his study undisturbed. Nor was domestic responsibility shared equally on account of his being at home. When he was left in charge of the household during Lidian's visits to Plymouth, he pleaded their helplessness without her—"nobody could do anything . . . until Asia returned to her seats"—and reiterated how much they missed her —"Waldo begins to be more pathetical & energetical in 'Der Mamma' & looks at doors, & greets me with unusual goodwill as if I could carry him to Mamma but failing he cares not for me"—which, however genuine the feeling, consigned the family to the woman's care and made her duty-bound to come home.[34]

The promise of marriage as mutual education also went unrealized. Their intellectual kinship based on Swedenborg proved superficial. Lidian, following Swedenborg, took "correspondence" to mean that nature and spirit were analogous but separate. Man depended for redemption on the supernatural intervention of Christ. But Emerson dismissed Swedenborg's attachment to the mechanism of Christianity as parochial "Hebraism": the individual saved himself by immediate insight. The result for their marriage was a truce eased by humor. Emerson reported to Plymouth that "your sinful household" skipped church in one letter, and in another, that the "conservatism" four-year-old Waldo demonstrated when he wanted the milk that he had just spilled was "hereditary on one side."[35]

---

32. Emerson objected to the "mechanical" social determinism of Fourier's plan for social reorganization: "This only [,] that Fourier has skipped no fact but one, namely, Life. He treats man as a fine Thing [,] something that may be put up & down, polished, moulded, roasted, made into solid or fluid or gas at the will of the owner or perhaps as a vegetable from which though now a poor crab, a very good peach can by manure & exposure be in time produced; but skips the faculty of Life which laughs at Circumstance & can make or supplant a thousand phalanxes & New Harmonys with one pulsation" (*Journals*, 8: 209).

33. LJE to EPP, Mar. 20, 1837.

34. RWE to LJE, Feb. 17, 1838, Emerson, *Letters*, 2:112.

35. RWE to LJE, June 14, 1841, and Nov. 10, 1840, Emerson, *Letters*, 2: 404, 358. Although Lidian made no complete statement of her theological opinions (her 1835 letter to Elizabeth Peabody was concerned mainly with ethics), she revealed the relative conservatism of her views when she wrote to Peabody on Jan. 20, 1839: "I must believe that Sin will finally

Thus the Emersons' marriage was one of affection but not of minds, and the "community of souls" who could answer yes to the question "Do you see the same truth?" was, as Emerson said in "Swedenborg," at once broader and more unstable than the family. Emerson's community ideal grew in part from his relationship with Margaret Fuller and her women friends. Thus he owed a debt, intellectual as well as personal, to the special bonds of friendship formed by antebellum women.

FEMININE FRIENDSHIPS

Margaret Fuller insisted that friendship required both intimacy and growth, much as the Emersons conceptualized their marriage. "Without full confidence no friendship can subsist," she wrote in the *Dial* in 1842, nor "without mutual stimulus, without infinite promise, a stern demand of excellence from either side, and revelations of thoughts, not only hoarded from the past, but constantly new-born from intercourse between two natures."[36] The occasion of her remarks was the publication in Germany of two sets of correspondence, one between Goethe and a young woman named Bettina Brentano and the other of Bettina and her friend Caroline Gunderode, and Fuller went on to judge whether the relationship of a man and a woman or of two women better met her ideal.[37] The bond between Goethe and Bettina was "too unequal," she concluded, more like "Idol and Idolator" than friends. But between the women, there was "great genius and beauty on both sides" (pp. 314, 320). Just so, Nancy Cott has argued in *The Bonds of Womanhood* that women's friendships were a source of mutual respect and open communication, blocked between the sexes by their unequal status in nineteenth-century society.[38]

---

work out a greater good than could have existed without its commission. My understanding fails to show me how things can be so—yet my Reason when I will listen steadfastly affirms—All must be for the Best—or that which we call God is a phantasm." I have seen no evidence to support Rusk's conclusion (*Life*, pp. 225–26) that Lidian became more orthodox in reaction to her husband's increasing religious radicalism. In fact, her interest in Fourierism suggests that from the point of view of applied ethics, she was bolder than he.

36. "Bettine [*sic*] Brentano and her Friend Gunderode," *Dial* 2 (Jan. 1842): 349–50. Subsequent page citations in the text refer to this article.

37. The first English translation of Bettina's letters to Goethe appeared as *Goethe's Correspondence with a Child* (London: Longman, Orme, Brown, Green, and Longmans, 1837–39). Fuller began the first translation of the correspondence of the two women in the present article, and it was completed by a Mrs. Wesselhoeft as *Correspondence of Fraulein Gunderode and Bettine [sic] von Arnim* (Boston: T. O. H. P. Burnham, 1861).

38. See Cott's chapter on "Sisterhood," *Womanhood*, pp. 169–96 and esp. pp. 187–91. See also Carroll Smith-Rosenberg's excellent "The Female World of Love and Ritual: Relations between Women in Nineteenth-Century America," in Michael Gordon, ed., *The American Family in Social-Historical Perspective*, 2d ed. (New York: St. Martin's Press, 1978), pp. 334–58.

But what neither Cott nor Fuller has measured is the extent to which these friendships changed in the context of social reform.

Lidian Emerson's friendship with her sister Lucy Brown was affected very little by Transcendentalism and may serve as a point of contrast to the more complex relationships of Elizabeth Peabody and Margaret Fuller. Her marriage changed her intimacy with her sister only with respect to the distance between them, and even that change was accommodated reluctantly, since Lucy's return to Plymouth following her separation from her husband was an important reason for Lidian's desire to settle in the town. A comparison of Lidian's letters to her husband and sister explains why the marriage did not disrupt the friendship. Although she sent "family" news to both, writing on children, servants, and friends and reserving more philosophical subjects for occasional letters to Elizabeth Peabody, there was a certain restrained formality in her correspondence with Emerson. She ended an account of a talk with Margaret Fuller in 1843, for example, with this well-chosen and depersonalized thought: "Every body [sic] who loves my husband likes to meet my husband's wife—and it is dear to me to be recognized as belonging, in any sense, to him."[39] But her feelings were an integral part of her narrative of events to Lucy. Skipping from Emerson's homely metaphors in his Phi Beta Kappa oration in 1837 to his domestic inclinations, she reflected that it is "beautiful to me however to witness the childlike, (not *childish*) as well as philosophic interest, he takes in his garden, & all the corners of our small household."[40]

Thus Lidian's habitual deference imposed a distance between the Emersons, and the friendship with Lucy better answered her idea of marriage, as well as her very human need, for a spontaneous reciprocal relation. Over the years, Lidian's disappointment in marriage made Lucy's confidence and affection more important. With "the thin critical man removed so far away," Emerson wrote from Baltimore in 1843, do not give in to the "somber Spirit that loves you so well": "The Good Spirit is always nearest do not harken to that Sad brother." And when visits to Plymouth, "where all should be so fresh, & wonted, & affectionate," did not help, Emerson contributed over a thousand dollars to build Lucy a house in Concord.[41]

Cott has proposed, as a corollary of the foregoing thesis, that the bonds women formed in self-defense laid a basis for the sex consciousness and solidarity needed for feminist action. It is significant, therefore, that Lidian seems to have depended on Lucy's support in the reform activity she pursued independent of her husband in the late 1840s. "I planned to

39. LJE to RWE, Jan. 30, 1843.
40. LJE to LB, Oct. 6, 1837.
41. RWE to LJE, Jan. 18, 1843, and Sept. 18, 1846, Emerson, *Letters*, 3:118, 349. On Lucy's house, see Rusk, *Life*, p. 308.

come to Boston today that I might attend the Fourier festival," she wrote,
"but my courage to do this has failed—not having heard from you that I
had best make the effort."[42] She admired what the women in the Fourier
movement accomplished together when they "consecrated their time,
talents, strength, indeed their whole being—of what they with calm enthusiasm believe to be the regeneration of the human race."[43] But for the
most part, Lidian's friendship with Lucy remained a refuge from a social
dilemma she did not wholly understand and did little to change.

There was more friction between Elizabeth and Mary Peabody than
ever appeared in the Jackson sisters' relations because of the Peabodys'
changing social roles. Though domestic writers insisted on the sanctity of
the home, the same emphasis on women's spiritual mission encouraged
participation in the voluntary associations which flourished with evangelical religion. For unmarried women especially, the result was an active
public life. In a single letter to Mary, written in spare moments between
December 25, 1834, and January 4, 1835, Elizabeth reported that she had
attended a Sunday school teachers' meeting at R. C. Waterston's chapel
for the poor, had visited Dr. Channing, had dined with Mr. Taylor and
talked about a charity school, had read the *Faerie Queene* to Alcott's class,
and had worked on plans for the sisters to gather a school of their own.[44] It
is little wonder that she apologized in the first entry on Wednesday that
she couldn't remember anything before the previous Thursday.

The reform context affected the sisters most practically by turning
their friendship into a business partnership. Both earned their living as
teachers, and with education and regeneration virtually synonymous in
the Liberal mind, the Peabodys recognized an opportunity. But the effort to start a school brought out Elizabeth's tendency to boss her sister.
You keep school at home in Salem, she advised as an expedient in 1834,
while I work for Alcott, "for as to living in Salem *I will not* if I *can live in*

42. LJE to LB, [Apr. 1850]. No list of members of the Women's Associative Union has
survived, but Lucy Brown may have been one, since she sent her son to the Brook Farm
school as early as 1841 (see LJE to LB, Sept. 19, 1841). Cott points out the connection
between woman's sphere and women's rights in *Womanhood*, pp. 201–06. Smith-
Rosenberg discusses the importance of such "intermediate" organizations as the New York
Female Reform Society for the reformation of prostitutes and abolition of the double
standard. These groups, in which women's "rights" were a secondary or even a covert
objective, are seen by Smith-Rosenberg as a means of expression for emerging feminine
self-consciousness (see "Beauty, the Beast, and the Militant Woman: A Case Study of Sex
Roles and Social Stress in Jacksonian America," *American Quarterly* 23 [1971]: 562–84).
The Women's Associative Union belongs in this category, as I explain below.
    43. LJE to RWE, June 4–13, 1848.
    44. EPP to MP, [Dec. 25, 1834]–Jan. 4 [1835], Berg, NYPL. All of Elizabeth's letters to
Mary cited in this chapter are located in this collection. On women's participation in
religious reform associations, see Cott, *Womanhood*, pp. 126–59, and Carroll Smith-
Rosenberg, *Religion and the Rise of the American City, 1812–1870* (Ithaca: Cornell Uni-
versity Press, 1971), esp. pp. 97–124.

Boston." The pattern of domination typical of male–female relations appeared, it seemed, when the friendship was exposed to market pressures, and Elizabeth worried continually that she "tyrannized" over Mary. Indeed, "it is the chief delight of my life to think of you," she wrote to Salem, exactly as Emerson had written from Baltimore, "unfolding your faculties and applying your talents—unshadowed by the queen of *Mal-aprespos.*"[45]

Mary contested Elizabeth's authority, however, as she would not have if her sister had in fact been a man. Elizabeth's idea of education as the formation of character had led her to the "fearful experiment" of giving her pupils truthful estimates of their failings, telling some they were "unfeminine and indelicate—some that they acted without principle —some that they were vain—some that they were wickedly passionate." Mary used the same method to correct Elizabeth's self-assertion.[46] When Elizabeth told Mary that she planned to keep a journal, Mary advised her rather "not to think of myself for three years" and to cultivate instead "forgetfulness of one's self in some active duty."[47] It was clear as Elizabeth continued her reply that more was at stake than Mary's injured pride or even her desire to restore equality to the friendship. She answered as if Mary questioned her right to a personal life independent of the family, precisely what reform activities offered women: "My own peculiar intellectual life has been *sacrificed—consciously sacrificed* my whole life . . . & at *thirty two years of age* & [*about?*] *commencing a life of study*—I hardly can see what can be your imagination of the possibility of such a thing—& still less—what advantage you think can be gathered?" Mary's concern, though differently phrased, came to much the same issue, that Elizabeth was becoming unfeminine.

Mary's doubts were confirmed when Elizabeth ignored the customary reserve toward men and brought Horace Mann into the sisterhood on equal terms. All three were living in a Boston boardinghouse for the sake of their work when they met in 1833 (Mann was a member of the Massachusetts legislature), a situation unusual enough for single women for Elizabeth to have to defend "our freedom in New England," which "as Miss Sedgwick says in her letter to me 'occasionally exposes a young lady to calumny'—but it is 'the expression and best safeguard of purity of manners.' "[48] The recent death of Mann's wife had precipitated a crisis of faith, and he turned to the Peabody sisters for consolation.

It was as natural for the erudite Elizabeth to respond with theological instruction on Sunday evenings, to revive "those higher views of the *destiny* of man . . . which only the supernatural part of Christianity can

45. EPP to MP, [Sept. 14–19, 1834]; Jan. 5–[7, 1835]; [week of Apr. 11?, 1836].
46. Elizabeth described her experiment to her sister Sophia, Aug. 23, 1825, Berg, NYPL.
47. EPP to MP, [week of May 16, 1836].
48. EPP to MP, Mar. 15–[17, 1835].

give him," as it was, in light of the personal nature of his difficulty, for her
to invite an intimacy usually reserved for other women. *"The first time* he
laid his head upon my bosom & begged my pardon for taking such liberty
with his grief—I told him *I needed a friend to my shattered mind &
nerves,*" she wrote to Mary in 1835, referring to her various professional
problems and gossip about her friendship with William Ellery Channing,
"& would he be sincere with me always—& let me tell him all my
troubles—and never flatter me—and never keep back a truth which an
elder brother would tell me."[49] The relationship brought Elizabeth's own
worries about her femininity to the surface. Was I "ever betrayed into an
overbearing—intrusive—masculine manner" by my "earnestness" or
"enthusiasm," she asked Mann on one occasion, and on another she
felt compelled to insist to Mary that her *"torrent-feelings . . .* are
feminine—they are *sentiments*—not *passions*—& they are *pure."*[50] But it
was Mary, writing from Cuba, where she had accompanied their younger
sister Sophia for the sake of her health, who pointed out that neither
Elizabeth's intellectual nor her emotional intensity was as improper as her
willingness to reveal herself so openly to a man. The licenses of feminine
friendships were one thing; relations between the sexes were governed by
other rules.[51]

Elizabeth took religious ground in her defense, and her argument
showed how the awakening in Boston, which helped create the conditions
for freer interaction between men and women, might also provide a
rationale. Artificial barriers between the sexes might be necessary in
Cuba, Elizabeth wrote, since "the conventions of french society & the
moral philosophy of Rochfoucauld" taught that there was no higher
principle in the soul than unstable human passions. But the "moral atmosphere Platonism & Christianity breathes around me" gives assurance
"that *infinite spirits* may deal with each other without *managements*—&
in the spirit of a love which is greater than even the Faith that moves
mountains."[52] "From all that I have suffered—& may yet have to suffer
for the precept of 'communicate,' " she concluded, "the more I feel *it is
true.*"

But the prospect of free and equal friendships between women and
men was frustated, in the end, as much by Elizabeth's more conventional

49. EPP to MP, [late May–early June?, 1836]; Jan. 16–21, [1835].
50. EPP to MP, Jan 5–[7, 1835]; Jan 16–21, [1835].
51. Louise Tharp suggests that the sisters' rivalry for Mann's affection was the cause of
tension between them, in *The Peabody Sisters of Salem* (Boston: Little, Brown, 1950), esp.
pp. 60–86. This may have been one factor, but the interpretation tends to impose
twentieth-century categories on the triangular friendship and thus obscures the importance
of the bond between the women and the way Mann's appearance disrupted it. For a good
discussion of the need to evaluate these friendships in terms of their historical context rather
than our own, see Smith-Rosenberg, "Female World," pp. 334–39.
52. EPP to MP, Mar. 15–[17, 1835].

feelings as by those of Mary and Horace Mann. Mann assured Elizabeth that her force of personality was not unfeminine, but he still admired Mary's "humility & sweetness—and self-sacrifice," a preference in which Elizabeth concurred: "*We agreed* that *you* were a rare specimen of perfection for the world—& that I was very much improved!"[53] Thus it is not surprising that the triangular friendship Elizabeth envisioned when she said, "It is the supreme delight of my heart when one of us has a friend that the other may have the same," ended in the marriage of Mary Peabody and Horace Mann in 1843.[54]

Margaret Fuller's friendships were more intricate than either Lidian's or Elizabeth's, since none of the friends was natural kin and because the emotion invested was so great that at times she was prostrated by "the nights of talk and days of agitation, the tides of feeling which have poured upon and from my soul," taking to her bed after visits that were "too much for my strength of body or mind."[55] Yet the intellectual results duly compensated for this expenditure of feeling. Fuller's ties with Caroline Sturgis, Waldo Emerson, Anna Barker, and Samuel Ward shaped her argument in *Woman in the Nineteenth Century* in 1844, the only major feminist statement produced by the Transcendentalist movement.

The friendship of Caroline Sturgis gave Margaret a sense of self-importance otherwise denied by a combination of social attitudes and practical circumstances. The death of her father in 1835 left her, as the oldest child, responsible for the support of the family and demanded the sacrifice of her intellectual ambitions to family duty. "Three precious years at the best period of my life, I gave all my best hours to you children," she later told one brother. To another she wrote, "from my birth [I] longed to rise, but I felt crushed to earth."[56] Thus leaving Boston to teach in Providence in 1837 had all the qualities of a forced exile, and it was then that Caroline's loyalty became critical.

Behind the "disinterested and uncommon kindness" Margaret professed for her eighteen-year-old friend was the need to be valued at her true worth. "I feel as if I might be of use to you *now*, more use than any other person," she wrote from Providence, urging Caroline to come board with her and study under her direction. The test of Caroline's esteem was her willingness to share Margaret's sacrifice: "In coming to me you know what you give up: your old friends, your old resources, and perhaps, what I mourn so much for myself, a new course of lectures from Mr.

53. EPP to MP, Jan. 5–[7, 1835]; Jan. 16–21, [1835].
54. EPP to MP, Jan. 16–21, [1835].
55. MF to CS, Oct. 7, 1839, Tappan Papers, Houghton. All the letters between Fuller and Sturgis cited below are located in this collection.
56. MF to Arthur Fuller, Dec. 31, 1837, and MF to Richard Fuller, Aug. 11, 1842, in *The Writings of Margaret Fuller*, ed. Mason Wade (New York: Viking Press, 1941), pp. 550, 561.

Emerson."[57] So, too, would she have to renounce the comforts of her
social position as the daughter of one of Boston's wealthiest merchants.
"Yesterday I had a beautiful day," Caroline typically wrote from the
family's summer home in Newburyport. "The sunlight and showers had
little love quarrels all the morning, & I alternated from my elm-tree
window to the mill-door by the riverside, from Italian to painting."[58]
Margaret suffered by the contrast in their lots. She felt "so homeless, so
forlorn" teaching in the ninety-nine-degree heat of the Providence summer
of 1838, while Caroline vacationed at the shore in New Bedford.[59] But
Fuller's ability to command the friendship of this rich young woman
contested, emotionally and symbolically, the circumstances that seemed
to conspire against her own achievement.

Definite rules set by Margaret governed the relationship and put her in
control. Unrestrained confidence was the first. When she came away from
one visit feeling "estranged," she warned it is "doubtful to me whether we
can continue *intimate; friends* we shall always be, I hope, after all we have
known of one another." Elevated conduct was the second condition.
Hitherto you have always been "right," was Margaret's reproval after a
party, but "it is beneath you to amuse yourself with active satire" and "to
laugh at such people as you did." I, she added with ominous implications
for the friendship, was "repelled." Exclusivity was the final stipulation.
Margaret responded to a hint of Caroline's disloyalty in a way that
confirmed her own importance and aimed to regain straying affections:
"If Fate has in store for my Caroline a friend of soul and mind like mine of
more equal age and fortunes, as true and noble, more beautiful and pure, I
should accept what I have known of her as an equivalent for the little one
situated like me can give."[60]

Transcendentalism initially threatened this friendship, when talk of
Transcendentalist radicalism made William Sturgis forbid his daughter to
live with Margaret in Providence in 1837. Margaret reacted with "strong

57. MF to CS, Nov. 2, 1837; Oct. 14, 1837.

58. CS to MF, Sept. 5, 1841. For biographical information on Caroline Sturgis, see
George Willis Cooke, *An Historical and Biographical Introduction to Accompany the Dial*,
2 vols. (1902; reprint ed., New York: Russell and Russell, 1961), 2:56–61, and *Notable
American Woman, 1607–1950*, ed. Edward T. James, Janet Wilson James, and Paul S.
Boyer, 3 vols. (Cambridge, Mass.: Harvard University Press, 1971), 2:214–15 (under Ellen
Hooper, Caroline's sister).

59. MF to CS, July 1838.

60. MF to CS, [1839]; Jan. 27, 1839; [July 11, 1839]. Smith-Rosenberg notes that
conflict was minimized in "woman's sphere" because of the empathetic function of the
relationships ("Female World," p. 342). But if Fuller's case is at all typical, it seems that
precisely because the friendships were so highly charged in emotional terms, in lieu of wider
sources of self-fulfillment, they were extremely volatile and susceptible to numerous va-
rieties of stress. One feels after reading Fuller's letters to her friends that she virtually made a
career of nurturing these very fragile relations.

indignation." If "transcendentalism" means "that I have an active mind frequently busy with large topics I hope it is so. If it is meant that I am honored by the friendships of such men as Mr Emerson, Mr Ripley, and Mr Alcott, I hope it is so. *But* if it is meant that I cherish any opinions which interfere with domestic duties, cheerful courage and judgement in the practical affairs of life, I challenge any or all in the little world which knows me to prove such deficiency from any acts of mine since I came to woman's estate."[61] Transcendentalism and feminism were not synonymous at the time, as Caroline's father feared; but the freedom of the movement did allow Fuller to build up an unusual nexus of relationships which included men as well as women.

Margaret cultivated Emerson's friendship in the late 1830s much as she did Caroline's. He recognized that he had been drawn into a social circle unique in his experience. "Have I been always a hermit, and unable to approach my fellow men, & do the Social Divinities suddenly offer me a *roomfull* of friends," he wrote to Elizabeth Hoar in 1840. "So consider me now quite friendsick & lovesick, a writer of letters & sonnets."[62] As his emphasis on quantity suggests, Fuller brought her various friends into mutual relation, and Emerson's studied tone of adolescent giddiness was as appropriate to the ages of the participants as to the nature of their intercourse. Caroline Sturgis was then twenty-one. Samuel Ward was the twenty-three-year-old son of a Boston banker, nicknamed "Raphael" for his interest in art. Anna Barker, affectionately known as "Récamier" after the virginal friend of Mme. de Stael, was a well-to-do Southern woman also in her early twenties. Not surprisingly, Emerson began one letter to Caroline "dear sister" but ended "dear child." To his mind, moreover, the friendships were valuable for their childlike simplicity and honesty, pursued "without lagging for the dull convoy" of convention or "bending to please or to explain."[63] But he came closest to the truth when he told Margaret that he had been "raised out of the society of mere mortals by being chosen the friend of the holiest nun & began instantly to dream of pure confidences & 'prayers of preserved maids in bodies delicate.' " Emerson had been invited into woman's sphere.[64]

61. MF to CS, Nov. 16, 1837.
62. RWE to Elizabeth Hoar, Sept. 12, 1840, Emerson, *Letters*, 2:330.
63. RWE to CS, c. Aug. 20, 1840?, Emerson, *Letters*, 2:326.
64. RWE to MF, Aug. 29, 1840, Emerson, *Letters*, 2:327. On Ward, see Cooke, *Introduction*, 2:36–39, and Emerson's letters to Ward, published as *Letters from Ralph Waldo Emerson to a Friend, 1838–1853*, ed. Charles Eliot Norton (1899; reprint ed., Port Washington, N.Y.: Kennikat Press, 1971). Anna Barker was a relative of Fuller's friend Eliza Farrar, the wife of Harvard astronomy professor John Farrar and an author in her own right. See Thomas Wentworth Higginson, *Margaret Fuller Ossoli* (Boston: Houghton Mifflin, 1884), pp. 35–36. One recent attempt to explain this circle of friends, which suffers from the author's emphasis on the heterosexual relationship of Fuller and Emerson without taking the dynamics of the entire group into account, is Carl F. Strauch, "Hatred's Swift Repulsions: Emerson, Margaret Fuller, and Others," *Studies in Romanticism* 7 (1968): 65–103.

The friendships were not a "castle in the air" to Fuller as they were to Emerson, however, but an essential part of her effort to establish herself in the movement, as if, as a woman, she needed to carry her house with her to feel sure of her power. The structure of the relationships in her mind, suggested in a letter to Caroline, was indicative of the sense of order and control they gave: "I thought of all women but you two as my pupils, my playthings or my acquaintances. You two alone I would have held by the hand. And with Mr. E for the representative of religious inspiration and one other of Earth's beauty I thought my circle would be as complete as friendship could make it."[65] The men, flanking the women Margaret admitted as equals, seemed little more than interlopers included only because they served a useful function. They were subject to the same rules laid down earlier for Caroline moreover. Emerson had been "taxed" by Margaret on the count of intimacy, he told Caroline, for "a certain inhospitality of soul inasmuch as you were both willing to be my friends in the full & sacred sense & I remained apart critical, & after many interviews still a stranger."[66]

But when a crisis brought this delicately balanced structure tumbling down in August 1840, the reason was not the reserve which betrayed Emerson's inability to grasp the emotional demands of feminine friendship but the lapse of Anna Barker and Samuel Ward into conventionality by engaging to marry. It is a fascinating commentary on Victorian marriage that everyone assumed the conjugal bond would prevent the free interaction of either husband or wife with the group. "Farewell, my brother, my sister," Emerson wrote in a strange celebration of marriage, "I can only assure myself of your sympathy late late in the evening when we shall meet again far far from Here." And to Margaret he sent condolences for the loss of her friends, which challenged, as he knew, the social control on which her identity depended:

> But ah! my friend, *you* must be generous beyond even the strain of heroism to bear your part in this scene & resign without a sigh two Friends;—you whose heart unceasingly demands all, & is sea that hates an ebb. I know there will be an ardent will & endeavor on their parts to prevent if it were possible & in all ways to relieve & conceal this bereavement but I doubt they must deal with too keen a seer and a heart too thoroughly alive in its affections to cover up the whole fact with roses & myrrh.[67]

65. MF to CS, Oct. 7, 1839.
66. RWE to MF, Aug. 16?, 1840, Emerson, *Letters*, 2:325.
67. RWE to Anna Barker and Samuel Ward, Sept. 1840, Emerson, *Letters*, 2:339; RWE to MF, Aug. 29, 1840, 2:33. One can only speculate that Emerson did not feel that his own marriage interfered with the friendships because he was considerably older and his marriage was relatively free of romantic conventions. He did continue to write to Ward (see n. 64), and Elizabeth Peabody corresponded with Anna as well as her husband after their marriage

Yet it was only when Fuller felt deserted and alone that she escaped these social dependencies. The events of the summer precipitated a conversion experience, unorthodox but still essentially religious in nature, which confirmed her individuality. It was as if "from the very blackness of the yawning gulf" rose "a star, pale, tearful, still it shone," she told Caroline on October 22. She exulted in her new freedom and used the incarnation of Christ as a symbol for the promise it offered:

> I cannot plunge into myself enough. I cannot dedicate myself sufficiently. The life that flows in upon me from so many quarters is too beautiful to be checked . . . It all ought to be; if caused by any apparition of the Divine in me I would bless myself like the holy Mother. But like her I long to be virgin. I would fly from the land of my birth, I would hide myself in night and poverty. . . . The gifts I must receive, yet for my child, not me. I have no words, wait till he is of age, then hear *him*.

Fuller expected her friends to acknowledge her independence. "I am now so at home, I know not how again to wander & grope, seeking my place in another soul," she wrote to Emerson. "I need to be recognized."[68] Emerson warned that one must relinquish such praise of friends and instead "be divorced & childless & houseless & friendless a churl & a fool if he would accompany with the Cherubim"; but he also sensed that she had finally appropriated his doctrine of the "infinitude of the private man" and that he, in consequence, would lose the essentially sociable woman he knew: "I thought you a great court lady with a Louis Quatorze taste for diamonds & splendor, and I find you with a 'Bible in your hand,' faithful to the new ideas, beholding undaunted their tendency, & making ready your friend 'to die a beggar.' "[69]

Caroline Sturgis accepted the change in her friend without reservations, and "I would fain bless you," Margaret replied, "for your recognition."[70] But Sturgis never really understood Margaret's experience. She criticized *Woman in the Nineteenth Century* in 1845 for concentrating on "such outward things" as the social condition, education, and

---

(she became acquainted with Ward in 1840 when she needed practical advice on running her bookstore, which the other Transcendentalist men could not give). There is some evidence from the correspondence that Anna was one of a number of Transcendentalists who converted to Catholicism (see n. 113). In an undated letter on kindergarten education, probably in the early 1850s, Peabody told Anna "that you can work for this cause with all your heart" because Cardinal Wiseman and other prominent Catholics approve it. Peabody's letters to the Wards are located in Houghton Library.

68. MF to RWE, Sept. 29, 1840, cited in Emerson, *Letters*, 2:341.
69. RWE to MF, c. Oct. 2, 1840? and Sept. 25, 1840, Emerson, *Letters*, 2:342, 337.
70. MF to CS, Oct. 22, 1840.

rights of women, instead of the more introspective thoughts and feelings they had exchanged in their letters.[71] But this was precisely what Fuller's conversion meant: she took her place in society both as a person and as a woman and turned her attention increasingly from private to public issues.

Fuller commented at the end of *Woman in the Nineteenth Century* that to become more of a soul did not make one any less a woman. The scope of the book, ranging, as Caroline said, over the work, education, and social position of women, was proof that she did not dismiss women's interests along with the defensive intricacies of feminine friendships but rather was able to set women's difficulties in historical perspective and to identify a solution. There must be one law for souls, she wrote, the "law of liberty."[72] Quarreling not only with the advocates of domesticity but also with the deeply rooted "prejudices and passions" which frustrated this goal, Fuller argued that men as well as women, "twin exponents of a divine thought," suffered from the bonds of womanhood that kept humanity as a whole from its destiny.

Margaret Fuller's contribution to Transcendentalism and to feminism was her balanced respect for a woman's individual identity, essentially above her sex, and her awareness that together women shared a problem rooted in the structure of society. If she finally understood the Transcendentalist idea of individual inspiration, her experience in the subculture women created gave her a sense of kinship with other women and of their dilemma as a class. Fuller's writings on religion, slavery, Fourierism, and health reform as well as women, when she worked as the literary critic of the *New York Tribune* from 1845 to 1847, were far different from the mood pieces and literary commentary she wrote for the *Dial* and demonstrated the practical potential of her views.[73] But as the foregoing discussion has shown, the transition from sisterhood to feminism was extremely difficult, even in the context of a reform movement, and in Fuller's case alone was there significant progress.

71. MF to CS, Mar. 13, 1845.
72. *Woman in the Nineteenth Century, and Kindred Papers relating to the Sphere, Condition, and Duties of Woman*, ed. Arthur B. Fuller (1874; reprint ed., New York: Greenwood Press, 1968), p. 38. See also my discussion of the religious dimension of her crisis and her book, in chap. 2.
73. Compare, for example, "The Magnolia of Lake Pontchartrain," *Dial* 1 (Jan. 1840): 299–305, and "Leila," *Dial* 1 (Apr. 1841): 462–67, with "Our City Charities," *Tribune*, Mar. 19, 1845; "Swedenborgianism," June 25, 1845; "The Water Cure," June 27, 1845; and "Prison Discipline," Feb. 25, 1846; or the following *Tribune* articles on women, collected in *Woman and Kindred Papers:* "The Wrongs of American Women; The Duties of American Women," pp. 217–27; "Woman in Poverty," pp. 315–19; "The Irish Character," pp. 321–35. For a complete bibliography of Fuller's articles, see *Writings*, ed. Wade, pp. 595–600.

WOMEN, FAMILIES, AND
COMMUNITARIAN REFORM

Sophia Ripley (1803–61) was a regular participant in Margaret Fuller's conversations. In January 1841, four months before Brook Farm began, she published an article on "Woman" in the *Dial* that reflected the direction of the discussions as well as her hopes for women in the community. "In our present state of society woman possesses not; she is under possession," Ripley wrote.[74] Nor was this merely an economic or legal condition, but also a spiritual dependence, since she "is educated with the tacit understanding that she is only half a being, and an appendage" and takes her "opinions, perhaps prejudices" first from her parents, then from her husband, "instead of moulding herself to her own ideal" (p. 364). To be free, Sophia like Fuller concluded, a woman must realize that her "individuality should be as precious to her as his love" (p. 365). In light of such outspoken feminism, Sophia's development at Brook Farm raises an important question. She professed her faith in Catholicism in 1846 and dedicated her work that year, she told her cousin Charlotte, to "our blessed mother."[75] After her conversion in New York in 1847, her letters to Charlotte were concerned almost exclusively with her relationships with the "Fathers" and "Sisters" of the church, who directed her in a way she thought "inexpressibly sweet," as if "I were a servant or a little child."[76] To say that the disappointing failure of Brook Farm caused her movement from feminism to Catholicism might be possible were it not for the fact that the anarchism of Bronson Alcott's Fruitlands coexisted, in even more unresolved tension, with the idea that the community was a "consociate family." There was a double impulse behind both social experiments, toward freedom on the one hand and community on the other, which equally tested the strength of Transcendentalist families.

In the years before the conversion to Fourierism at Brook Farm, the importance of the nuclear family declined, while the equality of the sexes

74. "Woman," *Dial* 1 (Jan. 1841): 363. Subsequent page citations in the text refer to this article.

75. SDR to CD, Sept. 12, 1846, Dana Papers, MHS. All of Sophia's letters to Charlotte cited below are located in this collection.

76. SDR to CD, [June 28, 1851]. Sophia signed one letter to Charlotte "your loving cousin & sister" (July 18, 1848), and their friendship was an important element in Sophia's sense of belonging to the larger Catholic "family" (Charlotte seems to have converted before Sophia and may have helped bring her into the church). Since the reactions of her Protestant kin to her conversion ranged from virtual disinheritance by her father to emotional estrangement from her husband, the intensity of Sophia's relationship with her cousin is not surprising. "I never expect to see him any more," she told Charlotte after her father refused repeatedly to see her (Oct. 18, [1852]), and on her relationship with George, she wrote, "we have been so long separated" (Oct. 26, [1852]).

was enhanced. Husbands and wives were recognized as autonomous members in an economy organized to guarantee individual freedom, and thus women became stockholders in the community. Sophia's investment of 1,000 dollars made her one of four women among the original ten associates, an arrangement clearly in advance of contemporary society, where married women had no legal existence apart from their husbands until 1848, when New York passed the first law establishing their right to control the property they brought into the marriage. Women also gained suffrage. Voting and officeholding privileges extended to all stockholders, and thus Ripley was a director of education every year for which a record exists, from 1841 to 1846. But social custom did set tacit limits on equality. No woman ever served on the Committee of General Direction, and in money matters, only men were elected directors of finance to supervise outside loans, while a majority of women took charge of the retrenchment program in 1843 to restrict consumption of meat, butter, coffee, and tea as directors of domestic economy.[77]

Indeed, if we look at the social reality behind the community's formal organization, the continuing disabilities of women are clear. For Sophia Ripley, the hardships of farm life brought out a self-sacrificing strain approaching willful martyrdom in what Emerson called her "somewhat hard nature," qualifying her gain in outward status by an intensification of traits she knew were imposed on women by their socialization. Thus almost every reminiscence of Brook Farm contains an account of Sophia's heroism as "a truly Christian woman": how she missed only two classes in six years despite the illnesses which afflicted everyone who lived in the drafty houses on the farm, how she faithfully nursed the sick, how she worked eight to ten hours a day in the laundry.[78]

The social structure of the community compounded the demand for selflessness. The disproportionate number of men at Brook Farm throughout its history (sixty of the ninety-nine people who became members between 1841 and 1845), as well as the boarders who did no work and the children in the school, all contributed to the women's domestic chores. "There are so many, and so few women to do the work that we have to be nearly all the time about it," Marianne Dwight wrote to her

77. For the investments of the original associates, see Octavius Brooks Frothingham, *George Ripley* (Boston: Houghton Mifflin, 1882), p. 115. Officers for 1842 (elected Sept. 29, 1841) are listed in Frothingham, p. 115, and the names of those elected for subsequent years were recorded in the minutes of meetings for Dec. 31, 1842, Jan. 11, 1844, and Jan. 7, 1845, MHS. On the legal status of women during this period, see Eleanor Flexner, *Century of Struggle: The Woman's Rights Movement in the United States*, rev. ed. (Cambridge, Mass.: Harvard University Press, 1975), pp. 62–102 and esp. pp. 62–65.

78. These examples are mentioned in [Amelia Russell], "Home Life in the Brook Farm Association," *Atlantic Monthly* 42 (1878): 463, and Lindsay Swift, *Brook Farm* (New York: Macmillan, 1900), p. 141. Emerson commented on Sophia's character in June 1843 in his *Journals*, 8:428.

friend Anna Parsons, hoping sympathizers like Anna would come and share the labor to give the women the "leisure" they deserved, "or rather, we should like" to have.[79] But although Parsons became the secretary of the Women's Associative Union in Boston in 1847, her parents questioned the propriety of a single woman living in the community, a fact which helps explain why, of the sixty-one unmarried members of Brook Farm, forty-one were men and only twenty women.[80]

This high proportion of unmarried people was one reason Brook Farm seemed like an extended family, where affections uninhibited by conjugal bonds might be more widely shared. Although the care of family bore most heavily on Sophia Ripley as cofounder with her husband, she also gained a certain authority through her maternal role. Precisely because the Brook Farmers initially minimized government to make "each master & mistress of their own actions," as Emerson noted, the importance of informal power increased: "At Brook-Farm again, I understand that the authority of G[eorge]. & S[ophia]. R[ipley]. is unconsciously felt by all: and this is the ground of regret to individuals, who see that this patriarchal power is thrown into the conservative scale."[81]

Kinship ties among both leaders and followers in fact lent considerable stability to a community composed in theory of "happy hapless Sansculottes." Although only nineteen couples joined between 1841 and 1845, fifty-four of the ninety-nine members belonged to some kinship group. The Ripley family was most extensive. George and his sister Marianne Ripley, Sophia and her cousin Charles Dana and her niece Sarah Stearns, accounted for half of the ten original members, and Dana's sister Anne came in 1844. Their combined investment of 6,500 dollars of the initial 12,000 dollars and their control, through plural officeholding, of six of the twelve directors' positions until 1843 indicate that their "patriarchal power" was substantial. Nor did it disappear with growing membership, since George, Sophia, and Charles Dana all occupied one or more offices every year of the community's history. There were extended families among the working people, too, however. Three Hosmer brothers, all

79. MD to AP, Apr. 14, 1844, in *Letters from Brook Farm, 1844–1847*, ed. Amy L. Reed (Poughkeepsie, N.Y.: Vassar College, 1928), p. 8.

80. See appendix E for a table on kinship at Brook Farm. Where the marital status of members is not designated in the descriptive literature on the community (see chap. 4, n. 58), I have used the following criteria available in the membership lists appended to the two editions of the Articles of Association (Sept. 29, 1841, and Feb. 17, 1842) and the Constitution (Feb. 11, 1844): (1) same surname, (2) proximate ages, (3) proximate birthplaces, (4) proximate dates of arrival at Brook Farm. These documents are located in the Massachusetts Historical Society. In two cases, those of George Leach and Mary Dwight, members were married, but the spouse was not a member and may not have lived in the community. I have counted both as single.

81. May 7, 1843, Emerson, *Journals*, 8:393.

shoemakers in their early twenties, and the wives of two joined in 1844, and James Clapp, a bricklayer, brought a younger sister, who worked as a seamstress, along with his wife.

While this pattern shows the continuing importance of kinship in New England for economic and practical support, it is also true that the idea of a perfect society was never far removed from the hope of reuniting families scattered by geographic mobility. "Come and live with me," Bronson Alcott wrote to his brother in New York in a way perhaps indicative of the feelings of the Brook Farmers as well, "and let us become more and more one in purpose, thought and deed—brothers in life, and workers together in the great Reforms of our Day."[82] Similarly, Brook Farm attracted families broken by death or separation who apparently viewed the community as a means of reconstructing the home. Icabod Morton came from Plymouth with his daughter, Amelia Russell was the guardian of her niece Anna Foord, John Allen was a widower with a son, and Almira Barlow, separated from her ex-minister husband, boarded at Brook Farm with her sons.[83]

There was a distinct hostility between the middle-class nuclear family and community life. The fact that Emerson had decided to reform his family "without pulling down my house," as he told his brother after he turned down Ripley's invitation to join Brook Farm, shows how economic self-sufficiency combined with the sense of well-being gained by the presence of both parents to argue against social experimentation. That thirteen of the nineteen couples at Brook Farm belonged to the working class proves, conversely, the importance of economic instability as a motive for reform.[84] But there was an ideological dimension to the prob-

82. ABA to Junius Alcott, Sept. 28, 1841, Alcott, *Letters*, p. 57. For suggestive evidence on the continuing importance of kin for economic support in urban industrial society, see Michael Anderson, "Family, Household, and the Industrial Revolution," in Gordon, *American Family*, pp. 38–51, and Thomas Dublin, "Women, Work, and the Family: Female Operatives in the Lowell Mills, 1830–1860," *Feminist Studies* 3 (1975): esp. 35–38. Interestingly, Peter Dobkin Hall demonstrates that kinship became less important from an economic point of view to the Boston elite as alternative means of capitalization such as banks, corporations, and insurance companies developed (in "Marital Selection and Business in Massachusetts Merchant Families, 1700–1900," in *American Family*, pp. 101–14). Thus both the reformers at Brook Farm who were critical of the economic status quo and the working people who joined them were, in contrast to other segments of contemporary society, more dependent on precapitalist economic institutions such as the family. From a practical point of view, moreover, the community offered a way to reorganize the family for mutual support in a time when geographic mobility was diminishing its effectiveness. On mobility, see Peter Knights, *The Plain People of Boston* (New York: Oxford University Press, 1971), esp. pp. 48–77.

83. Swift, *Brook Farm*, pp. 120, 127–28, 181–84.

84. I have counted all manual trades in the working group, so that the occupations of the husbands are as follows: four shoemakers (Ryckman, Colson, Castalia Hosmer, Granville Hosmer), two carpenters (Cheswell, Patterson), two farmers (Allen, Brown), one tallow chandler (Holland), one mechanic (Codman), one bricklayer (Clapp), one gardener (Klein-

lem, too. "Objections are often made to Association on the ground that the family sphere will be destroyed, that the individuality of persons and of families will be merged in a common mass," Swedenborgian Otis Clapp told the members of the New Church in Boston when they contemplated a community in 1843.[85] Clapp dismissed this scruple with the observation that harmonious surroundings would increase family affections. But respect for the ideal Victorian family apparently kept many such couples away from Brook Farm and gave the community an unusual social composition—a large number of unattached adults, who were often part of extended families—which encouraged everyone to behave toward one another as kin.

Family feeling took time to develop, however, because the community was an artificial construction. For Sophia Ripley, moving to Brook Farm meant leaving Boston, where she had always lived, to "be ready to dwell no where [sic], to encamp any where [sic], & give to our work that devoted, loyal love, which we have hitherto given to our localities, friends, & environments." Principle rather than affection united the Brook Farmers. "This oneness of purpose, including of course much kind consideration & tolerance is the closest tie which can bind us to the majority of men," she wrote to Margaret Fuller.[86] But by the time Fuller visited in late 1841 or 1842, Brook Farm felt more like a home. She felt "desolate" the day she arrived, seeming "to belong to nobody—to have a right to speak to

---

strup), and one printer (Pratt). The occupations of the other couples are: two ministers (Ripley, Robbins), one manufacturer (Palisse), one grocer (Hastings), and two unknown (Mack, Smith). For biographical data on these people, see appendix C. For Emerson's rationale, see RWE to William Emerson, Dec. 21, 1840, Letters, 2:371.

85. The address was reprinted as "The Family Sphere," Harbinger 1 (July 12, 1845): 70. As I suggested above (n. 14), there was significant interest in Fourierism among Swedenborgians because of the similar emphasis on universal harmony and because of the millennialism of the Swedenborgians, who gathered themselves into "New Churches" on the assumption that the Second Coming of Christ had occurred already in 1757 (see Block, New Church, p. 36). Although the Boston Swedenborgians did not establish a community, two phalanxes were founded by members of the New Church, the Leraysville Phalanx in Pennsylvania and the Canton Phalanx in Illinois (Block, pp. 153–54). Several writers pointed out the similarities in the two systems, moreover, in an effort to bring the groups closer together. See Parke Godwin, A Popular View of the Doctrines of Charles Fourier, 2d ed. (New York: J. S. Redfield, 1844), pp. 106–09, and Charles Hemple, The True Organization of the New Church as indicated in the Writings of Emanuel Swedenborg and demonstrated by Charles Fourier (New York: William Radde, 1848), esp. pp. 2–30. Often, however, Swedenborgians complained that Fourierists sacrificed spiritual progress to social reorganization, and Fourierists criticized Swedenborgians as "quietists and exclusivists" who gave insufficient weight to reform activity. For a good exchange on the subject by two men who were more than commonly sympathetic to the opposite system, see Henry James's letter and Charles Dana's reply, in "The Social and Religious Movements," Harbinger 2 (May 23, 1846): 378–81.

86. SDR to MF, probably fall 1841, Fuller Papers, Houghton.

nobody," in part because "the freedom of the place" sent everyone his or her separate way, as she concluded, but also because she was the guest in a family whose habits she did not understand and, when she did, did not approve. "The people showed a good deal of *sans-culotte* tendency in their manners," she observed after the conversation she led, "throwing themselves on the floor, yawning, and going out when they had heard enough."[87] Relaxed standards of dress were another sign of domestic comfort. The men wore tunics instead of coats during the day and the women bloomers under their skirts, though everyone dressed conventionally for dinner.[88]

More seriously, the prevailing informality, as well as the close living quarters, encouraged greater intimacy between unmarried men and women than was commonly acceptable, and Sophia Ripley repeatedly voiced her disapproval of the "prodigality of life" of "the children of the Tunic" in letters to Emerson. Emerson was sufficiently disturbed to seek out Brook Farmer George Partridge Bradford to clear up "some of the mists which gossip had made," but accepted Bradford's rationale that "plain dealing was the best defense of manners & morals between the sexes" and concluded himself, "I suppose that the danger arises whenever bodily familiarity grows up without a spiritual intimacy."[89] At least one couple was all but forced to leave because of their behavior, however.[90] But the marriages that resulted were even more disruptive of the larger family sphere.

In 1846, Charles Dana and Eunice Macdaniel were secretly married during a trip to New York. They threw a wedding party when they returned, but "about a dozen of our best people preferred to stay away" for reasons that became clear when Marianne Dwight told her friend Anna why she did attend: "Others of us felt and thought, that altho' the privacy of the wedding and other circumstances were unpleasant, or perhaps worse than that, this public announcement was, at least, a right step; it was best to go, and in kindness and justice make it as agreeable as we could."[91] The affair violated the expectation of "plain dealing" with everyone that had grown up in the community and was especially ironic in light of Dana's critique of the selfishness of the nuclear family in the *Harbinger* the year before. "The incoherence and antagonism which civilization establishes between individuals, it establishes between families in a higher and worse degree," he had written, because the "truer the man's love for his wife and children, the more it urges him into deadly

87. Undated journal, quoted in *Memoirs of Fuller,* 2:73–74.
88. Swift, *Brook Farm,* pp. 64–65.
89. May 7, 1843, Emerson, *Journals,* 8:391–92. He mentioned Ripley's letters in a letter to Margaret Fuller, Aug. 7, 1843, *Letters,* 3:196.
90. See my discussion of Abigail Morton and Manuel Diaz in chap. 4.
91. MD to AP, Mar. 22, 1846, Dwight, *Letters,* p. 159.

competition with his brethren."[92] Yet here was Dana acting like a "civilize" in an association, less from unregeneracy, it seemed, than to protect the privacy of love and marriage from intrusion by his adopted family. Fourierism, from which Dana borrowed his analysis, brought more serious contradictions than this, however.

An elaborately stated feminism and critique of the nuclear family were corollaries of Fourier's economic theory. But women gained no new ground at Brook Farm after 1844, and the community functioned increasingly less as an extended family as it grew in size and social complexity. Because the Brook Farmers adopted Fourierism to institute a millennium of universal unity and love, this lack of progress, if not regress toward conventional domesticity, is all the more dramatic.

Fourier argued that the key to social harmony was the economic liberation of women. Brisbane summarized Fourier's view of the destructive effect of restricting women to the single career of marriage in *The Social Destiny of Man*: "*Pecuniary dependency* poisons all social relations, and causes to a greater or less extent the renouncement of liberty, of that liberty which is most cherished,—*the Liberty of the heart with its sympathies and affections.*"[93] Independence through work was the obvious solution, and this socioeconomic emphasis led one Fourier advocate, Francis Shaw, to a wide view of women's rights, "not only freedom to speak in public, to vote, or to do many other things which are of trifling importance," but "social freedom also."[94]

But with "Liberty of the heart" the highest priority, in striking contrast to Sophia Ripley's insistence in 1841 on freedom of thought, Fourier did not question the sentimental stereotype of women but simply guaranteed their moral "influence" a broader field of action than the isolated home. Although Brisbane observed that women would be more inclined to work when industrial conditions were "enticing," the general tendency of Fourier's reasoning made it clear that the voluntary system of labor depended on the presence of women to make it "attractive." And in the moral sphere, Francis Shaw reached a conclusion indistinguishable from the rhetoric of domesticity: "We look, indeed, to woman for the regeneration of humanity, and to her social condition as the gauge of the progress which the race has made."[95] Nor, Brisbane added on the conservative side, should women be allowed to exercise their rights immediately, for fear

92. "The Isolated Family," *Harbinger* 1 (Sept. 27, 1845): 253. Dana may have been especially concerned about the family because he was one of the Brook Farmers interested in Swedenborg. He regularly attended the Swedenborgian church when he later lived in New York (Block, *New Church*, p. 158).
93. *The Social Destiny of Man; or, Association and Reorganization of Industry* (Philadelphia: C. F. Stollmeyer, 1840), p. 299.
94. "The Women of the Boston Anti-slavery Fair," *Harbinger* 1 (Sept. 27, 1845): 269.
95. Ibid., p. 269.

they would be contaminated with the "selfishness and duplicity" of civilization. Instead, industry must be "ennobled and refined,—*it must be elevated to woman*" so "she can then enter it with honor and advantage to herself."[96] Much less than the liberation of women, Fourierism promised the feminization of culture.

Freeing women's affections by the destruction of the family as an economic unit was the "pivot," then, in the movement from a society based on authority, subordination, and force to one ordered by "passional" attraction. "The passions tend from their nature," Brisbane wrote, "to social unity, concord, and the development of all the sympathies" and perfection required only the substitution of false institutions, which cramped and perverted the feelings, with the true one of association.[97] Thus it is hardly surprising that Fourier questioned the value of marital constancy and fidelity, along with the economics of the relationship, or that the Brook Farmers, practical reformers in Victorian society rather than theoreticians of the Enlightenment, rejected his conclusions.

Parke Godwin, a leading advocate of Fourierism in New York, broached the "delicate" subject of "manners and customs" in *A Popular View of the Doctrines of Charles Fourier* in 1844. Since Fourier viewed "the passion of Love as good, useful, and innocent in itself," Godwin wrote, he saw no reason to forbid divorce in a community where there was no question of abandoning dependent women and children.[98] Furthermore, not everyone was temperamentally suited for marriage, and thus young men and women would choose among the various "Corporations of Love" after puberty, some entering the corporation of "Constancy" to be sure, but others preferring a group like the "Bacchantes" (pp. 88–89). Godwin's defense against possible charges of licentiousness was the standard one adopted by the movement: American Associationists united in their support of Fourier's "positive doctrines" on labor organization, but "the mere conjectural opinions of their Master" were left to individual discretion (p. 84).

There was public criticism, however, and the Brook Farmers stated their position in response to a review of *The Wandering Jew,* a novel by Eugène Sue, one of Fourier's French followers, in the *Democratic Review* in 1845. Excerpts from the book quoted by John Dwight in the *Harbinger* in November explain the objections raised by the *Democratic Review* the following month. A "love like ours is so noble, grand, and divine, that it may well dispense with a divine consecration," the heroine told her prospective lover; indeed, "I will never take a vow to observe a law made by man *against* woman with contemptuous and brutal selfishness; . . . and as a *human creature,* enchains and enslaves her forever at the good will

96. Brisbane, *Social Destiny,* p. 300.
97. Ibid., p. 3.
98. *Popular View,* p. 86. Subsequent page citations in the text refer to this edition.

and pleasure of another human creature, her fellow and her equal before God."[99] Sue clearly embellished Fourier's ideas by making the licenses granted in an association into an antinomian doctrine with respect to existing law. Dwight was more intent on pointing out, however, that the book was "sensuous, not *sensual*," but in the process he revealed how much he was bound by the sensibilities of his culture when he admitted that it verged on "voluptuousness"—"a little too much perhaps for good taste" (p. 382).

The writer in the *Democratic Review* was obviously familiar with more of the works of Fourierism than *The Wandering Jew* and asked, quite reasonably, how "Honorable Divorce" and "promiscuous concubinage" could be reconciled with the biblical law that marriage was indissoluble except in cases of adultery.[100] Thus Ripley's overreaction is the most significant feature of his reply. For "barefaced and atrocious misrepresentation of the Associative movement in this country," this article is "without parallel among the productions of a partizan and bigoted press," he wrote, "an excitement of blind and infuriated passion" such as "would disgrace the most vulgar writer who could be hired to serve the cause of a vindictive personal controversy."[101] Although his vehemence was due in part to his understanding that any hint of radicalism on sex and marriage would discredit the movement, it also betrayed his uneasiness with the fact that there was an element of truth to the charge that Fourierists harbored heterodox opinions. It was impossible for Ripley to hide his admiration for what he took to be Sue's belief that marriage was "a union of two souls in the sight of God" and anything less "is not entitled to the sacred name of marriage, and though sanctioned by human law is an abomination before God" (p. 61). Nor could he help casting a hopeful glance with Fourier to a future "reign of harmony, purity, and truthfulness" when the affections "will develop more beautiful fruits, in freedom of action, than are now produced under legal restraints" (pp. 61–62).

But even now there were definite limits to his ideas. Ripley questioned neither the exclusivity of marriage nor the constancy of the relation, dismissing only the need for legal sanction. He was careful, too, to substitute "affections of the soul" for Fourier's "passions." Perhaps he sensed how easy it would be for John Humphrey Noyes and the Oneida community to conclude, after 1847, that the "amative part of the sexual relation, separate from the propagative, is eminently favorable to life" and to

99. "Eugène Sue—No. II," *Harbinger* 1 (Nov. 22, 1845): 382. Subsequent page citations in the text refer to this article. See also "Eugène Sue—No. I," *Harbinger* 1 (Nov. 15, 1845): 364–66.

100. "The Wandering Jew," *Democratic Review* 17 (1845): 418.

101. "The Democratic Review and Association," *Harbinger* 2 (Jan. 3, 1845): 60. Subsequent page citations in the text refer to this article.

institute "complex marriage" so that "all believers might be one, even as he [Christ] and the Father are one" in the bonds of love.[102] Ripley, in contrast, restricted his concept of universal love to the spiritual meaning intended by the Christian tradition and, with respect to Fourier, concluded that his speculations on marriage "are independent of his views concerning a reform in the relations of commerce and industry; and in no respect, do we hold ourselves responsible for their character" (p. 61).

In fact, the Brook Farmers' activities to promote Fourier's economics affected women and families more decisively than any theory. The prevailing assumption in antebellum society that women did not participate as equals in reform organizations made Brisbane's warning that their purity might be injured by social exposure superfluous. No woman from the community ever held elective office in any of the Fourier or labor associations, nor is there any solid evidence that they even attended the conventions, though if they refrained from speaking, as was customary in all but the New England Antislavery Society and certain come-outers' meetings, there would be no record of their presence.[103] At home, as new men joined the community, women officeholders tended to be displaced, Marianne

102. John Humphrey Noyes, *History of American Socialisms* (1870; reprint ed., New York: Dover, 1966), pp. 631, 624. At the Modern Times community on Long Island in the 1850s, in contrast, free love was sanctioned as one of the rights of "individual sovereignty" rather than as a duty of spiritual marriage, suggesting how nineteenth-century reformers could arrive at the same conclusion by the different routes—toward freedom and community—both inherent in the utopian impulse. On Modern Times, see Perry, *Radical Abolitionism*, pp. 208–16.

103. Several women who were not members of Brook Farm did participate in the Fourier movement, however. Mary Johnson and Rebecca Codman (probably not the forty-seven-year-old wife of a mechanic, also named Rebecca Codman, who joined Brook Farm in June 1844) were on the executive committee of the New England Fourier Society that issued the call to the Jan. 1845 convention in the *Phalanx* 1 (Dec. 9, 1844): 307–08. The previous year, three of the twenty people who signed the call to the original convention to organize a Fourier movement in New England were women (*Phalanx* 1 [Dec. 5, 1843]: 44), and one woman, Eliza Kenny of Salem, was a secretary of the convention which subsequently met on Dec. 27 and 28 (*Phalanx* 1 [Jan. 5, 1844]: 46). Generally, however, the women were not members of a community, their tenure was short, and their power decreased as the movement became more organized and claimed a national, rather than regional, constituency. In 1845, for example, no woman was elected to office for the coming year at the New England convention Johnson and Codman had called (*Phalanx* 1 [Feb. 8, 1845]: 309), and there were no women among the leaders of the national organization begun in New York in Apr. 1844 (*Phalanx* 1 [Apr. 20, 1844]: 103). The labor movement, at least as represented by the New England Workingmen's Association, was even more thoroughly male-dominated because it was based on traditions of trade unionism at the local level. The Female Labor Reform Association of Lowell was allowed to report on its activities at the Mar. 1845 convention of the NEWA, for example, but not to seat delegates, even though women operatives in the Lowell mills outnumbered men by three to one. See Norman Ware, *The Industrial Worker, 1840–1860* (Boston: Houghton Mifflin, 1924), p. 207. A survey of the *Phalanx, Harbinger*, and the private papers of Brook Farm women suggests, finally, that the women in the community had no contact with the labor movement.

Ripley, for example, losing the position she had occupied as a director of education since 1841 to John Dwight in 1845.[104]

In light of these trends, the Women's Associative Union established in Boston in 1847 seems as much an attempt to preserve the "bond of union" formed at Brook Farm, in anticipation of the community's dissolution, as an indication of the women's self-assertion. Although an anonymous "sister" had urged women in the *Harbinger* to become "active co-operators" with men rather than "mere passive recipients of the light," caution was the watchword for the ten to twelve women who met privately after the convention on May 25 to form the Union. "It may be that we are not yet prepared for any organization, nor would *we* rashly assume to define what such an organization should be" and certainly "not draw a strong line of separation between our brothers and ourselves."[105] Thus, comparing themselves to "the sisters of charity of the Roman church," they made the Union a ladies' auxiliary:

> Its purpose shall be to bring into active sympathy and hearty co-operation all women interested in the cause of Association, that each quickened by the hope, faith and zeal of all, may receive a new impulse of devotedness to the work, and be led to give freely of her time, talents, influence and means, to the spread of this gospel of glad tidings to a waiting people.[106]

Economic independence for women was part of the plan, however. They hoped that the store they opened in 1848 to sell needlework contributed by the members would be the beginning of a system to guarantee women employment. Similarly, at the end of the year, they put 25 dollars of their 169-dollar profit into a mutual insurance fund, after donating the rest, short of operating expenses, to the *Harbinger,* the Boston Union of Associationists, the Religious Union, and the American Union.[107] But in contrast to the Declaration of Sentiments issued by the first women's rights convention at Seneca Falls, New York, the same year, their ambitions were extremely modest. Whether the prolonged retirement of women in the community was to blame or the ambiguity of Fourier's theory, women made little progress in a movement that promised to revolutionize society.

It was just as true that while unity and love took the place of individual freedom as preeminent values, Brook Farm functioned less as a family after 1844. Anticipating further growth on the basis of the sixty-seven members

104. Jan. 7, 1845, minutes of meetings, MHS.

105. "Union of Women for Association," *Harbinger* 5 (June 12, 1847): 14. See also the "sister's" "A Woman's Call to Women," *Harbinger* 4 (May 8, 1847): 351.

106. "First Annual Report of 'The Women's Associative Union,' " *Harbinger* 7 (June 24, 1848): 61.

107. Ibid., p. 61.

admitted that year, the Brook Farmers wrote a new constitution in 1845 to implement a decentralized democracy. Elected chiefs of the industrial groups were to appoint representatives to a council of industry; a council of science would be similarly selected by the educational, literary, and scientific series; and stockholders would choose a council of finance, all together forming a general council to govern the phalanx. The plan was never put into effect, but the relative autonomy of the shoemakers, carpenters, and other workers' groups was evidence of the centrifugal pull of increasing size and specialization. Division of labor by sex, though practiced before, was now given formal sanction. The Constitution specified that a majority of women would sit on the council of "arbiters" to decide cases of "morals and manners," presumably a compliment to their moral superiority, but in fact restricting the open-ended authority Sophia Ripley had exercised as cofounder.[108]

Sophia Ripley's conversion to Catholicism was at least in part the result of the ambiguous status of women and the family at Brook Farm after 1844. Intellectually, her decision was perfectly consistent with the community's new commitment to universal unity. She came to believe that the spiritual independence of Protestantism, taken to a logical extreme in the original plan of Brook Farm, was "childish, empty, & sad": "I saw that all through my life my ties with others were those of the intellect & imagination, & not warm heart ties; that I do not love anyone & never did, with the heart, & of course never could have been worthy in any relation [without the Catholic church]."[109] Yet Catholicism was her private expression of this common feeling, a way of establishing her identity in a community where women had increasingly less of a meaningful role. And along with the several others who were also drawn to the church, she formed a small circle within the community, no longer itself a family. In New York in the 1850s, the Catholic church continued to provide Sophia with a community outside the home and, just as important, offered opportunities for charity and literary work on religious publications which gave her a sense of her own value, precisely what she had hoped to find at Brook Farm in 1841 and in some ways had found.[110]

108. The constitution was published in the *Phalanx* 1 (May 28, 1845): 343–49.
109. SDR to CD, [Mar. 1848].
110. Sophia discussed her charity work in a letter to Charlotte dated June 9, 1852. She also translated French articles for the Catholic press, wrote a tract on spiritual exercises, and translated a devotional manual. See her letters to CD, July 14, [1850], and June 9, 1852. Although it is difficult to trace Catholic converts at Brook Farm from existing sources, the following evidence suggests considerable interest in Catholicism. Sophia mentioned meeting several Brook Farmers returning from mass in Boston in a letter to Charlotte, Sept. 12, 1846; her niece Sarah Stearns, one of the original members, entered a convent in 1850 (SDR to CD, Sept. 26, 1850); and Linsday Swift noted in *Brook Farm* that George Leach, an abolitionist who operated a Graham hotel in Boston after he left Brook Farm, became a Catholic (p. 183). Charles Newcombe, a boarder from 1841 to 1845, kept a crucifix in his room and

CONSOCIATE FAMILY LIFE

The Fruitlands community was built on paradoxes. It was an experiment in practical anarchy, since the reformers sought total freedom from worldly restraints; but it was also a "consociate, or universal family," where the members were to be wedded in the bonds of the spirit. Even more perplexing to the uninitiated observer, the construction of the consociate family required the renunciation of marriage. Or so it seemed to Charles Lane. Between the potency of the "conjugal mixture" and the way the well-being of the family was commonly "used to justify every glaring and cruel act of selfish acquisition," he argued, the "all-absorbing influence of this union is too obvious to be dwelt upon."[111] The necessity of a choice to Lane at least was clear, and when Fruitlands disbanded in January 1844, he joined the Shaker community nearby because they practiced celibacy. But the Alcott family did not follow Lane's logic to the ultraindividualism at the heart of the consociate idea. They, indeed, were Lane's evidence for the unfortunate tenacity of family affections.

Bronson Alcott's interest in family reorganization began in the 1830s as a result of his commitment to education. Because Alcott was a teacher, the central theme of his Transcendentalism was the perfect intuition of children, which, despite his claim that their exemplary innocence would regenerate their elders, had to be carefully nurtured by teachers and parents alike. He arranged for some of his students at the Temple School to board with his family in order to benefit from a thorough integration of school and home, and it was perhaps inevitable that Elizabeth Peabody, Alcott's assistant, would be similarly cast in a parental role. In 1836, she

---

practiced devotional exercises, and Isaac Hecker, who lived at Brook Farm before moving on to Fruitlands, became a priest. See *The Journals of Charles King Newcombe,* ed. Judith Johnson (Providence: Brown University, 1946), p. 27, and Walter Elliott, *The Life of Father Hecker,* 2d ed. (New York: Columbus Press, 1894), pp. 47–66. I have already discussed William Henry Channing's affinity for Catholicism, because of its recognition of the unity of the race, in chap. 4, n. 94, and according to Sophia Ripley, his wife Julia almost converted in 1849 (SDR to CD, Oct. 29, 1849). Also relevant are Channing's "Unity in Catholicity in the Church," *Harbinger* 2 (May 16, 1846): 365–67, and two unsigned articles both entitled "The Catholics and Associationists," *Harbinger* 3 (July 25, 1846): 102–04, and 3 (Sept. 5, 1846): 193–95. Despite the importance of the idea of universal unity or kinship to these people, temperamentally they seemed more inclined than others toward withdrawal from the world for purity's sake, and they reveal the monastic quality of community life. It is significant, therefore, that other communities also produced Catholic converts. In 1857, there were eight converts at the Yellow Springs community in Ohio, founded by one-time Fourierist Mary Gove Nichols and her husband Thomas, after the group had passed through such preliminary practices as fast days, penances, and obedience to the authority of the leaders. See Bertha-Monica Stearns, "Two Forgotten New England Reformers," *New England Quarterly* 6 (1933): 59–85.

111. "The True Life," *Present* 1 (Mar. 1, 1844): 316.

moved in with the Alcotts on Front Street to begin what Emerson called the "Family School."[112] It was the Alcotts' first experiment with an extended family for the sake of spiritual culture.

The result was a particularly intense and, in Peabody's opinion, illiberal form of domesticity in this child-centered house. The fact that she began a diary the day she arrived was a sign that she expected greater freedom in a home dedicated to culture. But after airing her not altogether sympathetic view of Sylvester Graham at dinner, she was warned not to discuss controversial subjects in front of the children. Alcott "rather avoids than seeks any communication with persons who differ from himself," she concluded from the episode, without quite realizing that she, now a woman of the house, had simply felt the weight of paternal authority.[113]

Abigail Alcott (1800–77) was used to the extra demands of motherhood that came with a philosophy of child-rearing. The "Observations on the Phenomena of Life," which her husband began with Anna's birth in 1831 and which filled 2,500 manuscript pages five years and two daughters later (Louisa was born in 1832 and Elizabeth in 1835), contained directions for parental behavior as well as notes on the progress of the child's soul. The capacity for affection, reason, and conscience must be drawn out in an atmosphere of love, while selfishness, jealousy, and aggression should be given no occasion to appear by anticipating and satisfying the child's legitimate wants. Abba was responsible for administering this protective environment. "Mr. A aids me in general principles, though nobody can aid me in the detail," she wrote in 1833, although as Anna's timidity and Louisa's hot temper became more pronounced, Bronson began to supervise the girls himself and blamed his wife's impatience with Anna and indulgence of Louisa for their faults.[114]

There were psychological burdens of Transcendental motherhood as well. Alcott's conversations with the children at the Temple School are particularly revealing. Since every child was the spiritual equal of Christ, every mother was another Mary, an object of reverence to be sure, but subject, too, to the absorbing concerns and anxieties of raising a redeemer. "Good mothers, spiritually minded mothers, are very happy, when they find a child is going to be given them" and "feel disposed to keep hidden, or retired, and think about it," Alcott told his pupils. Only thankless mothers "think of the care and trouble these will give them."[115] The

112. RWE to EPP, Nov. 15, 1836, Emerson, *Letters*, 2:46.
113. Quoted in Tharp, *Peabody Sisters*, p. 100.
114. Quoted in Charles Strickland, "A Transcendentalist Father: The Child-rearing Practices of Bronson Alcott," *Perspectives in American History* 3 (1969): 35. I am indebted to Strickland's excellent analysis for my understanding of Alcott's practice as a father.
115. *Conversations with Children on the Gospels*, 2 vols. (Boston: James Munroe, 1836–37), 1:46, continued in a note on p. 220.

biblical fathers of John the Baptist and Jesus paled, in Alcott's recounting of the Gospels, in comparison with Elizabeth and Mary: Zacharias was struck dumb after learning of his wife's pregnancy from an angel, and Joseph married Mary after the fact of immaculate conception. But not to see, as Abba Alcott surely did, that these human fathers were replaced by God the Father was to miss the point: "I believe there will be a great educational regeneration and I believe that my husband is to be the Messiah to announce to the world a new revelation."[116]

Abigail did not fundamentally question the domestic order in the Alcott home. She was well prepared by contemporary beliefs about the family to endure the strains that arose from the glorification of motherhood and the real power of fatherhood, which Alcott's ideas, despite their theological radicalism, reaffirmed. "He shall be my moral mentor, my intellectual guide," she vowed during their engagement in 1828 and in 1848 could still write, "his spirit-culture has been the best blessing of my life."[117] Nor do hints of rebellion change the fact that the children, too, were faithful to their father's system.

The lot of the Alcott girls was not an easy one precisely because the home existed for their benefit. Their behavior was subject to close and continual scrutiny. No deviation in mood could pass without analysis in Alcott's voluminous "Observations," and by the same logic, the journals the children kept when they grew older were open to their parents' inspection. Thus in a family where the child's every thought and feeling was common property, Anna's possessiveness when she was finally given a room of her own at Fruitlands was a natural response: "It is to be my room and I to stay by myself in it."[118] Nor is it surprising that Louisa gave her first novel the self-indulgent title *Moods*.

More seriously, the girls were caught in the paradox of their father's philosophy. Although innate perfection entitled the child to respect as a free moral agent, the means needed to cultivate goodness required a didacticism so overbearing as to verge on psychological and physical (though nonviolent) coercion. "The *child* must be *treated* as a *free, self-guiding, self-controlling being*," Alcott emphatically stated, but he suggested the problem of making the child strictly moral as well when he concluded: "He must be free that he may be truly virtuous, for without freedom there is no such thing as virtue."[119] No occasion passed without a moral lesson. It was natural enough on Louisa's fourth birthday to make

116. AMA to SJM, Sept. 7, 1834, quoted in Strickland, "Father," p. 44.

117. Quoted in Martha Saxton, *Louisa May: A Modern Biography of Louisa May Alcott* (Boston: Houghton Mifflin, 1977), p. 42; AMA to SJM, June 14, 1848. See also Saxton's excellent discussion of the courtship of Abigail and Bronson, pp. 35–49.

118. Journal, July 26, 1843, quoted in Clara Sears, *Bronson Alcott's Fruitlands* (Boston: Houghton Mifflin, 1915), p. 102.

119. "Observations," quoted in Strickland, "Father," p. 22.

the necessity of giving her cake away when there was not enough her "first lesson in the sweetness of self-denial," but her father also set up deliberate tests of her will, such as leaving apples she was forbidden to touch where she was sure to find them. His Socratic conversations on religion and morals, moreover, bothered Abigail because the weightiness of the topics seemed inappropriate to children, despite her husband's assurance that "nothing is too metaphysical for the mind of a child." Finally, Alcott manipulated the children's diet and sleeping habits to aid in character formation. He tried to weaken the obstinate willfulness Anna showed at the age of a year, for example, by feeding her no meat and engaging her in games during some of the hours she usually slept.[120]

By 1839, there was a plan for Bronson's cousin William Alcott, the author of numerous books of the family such as *The Young Wife*, to replace Elizabeth Peabody as the third adult in the Alcott home, and all were to conform to "the strictest Graham principles."[121] William never arrived, but the dietary rules were strictly kept, and Abba occasionally rebelled against the new regime. "Oh these physiologists," she wrote to her brother just before Thanksgiving, "may their bowels never yearn as mine do for [plum-loaves?] and cranberry sauce," expecting to see nothing better on her table than a "Carolina potato or boiled rice."[122] But the children lacked her standard of comparison, and in 1860 Louisa was proud that the Alcott girls, mere "vegetable productions," outperformed their neighbors when gymnastics became the rage in Concord.[123] The intense pattern of family life that Bronson Alcott instituted in the 1830s made converts of the children. There was only a shade of deviance from the father's values when Louisa wrote on her mother's birthday in 1843, "I wish I was rich, I was good, and we were all a happy family this day."[124] It

120. On Louisa's birthday lesson, see "Sketch of Childhood, by Herself," quoted in Ednah D. Cheney, *Louisa May Alcott: Her Life, Letters, and Journals* (1889; reprint ed., Boston: Little, Brown, 1928), p. 18, and on her temptation with apples, see Strickland, "Father," 68–69. Alcott's justification of his Socratic dialogues and his experiments with the children's eating and sleeping habits are discussed in Strickland, pp. 70, 25–26. A number of historians have emphasized the greater freedom given to children by Alcott's educational reforms. Dorothy McCuskey notes, for example, that he introduced physical exercise in schools, encouraged imagination rather than learning by rote, and did away with corporal punishment, in *Bronson Alcott, Teacher* (New York: Macmillan, 1940), pp. 19–39. But it is important to recognize the degree to which indirect control to instill internalized standards of behavior replaced these direct methods. The intense inward focus of Alcott family life, moreover, tends to support Philippe Aries's thesis that the "discovery" of childhood was the crux of the transition from the sociable medieval family to the insular modern one. See his *Centuries of Childhood: A Social History of Family Life*, trans. Robert Baldick (New York: Knopf, 1962), esp. pp. 33–49, 356–404.

121. AMA to SJM, Oct. 3, 1839.

122. AMA to SJM, Nov. 29, 1839.

123. Louisa May Alcott to Louisa Bond, Sept. 17, 1860, quoted in Cheney, *Louisa May Alcott*, p. 92.

124. Journal, Oct. 8, 1843, quoted in Sears, *Fruitlands*, p. 108.

was precisely such conviction that kept the Alcotts together in the 1840s when changes in Bronson's domestic philosophy threatened the integrity of the family.

The idea of "consociate family life" was stated most clearly by Charles Lane in August 1843:

> The human beings in whom the Eternal Spirit has ascended from low animal delights or mere human affections, to a state of spiritual chastity and intuition, are in themselves a divine atmosphere, they *are* superior circumstances, and are constant in endeavoring to create, as well as to modify, all other conditions, so that these also shall more and more conduce to the like consciousness in others. Hence our perseverance in efforts to attain simplicity in diet, plain garments, pure bathing, unsullied dwellings, open conduct, gentle behavior, kindly sympathies, serene minds. These and several other particulars needful to the true end of man's residence on earth, may be designated Family Life. . . . The Family, in its highest, divinest sense, is therefore our true position, our sacred earthly destiny.[125]

Not yet questioning the compatibility of the nuclear and consociate families, Lane may have seen that this was a logical conclusion of the perfectionist educational theories of Pestalozzi, Greaves, and Bronson Alcott. Gradualism had simply given way to immediatism, and the family had been transformed from an agency for the spiritual nurture of children to a standard for adult society.

In Alcott's case, the catalyst was his alienation. There seemed to be a fatality in the newspaper charges that his *Conversations with Children on the Gospels* was subversive of social order. Did not the doctrine of the child's spiritual insight, the critics asked in 1837, challenge not only parental but all authority? And although his practice as a father proved that such fears were then unfounded, Alcott's conviction that there was a perfect standard of judgment gave him a weapon against a society which refused to recognize his genius and underwrote his anarchic critique of the institutions of property, state, and church. But just as the child's legitimate freedom consisted of voluntary self-submission, Alcott's anarchism required, by definition, obedience to the divine laws of humility and charity, laws embodied most perfectly in the family. By 1841, the family had emerged as a positive social ideal: "Great is the house, fair the household; the cope of heaven does not cover a holier fact; and whoso restores its order and divines its law solves life's problem, and recovers to man his lost Eden."[126] The consociate family at Fruitlands was an inevitable step.

But the tension between the natural and spiritual family was already apparent. Abba wrote in January 1842: "His family is the stumbling

125. "The Consociate Family Life," *New Age* 1 (Nov. 1, 1843): 117.
126. Journal, Jan. 1, 1841, in "Days from a Diary," *Dial* 2 (Apr. 1842): 410.

block—and I sometimes feel as if I could live on [leaves?] to effect his emancipation from the tyranny of physical wants."[127] Alcott's own family was inescapably part of the social, economic, and indeed material order he rejected. Thus his search for the consociate family loosened the bonds between husband and wife and father and children.

From an economic and emotional standpoint, Abigail was effectively widowed by her husband's social opinions. The separation of woman at home from the debasing influences of the marketplace was a standard theme in the domestic literature. But when Alcott refused to be employed "in the usual way" for purity's sake, first experimenting with farming and day labor in Concord and by 1842 abstaining from wage labor entirely, Abigail was left to depend for subsistence on the charity of relatives and friends. It was a humiliating experience, the "worm gnawing at the vitals of my tranquility," she told her brother.[128] What made the situation worse than common widowhood was that her husband was alive to censor possible remedies on ethical grounds. When she proposed investing the money she inherited from her father in property for the children, "Mr. A thought any action which would seem to be enriching ourselves and impoverishing others would not be justifiable on any principle of equitable dealing."[129] The acerbic humor she turned on the irony of their position was a sign of her inability to solve the moral dilemma: "We are as poor . . . as church mice (and as *good* too)."[130]

There were other ironies she missed, however. As Alcott became indifferent to the source of his family's subsistence, accepting charity in good conscience, as I explained in chapter 4, as offerings to the spirit, his wife entered the market as a manual laborer. During their residence in Concord, Abigail did piecework on shoes, took in sewing, and considered putting the girls out as apprentices to do domestic chores in other homes. Her experience made her see the value of economic independence for women: "My girls shall have trades—and the mother with the sweat of her brow shall earn an honest subsistence for herself and them. I have no accomplishments for I never was educated for a fine lady—but I have handicraft *wit* and *will*, enough to feed the body and save the souls of myself and children."[131] But actually to "adopt some scheme of life giving me more labor," Abba would have had to recognize and accept the economic breakdown of the family. This she could not do. She clung to them more tenaciously than ever in adversity. "It is your life has been more

127. AMA to SJM, Jan. 18, 1842.
128. AMA to SJM, Apr. 4, 1841.
129. AMA to SJM, Apr. 26, [1841]. The date on the letter, 1840, must be erroneous, since her father died in Mar. 1841.
130. AMA to SJM, Jan. 24, 1841.
131. AMA to SJM, Apr. 4, 1841. See also her letter to SJM of Aug. 30, 1840, on her plan to work.

to me than your doctrine or theories," she wrote of her husband in 1842, and of her children said, "they are the threads wrought into the texture of my life—the vesture with which I am covered."[132] Instead of taking steps toward self-support, therefore, Abigail set her hopes for her family's salvation on the plan for common labor and ownership in the consociate household.

In sharp contrast to her husband's intention to eliminate economic activity by restricting production, consumption, and exchange, Abigail valued Fruitlands as an instrument of practical survival, as much as an "association" of interests (as the Fourierists would say) as a "consociation" of souls. The connection of competence and community in her mind was clear in 1844, when, soon after the failure of the experiment, she reluctantly resolved to "take up the family cross and work on, isolated and poor, a while longer."[133] When she worked as a visitor to the poor in Boston in 1849, she further demonstrated her grasp of the economics of combination: "I try to get up a more neighborly feeling—and introduce on a small scale the association principle—if one woman has 2 flat irons and one tub [and] her neighbor has 2 tubs and 1 flat iron I demonstrate to them the economy and gain, by interchanging their tools."[134] It would be misleading to suggest that Abba shared none of Bronson's idealism. Inspired by the physical beauty of Fruitlands in 1843, she wrote that the "true life *ought* to be lived here if any where [sic] on earth—away from the false and degrading customs of society as now *fashioned;* apart from observation; no ambitious motive stimulating us to a false action; we may fail, but it will be something that we have ventured which so few have dared."[135] It was simply that she saw, as she told the women in Boston, that "love was economical as well as beautiful."

Nor was she any less vitriolic than her husband in her criticism of society—"a false compact [of] Cunning, competition,—force and fraud." But while the source of Bronson Alcott's bitterness was his frustrated aspiration after "principle and salvation," Abigail's came instead from her inability to satisfy her "simple and superficial" desire for "competence and rest."[136] Hers was a working-class critique of a society that failed to supply basic human needs, a point of view that she understood precisely because her husband's quest for spiritual perfection left her, a woman with few marketable skills and responsible for the care of four young children, to contend with the facts of material existence. Only a person who in 1841

132. Journal, July 21, 1842, and Sept. 16, 1842, cited in Alcott, *Journals*, pp. 144, 147. Shepard included selections from Abigail's journals in his edition of Alcott, *Journals*, pp. 141–58.
133. Mar. 31, 1844, cited in Alcott, *Journals,* p. 158.
134. AMA to SJM, July 29, 1849.
135. AMA to SJM, June 14, 1843.
136. AMA to SJM, Feb. 15, 1846; Apr. 15, 1841.

had written, "We must [get money], or starve, freeze, go thirsty and naked," could pass this judgment on Unitarian benevolence in 1849: "I am dis-gusted with the lack of strength and simplicity in our own priests and the 'ministry at large' is a Sinecure—Our charitable societies are too complex—the poor are freezing and starving, while wrapped in our Sables, and Picknicking on Tea and Toast we dis-cuss resolutions."[137]

It is little wonder Charles Lane concluded after living with Abigail Alcott that the nuclear family was a remnant of an acquisitive society. By the time Fruitlands began in 1843, she was virtually obsessed with money, and the fact that the subsistence of her family was a condition of her commitment to the community must have formed an undercurrent of feeling hostile to Lane's otherworldly aspirations. Lane's second charge, that family affections inhibited universal love, was equally well founded, for at Fruitlands Abigail hoped to reconstruct the emotional bonds of her family.

When the English reformer Robert Owen visited the Alcotts in 1845, he "analysed the 5 great Evils from which society is suffering and which are working out the great disharmony—disorganization and sin [:] 'Religious Perplexities, Disappointment of the Affections, Pecuniary Difficulties—intemperance—Anxiety for the welfare of Offspring.' " "*I believe it I know it* at least from my experience of 4 of these evils," Abigail stated emphatically, the one exception being intemperance.[138] Even though Abigail long resisted the suggestion that there had been any weakening of domestic ties, the combination of perfectionism and poverty could not help but affect family relationships. She commented on her marriage in 1842: "We have in no wise been aliens in affection—but our diversity of opinion has at times led us far and wide of a quiet and contented frame of mind—but I can say through *all*, I have known no change in my affections."[139] But the occasion of her remarks cast doubt on the reassurance she gave her brother. When Alcott left for England within the month, Abba sensed that this was simply the climax of his emotional withdrawal from American society and from his family as part of the social order. Hence her relief at his letters home: "He does not forget his home, though surrounded by those spiritual affinities which he has so long desired to enjoy."[140]

The children, too, felt the competition between their father's longing for "spiritual affinities" and the claims of natural affections. The careful calculation of Alcott's child-rearing practices confirms Abba's judgment that for him love had always been "a principle and not a passion"; but

137. AMA to SJM, Apr. 4, 1841; July 29, 1849.
138. AMA to SJM, Dec. 10, 1845.
139. AMA to SJM, Apr. 15, [1842]. In light of her allusions to Bronson's coming trip to England, the date on the letter, 1841, is in error.
140. Journal, July 21, 1842, cited in Alcott, *Journals*, p. 144.

now his daughters no longer even commanded his attention, as he turned from child nurture to adult regeneration as the means of perfection. The anarchist's state of mind, moreover, was hardly conducive to fatherhood: "He experiences at times the most dreadful nervous excitation his mind distorting every act however simple into the most complicated and adverse form."[141] Indeed, it must have been a relief to the children to have Bronson's brother, Junius, stay with the family during his absence in England, a surrogate father who could enjoy taking "us all—being Abba's birthday, July 26—into his little boat *Undine* (or 'Water Spirit') and [rowing] up there [to the Cliffs]." And the girls were free to release their pent-up affection by "decorating their father's miniature with all sorts of everlasting flowers," treating him with a reverence usually reserved for the dead.[142]

It was perfectly reasonable for Abigail to conclude that her husband would be reconciled to the family only if his longing for spiritual companionship was met as well. The consociate family promised to satisfy both conditions. Her contentment, two days after his return with Lane and another English reformer, seemed to confirm her logic: "I wished to breathe out my soul in one long utterance of hope that the causes which were conspiring just then to fill us with such pure joy might never pass away—the presence of my dear husband, the gentle sympathy of kind friends, and the inspiring and exhilerating influence of Nature, who so lovingly embraces us the moment we approach her."[143]

But in practice the consociate family meant a multiplication of husbands whose authority was not easily borne without the inexhaustible patience of which Abigail's love seemed capable. In the 1830s, her devotion to Bronson had obscured her subordinate role in the family. But although she was "sad to see greatness so subject to contemptible pitiable meanness" in Charles Lane at Fruitlands, she was far from blind to the reality of their relationship: "No man is great to his valet says Sterne or somebody else—neither is he always *sublime* to his *house maid*."[144] Similarly, the "stiff quiet and peaceless order" consistently demanded for spiritual purity was not different in kind from the rules of parenthood laid down by her husband. But now Abba rebelled, at least in her journal, against "this invasion of my rights as a woman and a mother." Even more than the recent "five months of liberty and option" which she saw made it difficult once again to bow to authority, Alcott's gradual withdrawal from the family over the past several years had given Abigail habits of self-determination not easily broken.[145]

141. AMA to SJM, Jan. 18, 1842.
142. AMA, Journal, July 26, 1842, and Aug. 22, 1842, cited in Alcott, *Journals*, p. 145.
143. Journal, Oct. 23, 1842, cited in Alcott, *Journals*, p. 148.
144. AMA to SJM, [Nov. 4, 1843].
145. Journal, Nov. 29, 1842, cited in Alcott, *Journals*, p. 148.

Nor, finally, were either husband and wife or father and children reunited in the consociate family. Bronson Alcott is a shadowy figure at Fruitlands, in part because he lost his journals for 1840 to 1845 (and probably destroyed them) but also because he rarely appears in the papers of his wife and daughters. The evidence suggests that he devoted much of his time to integrating the other members of the community into the family, a thankless task in light of their transient habits of coming and going and their idiosyncratic behavior.[146] Thus with Bronson still wedded to "the Unseen and Eternal," it was primarily Abigail's loyalty that made Lane complain at the tenacity of conjugal affections. The family united only in their disappointment and decision to leave. "Mr. L. was in Boston and we were glad," Louisa wrote in her journal on December 10: "In the eve father and mother and Anna and I had a long talk. I was very unhappy and we all cried. Anna and I cried in bed, and I prayed God to keep us together."[147]

Little Women has long been read as a paradigm of nineteenth-century domestic values. But precisely because the story was true to the author's life, the implications of the novel, at least for her own family, are anything but clear. While the dominating presence of Mrs. March and the absence of the father fit the common notion that women cared for the home and men went out to work, the roles of Louisa's parents were in fact reversed. Bronson was indeed away, but on the Lord's business, which left Abigail to provide economic as well as emotional support for the family. Religion, moreover, by convention woman's concern and valued for the stability it promised social life, produced revolutionary results in the hands of a man with the idea of the consociate family. But consociation was also an indication of the Transcendentalists' conservatism. If the philosophy behind Fruitlands raised basic questions about the nuclear family as well as about the free market economy, it was also a reflection of the reverence for the home at the heart of antebellum culture.

146. See Sears, *Fruitlands*, p. 100, and Elliott, *Hecker*, pp. 85–86.
147. Quoted in Sears, *Fruitlands*, p. 111.

6 Epilogue: Transcendentalism at Mid-century

No event in America as dramatic as the European Revolution of 1848 divides what E. J. Hobsbawm has called the "age of revolution" from the "age of capital." But by 1850, there was a feeling among reformers that urban industrial society in its present form was here to stay. The sense of social flexibility that in the transitional years of the 1830s and 1840s made the Transcendentalists active seekers of Christian, Anarchist, or Fourierist alternatives to the emerging system, quietly dissolved. Quite accurately, Bronson Alcott observed in 1850: "Extremes are getting less extreme; conservatism concedes a little and reform softens somewhat; and one feels, amidst the transition of our time, the sure signs of an improved order of things."[1]

Behind this mood of accommodation, however, something of the old radical spirit remained, setting Transcendentalists apart from the bustling complacency of a nation buoyed up by gold, railroads, and trade, as well as against themselves. After Alcott spent nearly four months in New York in 1856, indulging in such innocent pleasures as ice cream at the "princely" International hotel and endless talk with acquaintances ranging from Stephen Pearl Andrews, the advocate of free love, to Henry

---

1. Alcott, *Journals*, p. 227. For Hobsbawm's thesis that the success of the industrial revolution, in the form of free market capitalism, impeded social revolutionary movements after 1848, see *The Age of Revolution: Europe, 1789–1848* (New York: Praeger Publishers, 1962), pp. 297–308, and *The Age of Capital, 1848–1875* (London: Weidenfeld and Nicholson, 1975), pp. 1–5. On the comparable development of the American economy, see Douglass C. North, *The Economic Growth of the United States, 1790–1860* (Englewood Cliffs, N.J.: Prentice-Hall, 1961), pp. 204–15, and David T. Gilchrist and W. David Lewis, eds., *Economic Change in the Civil War Era: Proceedings of a Conference on American Economic Institutional Change, 1850–1873, and the Impact of the Civil War, Held March 12–14, 1964* (Greenville, Del.: Eleutherian Mills-Hagley Foundation, 1965), esp. pp. 94–108, 137–51. Consider also Robert Fogel's and Stanley Engerman's evidence on the increasing profitability of the Southern slave economy in the 1850s, to which the North owed much of its prosperity throughout the antebellum period, in *Time on the Cross: The Economics of American Negro Slavery*, 2 vols. (Boston: Little, Brown, 1974), 1:89–94.

Bellows, the proponent of Unitarian orthodoxy, suddenly and unexpec-
tedly the voice of the prophet returned to denounce the "noxious evils" of
the city, whose "foul fields [cannot] be cleansed save by fire unquenchable
consuming the chast [*sic*]."[2] The uneasy fit of the Transcendentalists into mid-century society is clearly seen in their strained relations with a
younger generation of reformers such as James Russell Lowell, Thomas
Wentworth Higginson, and Franklin Benjamin Sanborn. While Alcott
wondered at Lowell's "ruddy health and flowing spirits"—traits "so rare
to be met with here amongst this severe and staid Puritan people"—and
Sanborn declared Thoreau's philosophy "not worth a straw," the difference between young and old was less their worldly or abstracted character
than their view of reform—whether society, basically sound, could be
changed piecemeal or required an immediate, total conversion.[3] The issue
was muted, since the Transcendentalists were no longer zealous reformers; but it did appear in their respective approaches to the most crucial
reform of the decade, antislavery.

The Transcendentalist movement ended in deflated hopes and
cheerful acquiescence, suppressed doubts and self-congratulation, precisely such paradoxical traits as those Walter Houghton calls typically
"Victorian" in *The Victorian Frame of Mind*.[4] To explain the rise of
American Victorianism after 1850 would require another book.[5] But to
sketch the Transcendentalists' change from reformers of boundless visions
and ambitions to quite respectable citizens is an appropriate way to end
this one.

The most striking aspect of the transformation was the speed with
which it occurred. By the early 1850s, the Transcendentalists spoke of
their movement as history. "All that can be said," Emerson wrote of
Margaret Fuller after her accidental death in 1850, "is, that she represents
an interesting hour & group in American cultivation," because such
"quantities of rectitude, mountains of merit, chaos of ruins, are of no

2. ABA to AMA, Dec. 27, 1856, Alcott, *Letters*, p. 227.
3. Jan. 4, 1850, Alcott, *Journals*, p. 218; Sanborn to Thoreau, Jan. 30, 1855, in *The
Correspondence of Henry David Thoreau*, ed. Carl Bode and Walter Harding (New York:
New York University Press, 1958), p. 367.
4. *The Victorian Frame of Mind, 1830–1870* (New Haven: Yale University Press,
1957).
5. The best study of American Victorianism is Daniel Walker Howe, ed., *Victorian
America* (Philadelphia: University of Pennsylvania Press, 1976), especially Howe's introductory essay, "Victorian Culture in America," pp. 3–28. This is not the place to argue that
American Victorianism began in 1850, but two historians have recently shown that the
1850s were a decade of important reorientation in American politics and psychology.
Michael Holt demonstrates a new political consensus on socioeconomic issues, in *The
Political Crisis of the 1850s* (New York: John Wiley and Sons, 1978), and George B. Forgie
describes a "sentimental regression" back to a veneration of the Founding Fathers, in
Patricide in the House Divided: A Psychological Study of Lincoln and his Age (New York:
Norton, 1979), pp. 159–99.

account without result,—'tis all mere nightmare; false instincts; wasted lives."[6] Here was one motive for hastily dismissing the past. As an "eloquent talker," Margaret was a symbol of what Emerson saw as the movement's failure to produce anything of lasting artistic or social value and instead, only magazine literature, series of lectures, and short-lived utopias. To place Transcendentalism firmly behind him eased his painful feeling of wasted potential.

In a similar way, Alcott stifled the memory of his frustrated efforts by assuming the casual tone of an urbane observer. The "zealots" he had known, he wrote in his journal in 1850, with their "vague longings for a terrestrial Eden" and "adventures in endeavoring to actualize their dreams here in Yankee land," were good material for fiction: "I know of no better material than could easily be collected from this period for a philosophical romance that should vie with Sir Thomas More's *Arcadia* [*sic*] or Plato's *Republic*."[7] As recently as 1848 Alcott was close to despair: "Is it not much to front famine, nakedness, obloquy, insanity, family desertion, debt, alienation of friends, and be left to roam over the land an outcast, and a subject of pity, if not sometimes of contempt?"[8] Thus cutting his ties with both his history and aspirations was a way out of the emotional dilemma of caring too much.

The Transcendentalists' feeling of failure was nurtured by their changing standard of success. The triumph of European colonialism and the expansion of America to the Pacific with the acquisition of California took their toll, for example, in Emerson's 1851 estimate of Thoreau: "He is a boy, & will be an old boy. Pounding beans is good to the end of pounding Empires, but not, if at the end of years, it is only beans."[9] Although Emerson continued to advocate spiritual goals, as we will see, Thoreau's trade with the "Celestial Empire" at Walden could not help but look meager next to such global power.[10]

Closer to home, the financial and social success of the Transcendentalists after mid-century made their marginal existence as radical reformers seem, by contrast, almost unreal. The turning point for George Ripley was 1862. After working thirteen years for Greeley's *Tribune* at near-subsistence wages (he began at 12 dollars a week), he had finally paid off the Brook Farm debt of slightly more than 1,000 dollars. Sophia's death the year before had ended a marriage strained by religious differences. The

---

6. 1851, Emerson, *Journals*, 11:431. Fuller drowned when returning to America after the unsuccessful Italian revolution of 1848, in which she participated. See William Henry Channing's account of this period in *Memoirs of Fuller*, 2:206–352.

7. Alcott, *Journals* p. 226.

8. Ibid., p. 206.

9. Emerson, *Journals*, 11:404.

10. Henry David Thoreau, *Walden*, ed. J. Lyndon Shanley, *The Writings of Henry D. Thoreau*, vol. 1. (Princeton: Princeton University Press, 1971), p. 20.

reversal of Ripley's fortunes began with the publication of the *New American Cyclopedia*, which he edited with Charles Dana. By the time of his death in 1880, the book had earned royalties of nearly 1.5 million dollars.[11] Now literary critic of the *Tribune*, Ripley's insistence on high moral standards in literature, his good-natured praise of most works, and his avoidance of controversial subjects won him a national reputation. At age sixty-three he married a woman in her thirties and entered New York society, giving (as one example of his habits at the time) a champagne party in 1868 for 300 guests.

"Did he ruminate over so varied a life, recall the dramatic controversies of the 1820's and 30's, or remember the intensely romantic idealism of Brook Farm?" Ripley's biographer Charles Crowe asks. "One must suppose that he did not. . . . He had long since ceased to think of the good life in the context of the social Kingdom of Heaven on Earth, and he had lost so much belief in society that he hardly thought of it anymore. He became so completely George Ripley the scholarly but popular dean of American criticism, an institution, a pillar of letters and learning, that all the other George Ripleys ceased to exist."[12] It is impossible not to sympathize with Ripley's relief at finding social respectability after struggling most of his adult life for unpopular principles, even if the cost was his former convictions. And from the perspective of a one-man "institution," the incessant intellectual and social movement of the 1830s and 1840s might easily seem a confused "nightmare," as Emerson said, best forgotten.

The gulf between past and present was felt most strongly by the Catholic converts. By definition and experience, entering the church was a passage from error to truth, nature to grace, death to life. Like the shadowy quality her husband ascribed to their years as reformers, Sophia Ripley discerned a "coldness of heart in Protestantism" that forbade human relations deeper than those formed by "intellect & imagination."[13] It required "the profound REALISM of the Gospel," Orestes Brownson wrote, incarnated in the historical Christ and his church, to save this world.[14] Even the vocabulary of Brownson's conversion expressed his desire for a solid, comprehensive experience. The "doctrine of life" brought him into the church. Man can "be" alone, he

11. On Ripley's financial history, see Octavius Brooks Frothingham, *George Ripley* (Boston: Houghton Mifflin, 1882), pp. 199–223. The financial recovery of the Transcendentalists was due mainly to book royalties and lecture fees, though few prospered as much as Ripley. One interesting example of the nonliterary profits of Transcendentalism, however, concerns James Freeman Clarke. As a result of developments related to his ministry in Louisville in the 1830s, Clarke owned substantial property and railroad stock in the West and in 1850 was worth 46,000 dollars. See Arthur S. Bolster, Jr., *James Freeman Clarke* (Boston: Beacon Press, 1954), p. 187.

12. *George Ripley* (Athens: University of Georgia Press, 1967), pp. 262–63.

13. SDR to CD, Mar. 1848, Dana Papers, MHS.

14. "No Church, No Reform," *Brownson's Quarterly Review* 1 (1844): 183, 186.

explained in "The Mediatorial Life of Jesus" in 1842, but he "lives" only in communion with others, the most important of whom was Christ, whose sacrifice broke the chain of inherited sin to redeem the race.[15] Similarly, Catholicism answered Brownson's question on the source of saving "power." Here the real presence of Christ in the church was a force that Protestant preaching could not equal because "ideas in themselves are not powers, have no active force, and can be rendered real and active only as clothed with concrete existence by a power distinct from themselves."[16]

In his language and his logic, Brownson conveyed his awareness that by 1850 society was so complex and interdependent that only an institution with the authority of history could adequately direct its future. Indeed, the striking likeness of his views to the repudiation of idealism by Marx and Engels in *The German Ideology* in 1846, two years after Brownson's conversion, suggests his modernity. "Life is not determined by consciousness," they wrote to refute the Young Hegelians' premise that ideas could change the world, "but consciousness by life," and hence "we set out from real, active men" to understand and revolutionize society.[17] However great the difference between the realism of materialism and the realism of supernaturalism, all three writers agreed that urban industrial society had reached a stage where idealism was not enough.

In polemics such as "Transcendentalism, or Latest Form of Infidelity" in his *Quarterly Review*, Brownson cut himself off from his friends.[18] But he was never altogether at home in the church, and the dilemma of being caught between the cultural norms of two quite different historical periods was one that other Transcendentalists shared. In Brownson's case, his affinity for Catholicism was evidence of the Victorian's preference for intellectual systems as expressions of faith, on the one hand, in the supremacy of mind over matter so clearly demonstrated in technological power (even *Capital* thus paid tribute to mid-century capitalism) but also as dogmatic assertions of truth to smother persistent doubts about the new order with what Houghton has called a spirit of "earnestness."[19] The rigor of Catholic theology appealed to Brownson. But he was still too much a freethinker, a product of the transitional age of experimentation, to sub-

15. Brownson, *Works*, 4:154–56. Brownson acknowledged his debt to Pierre Leroux's idea of "life," which was neither altogether consistent with standard Catholic doctrine nor approved by the church, in *The Convert* (1854), in *Works*, 5:169.

16. *Convert*, in Brownson, *Works*, 5:122.

17. *The German Ideology*, ed. C. J. Arthur (New York: International Publishers, 1947), pp. 15, 14.

18. *Brownson's Quarterly Review* 2 (1845): 273–323, 409–42.

19. See Houghton's excellent discussion of Victorian dogmatism and earnestness, in *The Victorian Frame of Mind*, pp. 137–60, 218–62. See also John Higham's discussion of the later revolt of the intellectuals against closed theoretical systems, in "The Reorientation of American Culture in the 1890's," in John Weiss, ed., *The Origins of Modern Consciousness* (Detroit: Wayne State University Press, 1965), pp. 35–48.

mit easily to authoritative dicta. Friction with Archbishop Fitzpatrick of Boston and Archbishop Hughes of New York over questions of dissent and progress within the church caused Brownson's successive moves to New York in 1854 and New Jersey in 1857.[20] Nor did religion subsume his secular interests, as plainly attested by the publication of *The American Republic* in 1865, a vigorous analysis of the nation's foundation in twin principles of "sovereignty of the people without social despotism and individual freedom without anarchy."[21]

Thus to some extent Brownson remained a critic and an outsider throughout his life and was, in that sense, an inexorable Transcendentalist. But the fact that he accommodated himself sufficiently to one institution to die a Catholic in 1876 was a sure sign that the age of revolution had passed.

The Transcendentalists who stayed in Boston in the 1850s became members of a new cultural elite, although, as in Brownson's case, their assimilation was not complete.[22] Composed of such diverse professionals as poets, historians, scientists, lawyers, and ministers, the elite took shape against a background that made social and intellectual life precarious for native educated Bostonians, specifically the influx of Irish immigrants in the early and middle years of the decade and the publication of Darwin's *Origin of Species* in 1859. Indeed, R. H. Dana, Jr., one of the founding members of the Saturday Club in 1856, felt the brunt of Irish political power when he polled less than 10 percent of the vote in an 1868 election against Benjamin Butler's anti-Yankee platform, and Louis Agassiz, Harvard professor of zoology and another of the club's original members, discovered the hazards of defending the divine creation of species, since his students had abandoned his position by the time of his death in 1873.[23]

20. See Arthur M. Schlesinger, Jr., *Orestes A. Brownson* (Boston: Little, Brown, 1939), pp. 194–234 and passim.

21. *The American Republic; Its Constitution, Tendencies, and Destiny*, in Brownson, *Works*, 18:8.

22. I have called this group a "cultural" elite because they did not necessarily control the wealth of the city but did set the tone of literary and social life for the more prosperous classes. James T. Fields, for example, worked his way up from a job as a bookstore clerk to become a partner in Ticknor and Fields, publishers of Emerson, Thoreau, Hawthorne, Longfellow, Lowell, Harriet Beecher Stowe, and others, and is remembered for his lavish entertainment of American and English notables. I have called the elite "new" in contrast to the conservative coalition of newspaper editors and clergymen who denounced Transcendentalism in the 1830s, which I have discussed in chap. 3. The best general discussion of elite culture is Martin Green, *The Problem of Boston: Some Readings in Cultural History* (London: Longmans, 1966), pp. 102–21 and passim.

23. Green, *Boston*, pp. 104–05; Bruce Kuklick, *The Rise of American Philosophy: Cambridge, Massachusetts, 1860–1930* (New Haven: Yale University Press, 1977), pp. 22–23. The best study of the Irish in Boston remains Oscar Handlin, *Boston's Immigrants: A Study in Acculturation*, rev. ed. (Cambridge, Mass.: Harvard University Press, 1959). On the implications of science and Darwin in particular for American philosophy and religion, see Kuklick, *Philosophy*, pp. 21–26, and Sydney E. Ahlstrom, *A Religious History of the American People* (New Haven: Yale University Press, 1972), pp. 767–72.

In light of these trends, the observation made by Emerson's son Edward in 1918 that "in the early 'fifties' times were pleasanter to live in" than the "uncomfortable" thirties and forties is somewhat surprising.[24] But from his perspective, which encompassed little more than the day-to-day life of genteel Bostonians, there were improvements. Against external threats, old animosities were sufficiently submerged for his father to list Samuel Kirkland Lothrop of the Brattle Street Church as a prospective member of the Town and Country Club in 1850, along with such erstwhile heretics as Bronson Alcott, Theodore Parker, and Emerson himself.[25] And club life, the characteristic form of organization of the new elite, was definitely comfortable. In contrast to the discussions of the Transcendentalist Club in the 1830s, where, as Edward Emerson noted, "no refreshments were served," the Saturday Club met at Parker's Hotel for a three o'clock dinner of seven courses, sherry, sauterne, claret, and cigars.[26] "It was all smoke, and no salt," Thoreau concluded on his way to his own "Town and Country Club" at the "Fitchburg Depot, where I wait for the cars, sometimes for two hours, to get out of town."[27]

There was a sharp difference between the Transcendentalists' city and country life, in fact, which reveals the reserves of thought and feeling behind the affability of Saturday dinner. Concord was an enclave where relationships persisted unchanged. Though Emerson's list of correspondents grew in the 1850s to include men as diverse as Charles Eliot Norton, as conservative in his social opinions as his father had been in religion, and Charles Sumner, who borrowed time from antislavery politics to forward the government's latest scientific reports, Emerson husbanded his praise, in the privacy of his journal, for such old friends as Bronson Alcott. The "most advanced soul we have had in New England, who makes all other souls appear slow & cheap & mechanical," he reflected in 1853.[28] His letters to Alcott, who lived in Boston and then New Hampshire before settling in Concord in 1857, were infrequent, cursory—and rich in significance: "I hear gladly that you will come & see me, as you promised,

24. *The Early Years of the Saturday Club* (Boston: Houghton Mifflin, 1918), pp. 3–4.

25. Emerson, *Journals*, 11:237. Apparently old wounds had not healed enough for Lothrop to join. He did not sign the club's constitution, which has been published in Kenneth Cameron, "Emerson, Thoreau, and the Town and Country Club," *Emerson Society Quarterly*, no. 8 (1957): 16–17. In 1853, moreover, he sponsored the adoption of a Unitarian confession of faith that defended Christianity from Transcendentalist relativism, as William R. Hutchison explains in *The Transcendentalist Ministers* (New Haven: Yale University Press, 1959), pp. 128–33. The proper relationship between Christianity and Unitarianism continued to divide the denomination, however, and led to the formation of the schismatic Free Religious Association in 1867. On this later version of the Transcendentalist controversy and its effects, see Stow Persons, *Free Religion: An American Faith* (New Haven: Yale University Press, 1947).

26. Edward Emerson, *Saturday Club*, pp. 4, 23.

27. Quoted in F. B. Sanborn and William T. Harris, *A. Bronson Alcott*, 2 vols. (Boston: Roberts Brothers, 1893), 2:465.

28. Emerson, *Journals*, 13:139.

& send a ticket for the road."[29] Long conversations on walks through the woods were the staple activity of the host and his guest, and as the decade wore on, Emerson's rambles, in company or alone, increasingly served as a kind of therapy to "forget my affairs & my books": "I do not hurry homewards for I think all affairs may be postponed to this walking. And it is for this idleness that all my businesses exist."[30] When society weighed as an "immense Boston," with "mountains of ordinary women" and "leathern men all immoveably bounded," sauntering, as Thoreau put it in "Walking," was a way to escape to the Holy Land—"Sainte Terre"—of free souls.[31]

Young people were rarely included in these excursions. Indeed, Emerson was puzzled that "I have been writing & speaking what were once called novelties, for twenty five or thirty years, & have not now one disciple."[32] Though he reasoned that he never intended "to bring men to me, but to themselves," he betrayed a secret regret when he made a special trip to New York in 1857 to meet an Ohio admirer named Peter Kaufmann, who, to Emerson's chagrin, turned out "invariably *bourgeois*."[33] To some extent, Emerson exaggerated the absence of a Transcendentalist tradition. All who later wrote the Transcendentalists' memoirs and published their papers—John Weiss, Moncure Conway, James Elliot Cabot, Franklin Benjamin Sanborn, Thomas Wentworth Higginson, and Octavius Brooks Frothingham, to name the most important—were acquainted, as young men in their twenties and thirties, with the Transcendentalists in the 1850s.[34] Still, communication between old and young was

29. RWE to ABA, Sept. 16, 1853?, Emerson, *Letters*, 4:385.

30. 1857, Emerson, *Journals,* 14:145.

31. RWE to Caroline Sturgis Tappan, July 27, 1853, Emerson, *Letters*, 4:376; Henry D. Thoreau, *Excursions* (Boston: Houghton Mifflin, 1881), p. 161. Intellectually, Emerson accommodated himself to Victorian culture by mulling over the problem of England in his journal between his visit there in 1848 and the publication of *English Traits* in 1856. Though he worried that the English cared more for trade than freedom, lived apart from nature, and were not sufficiently individualized to stand out from their class (*Journals*, 13:118, 70, 65), he was enough impressed by the wealth and power of mid-century Britain to judge it the best of actual nations in *English Traits*, in *Works*, 5:299. But an underlying disaffection remained, and he wrote to Caroline Sturgis Tappan on Oct. 13, 1857, that we "still find colleges & books as cramp & sterile as ever, & our discontent keeps us in the selfsame suspicious relation to beauties & elegant society" (*Letters*, 5:86). Walks with his Concord neighbors Henry Thoreau and Ellery Channing became more frequent in the latter half of the decade. See his *Journals*, 14: passim.

32. 1859, Emerson, *Journals*, 14:258.

33. May 1857, Emerson, *Journals*, 14:142. See also Emerson's letter to Kaufmann to arrange this visit, *Letters*, 5:77.

34. Information on individuals in this group varies in quantity, from a great deal on Higginson, who commanded the first regiment of freed slaves during the Civil War, to almost nothing on Cabot. The autobiographies of those who wrote them can be mentioned here, while supplementary sources are cited in the notes below: Moncure Daniel Conway, *Autobiography, Memories and Experiences of Moncure Daniel Conway*, 2 vols. (London:

curiously meager. "My dear sir," wrote Emerson to Higginson to confirm
a speaking engagement in 1858, clearly making this one of the"oppressive
miscellany of *business-letters*," which, he complained to his aunt Mary,
"long ago destroyed almost all inclination to write."[35] Even more, there
was a positive lack of mutual appreciation between generations. Alcott
was an "innocent charlatan" to Higginson, while Sanborn's school, observed Alcott, taught "gentlemanly manners," but "Tis not all one
desires."[36] It was a telling indictment, however mild, from the father of
spiritual culture.

The younger generation was in truth a new breed of men. What had
been most exciting about Transcendentalism in the 1830s and 1840s was
the reformers' demand for integrity: the social revolution must begin by
making one's own life consistent with principle. Once that personal rigor
was gone, reform lost its radical edge and slid toward philanthropy. It is
hard to imagine a more conventional set of occupations than those of the
Transcendentalists' young friends. All the aforenamed were ministers,
with the exception of Cabot, a lawyer, and Frank Sanborn. Sanborn's life
in Concord after his graduation from Harvard in 1855 was a model of
decorum. He conducted a private school, kept house with a maiden sister,
and kept company with Mary Moody Emerson and Sarah Alden Ripley,
Emerson's aunts, over afternoon tea. There were disharmonies in

---

Cassell, 1904); Octavius Brooks Frothingham, *Recollections and Impressions* (New York:
G. P. Putnam's Sons, 1891); Thomas Wentworth Higginson, *Cheerful Yesterdays* (Boston:
Houghton Mifflin, 1898); and F. B. Sanborn, *Recollections of Seventy Years*, 2 vols.
(Boston: Richard G. Badger, 1909). Another who shared the perspective of this group but
did not contribute to Transcendentalist historiography, with the exception of his "A Fable
for Critics," is James Russell Lowell. See Martin Duberman, *James Russell Lowell* (Boston:
Houghton Mifflin, 1966). Several women might also be included in the group, the most
important of whom is Ednah Cheney, the first biographer of Louisa May Alcott, whose
autobiography is *Reminiscences of Ednah Dow Cheney* (Boston: Lee and Shepard, 1902).

35. RWE to Higginson, Apr. 8, 1858, and to Mary Moody Emerson, Dec. 10, 1857,
Emerson, *Letters*, 5:102, 91. Higginson later recalled that he read Emerson over and over as
a young man (*Yesterdays*, p. 92). Similarly, Sanborn and his fiancée shared a strong interest
in Emerson (*Recollections*, 2:272, 304–05), while Conway was all but converted from
Methodism to Transcendentalism by Emerson's essays (*Autobiography*, 1:91, 97). But two
circumstances support my contention that relations at the time were distant. First, the young
men were influenced primarily through books, while intimate personal relations with the
Transcendentalists did not develop. Second, as they came to value the Transcendentalists
more in later life, they exaggerated their earlier appreciation. Tilton G. Edelstein concludes,
for example, that Higginson found Emerson too abstract in the 1840s, in *Strange Enthusiasm: A Life of Thomas Wentworth Higginson* (New Haven: Yale University Press,
1968), pp. 40–41.

36. Journal, c. 1857, *Letters and Journals of Thomas Wentworth Higginson*, ed. Mary
Thacher Higginson (Boston: Houghton Mifflin, 1921), p. 94; ABA to SJM, Aug. 24, 1860,
Alcott, *Letters*, p. 315.

Sanborn's character, however. As a member of the town, county, and state Kansas Aid Committees and one of the "Secret Six" who sponsored John Brown, he promoted armed opposition to slavery.[37] Yet this marriage of violence and gentility can be explained. Free soil commitments, Eric Foner has shown, thrived on faith in the free labor of capitalism.[38] Just so, on an 1856 trip to Nebraska to inspect the progress of Kansas immigration, Sanborn made notes on soaring land values and the need for a railroad, to be urged on "Eastern capitalists as a most important object."[39] Thus it is not surprising that in 1866 when he was head of the state board of charities, he helped defeat a bill in the legislature for the eight-hour day.[40] Needless to say, Sanborn shared none of the Transcendentalists' distress at the injustices of free trade.

To say that the horizons of the young reformers were bounded by a basic commitment to the Northern status quo need not impugn their sincerity or suggest that their activities were limited. Indeed, the catholic sympathies of Wentworth Higginson are truly impressive. He ran an evening school for workers in Newburyport and, as a Free Soil candidate for Congress in 1850, supported the ten-hour day. In 1853, he made an eloquent plea for women's suffrage at the state constitutional convention. He led the assault on the Boston courthouse to rescue Anthony Burns the following year.[41] Through all these efforts, Higginson was confident that the normal workings of political democracy gradually would correct abuses, for even after he used mob tactics in the Burns affair, he still refused "to admit that there is any evil in the world that next year's

37. The arrangement of Sanborn's *Recollections* conforms perfectly to this split in his character. Nearly all of the first volume, on "Political Life," concerns Kansas and John Brown's raid, while the second, on "Literary Life," is reminiscences of the Concord authors. It is a fascinating commentary on Sanborn's evaluation of his own life that of the four careers he says he pursued—politics, literature, reform, and journalism—he judged only the first two, which belonged to the antebellum period, worthy of exposition in his autobiography. On John Brown's raid and its Northern sponsors, see Stephen B. Oates, *Our Fiery Trial: Abraham Lincoln, John Brown, and the Civil War Era* (Amherst: University of Massachusetts Press, 1979), esp. pp. 9–21; Tilton G. Edelstein, "John Brown and his Friends," in Hugh Hawkins, ed., *The Abolitionists: Means, Ends, and Motivations*, 2d ed. (Lexington, Mass.: D. C. Heath, 1972), pp. 120–33; and C. Vann Woodward, "John Brown's Private War," in Daniel Aaron, ed., *America in Crisis: Fourteen Episodes in American History* (New York: Knopf, 1952), pp. 109–30.

38. *Free Soil, Free Labor, Free Men: The Ideology of the Republican Party before the Civil War* (New York: Oxford University Press, 1970), esp. pp. 11–39.

39. Sanborn to his mother, Aug. 17, 1856, quoted in *Recollections*, 1:61.

40. See David Montgomery, *Beyond Equality: Labor and the Radical Republicans, 1862–1872* (New York: Knopf, 1967), pp. 266–67.

41. On these activities, see Higginson, *Yesterdays*, pp. 132–66, and Edelstein, *Enthusiasm*, pp. 84–173. Higginson's suffrage speech is *Woman and her Wishes: An Essay, enscribed to the Massachusetts Constitutional Convention* (London: John Chapman, 1854).

election cannot cure."[42] The border war in Kansas finally made him an advocate of violence; but this resort to extralegal methods cannot be separated from his patriotism: "We see but one obstacle in the way of this nation's greatness. That obstacle is the influence of slavery."[43] It is just as important to see that there was a streak of rebelliousness in Higginson which made him unsuited for Sanborn's work of administering armed resistance. But while the Transcendentalists had chafed at bourgeois restraints on ethical grounds, Higginson's discontent was visceral. Kansas, he reported home to a friend, was "as genuine a sensation as we expected it to be; things and people are very real there."[44] The Transcendentalists' frustrations may have built castles in the air, but Higginson's were burned up in physical culture: "It is hard for me to imagine how any person gets through the winter happily without a gymnasium."[45]

The cause in which both young and old participated was antislavery. The Transcendentalists' concern with slavery has led George Fredrickson to conclude in *The Inner Civil War* that they first relinquished the detachment of Emersonian "individualism" for political responsibility in the decade before the war.[46] It is true that the 1850s were a turning point, but the change was not from indifference to commitment, as the present study

42. "Celebration of W[est]. I[ndes]. Emancipation at Abington, August First, 1854: Speech of Rev. Thomas W. Higginson," *Liberator* 24 (1854): 126.

43. *To the Young Men of Worcester County* (1852), quoted in Edelstein, *Enthusiasm*, p. 134.

44. Higginson to a friend, Sept. 16, 1856, *Letters and Journals*, p. 142.

45. "Saints and their Bodies" (1858), in *Out-door Papers* (Boston: Ticknor and Fields, 1863), p. 23. Higginson's passion for physical activity drew him into an otherwise unlikely friendship with Thoreau. He first sought out Thoreau after reading *A Week on the Concord and Merrimack Rivers* in 1849 (Edelstein, *Enthusiasm*, pp. 96–97), and in 1858 asked Thoreau's advice about a hiking trip to Canada, to which Thoreau replied at length (see *Correspondence of Thoreau*, pp. 506–07). Similarly, though Sanborn dismissed Thoreau's philosophy, he admired his knowledge of nature (*Correspondence of Thoreau*, p. 367).

46. *The Inner Civil War: Northern Intellectuals and the Crisis of the Union* (New York: Harper and Row, 1965), esp. pp. 7–22. Fredrickson's thesis on this intellectual reorientation pertains to Northern intellectuals generally, but the Transcendentalists and Emerson in particular are central to his argument. In this, he follows Stanley Elkins, who claims that since Transcendentalism was "the closest thing to a concerted intellectual effort to be found in pre–Civil War America," it must have been the source of contemporary antiinstitutional attitudes. See his *Slavery: A Problem in American Institutional and Intellectual Life*, 2d ed. (Chicago: University of Chicago Press, 1968), pp. 146–206. Their position is based on two errors. First, Transcendentalism cannot be identified with selected public statements of Ralph Waldo Emerson. One need only look at Emerson's private papers, examine other Transcendentalists, and consider their ideas in the context of their actions to see that they were serious social reformers. Second, the Transcendentalists were simply not as influential as these historians suppose. They were more often denounced than heeded in the 1830s and 1840s, their most active period of reform, and their direct impact on antislavery in the 1850s was surprisingly small, as I show below.

amply has shown. Rather, the Transcendentalists' challenge to such basic institutions as free markets, private property, and the individual family gave way to a reform which assumed the superior virtue of free society.[47] Even so, antislavery continued to raise large questions about freedom and order which brought out the old strain of skepticism in Transcendentalist thinking.

For Emerson, the decision to address antislavery meetings was difficult, in fact, because "these temporary heats" scarcely touched the problem of the age.[48] "Slavery & unbelief," he jotted in his journal and elucidated his meaning in this stunning statement of purpose: "I have quite other slaves to free than those negroes, to wit, imprisoned spirits, imprisoned thoughts, far back in the brain of man,—far retired in the heaven of invention, &, which, important to the republic of Man, have no watchman, or lover, or defender, but I."[49] Slavery was the extension of the moral imperfection of the free society which tolerated it and thus, when Emerson did speak, he lectured on character. More than once he preached against the time-serving politics of Daniel Webster ("The fairest American fame ends in this filthy [Fugitive] law"), until he discovered John Brown, "the rarest of heroes, a pure idealist, with no by-ends of his own."[50] Yet

47. In addition to Foner's demonstration that the political antislavery of the 1850s was built on faith in free enterprise (see n. 38), I am indebted to David Brion Davis's persuasive analysis of the multiple ways in which antislavery supported the rise of capitalism—by displacing anxieties about the dislocation and coercion of labor, by defining (by contrast) the permissible limits of dominion as internalized self-control, and, when antislavery received official sanction, as it did in Britain, by investing state authority with moral legitimacy—in *The Problem of Slavery in the Age of Revolution, 1770–1823* (Ithaca: Cornell University Press, 1975), esp. pp. 343–468. To see the interdependence of antislavery and capitalism is not to deny, as Davis says, that "the rise of antislavery sentiment represented a major advance in the moral consciousness of mankind" (p. 455) or that in significant cases antislavery was wedded to radical reform. This was especially true of contemporaries of the Transcendentalists in the 1830s and 1840s, such as Garrison, Wendell Phillips, and Adin Ballou. Though he does not probe the social roots of their disaffection, Lewis Perry has ably shown how their critique of slavery led to the endorsement of various forms of anarchy, in *Radical Abolitionism: Anarchy and the Government of God in Antislavery Thought* (Ithaca: Cornell University Press, 1973). But by the 1850s, as I argue below, radical abolitionism had been largely displaced by free soil moderation.

48. 1855, Emerson, *Journals*, 13:405. For a good survey of Emerson's views on slavery, see Marjory M. Moody, "The Evolution of Emerson as an Abolitionist," *American Literature* 17 (1945): 1–21.

49. 1854 or 1855 and 1852, Emerson, *Journals*, 14:375 and 13:80. Emerson never did dedicate himself to antislavery to the exclusion of other interests. For example, he offered a lecture series on "American Slavery" in the winter of 1854–55 but returned to a more varied program the following year.

50. "Remarks at a Meeting for the Relief of the Family of John Brown, at Tremont Temple, Boston, November 18, 1859," in Emerson, *Works*, 11:268. Emerson discussed Webster in "The Fugitive Slave Law: Address to Citizens of Concord, 3 May 1851" and "The Fugitive Slave Law: Lecture read in the Tabernacle, New York City, March 7, 1854, on

what is most striking about Emerson's Brown is his handling of the murders at Harpers Ferry: he didn't even see them, rapt as he was by Brown as an individual, who "believed in his ideas to that extent that he existed to put them all into action," or, in Brown's homely words, "putting the thing through."[51] Much as Emerson marveled at the perfect dialectic of Brown's idea and act, there was an abstraction in his approach to slavery which made his occasional musings on agencies of abolition —providence, commercial progress, purchase, disunion—comparatively desultory.[52] When confronted with slavery, a problem that resisted solution by such immediate social reorganization as typified Transcendentalist reform (though not impervious, as Thoreau will show, to all voluntary means), Emerson fell back, rather lamely, on the moral mechanism of character.

This failure of political imagination has caused Stanley Elkins to blame the Transcendentalists for the Civil War. Their disdain of institutional methods, he argues, precluded the peaceful abolition of slavery.[53] To answer Elkins's charge, one need not review the case that to work outside established channels is not to abandon serious reform. One should instead begin by showing that the Transcendentalists' influence on antislavery in the 1850s was extremely small. Ripley avoided reform; Brownson defended slavery when he first became a Catholic and continued to denounce abolitionism as a threat to social order; Peabody spent her energies on causes as far-flung as educational reform and Hungarian nationalism; and Alcott declined a rare invitation to speak on slavery because he preferred "to meet private companies," where he discussed such topics as housekeeping and health, and besides, "I am not sure of having anything to propose adequate to the subject, the company, and occasion."[54] Alcott did make a dramatic appearance during a lull in the fighting over Anthony Burns ("Why are we not within?" he asked from the courthouse steps), and Peabody traveled as far as Virginia to plead for the life of a follower of John Brown.[55] Of the original Transcendentalists, however, only Emerson

---

the Fourth Anniversary of Daniel Webster's Speech in favor of the Bill," in *Works*, 11:179–214, 217–44.

51. "Relief of Brown," in Emerson, *Works*, 11:270.

52. Emerson considered these alternatives in his *Journals*, 13:80, and 14:413, 400, 298.

53. See n. 46.

54. ABA to James Redpath, Nov. 19, 1860, Alcott, *Letters*, p. 317. For Brownson's changing views of slavery and abolition, see "Slavery and the Mexican War," *Brownson's Quarterly Review*, n.s. 1 (1847): 334–67; "Slavery and the Incoming Administration," *Brownson's Quarterly Review*, New York ser. 2 (1857): 89–114; and "Emancipation and Colonization," *Brownson's Quarterly Review*, 3d New York ser. 3 (1862): 220–40.

55. Higginson recalled Alcott's almost ghostly appearance in *Cheerful Yesterdays*, p. 185. On Peabody's mission, see Louise Hall Tharp, *The Peabody Sisters of Salem* (Boston: Little, Brown, 1950), pp. 283–85.

publicly opposed slavery with any regularity; but the same philosophical bent which made him a powerful speaker ran against the grain of the most important development of the decade, antislavery politics. What John Thomas says of Garrison, who stood by moral suasion, nonresistance, and disunion, no doubt holds true for Emerson, too: "During the decade before the Civil War, Garrison's prestige rose as his personal influence began to decline."[56] The nonextensionist argument of free soil politics made antislavery respectable—and eclipsed moral tactics.[57] It is much more likely that violence came from this new political realism, which refused to dally with character, than from Transcendentalism.

Theodore Parker is a case in point. Parker was nearly a contemporary of the older Transcendentalists (he was seven years younger than Emerson), but his national fame as an abolitionist in the 1850s had less to do with his kinship with the others than, as Frothingham said, with his difference: "He was as thorough a Transcendentalist as Emerson; but the same people who called Emerson a mystic, called Parker a preacher of common sense."[58] While Emerson fought slavery in its universal relations, Parker took practical action. He wrote countless letters to cajole politicians, made his home a station on the underground railroad, and was an executive member of the Boston Vigilance Committee to resist the rendi-

56. *The Liberator: William Lloyd Garrison* (Boston: Little, Brown, 1967), p. 367.

57. The basic position of Republican politicians in the 1850s was to respect the institution of slavery in the states where it was established while withholding federal sanction of slavery in the territories, in the expectation that if slavery were contained, it would die a natural death. See Foner, *Free Soil*, pp. 73–102. Although I have contrasted this stance to the moral absolutism of the radical abolitionists, one should call attention to David Potter's argument that the free soil position was moral, that is, based on a sincere oppostion to slavery but that its proponents were willing to limit the issue to slavery in the territories because they respected the Constitution's guarantees to slaveholders and the Union these ensured, in *The Impending Crisis, 1848–1861* (New York: Harper and Row, 1976), pp. 36–50. Even if this is true, I think it is fair to say, first, that moral principles had been compromised for the sake of political ones, and second, that the later antislavery advocates did not feel compelled to reconcile their methods with conscience to the same extent that earlier abolitionists did. Another way to express the distinction between these two approaches is to contrast "abolition" and "antislavery," although David Brion Davis rightly points out that these categories should not obscure subtle differences among reformers, in "Antislavery or Abolition?" *Reviews in American History* 1 (1973): 95–99. One should also call attention to John Demos's excellent discussion of the transition in the 1850s, in "The Antislavery Movement and the Problem of Violent Means," *New England Quarterly* 37 (1964): 501–26.

58. *Theodore Parker: A Sermon preached in New York, June 10, 1860* (Boston: Walker, Wise, 1860), p. 9. On Frothingham's antislavery activities, see J. Wade Caruthers, *Octavius Brooks Frothingham: Gentle Radical* (University, Ala.: University of Alabama Press, 1977), pp. 32–52. Frothingham was not as active an opponent of slavery as Sanborn and Higginson, although Caruthers speculates that his antislavery preaching contributed to his resignation from his pulpit in Salem in 1855. For an example of his views, see *Speech of the Rev. O. B. Frothingham, before the American Anti-Slavery Society, in New York, May 8th, 1856* (New York: American Anti-Slavery Society, 1856).

tion of fugitive slaves. He condoned legal or extralegal methods interchangeably: R. H. Dana's plea for Anthony Burns, for example, was still pending before the U. S. commissioner when Parker approved the attack on the courthouse which led to two deaths.[59] But he admired militance enough to "keep in my study two trophies of the American Revolution," the gun his grandfather used in the Battle of Lexington and the one which he captured.[60] Ethics, moreover, could be measured by results, since slavery condemned itself by the South's sluggish progress: South Carolina had only 364 ministers to Connecticut's 498 and 12,520 primary school students to Ohio's 218,609, while Virginia had an annual income of only 76,769,032 dollars, as compared with New York's 193,806,433 dollars.[61] Here indeed was a man of common sense, ready to use violence and to rationalize it: "A man held against his will as a slave has a natural right to kill every one who seeks to prevent his enjoyment of his liberty."[62]

It was to Parker that the young men turned for antislavery leadership. Higginson, who complained at a Unitarian ministers' meeting that the old offered "nothing *positive*" in religion, sought advice from Parker (whose abolitionism at least was substantial) when his antislavery preaching alienated his Newburyport congregation in 1848.[63] Similarly, Moncure Conway's relations with Emerson and Parker fell into a natural division of labor: he wrote to Emerson in 1851 about his spiritual troubles as a Southern Methodist minister but at Harvard Divinity School enlisted Parker's aid on behalf of a fugitive slave.[64] Not all of the young men were as hot-headed as Parker. In 1863, when Conway was the official emissary to England of a group of abolitionists, he proposed that the North end the

59. Higginson, *Cheerful Yesterdays*, p. 150. For examples of Parker's correspondence with politicians, see Octavius Brooks Frothingham, *Theodore Parker: A Biography* (Boston: James R. Osgood, 1874), pp. 376–447. Although Alcott and Thoreau occasionally harbored fugitive slaves, only Parker among the Transcendentalists did so with sufficient frequency to be included in Wilbur H. Siebert's list of agents, in *The Underground Railroad from Slavery to Freedom* (1898; reprint ed., New York: Arno Press, 1968), p. 412. On the rescues and attempted rescues of fugitive slaves in Boston, see Leonard Levy, "Sims' Case: The Fugitive Slave Law in Boston in 1851," *Journal of Negro History* 35 (1950): 39–74; Harold Schwartz, "Fugitive Slave Days in Boston," *New England Quarterly* 27 (1954): 191–212; and Samuel Shapiro, "The Rendition of Anthony Burns," *Journal of Negro History* 44 (1959): 34–51. See also Douglas C. Stange's interesting account of the ultimately futile effort of Parker and several other Unitarian ministers to make the Liberal clergy collectively oppose slavery, in *Patterns of Antislavery among American Unitarians, 1831–1860* (Rutherford, N.J.: Associated Universities Press, 1977), pp. 172–227.

60. Parker to James Martineau, Nov. 11, 1850, quoted in Frothingham, *Parker*, p. 408.

61. *Letter to the People of the United States* (1848), excerpted in *Theodore Parker: An Anthology*, ed. Henry Steele Commager (Boston: Beacon Press, 1960), pp. 237, 235, 238.

62. Parker to Francis Jackson, Nov. 24, 1859, in *Parker*, ed. Commager, p. 258.

63. Higginson to Samuel Longfellow, Mar. 1848, *Letters and Journals*, p. 16; Edelstein, *Enthusiasm*, p. 81.

64. *Autobiography*, 1:97, 119.

war and accept Southern secession, if the South abolished slavery.[65] But
the depth of his pacifism was exceptional (he was denounced by
abolitionists so universally that he permanently exiled himself to England), and in general, the Transcendentalists' successors accepted violence
readily, while their elders more reluctantly condoned it. The young men
viewed slavery much more as an institutional problem than a moral one. It
is not that they did not condemn slavery as contrary to a higher law but
that the higher law had limited applications. This helps explain, on the one
hand, why their critique of slavery did not turn back on the various forms
of moral and social bondage in Northern society, which had occupied the
Transcendentalists for nearly two decades: beyond the institutional
bounds of slavery, society, by definition, was free. On the other hand, this
political mind-set casts light on their embrace of force. For the less the
problem of slavery was comprehended in moral terms, the easier it probably was to sever means from ends and to live with immoral means.[66]

Only Thoreau was able to translate the spirit of Transcendentalist
reform into an antislavery program pertinent to the 1850s, and he did so
with extraordinary power. He knew, like Emerson, that few were really
free. No one died in America, he said in "A Plea for John Brown," for "to
die you must first have lived" and so we "deliquesce like fungi, and keep a
hundred eulogists mopping the spot where we left off."[67] But Thoreau's
moral imperative was also political: resist the state. Government was
subject to higher laws (the commissioner on the "case is God; not Edward
G. God, but simple God," he mocked, when Loring judged Anthony Burns
in 1854); but when the state turned accomplice to slavery, civil disobedience redeemed the individual from complicity and the state from crime.[68]
Far from the whim of a purist, civil disobedience was a plan to disrupt the
political mechanism by obstructionist tactics:

> A minority is powerless while it conforms to the majority; it is not even
> a minority then, but it is irresistible when it clogs by its whole weight. If
> the alternative is to keep all just men in prison, or give up war and
> slavery, the State will not hesitate which to choose. If a thousand men
> were not to pay their tax-bills this year, that would not be a violent and

65. See Peter F. Walker's discussion of this incident, in *Moral Choices: Memory, Desire,
and Imagination in Nineteenth-Century American Abolitionism* (Baton Rouge: Louisiana
State University Press, 1978), pp. 3–20.

66. Foner notes that some abolitionists, especially in New England, were uneasy with
the limited goals of political antislavery and continued to stress their opposition to slavery on
moral grounds, in *Free Soil*, pp. 81–82. Wendell Phillips exemplifies this persistence of
moral vision, as Irving H. Bartlett shows in *Wendell Phillips: Brahmin Radical* (Boston:
Beacon Press, 1961), esp. pp. 241–313.

67. "A Plea for John Brown" (1859), in *Reform Papers*, ed. Wendell Glick, *The
Writings of Henry D. Thoreau*, vol. 3 (Princeton: Princeton University Press, 1973), p. 134.

68. "Slavery in Massachusetts" (1854), in ibid., p. 96.

bloody measure, as it would be to pay them, and enable the State to commit violence and shed innocent blood. This is, in fact, the definition of a peaceable revolution, if any such is possible.[69]

Here was the nonviolent radicalism of Transcendentalism, restated for a new generation. Now the state, not society, was the principal obstruction to freedom. For Thoreau clearly saw that if men chose to resolve social issues by political means, then the state became a separate power, and radical reform could no longer afford to be simply personal, domestic, or communitarian but had to become political resistance.

During the war, in 1862, Thoreau died, a failure, if one measures by common standards of success (which Thoreau certainly did not) such as immediate popular appeal. But if Thoreau had not been able to change people's minds, neither did the war. Fredrickson has proposed that the war mobilization turned individualists already politically awakened by the slavery issue into staunch defenders of institutions.[70] But we have seen that the Transcendentalists' conversion from secession to loyalty involved more than their political attitudes and was complete by 1861: the renunciation of radical social reform and acceptance of free market capitalism, the lapse of family experiments in respectable domesticity, and the rise of political pragmatism, dissociated from morality and wed to a vigorous Northern nationalism conducive to the use of force. What did change after the war was the mood, though not the basic commitments, of the Transcendentalists' young followers. More wholeheartedly than the Transcendentalists themselves, they had embraced Victorian America; but as the century wore on, they fell prey to the ill-focused anxiety of people cast adrift in a sea of immigrants, machine politics, and new wealth. The Boston where Henry Adams was born in 1843, he wrote in his *Education*, might as well have been ancient Jerusalem, so little did it resemble America of 1905.[71] But it was back to that Boston that the second and even third

69. "Resistance to Civil Government" (1847), in ibid., p. 76.

70. *Inner Civil War*, esp. pp. 65–78, 98–112. One difficulty with this interpretation, to which Fredrickson alludes on pp. 190–98, is that many of these intellectuals accepted the laissez-faire assumptions of Social Darwinism by the 1870s. David Montgomery casts some light on this point in *Beyond Equality*, pp. 379–86, when he explains that there had always been implicit limits to government action, i.e., reforming but not revolutionizing the status quo. As I note below, the Transcendentalists were first portrayed as individuals outside the bounds of institutions in the postbellum works of their followers. It is more likely that the laissez-faire premises of these writers, which made them more antiinstitutional than the Transcendentalists themselves, contributed to this image.

71. *The Education of Henry Adams: An Autobiography* (Boston: Houghton Mifflin, 1918), p. 3. The best social history of late nineteenth-century Boston is Stephan Thernstrom, *The Other Bostonians: Poverty and Progress in the American Metropolis, 1880–1970* (Cambridge, Mass.: Harvard University Press, 1973). On intellectuals and reformers in this period, see Green, *Boston*, pp. 102–96, and Nathan Irvin Huggins, *Protestants against Poverty: Boston's Charities, 1870–1900* (Westport, Conn.: Greenwood Publishing, 1971).

generations looked, in part out of simple nostalgia, in part for a glimpse of "the high, vertical moral light," as Henry James put it, of simple integrity.[72] As a group of writers, they were as influential as they were prolific (Higginson alone takes up nearly twenty pages in the National Union Catalogue) and it is in their works that the myth of Transcendentalist individualism began.

The Transcendentalists loomed to heroic proportions on an uncomplicated social landscape in the late nineteenth-century writings. More often than not, they were pictured in such pastoral settings as Concord and Brook Farm rather than Boston proper, making it seem that all the world was then a paradise for "happy hapless Sansculottes."[73] "A Boy's Recollections of Brook Farm," typical of the memoirs of community life which appeared in New England magazines from the 1870s on, may have been true to the child's perceptions but told nothing of the adults' critique of competition or plan for a peaceable revolution.[74] Yet the Transcendentalists stood out as magnificent personalities against this tranquil background. Biography was the principal vehicle for these writers, and in their presentation of their subjects' values, their historical accuracy was flawless. As the Transcendentalists died one by one, long extracts from their private and public papers were laced together by no more than the barest commentary, to produce such works as Frothingham's *Theodore Parker* (1874) and *George Ripley* (1882), Sanborn's *Henry D. Thoreau* (1884) and *A. Bronson Alcott* (1893), Higginson's *Margaret Fuller Ossoli* (1884), Cabot's *Memoir of Ralph Waldo Emerson* (1887), and Henry Brownson's *Orestes A. Brownson* (1898–1900), until only Elizabeth Peabody, who outlived them all until 1894, lacked a biographer. Their unobtrusive style, a clear sign of the writers' self-distrust, made their work seem almost like historiographical spiritualism, an attempt to raise the dead as whole as possible for reassurance and guidance.[75] More important, just as the quotations dominate the text, so the Transcendentalists, in the imagination of their successors, managed to conquer circumstance and stand alone.

There is no question that the Transcendentalists were the powerful individuals their successors believed, not, however, because they stood apart from history, but because they came to grips with the realities of their time. The urban industrial revolution in New England made the two

72. "Emerson (1888), in Brian M. Barbour, ed., *American Transcendentalism* (Notre Dame, Ind.: University of Notre Dame Press, 1973), p. 259.

73. Emerson made this quip about the Brook Farmers on May 7, 1843, *Journals*, 8:392.

74. Horace Sumner, "A Boy's Recollections of Brook Farm," *New England Magazine* 16 (1894): 309–13.

75. The allusion to spiritualism is not as far-fetched as it might seem, since Higginson, among others, was seriously interested in spiritualism, as Edelstein notes in *Enthusiasm*, p. 80.

decades after 1830 an age of tremendous transition, and the Transcendentalists changed in kind. They began as radical intellectuals, with a religious philosophy adapted to the dynamics of history, and became social reformers aware of the need for structural change to achieve ethical ends. That they did not turn to politics should be no indictment, for their goal was too immediate and too comprehensive to tarry for reform by the state. They aimed to reconstruct all aspects of life according to principle, as individuals, in families, and in cooperative groups. When Transcendentalism ended at mid-century, the reason was the failure of this vision. Capitalism came of age in America when it became clear that the Transcendentalists, and other radical reformers, had not been able to communicate to their contemporaries the belief in a social alternative, and had lost faith themselves. But for us, the record of Transcendentalism as a movement of great humanity must remain of lasting value.

Appendixes

Note to Appendixes A and B

The first two tables have been compiled from partial and sometimes conflicting accounts of Boston churches and thus claim no more than approximate accuracy. Two sorts of difficulties were involved, one with the sources and the other with the churches themselves. Written at approximately twenty-five year intervals (between 1828 and 1881), the sources at times contradict one another on the dates of founding and dissolution and on the names of churches, since colloquial or descriptive names tend to be substituted for official titles. This is especially true when the church in question was either newly formed or had ceased to exist when the author was writing. In some cases, I have had to piece together the history of a church through several sources on the basis of its succession of ministers or location, in lieu of consensus on names and dates.

The second problem concerns the churches themselves. Procedures of establishment, with implications for dating, differed according to denominational practice and circumstance. Congregational churches (Unitarian or Orthodox) may be considered "founded" when a covenant is signed, but they may lack a church building, minister, and regular worship for a significant period. Episcopal and Catholic churches probably should not be considered "founded" until the building is consecrated, but a group of subscribers might exist years before the ceremony. Thus establishing the dates of founding according to denominational standards would have produced misleading discrepancies. I have chosen instead to date the founding from the beginning of sustained church life, that is, from the start of regular services with a settled minister and a stable congregation. Circumstances, too (e.g., lack of funds, disagreements within the congregation, legal difficulties), in some cases significantly delayed formal establishment of an emerging congregation, and I have judged again by a standard of sustained activity.

Despite these problems, in only a few cases would the decade of founding have been changed by a different judgment on my part. When I have left a question mark in place of the date, I am reasonably sure of the decade, though not the year.

APPENDIX A   Establishment and Dissolution of Boston Churches to 1860

			Decade of founding		
Denomination	Prior to 1820	1820–1829	1830–1839	1840–1849	1850–1859
Unitarian	First Ch (1630) Second Ch (1650) King's Chp (1686) Brattle St (1699) New North (1714) New South (1719) Federal St (1727) Hollis St (1732) West Ch (1737)	Hawes Pl Ch (1823) Twelfth Congregational Society (1825) Thirteenth Congregational Society (1826) South Congregational Ch (1827) Friend St Chp (1828)	Warren St Chp (1835) Pitts St Chp (1836) [Friend St Chp] (1836) Suffolk St Chp (1839) Bulfinch St Ch (1839)	Ch of the Disciples (1841) Twenty-eighth Congregational Society (1845) Second Hawes Ch (1845) Ch of our Savior (1845) Indiana St Ch (1845) East Boston Congregational Ch (1846) Harrison Sq Ch (1848)	[Second Hawes Ch] (1853) Hanover St Chp (1854) [Ch of our Savior] (1854) [Bulfinch St Ch] (1855) [Indiana St Ch] (1855) Ch of the Unity (1857)
Orthodox	Third Ch (Old South) (1669) Park St (1809) Hawes Pl (1819) Essex St (1819) (became Union Ch, 1822)	Mission House (1821) (became Mariner's Ch, 1830) Green St Ch (1823) Phillips Ch (1823) [Hawes Pl] (1823) Hanover St Ch (1825) Salem St Ch (1827) Pine St Ch (1827)	Central Ch (1835) Maverick Ch (1836) Marlborough Chp (1836)	[Marlborough Chp] (1841) Mt. Vernon Ch (1842) Payson Ch (1845) Shawmut Ch (1845) Pilgrim Congregational Soc (1846) [Green St Ch] (1846) Edwards Ch (1849)	[Pilgrim Cong Soc] (1852) [Edwards Ch] (1853) Ch of the Unity (1857)

		Decade of founding			
Denomination	Prior to 1820	1820–1829	1830–1839	1840–1849	1850–1859
Baptist	First Baptist (1679) Second Baptist (1743) Free Will Baptist (1803) (became First Christian Ch) African Baptist (1805) Third Baptist (1807)	Fourth Baptist (Rowe St) (1827) South Baptist (1828)	North Baptist (1835) Harvard St Ch (1839) Tremont St Ch (1839)	Bowdoin Sq. Ch (1840) [North Baptist] (1840) Free Will Baptist (1843) Winthrop Ch (1844) Union Ch (1844) Central Sq Ch (1844) Boston Baptist Bethel (1845) Twelfth Baptist Ch (1848)	First Mariner's Ch (1851) Shawmut Ave Ch (1856) Fourth St Ch (1858)
Methodist	First Methodist (1796) Second Methodist (1806) First African Methodist (1818)	Second African Methodist (Revere St) (1826) Bethel Ch (1828)	Third Methodist (Church St) (1834) Fifth Methodist (South Boston) (1835) Zion Ch (1836) Fourth Methodist (N. Russell St) (1837) Bethel Ch (Charles St) (1839)	Sixth Methodist (Meridian St) (1840) Wesleyan Methodist (1846) Eighth Methodist (Suffolk St) (1846) Hedding Ch (Canton St) (1846) Bethel Ch (1848)	Bennington St Ch (1853)

Universalist	First Universalist (1785) Second Universalist (1816)	Third Universalist (Bulfinch St Ch) (1822)	Fourth Universalist (South Boston) (1830) Fifth Universalist (1835) Webster St Ch (1839) [Bulfinch St Ch] (1839)	Sixth Universalist (1840) South Universalist (1845)	
Episcopal	Christ Ch (1722) Trinity Ch (1734) St. Matthew's Chp (1816)	St. Paul's Ch (1820)	Grace Ch (1830)	St. Stephen's Ch (1843) Ch of the Messiah (1843) Ch of the Advent (1844) Seaman's Chp (1845) St. John's Ch (1846)	St. Mark's Ch (1851) St. Batolph Ch (1851)

Denomination		Decade of founding				
	Prior to 1820	1820–1829	1830–1839	1840–1849	1850–1859
Catholic	Ch of the Holy Cross (1803)	Chp of the Holy Cross (1827)	St. Augustine's Ch (1833) St. Mary's Ch (1836) St. Patrick's Ch (1837)	St. Stephen's Ch (1842) St. John the Baptist (1844) Ch of St. Peter and St. Paul (1844) [St. Augustine's Chp] (1844) Ch of St. Nicholas (1844) Ch of the Holy Trinity (1844) St. Vincent de Paul's Ch (1849)	Ch of the Holy Family (1851) St. Francis de Sales Ch (1853) St. James' Ch (1854)

Sources: Caleb H. Snow, *A History of Boston*, 2d ed. (Boston: Abel Brown, 1828), pp. 338–47; [I. S. Homans], *Sketches of Boston* (Boston: Phillips, Sampson, 1851), pp. 66–129; Thomas C. Simonds, *History of South Boston* (Boston: David Clapp, 1857), pp. 154–82; William H. Sumner, *A History of East Boston* (Boston: J. E. Tilton, 1858) pp. 643–63; and Justin Winsor, ed., *The Memorial History of Boston*, 4 vols. (Boston: James R. Osgood, 1881), 3: 401–546.

Notes: The geographical area included is the Boston penisula proper, South Boston, and East Boston. Brackets indicate that the church ceased to exist at the date in parentheses. Abbreviations: Church, Ch; Chapel, Chp.

APPENDIX B Growth Rates of Boston Churches, 1820–1860

Denomination	Decade				Total
	1820–1829	1830–1839	1840–1849	1850–1859	
Unitarian	55.6	28.6	38.9	−16.0	133.3
Orthodox	150.0	30.0	70.0	− 5.6	325.0
Baptist	40.0	57.1	42.8	18.2	300.0
Methodist	66.7	100.0	66.7	6.7	433.3
Universalist	50.0	100.0	33.3	0	300.0
Episcopal	33.3	25.0	100.0	20.0	300.0
Catholic	100.0	150.0	100.0	30.0	1200.0
TOTAL	63.0	47.7	50.2	6.2	

APPENDIX C Members of Brook Farm, September 1841 to April 1845

Date of admission	Name	Birthplace	Birthdate	Occupation
Sept. 1841	George Ripley	Greenfield, Mass.	1802	minister
	Sophia Ripley	Cambridge, Mass.	1803	wife (minister)
	Marianne Ripley	Greenfield, Mass.	1797	teacher
	Charles Dana	Hindsdale, N.H.	1819	student
	Minot Pratt	Weymouth, Mass.	1805	printer
	Maria Pratt	Boston, Mass.	1806	wife (printer)
	Nathaniel Hawthorne	Salem, Mass.	1804	writer
	Sarah Stearns	Mass. ?	c. 1820	student
	William Allen	Vermont	?	farmer
	Charles Whitmore	?	?	?
Feb. 1842	Georgiana Bruce	England	c. 1820	teacher
	Samuel D. Robbins	Lynn, Mass.	1812	minister
	Mary Robbins	Lynn, Mass. ?	c. 1812	wife (minister)
	David Mack	Cambridge, Mass. ?	?	?
	Maria Mack	Cambridge, Mass. ?	?	wife (occupation unknown)
	Lemuel Capen	?	?	minister
	Warren Burton	Wilton, N.H.	1800	minister
	George Leach	Glouchester, Mass. ?	?	hotelkeeper ?
	Francis Farley	?	?	farmer
	Sylvia Allen	Vermont ?	?	wife (farmer)
June	Anna Foord	?	c. 1820	student
	Abigail Morton	Plymouth, Mass. ?	c. 1820	student
	James Hill	?	?	?

Aug.	James Curtis	Providence, R.I.	1824	student
Sept.	Eleanor Garrith	?	?	?
	John Brown	?	?	farmer
Oct.	Manuel Diaz	?	?	student
Dec.	Icabod Morton	Plymouth, Mass. ?	?	commercial fisherman
Jan. 1843	Amelia Russell	Dunkirk, France	1798	teacher
	Lewis Ryckman	New York, N.Y.	1796	shoemaker
	Jane Ryckman	New York, N.Y.	1799	wife (shoemaker)
	Mary Brown	?	?	wife (farmer)
Feb. 1844	John Cheever	Ireland	1802	domestic servant
	Marianne Williams	England	1806	?
	John Mitchell	Scotland	1818	shoemaker
	John S. Dwight	Boston, Mass.	1813	minister
	Christopher List	Wurtemburg, [Ger. ?]	1816	lawyer
	William Davis	Sutton, Mass.	1816	carpenter
	Anne Dana	Gaines, N.Y.	1825	sister (student)
	Charles Salisbury	Walpole, N.H.	1819	farmer
	Deborah N— ?	?	?	?
	Mary Holland	Belfast, Me. ?	c. 1817	wife (tallow chandler)
	Mary Ann Willard	?	?	?
Apr.	William Teel	Jersey City, N.J.	1822	shoemaker
	Porter Holland	Belfast, Me.	1817	tallow chandler
	Jeremiah Reynolds	Sterling, Conn.	1820	carpenter
	Peter Baldwin	Boston, Mass.	1806	baker
May	Ephraim Capen	Dorchester, Mass.	1813	pewterer
	Job Tirell	Boston, Mass.	1795	carpenter

Date of admission	Name	Birthplace	Birthdate	Occupation
	Charles Fuller	Boston, Mass.	1822	shoemaker
	Frederick Burnham	Roxbury, Mass.	1821	shoemaker
	William Cheswell	Boston, Mass.	1818	carpenter
	Mary Ann Cheswell	Boston, Mass.	1822	wife (carpenter)
	Robert Westacott	England	1818	cabinet maker
June	Frederick Cabot	Boston, Mass.	1822	clerk
	Mary Dwight	West Newbury, Mass. ?	1792	mother (minister)
	Marianne Dwight	Boston, Mass.	1816	teacher
	Benjamin Fitch	Temple, N.H.	1810	farmer
	Francis Dwight	Boston, Mass.	1819	sister (minister)
	Flavel Patterson	Lunenburg, Mass.	1806	carpenter
	Caroline Patterson	Charlestown, Mass.	1815	wife (carpenter)
	Rebecca Codman	Charlestown, Mass.	1798	wife (mechanic)
	Jonathan Butterfield	West Cambridge, Mass.	1818	printer
July	Nathaniel Colson	Abington, Mass.	1815	shoemaker
	Hannah Colson	Athens, Me.	1821	wife (shoemaker)
	George Houghton	Stillwater, N.Y.	1809	printer
	Buckley Hastings	Franklin [County ?], Mass.	1814	grocer
	Hiram Haskell	St. Johns, New Brunswick	1823	apothecary
	Julia Whitehouse	Assumption Point, [N.J. ?]	1799	?
Aug.	John Codman	Boston, Mass.	1794	mechanic
	Cynthia Hastings	Whitingham, [Vt. ?]	1818	wife (grocer)
	John Drew	Plymouth, Mass.	1821	?
	Catharine Sloan	Dunstable, Mass.	1822 ?	seamstress

	Name	Place	Year	Occupation
	Caleb Smith	Hallowell, Me. ?	c. 1822	?
	Benjamin Clark	Townsend, Mass.	1822	farmer
	Edmund Farrington	Medway, Mass.	1822	mechanic
	Thomas Blake	Hallowell, Me.	1823	printer
	John Orvis	Ferrisburgh, Vt.	1816	farmer
	Castalia Hosmer	Bedford, Mass.	1819	shoemaker
	Mary Hosmer	Townsend, Mass.	1820	wife (shoemaker)
Sept.	Charles Hosmer	Medford, Mass.	1820	shoemaker
	Elmira Daniels	Keene, N.H.	1819	seamstress
	Alex Murray	St. Johns, New Brunswick	1820	cabinetmaker
	James Clapp	Smithfield, R.I.	1816	bricklayer
	Peter Kleinstrup	Denmark	1800	gardener
	George Pierce	?	?	?
Oct.	Alpha Clapp	Cumberland, R.I.	1820	wife (bricklayer)
	Caroline Clapp	Boston, Mass.	1824	seamstress
	Augustina Kleinstrup	Denmark	1808	wife (gardener)
Nov.	Ann Hosmer	Bedford, Mass. ?	c. 1822	wife (shoemaker)
	Granville Hosmer	Bedford, Mass.	1822	shoemaker
Dec.	John Hoxie	Boston, Mass. ?	?	?
	Jeanne Palisse	Switzerland	1802	manufacturer
	Eunice Macdaniel	Washington, D.C.	1824	sister (journalist who was not a member)

Date of admission	Name	Birthplace	Birthdate	Occupation
	Francis Macdaniel	Washington, D.C.	1815	sister (journalist)
	Eliza Palisse	Weymouth, Mass.	1806	wife (manufacturer)
	John Sawyer	Lancaster, Mass.	1814	broker
	Lydia Smith	Clinton, Me.	1822	wife (occupation unknown)
	Henry Trask	Cambridgeport, Mass.	1820	carriage maker
Jan. 1845	Sarah Codman	Boston, Mass.	1825	daughter (mechanic)
Mar.	Charles Curtis	Newtown, Conn.	1820	?
Apr.	Alfred Peppercorn	England	?	butcher

Sources: Articles of Association, September 29, 1841; Articles of Association, February 17, 1842; Constitution, February 11, 1844; minutes of meetings. All these documents, with appended lists of signatures, are located in the Massachusetts Historical Society.

Notes: See chap. 4, n. 58, on the criteria for membership.

APPENDIX D   A Demographic Profile of Working People Who Joined Brook Farm in 1844

Urban	Rural	Foreign
Charles Fuller, shoemaker[a]	Castalia Hosmer, shoemaker	John Mitchell, shoemaker
Nathaniel Colson, shoemaker[a]	Mary Hosmer	
Hannah Colson[a]	Charles Hosmer, shoemaker	
William Teel, shoemaker[b]	Granville Hosmer, shoemaker	
Frederick Burnham, shoemaker	Ann Hosmer	
Job Tirell, carpenter[a]	William Davis, carpenter	
William Cheswell, carpenter[a]	Jeremiah Reynolds, carpenter	
Mary Ann Cheswell[a]		
Flavel Patterson, carpenter		
Caroline Patterson		
Alex Murray, cabinetmaker		Robert Westacott, cabinetmaker
George Houghton, printer	Jonathan Butterfield, printer	
Thomas Blake, printer		
Caroline Clapp, seamstress[a]	Catharine Sloan, seamstress	
Elmira Daniels, seamstress		
John Codman, mechanic[a]	Edmund Farrington, mechanic	
Rebecca Codman[a]		
Porter Holland, tallow chandler	Charles Salisbury, farmer	John Cheever, domestic servant
Mary Holland	Benjamin Clark, farmer	
	Benjamin Fitch, farmer	Peter Kleinstrup, gardener
Peter Baldwin, baker[a]	John Orvis, farmer	Augustina Kleinstrup

239

Urban	Rural	Foreign
James Clapp, bricklayer		
Alpha Clapp		
Henry Trask, carriage maker		

Sources: Constitution, February 11, 1844, and minutes of meetings, Massachusetts Historical Society; U.S. Census Office, *Sixth Census or Enumeration of the Inhabitants of the United States, as Corrected at the Department of State in 1840* (Washington, D.C.: Blair and Rives, 1841).

Notes: See chap. 4, n.128, on the classification procedure.

[a] Born/residing in Boston.
[b] Residing in New York City.

APPENDIX E Kinship at Brook Farm, September 1841 to January 1845

Family groups	Unattached individuals
George Ripley (hus)	Nathaniel Hawthorne
Sophia Ripley (wi)	Charles Whitmore
Marianne Ripley (GR's sister)[a]	Georgiana Bruce
Sarah Stearns (SR's niece)[a]	Lemuel Capen
Charles Dana (SR's cousin)[a]	Warren Burton
Anne Dana (CD's sister)[a]	George Leach
	Francis Farley
Castalia Hosmer (hus)	James Hill
Mary Hosmer (wi)	James Curtis
Charles Hosmer (CH's brother)[a]	Eleanor Garrith
Granville Hosmer (CH's brother)	Manuel Diaz
Ann Hosmer (GH's wi)	John Cheever
	Marianne Williams
Mary Dwight (mother)[a]	John Mitchell
John Dwight (son)[a]	Christopher List
Marianne Dwight (daughter)[a]	William Davis
Francis Dwight (daughter)[a]	Charles Salisbury
	Deborah N—
James Clapp (hus)	Mary Ann Willard
Alpha Clapp (wi)	William Teel
Caroline Clapp (JC's sister)[a]	Jeremiah Reynolds
	Peter Baldwin
Amelia Russell (aunt?)[a]	Ephraim Capen
Anna Foord (niece?)[a]	Job Tirell
	Charles Fuller
Icabod Morton (father)[a]	Frederick Burnham
Abigail Morton (daughter)[a]	Robert Westacott
	Frederick Cabot
Eunice Macdaniel (sister)[a]	Benjamin Fitch
Francis Macdaniel (sister)[a]	Jonathan Butterfield
	George Houghton
Minot Pratt (hus)	Hiram Haskell
Maria Pratt (wi)	Julia Whitehouse
	John Drew
William Allen (hus)	Catharine Sloan
Sylvia Allen (wi)	Benjamin Clark
	Edmund Farrington
Samuel Robbins (hus)	Thomas Blake
Mary Robbins (wi)	John Orvis
	Elmira Daniels
David Mack (hus)	Alex Murray
Maria Mack (wi)	George Pierce
	John Hoxie
John Brown (hus)	John Sawyer
Mary Brown (wi)	Henry Trask

Lewis Ryckman (hus)
Jane Ryckman (wi)

Porter Holland (hus)
Mary Holland (wi)

William Cheswell (hus)
Mary Ann Cheswell (wi)

Flavel Patterson (hus)
Caroline Patterson (wi)

John Codman (hus)
Rebecca Codman (wi)

Nathaniel Colson (hus)
Hannah Colson (wi)

Buckley Hastings (hus)
Cynthia Hastings (wi)

Caleb Smith (hus)
Lydia Smith (wi)

Peter Kleinstrup (hus)
Augustina Kleinstrup (wi)

Jeanne Palisse (hus)
Eliza Palisse (wi)

Sources: Lindsay Swift, *Brook Farm* (New York: Macmillan, 1900); Articles of Association, September 29, 1841; Articles of Association, February 17, 1842; Constitution, February 11, 1844; minutes of meetings, September 1841–January 1845. The documents are located in the Massachusetts Historical Society.

Notes: See chap. 5, n. 80, on the procedure for determining kinship. Abbreviations: husband, hus; wife, wi.

[a] Unmarried (single, separated, or widowed).

Abbreviations and Short Forms

ABA	Amos Bronson Alcott
Alcott, *Journals*	*The Journals of Bronson Alcott*, ed. Odell Shepard (Boston: Little, Brown, 1938)
Alcott, *Letters*	*The Letters of A. Bronson Alcott*, ed. Richard L. Herrnstadt (Ames, Ia.: Iowa State University Press, 1969)
AMA	Abigail May Alcott
AP	Anna Parsons
Berg, NYPL	Berg Collection, New York Public Library, New York, N.Y.
BPL	Boston Public Library, Boston, Mass.
Brownson, *Works*	*The Works of Orestes A. Brownson*, ed. Henry F. Brownson, 20 vols. (Detroit: H. F. Brownson and Thorndike Nourse, 1882–87)
CD	Charlotte Dana
CS	Carolyn Sturgis
Emerson, *Journals*	*The Journals and Miscellaneous Notebooks of Ralph Waldo Emerson*, ed. Ralph H. Orth et al., 14 vols. to date (Cambridge, Mass.: Harvard University Press, 1960–)
Emerson, *Letters*	*The Letters of Ralph Waldo Emerson*, ed. Ralph L. Rusk, 6 vols. (New York: Columbia University Press, 1939)
Emerson, *Works*	*The Complete Works of Ralph Waldo Emerson*, ed. Edward Waldo Emerson, 12 vols. (Boston: Houghton Mifflin, 1903–04)
EPP	Elizabeth Palmer Peabody
GR	George Ripley
Houghton	Houghton Library, Harvard University, Cambridge, Mass.
LB	Lucy Brown
LJE	Lidian Jackson Emerson
MD	Marianne Dwight

Memoirs of Fuller	William Henry Channing, James Freeman Clarke, and Ralph Waldo Emerson, *Memoirs of Margaret Fuller Ossoli*, 2 vols. (Boston: Phillips, Sampson, 1852)
MF	Margaret Fuller
MHS	Massachusetts Historical Society, Boston, Mass.
MP	Mary Peabody
OAB	Orestes Augustus Brownson
RWE	Ralph Waldo Emerson
SDR	Sophia Dana Ripley
SJM	Samuel J. May

Bibliography

The popularity of the Transcendentalists and the consequent availability of their writings in numerous editions is a definite asset to the general reader but clearly complicates the task of the bibliographer. Generally, I have tried to select the edition most commonly found in libraries, though at times I have listed two different editions, either to let the reader know that a new multivolume edition is in progress, which may not be sufficiently complete, however, to have superseded an old edition, or to indicate that a particularly good abridged edition of a writer's works exists. I have limited my citations on the Transcendentalists to major works, since the literature on Transcendentalism is perhaps the best known aspect of this study and may be found in other bibliographies, the most useful of which are Perry Miller, ed., *The Transcendentalists: An Anthology*, pp. 505–10, and Brian M. Barbour, ed., *American Transcendentalism: An Anthology of Criticism*, pp. 289–97 . Although many of their papers have been published, the principal manuscript collections for my six major Transcendentalists are located in the following libraries: Bronson Alcott, Houghton Library, Harvard University; Orestes Brownson, Notre Dame University Archives; Ralph Waldo Emerson, Houghton Library; Margaret Fuller, Boston Public Library and Houghton Library; Elizabeth Peabody, Berg Collection, New York Public Library; and George Ripley, Massachusetts Historical Society.

Other sources cited are grouped under topical headings: antebellum religion, antebellum society, reform, and women and families. Since I have not repeated all the references included in the notes, readers interested in more detailed information should use the notes to supplement the bibliography. Finally, I have given less space to modern secondary works than to primary sources and older histories, on the assumption that the latter are less widely known and thus could be collected in a single list to greater profit.

246   Bibliography

TRANSCENDENTALISM

1. GENERAL
Aesthetic Papers. Edited by Elizabeth Peabody. Boston, 1849.
Albanese, Catherine L. *Corresponding Motion: Transcendental Religion and the New America.* Philadelphia: Temple University Press, 1977.
Barbour, Brian M., ed. *American Transcendentalism: An Anthology of Criticism.* Notre Dame, Ind.: University of Notre Dame Press, 1973.
Boston Quarterly Review. Edited by Orestes Brownson. 1838–42.
Buell, Lawrence. *Literary Transcendentalism: Style and Vision in the American Renaissance.* Ithaca: Cornell University Press, 1973.
Cooke, George Willis. *An Historical and Biographical Introduction to Accompany the Dial.* 2 vols. 1902. Reprint. New York: Russell and Russell, 1961.
Dial. Edited by Margaret Fuller and Ralph Waldo Emerson. Boston, 1840–44.
Frothingham, Octavius Brooks. *Transcendentalism in New England.* 1876. Reprint. New York: Harper and Row, 1959.
Hochfield, George, ed. *Selected Writings of the American Transcendentalists.* New York: New American Library, 1966.
Hutchison, William R. *The Transcendentalist Ministers: Church Reform in the New England Renaissance.* New Haven: Yale University Press, 1959.
Miller, Perry, ed. *The Transcendentalists: An Anthology.* Cambridge, Mass.: Harvard University Press, 1950.
Stoehr, Taylor. *Nay-Saying in Concord: Emerson, Alcott, and Thoreau.* Hamden, Conn.: Archon Books, 1979.
Western Messenger. Edited by James Freeman Clarke and William Henry Channing. Louisville, Ky., and Cincinnati, Ohio, 1835–41.

2. MAJOR TRANSCENDENTALISTS
Alcott, Bronson. *Conversations with Children on the Gospels.* 2 vols. Boston: James Munroe, 1836–37.
———. *The Doctrine and Discipline of Human Culture.* Boston: James Munroe, 1836.
———. *Observations on the Principles and Methods of Infant Instruction.* Boston: Carter and Hendee, 1830.
———. *The Letters of Bronson Alcott.* Edited by Richard L. Herrnstadt. Ames: Iowa State University Press, 1969.
———. *The Journals of Bronson Alcott.* Edited by Odell Shepard. Boston: Little, Brown, 1938.
———. *Record of a School: Exemplifying the General Principles of Spiritual Culture.* 2d ed. Boston: Russell, Shattuck, 1836.

Blanchard, Paula. *Margaret Fuller: From Transcendentalism to Revolution*. New York: Delacorte Press/Seymour Lawrence, 1978.

Brownson, Henry F. *Orestes A. Brownson's Early Life, Middle Life, and Latter Life*. 3 vols. Detroit: H. F. Brownson, 1898–1900.

Brownson, Orestes. *Babylon is Falling: A Discourse Preached in the Masonic Temple, to the Society for Christian Union and Progress, on Sunday Morning, May 28, 1837*. Boston: I. R. Butts, 1837.

————. *A Discourse on the Wants of the Times*. Boston: James Munroe, 1836.

————. *The Works of Orestes A. Brownson*. Edited by Henry F. Brownson. 20 vols. Detroit: H. F. Brownson and Thorndike Nourse, 1882–87.

Cabot, James Elliot. *A Memoir of Ralph Waldo Emerson*. 2 vols. Boston: Houghton Mifflin, 1887.

Channing, William Henry, Clarke, James Freeman, and Emerson, Ralph Waldo. *Memoirs of Margaret Fuller Ossoli*. 2 vols. Boston: Phillips, Sampson, 1852.

Crowe, Charles. *George Ripley: Transcendentalist and Utopian Socialist*. Athens: University of Georgia Press, 1967.

Emerson, Ralph Waldo. *The Collected Works of Ralph Waldo Emerson*. Edited by Joseph Slater et al. 2 vols. to date. Cambridge, Mass.: Harvard University Press, 1971–.

————. *The Complete Works of Ralph Waldo Emerson*. Edited by Edward Waldo Emerson. 12 vols. Boston: Houghton Mifflin, 1903–04.

————. *The Early Lectures of Ralph Waldo Emerson*. Edited by Robert E. Spiller, Stephen E. Whicher, and Wallace E. Williams. 3 vols. Cambridge, Mass.: Harvard University Press, 1972.

————. *The Journals and Miscellaneous Notebooks of Ralph Waldo Emerson*. Edited by Ralph H. Orth et al. 14 vols. to date. Cambridge, Mass.: Harvard University Press, 1960–.

————. *The Letters of Ralph Waldo Emerson*. Edited by Ralph L. Rusk. 6 vols. New York: Columbia University Press, 1939.

————. *Selections from Ralph Waldo Emerson: An Organic Anthology*. Edited by Stephen E. Whicher. Boston: Houghton Mifflin, 1957.

————. *Young Emerson Speaks: Unpublished Discourses on Many Subjects by Ralph Waldo Emerson*. Edited by Arthur Cushman McGiffert, Jr. 1938. Reprint. Port Washington, N.Y.: Kennikat Press, 1968.

Frothingham, Octavius Brooks. *George Ripley*. Boston: Houghton Mifflin, 1882.

Fuller, Margaret. *Margaret Fuller, American Romantic: A Selection from Her Writings and Correspondence*. Edited by Perry Miller. New York: Doubleday, 1963.

————. *Woman in the Nineteenth Century, and Kindred Papers Relating to the Sphere, Condition, and Duties of Woman*. Edited by Arthur B. Fuller. 1874. Reprint. New York: Greenwood Press, 1968.

————. *The Writings of Margaret Fuller*. Edited by Mason Wade. New York: Viking Press, 1941.

Higginson, Thomas Wentworth. *Margaret Fuller Ossoli*. Boston: Houghton Mifflin, 1884.

McCuskey, Dorothy. *Bronson Alcott, Teacher*. New York: Macmillan, 1940.

[Peabody, Elizabeth]. "A Glimpse of Christ's Idea of Society." *Dial* 2 (1841): 214–28.

————. "Spirit of the Hebrew Scriptures." *Christian Examiner* 16 (1834): 174–202, 305–20, and 17 (1834): 78–92.

————. "The Way for a Child to be Saved." *Western Messenger* 1 (1836): 629–48.

Ripley, George. *The Claims of the Age on the Work of the Evangelist: A Sermon Preached at the Ordination of Mr. John Sullivan Dwight, as Pastor of the Second Congregational Church in Northampton, May 20, 1840*. Boston: Weeks, Jordan, 1840.

————. *Discourses on the Philosophy of Religion: Addressed to Doubters Who Wish to Believe*. Boston: James Munroe, 1836.

————. "Martineau's Rationale of Religious Inquiry." *Christian Examiner* 21 (1836): 225–54.

Rusk, Ralph L. *The Life of Ralph Waldo Emerson*. New York: Scribner's, 1949.

Sanborn, F[ranklin]. B[enjamin]., and Harris, William T. *A. Bronson Alcott: His Life and Philosophy*. 2 vols. Boston: Roberts Brothers, 1893.

Schlesinger, Arthur M., Jr. *Orestes A. Brownson: A Pilgrim's Progress*. Boston: Little, Brown, 1939.

Shepard, Odell. *Pedlar's Progress: The Life of Bronson Alcott*. Boston: Little, Brown, 1937.

Tharp, Louise Hall. *The Peabody Sisters of Salem*. Boston: Little, Brown, 1950.

3. OTHER TRANSCENDENTALISTS

Bolster, Arthur S., Jr. *James Freeman Clarke: Disciple to Advancing Truth*. Boston: Beacon Press, 1954.

Caruthers, J. Wade. *Octavius Brooks Frothingham: Gentle Radical*. University, Ala.: University of Alabama Press, 1977.

Clarke, James Freeman. *James Freeman Clarke: Autobiography, Diary and Correspondence*. Edited by Edward Everett Hale. Boston: Houghton Mifflin, 1891.

————. *The Letters of James Freeman Clarke to Margaret Fuller*. Edited by John Wesley Thomas. Hamburg, Germany: Cram, De Gruyter, 1957.

Commager, Henry Steele. *Theodore Parker*. Boston: Beacon Press, 1947.

Conway, Moncure Daniel. *Autobiography, Memories and Experiences of*

Moncure Daniel Conway. 2 vols. London: Cassell, 1904.

Cooke, George Willis. *John Sullivan Dwight: Brook-Farmer, Editor, and Critic of Music.* Boston: Small, Maynard, 1898.

Edelstein, Tilton G. *Strange Enthusiasm: A Life of Thomas Wentworth Higginson.* New Haven: Yale University Press, 1968.

Elliott, Walter. *The Life of Father Hecker.* 2d ed. New York: Columbus Press, 1894.

Frothingham, Octavius Brooks. *Memoir of William Henry Channing.* Boston: Houghton Mifflin, 1886.

_____. *Recollections and Impressions.* New York: G. P. Putnam's Sons, 1891.

_____. *Theodore Parker: A Biography.* Boston: James R. Osgood, 1874.

Higginson, Thomas Wentworth. *Cheerful Yesterdays.* Boston: Houghton Mifflin, 1898.

_____. *Letters and Journals of Thomas Wentworth Higginson.* Edited by Mary Thacher Higginson. Boston: Houghton Mifflin, 1921.

Holden, Vincent F. *The Early Years of Isaac Thomas Hecker (1819–1844).* Washington, D.C.: Catholic University Press, 1939.

Lebeaux, Richard. *Young Man Thoreau.* Amherst: University of Massachusetts Press, 1977.

Newcombe, Charles King. *The Journals of Charles King Newcombe.* Edited by Judith Johnson. Providence: Brown University, 1946.

Parker, Theodore. *Theodore Parker: An Anthology.* Edited by Henry Steele Commager. Boston: Beacon Press, 1960.

_____. *The Works of Theodore Parker.* 14 vols. Boston: American Unitarian Association, 1907–16.

Sanborn, F[ranklin]. B[enjamin]. *The Life of Henry David Thoreau.* Boston: Houghton Mifflin, 1917.

_____. *Recollections of Seventy Years.* 2 vols. Boston: Richard G. Badger, 1909.

Thoreau, Henry David. *The Correspondence of Henry David Thoreau.* Edited by Carl Bode and Walter Harding. New York: New York University Press, 1958.

_____. *The Journal of Henry D. Thoreau.* Edited by Bradford Torrey and Francis H. Allen. 14 vols. 1906. Reprint. Boston: Houghton Mifflin, 1949.

_____. *The Writings of Henry David Thoreau.* Edited by William Howarth et al. 4 vols. to date. Princeton: Princeton University Press, 1971–.

Weiss, John. *The Life and Correspondence of Theodore Parker.* 2 vols. New York: Appleton, 1864.

Wells, Ronald Vale. *Three Christian Transcendentalists: James Marsh, Caleb Sprague Henry, and Frederick Henry Hedge.* New York: Columbia University Press, 1939.

ANTEBELLUM RELIGION

1. GENERAL

Ahlstrom, Sydney E. *A Religious History of the American People.* New Haven: Yale University Press, 1972.

————. "The Scottish Philosophy and American Theology." *Church History* 24 (1955): 257–69.

Bozeman, Theodore Dwight. *Protestants in an Age of Science.* Chapel Hill: University of North Carolina Press, 1977.

Brown, Jerry Wayne. *The Rise of Biblical Criticism in America, 1800–1870: The New England Scholars.* Middletown, Conn.: Wesleyan University Press, 1969.

Cross, Whitney. *The Burned-over District: The Social and Intellectual History of Enthusiastic Religion in Western New York, 1800–1850.* Ithaca: Cornell University Press, 1950.

Johnson, Paul E. *A Shopkeeper's Millennium: Society and Revivals in Rochester, New York, 1815–1837.* New York: Hill and Wang, 1978.

McLoughlin, William. *New England Dissent, 1630–1833: The Baptists and the Separation of Church and State.* 2 vols. Cambridge, Mass.: Harvard University Press, 1971.

Mathews, Donald G. "The Second Great Awakening as an Organizing Process, 1780–1830: An Hypothesis." *American Quarterly* 21 (1969): 23–43.

Miller, Perry. *The Life of the Mind in America: From the Revolution to the Civil War.* New York: Harcourt, Brace and World, 1965.

Rosenberg, Carroll Smith. *Religion and the Rise of the American City: The New York City Mission Movement, 1812–1870.* Ithaca: Cornell University Press, 1971.

Scott, Donald M. *From Office to Profession: The New England Ministry, 1750–1850.* Philadelphia: University of Pennsylvania Press, 1978.

Smith, Timothy. *Revivalism and Social Reform: American Protestantism on the Eve of the Civil War.* New York: Harcourt, Brace and World, 1965.

2. UNITARIANISM

Allen, Katherine G., ed. *Sketches of Some Historic Churches of Greater Boston.* Boston: Beacon Press, 1918.

Channing, William Ellery. *The Works of William Ellery Channing.* Boston: American Unitarian Association, 1875.

Channing, William Henry. *The Life of William Ellery Channing.* Boston: American Unitarian Association, 1880.

Christian Examiner. Boston, 1824–69.

Christian Register. Boston, 1821–1961.

[Eliot, Ephraim]. *Historical Notices of the New North Religious Society.* Boston: Phelps and Farnham, 1822.

Eliot, Samuel A. *Heralds of a Liberal Faith.* 3 vols. Boston: American Unitarian Association, 1910.

Ellis, Arthur B. *History of the First Church in Boston.* Boston: Hall and Whiting, 1881.

Follen, Charles. *The Works of Charles Follen, with a Memoir of his Life.* [Edited by Eliza Cabot Follen]. 5 vols. Boston: Hilliard, Gray, 1841.

Foote, Henry Wilder. *Annals of King's Chapel.* 2 vols. Boston: Little, Brown, 1896.

Frothingham, Octavius Brooks. *Boston Unitarianism, 1820–1850: A Study of the Life and Work of Nathaniel Langdon Frothingham.* 1890. Reprint. Hicksville, N.Y.: Regina Press, 1975.

Gannett, William C. *Ezra Stiles Gannett: Unitarian Minister in Boston, 1824–1871.* Boston: Roberts Brothers, 1875.

Howe, Daniel Walker. *The Unitarian Conscience: Harvard Moral Philosophy, 1805–1860.* Cambridge, Mass.: Harvard University Press, 1970.

Lothrop, Samuel Kirkland. *A History of the Church in Brattle Street, Boston.* Boston: William Crosby and H. P. Nichols, 1851.

————. *Proceedings of an Ecclesiastical Council, in the Case of the Proprietors of Hollis-Street Meeting-House and the Rev. John Pierpont, Their Pastor.* Boston: W. W. Clapp and Son, 1841.

————. *Some Reminiscences of the Life of Samuel Kirkland Lothrop.* Edited by Thornton Kirkland Lothrop. Cambridge, Mass.: John Wilson and Son, 1888.

Lyttle, Charles H. *Freedom Moves West: A History of the Western Unitarian Conference, 1852–1952.* Boston: Beacon Press, 1954.

McColgan, Daniel. *Joseph Tuckerman: Pioneer in American Social Work.* Washington, D. C.: Catholic University Press, 1940.

Peabody, Elizabeth Palmer. *Reminiscences of Rev. William Ellery Channing.* Boston: Roberts Brothers, 1880.

Pray, Lewis G. *Historical Sketch of the Twelfth Congregational Society.* Boston: Committee of the Society, 1863.

Robbins, Chandler. *A History of the Second Church, or Old North, in Boston.* Boston: Committee of the Society, 1852.

Tuckerman, Joseph. *The Principles and Results of the Ministry at Large, in Boston.* Boston: James Munroe, 1838.

Ware, Henry, Jr. *The Works of Henry Ware. Jr.* 4 vols. Boston: James Munroe, 1846–47.

Ware, John. *Memoir of the Life of Henry Ware, Jr.* 2 vols. Boston: James Munroe, 1846.

The West Church and its Ministers: Fiftieth Anniversary of the Ordination of Charles Lowell. Boston: Crosby, Nichols, 1856.

ANTEBELLUM SOCIETY

1. GENERAL
Commons, John R., et al. *History of Labor in the United States*. 4 vols. New York: Macmillan, 1918–35.
————, eds. *A Documentary History of American Industrial Society*. 10 vols. Cleveland: Arthur H. Clarke, 1910–11.
Davis, David B. "Some Themes of Counter-subversion: An Analysis of Anti-Masonic, Anti-Catholic, and Anti-Mormon Literature." *Mississippi Valley Historical Review* 47 (1960): 205–24.
————, ed. *Antebellum American Culture: An Interpretive Anthology*. Lexington, Mass.: D. C. Heath, 1979.
Dawley, Alan. *Class and Community: The Industrial Revolution in Lynn*. Cambridge, Mass.: Harvard University Press, 1976.
Faler, Paul. "Cultural Aspects of the Industrial Revolution: Lynn, Massachusetts, Shoemakers and Industrial Morality, 1826–1860." *Labor History* 15 (1974): 367–94.
Fogel, Robert, and Engerman, Stanley. *Time on the Cross: The Economics of American Negro Slavery*. 2 vols. Boston: Little, Brown, 1974.
Forgie, George B. *Patricide in the House Divided: A Psychological Interpretation of Lincoln and His Age*. New York: Norton, 1979.
Gilchrist, David T., ed. *The Growth of the Seaport Cities, 1790–1825: Proceedings of a Conference Sponsored by the Eleutherian Mills-Hagley Foundation, March 17–19, 1966*. Charlottesville: University Press of Virginia, 1967.
Gilchrist, David T., and Lewis, W. David, eds. *Economic Change in the Civil War Era: Proceedings of a Conference on American Economic Institutional Change, 1850–1873, and the Impact of the Civil War held March 12–14, 1964*. Greenville, Del.: Eleutherian Mills-Hagley Foundation, 1965.
Hobsbawm, E. J. *The Age of Capital, 1848–1875*. London: Weidenfeld and Nicolson, 1975.
————. *The Age of Revolution: Europe, 1789–1848*. New York: Praeger Publishers, 1962.
Holt, Michael F. *The Political Crisis of the 1850s*. New York: John Wiley and Sons, 1978.
Houghton, Walter E. *The Victorian Frame of Mind, 1830–1870*. New Haven: Yale University Press, 1957.
Howe, Daniel, ed. *Victorian America*. Philadelphia: University of Pennsylvania Press, 1976.
Montgomery, David. "The Working Classes of the Pre-Industrial American City, 1780–1830." *Labor History* 9 (1968): 3–22.
North, Douglass C. *The Economic Growth of the United States, 1790–1860*. Englewood Cliffs, N.J.: Prentice-Hall, 1961.

Pessen, Edward. *Jacksonian America: Society, Personality, and Politics.* Rev. ed. Homewood, Ill.: Dorsey Press, 1978.

————. *Most Uncommon Jacksonians: The Radical Leaders of the Early Labor Movement.* Albany: State University of New York Press, 1967.

Rezneck, Samuel. "The Social History of an American Depression, 1837–1843." *American Historical Review* 40 (1935): 662–87.

Schlesinger, Arthur M., Jr. *The Age of Jackson.* Boston: Little, Brown, 1945.

Temin, Peter. *The Jacksonian Economy.* New York: Norton, 1969.

Thernstrom, Stephan. *Poverty and Progress: Social Mobility in a Nineteenth Century City.* Cambridge, Mass.: Harvard University Press, 1964.

Thompson, E. P. *The Making of the English Working Class.* New York: Random House, 1963.

Wallace, Anthony F. C. *Rockdale: The Growth of an American Village in the Early Industrial Revolution.* New York: Knopf, 1972.

Ware, Norman. *The Industrial Worker, 1840–1860: The Reaction of American Industrial Society to the Advance of the Industrial Revolution.* Boston: Little, Brown, 1924.

2. BOSTON

Boston Courier. Edited by Joseph T. Buckingham. Boston, 1824–64.

Boston Daily Advertiser. Edited by Nathan Hale. Boston, 1813–1929.

Buckingham, Joseph T. *Personal Memoirs and Recollections of Editorial Life.* 2 vols. Boston: Ticknor, Reed, and Fields, 1852.

Commager, Henry Steele. "The Blasphemy of Abner Kneeland," *New England Quarterly* 8 (1935): 29–41.

French, Roderick S. "Liberation from Man and God in Boston: Abner Kneeland's Free Thought Campaign, 1830–1839." *American Quarterly* 32 (1980): 202–21.

Green, Martin. *The Problem of Boston: Some Readings in Cultural History.* London: Longmans, 1966.

Handlin, Oscar. *Boston's Immigrants: A Study in Acculturation.* Rev. ed. Cambridge, Mass.: Harvard University Press, 1959.

[Homans, I. S.]. *Sketches of Boston, Past and Present.* Boston: Phillips, Sampson, 1851.

Kneeland, Abner. *A Review of the Trial, Conviction, and Final Imprisonment in the Common Jail of the County of Suffolk, of Abner Kneeland, for the Alledged Crime of Blasphemy.* Boston: George A. Chapman, 1838.

Knights, Peter R. *The Plain People of Boston, 1830–1860: A Study of City Growth.* New York: Oxford University Press, 1971.

Morison, Samuel Eliot. *The Maritime History of Massachusetts, 1783–1860.* Boston: Houghton Mifflin, 1921.

Simonds, Thomas C. *History of South Boston*. Boston: David Clapp, 1857.

Snow, Caleb H. *A History of Boston*. 2d ed. Boston: Abel Brown, 1828.

Story, Ronald. "Class and Culture in Boston: The Athenaeum, 1807–1860." *American Quarterly* 27 (1975): 178–99.

Sumner, William H. *A History of East Boston*. Boston: J. E. Tilton, 1858.

Tuckerman, Joseph. *An Essay on the Wages Paid to Females for their Labour*. Philadelphia: Carey and Hart, 1830.

Whitehill, Walter Muir. *Boston: A Topographical History*. Cambridge, Mass.: Harvard University Press, 1963.

Winsor, Justin, ed. *The Memorial History of Boston*. 4 vols. Boston: James R. Osgood, 1881.

REFORM

1. COMMUNITARIAN

Alcott, Bronson. "Days from a Diary." *Dial* 2 (1842): 409–37.

Bestor, Arthur E., Jr. "Albert Brisbane—Propagandist for Socialism in the 1840s." *New York History* 28 (1947): 128–58.

_____. "American Phalanxes: A Study of Fourierist Socialism in the United States (with Special Reference to the Movement in Western New York)." Ph.D. dissertation, Yale University, 1938.

_____. *Backwoods Utopias: The Sectarian Origins and Owenite Phase of Communitarian Socialism in America, 1663–1829*. 2d rev. ed. Philadelphia: University of Pennsylvania Press, 1970.

Brisbane, Albert. *Albert Brisbane: A Mental Biography, with a Character Study by His Wife Redelia Brisbane*. Edited by Redelia Brisbane. 1893. Reprint. New York: Burt Franklin, 1969.

_____. *A Concise Exposition of the Doctrine of Association, or Plan for a Re-Organization of Society, which will secure to the Human Race, Individually and Collectively, their Happiness and Elevation (Based on Fourier's Theory of Domestic and Industrial Association)*. New York: J. S. Redfield, 1844.

_____. *The Social Destiny of Man; or, Association and Reorganization of Industry*. Philadelphia: C. F. Stollmeyer, 1840.

Brook Farm Articles of Association, Constitution, Minutes of Meetings, and Other Papers. Massachusetts Historical Society. Boston.

Brownson, Orestes A. "Brook Farm." *Democratic Review* 11 (1842): 481–96.

Channing, William Henry. *The Christian Church and Social Reform: A Discourse delivered before the Religious Union of Associationists*. Boston: William Crosby and H. P. Nichols, 1848.

Clarke, James Freeman. "Fourierism." *Christian Examiner* 37 (1844): 57–78.

Codman, John. *Brook Farm: Historic and Personal Memoirs.* 1894. Reprint. New York: AMS Press, 1971.

Dwight, John Sullivan. Papers relating to Brook Farm. Boston Public Library. Boston.

Dwight, John Sullivan, and Dana, Charles Anderson. *Association, in its Connection with Education and Religion: Two Lectures delivered before the New England Fourier Society, in Boston, February 29th and March 7th, 1844.* Boston: Benjamin H. Greene, 1844.

Dwight, Marianne. *Letters from Brook Farm, 1844–1847.* Edited by Amy L. Reed. Poughkeepsie, N.Y.: Vassar College, 1928.

Emerson, Ralph Waldo. "English Reformers." *Dial* 3 (1842): 227–55.

————. "Fourierism and the Socialists." *Dial* 3 (1842): 86–96.

Foner, Philip S. "Journal of an Early Labor Organizer." *Labor History* 10 (1969): 205–27.

Fourier, Charles. *The Utopian Vision of Charles Fourier.* Edited by Jonathan Beecher and Richard Bienvenu. Boston: Beacon Press, 1971.

Godwin, Parke. *A Popular View of the Doctrines of Charles Fourier.* 2d ed. New York: J. S. Redfield, 1844.

Gohdes, Clarence. "A Brook Farm Labor Record." *American Literature* 1 (1929): 297–303.

Greeley, Horace. *Recollections of a Busy Life.* New York: J. B. Ford, 1868.

Guarneri, Carl Joseph. "Utopian Socialism and American Ideas: The Origins and Doctrine of American Fourierism." Ph.D. dissertation, Johns Hopkins University, 1979.

Haraszti, Zoltan. *The Idyll of Brook Farm as Revealed by Unpublished Letters in the Boston Public Library.* Boston: Trustees of the Public Library, 1937.

Harbinger. Edited by George Ripley. Brook Farm and New York, 1845–48.

Johnson, Christopher. *Utopian Communism in France: Cabet and the Icarians, 1839–1851.* Ithaca: Cornell University Press, 1974.

Lane, Charles. "The Consociate Family Life." *The New Age, and Concordium Gazette* 1 (1843): 116–20.

————. "A Day with the Shakers." *Dial* 4 (1843): 165–73.

————. "The True Life." *Present* 1 (1844): 312–16.

New York Tribune. Edited by Horace Greeley. New York, 1841–1924.

Noyes, John Humphrey. *History of American Socialisms.* 1870. Reprint. New York: Dover, 1966.

Peabody, Elizabeth. "Fourierism." *Dial* 4 (Apr. 1844): 473–83.

————. "Plan of the West Roxbury Community." *Dial* 2 (1842): 361–72.

Phalanx. Edited by Albert Brisbane. New York, 1843–45.

Present. Edited by William Henry Channing. New York, 1843–44.

Rozwenc, Edwin. *Cooperatives Come to America: The History of the Protective Union Store Movement, 1845–1867*. 1941. Reprint. Philadelphia: Porcupine Press, 1975.

Russell, Amelia. *Home Life of the Brook Farm Association*. Boston: Little, Brown, 1900.

Sears, Clara Endicott. *Bronson Alcott's Fruitlands*. Boston: Houghton Mifflin, 1915.

Sears, John Van Der Zee. *My Friends at Brook Farm*. New York: Desmond Fitzgerald, 1912.

Stoller, Leo. *After Walden: Thoreau's Changing Views on Economic Man*. Stanford: Stanford University Press. 1957.

Swift, Lindsay. *Brook Farm: Its Members, Scholars, and Visitors*. New York: Macmillan, 1900.

Thomas, John L. "Romantic Reform in America." In David Brion Davis, ed., *Ante-Bellum Reform*. New York: Harper and Row, 1967.

Thoreau, Henry D. *Walden*. Edited by J. Lyndon Shanley. The Writings of Henry D. Thoreau, vol. 1. Princeton: Princeton University Press, 1971.

Walters, Ronald. *American Reformers, 1815–1860*. New York: Hill and Wang, 1978.

2. ANTISLAVERY

Davis, David Brion. *The Problem of Slavery in the Age of Revolution, 1770–1823*. Ithaca: Cornell University Press, 1975.

Demos, John. "The Antislavery Movement and the Problem of Violent Means." *New England Quarterly* 37 (1964): 501–26.

Elkins, Stanley. *Slavery: A Problem in American Institutional and Intellectual Life*. 2d ed. Chicago: University of Chicago Press, 1968.

Foner, Eric. *Free Soil, Free Labor, Free Men: The Ideology of the Republican Party before the Civil War*. New York: Oxford University Press, 1970.

Fredrickson, George M. *The Inner Civil War: Northern Intellectuals and the Crisis of the Union*. New York: Harper and Row, 1965.

Kraditor, Aileen S. *Means and Ends in American Abolitionism: Garrison and His Critics on Strategy and Tactics, 1834–1850*. New York: Random House, 1967.

Montgomery, David. *Beyond Equality: Labor and the Radical Republicans, 1862–1872*. New York: Knopf, 1967.

Oates, Stephen B. *Our Fiery Trial: Abraham Lincoln, John Brown, and the Civil War Era*. Amherst: University of Massachusetts Press, 1979.

Parker, Theodore. *The Slave Power*. Edited by James K. Hosmer. The Works of Theodore Parker, vol. 11. Boston: American Unitarian Association, 1907–16.

Perry, Lewis. *Radical Abolitionism: Anarchy and the Government of God in Antislavery Thought*. Ithaca: Cornell University Press, 1973.

Stange, Douglas C. *Patterns of Antislavery among American Unitarians, 1831–1860.* Rutherford, N.J.: Associated Universities Press, 1977.

Thoreau, Henry. *Reform Papers.* Edited by Wendell Glick. The Writings of Henry D. Thoreau, vol. 3. Princeton: Princeton University Press, 1973.

Walker, Peter F. *Moral Choices: Memory, Desire, and Imagination in Nineteenth-Century American Abolitionism.* Baton Rouge: Louisiana State University Press, 1978.

WOMEN AND FAMILIES

Alcott, Abigail. Letters and Journals. Alcott Family Papers. Houghton Library, Harvard University. Cambridge, Mass.

Aries, Philippe. *Centuries of Childhood: A Social History of Family Life.* Translated by Robert Baldick. New York: Random House, 1962.

Cheney, Ednah D. *Louisa May Alcott: Her Life, Letters and Journals.* 1889. Reprint. Boston: Little, Brown, 1928.

Cott, Nancy F. *The Bonds of Womanhood: "Woman's Sphere" in New England, 1780–1835.* New Haven: Yale University Press, 1977.

Douglas, Ann. *The Feminization of American Culture.* New York: Knopf, 1977.

Emerson, Lidian. Letters. Emerson Papers. Houghton Library, Harvard University. Cambridge, Mass.

Flexner, Eleanor. *Century of Struggle: The Woman's Rights Movement in the United States.* Rev. ed. Cambridge, Mass.: Harvard University Press, 1975.

Gordon, Michael, ed. *The American Family in Social-Historical Perspective.* 2d ed. New York: St. Martin's Press, 1978.

Jeffrey Kirk. "The Family as a Utopian Retreat from the City: The Nineteenth-Century Contribution." In Sallie Te Selle, ed., *The Family, Communes, and Utopian Societies.* New York: Harper and Row, 1971.

————. "Marriage, Career, and Feminine Ideology in Nineteenth Century America: Reconstructing the Marital Experience of Lydia Maria Child, 1828–1847." *Feminist Studies* 2 (1975): 113–30.

Pommer, Henry. *Emerson's First Marriage.* Carbondale: Southern Illinois University Press, 1967.

Ripley, Sophia. Letters. Dana Papers. Massachusetts Historical Society. Boston.

Saxton, Martha. *Louisa May: A Modern Biography of Louisa May Alcott.* Boston: Houghton Mifflin, 1977.

Smith-Rosenberg, Carroll. "Beauty, the Beast, and the Militant Woman: A Case Study of Sex Roles and Social Stress in Jacksonian America." *American Quarterly* 23 (1971): 562–84.

Strauch, Carl F. "Hatred's Swift Repulsions: Emerson, Margaret Fuller, and Others." *Studies in Romanticism* 7 (1968): 65–103.

Strickland, Charles. "A Transcendentalist Father: The Child-rearing Practices of Bronson Alcott." *Perspectives in American History* 3 (1967): 5–73.

Index

Abbott, Jacob, 55

abolitionism, 71n, 103n; opposition to, 20–21, 71, 74n, 219; Alcott and, 118; contrasted with free soil politics, 220n, 222, 222n. *See also* antislavery; slavery

Adams, Henry, 223

Advertiser. See Boston Daily Advertiser

Agassiz, Louis, 212

agriculture, at Fruitlands, 124–26; as basis for original Brook Farm economy, 138–39

Alcott, Abigail May, 20, 119, 119n; on reform, 126, 127, 128n, 200, 203–04; on the family, 163; and domestic life, 198–202; on economic independence for women, 202; expectations for Fruitlands, 203–05; life at Fruitlands, 205–06

Alcott, Amos Bronson: and Boston elite, 20; Buckingham criticism of, 23, 81–82; and Elizabeth Peabody, 55, 197–98; biographical sketch, 60–65; on education, 62–63; and Temple School, 63–64; attacked for *Conversations*, 80–83; linked with Graham, 81–82; on diet reform, 82n; and Emerson, 94, 95, 96n, 213–14; in Concord, 94–96; on cities, 95n; anarchism of, 117–18, 118n; on labor and money, 118–19; progressive impoverishment of, 118n–19n; in England, 120–22; and Fruitlands, 122–30, 206; and Fourierism, 141; on child-rearing, 197–200, 200n; on family reorganization, 197–202; and his family in the *1840*s, 202–06; on end of Transcendentalism, 209; on slavery, 219, 219n

Alcott, Anna, 124–25, 198, 199

Alcott, Anna Bronson, 61

Alcott, Elizabeth, 198

Alcott, Joseph, 61

Alcott, Junius, 120n, 205

Alcott, Louisa May, 127n, 198, 199–200, 206, 215n

Alcott, William, 62, 200

Alcott House, 120, 121n, 128

Allen, John, 154, 154n, 188

The American Republic, 212

American Union of Associationists, 155n, 195

American Unitarian Association, 14, 32

anarchism: Karl Mannheim on, 117; of Alcott, 117–18; and the family, 201

Andrews, Stephen Pearl, 167n, 207

Antinomianism, 70, 71, 85

antislavery: elite opposition to, 19–21; W. E. Channing on, 21; Unitarians and, 29, 32, 221n; Clarke's stand on, 35; Ripley on, 105, 219; Pratt on, 134; Fourierism and, 141, 153–54; women's rights and, 162n; and the Transcendentalists' followers, 216–17, 220n, 221–22; and the Transcendentalists, 217–18, 219–20; Emerson on, 218–19; and rise of capitalism, 218n; Parker on, 220–21; Thoreau on, 222–23. *See also* abolitionism; slavery

Appleton, William, 16n

apprenticeship training, 110

Association of Delegates from the Benevolent Societies of Boston, 30

Austin, James T., 21, 73, 74n; in Kneeland trials, 74–75; Republicanism of, 75n

Awl (Lynn, Mass.), 155, 160n

Babylon is Falling, 78–79
Baldwin, Peter, 159n
Baldwin, Thomas, 7
Ballou, Adin, 105, 105n, 141, 218n
Ballou, Hosea, 7
Bancroft, George, 51, 106–07
Baptist Church, 7–8, 15, 72n
Barker, Anna, 179, 181, 181n, 182, 183n
Barlow, Almira, 133, 188
Barnard, C. F., 29n
Barrett, Samuel, 14
Beecher, Lyman, 14
Bellows, Henry, 207–08
benevolence: in Unitarian churches, 11; of
    Unitarian evangelicals, 29–31
Benevolent Fraternity of Christian
    Churches, 29, 31, 32
Bestor, Arthur, 152
Bible: Transcendentalists on, 42–44
biblical criticism: Unitarian practice of,
    11–12, 39–41; Transcendentalist
    criticism of miracles, 41, 79, 88;
    Andrews Norton on, 54, 79, 87–88
Billings, Samuel, 22n
Binney, Amos, 8n
Blake, Thomas, 157n
The Bonds of Womanhood, 174
Boston: preindustrial economy and
    society, 5–11; labor unions in, 8,
    25–26, 158, 158n, 159; churches in,
    14–17; impact of industrialization on,
    17–28; attack on Transcendentalism in,
    70–93; in *1850*s, 212–13;
    establishment and dissolution of
    churches to *1860,* 229–32; growth rate
    of churches, 233
Boston and Worcester Railroad
    Corporation, 75
Boston Athenaeum, 7, 20
Boston Courier, 22, 23, 76n; on
    Kneeland, 75, 76; on Alcott, 81–82
Boston Daily Advertiser, 75, 86, 87; on
    Kneeland, 75–76; on Alcott, 80–81
Boston Investigator, 27
Boston Morning Post, 72n; on Kneeland,
    75; on Emerson, 89–90, 90n
Boston Mutual Benefit Association, 159,
    160n
Boston Quarterly Review, 90, 102n, 106
Boston Trades' Union, 26
Boston Union of Associationists, 195
Boston Vigilance Committee, 220

Bowen, Francis, 83–85
Bower, Samuel, 128n
Bradford, George Partridge, 98n, 190
Brattle Street Church, 10, 16n, 22n, 74n,
    75, 77, 213
Brentano, Bettina, 174
Brisbane, Albert, 141, 142n–43n, 150,
    150n, 151, 191, 192
Bronson, Tillotson, 61
Brook Farm: plans for, 98n, 104–06;
    membership in, 98n, 132n, 132–33,
    135, 137–38, 138n, 152–54, 157,
    234–38; Emerson and, 106, 116;
    founding of, 130–33; religious goals of,
    131–32, 143–44; Fuller's relation to,
    133, 189–90; social goals of, 133–34;
    Peabody and, 134–35, 136; plan for
    reuniting social classes, 134–36,
    145–47; stockholders in, 135–36,
    136n, 158, 186, 187; working people at,
    135–36, 153, 157–61, 188; debts of,
    136n; labor system at, 136–38,
    147–48; agricultural basis of, 138–39;
    Brownson on, 139, 162–63;
    industrialization of, 139–40, 148–50;
    and Fourier's ideas, 140–50, 191–94;
    and Fourier movement, 150–61; reform
    activity of leaders, 154–55; disbanded,
    161; women and families at, 185–96;
    demographic profile of working people,
    239–40; kinship at, 241–42
Brooks, Peter Chardon, 9, 111n
Brown, John, 216, 216n, 218–19
Brown, John Stillman, 137
Brown, Jonas B., 22n
Brown, Lucy, 175–76
Brownson, Henry, 224
Brownson, Orestes Augustus: on
    Kneeland, 27n, 78; as Unitarian
    evangelical, 33–34; and Society for
    Christian Union and Progress, 34, 48;
    on religious institutions, 43; as a
    Catholic, 44, 142, 210–12; and
    Eclectics, 44n; biographical sketch,
    44–49; on history, 48–49; influence on
    Ripley, 51; and Democratic party, 92,
    106–07; on government, 107; influence
    on Hecker, 128; on community system,
    139; and Fourierism, 141, 142; on
    Brook Farm, 162–63; on slavery, 219
Buckeley, Peter, 170n
Buckingham, Joseph Tinker, 25, 73;